CINEMAS OF THE MOZAMBICAN REVOLUTION

Anti-Colonialism, Independence and Internationalism in Filmmaking, 1968–1991

AFRICAN ARTICULATIONS

ISSN 2054-5673

The series is open to submissions from the disciplines related to literature, cultural history, cultural studies, music and the arts.

African Articulations showcases cutting-edge research into Africa's cultural texts and practices, broadly understood to include written and oral literatures, visual arts, music, and public discourse and media of all kinds. Building on the idea of 'articulation' as a series of cultural connections, as a clearly voiced argument and as a dynamic social encounter, the series features monographs that open up innovative perspectives on the richness of African locations and networks. Refusing to concentrate solely on the internationally visible above the supposedly ephemeral local cultural spaces and networks, African Articulations provides indispensable resources for students and teachers of contemporary culture.

Please contact the series editors with an outline, or download the proposal form www.jamescurrey.com. Only send a full manuscript if requested to do so.

Stephanie Newell, Professor of English, Yale University stephanie.newell@yale.edu
Ranka Primorac, Lecturer in English, University of Southampton r.primorac@soton.ac.uk

Previously published volumes are listed at the back of this book

CINEMAS OF THE MOZAMBICAN REVOLUTION

Anti-Colonialism, Independence and Internationalism in Filmmaking, 1968–1991

Ros Gray

JAMES CURREY

James Currey
is an imprint of
Boydell & Brewer Ltd
PO Box 9, Woodbridge
Suffolk IP12 3DF (GB)
www.jamescurrey.com
and of
Boydell & Brewer Inc.
668 Mt Hope Avenue
Rochester, NY 14620-2731 (US)
www.boydellandbrewer.com

First published 2020

British Library Cataloguing in Publication Data
A catalogue record for this book is available on request from the British Library

ISBN 978-1-84701-237-1 (James Currey cloth)

This publication is printed on acid-free paper

MIX
Paper from responsible sources
FSC® C013056
www.fsc.org

Printed and bound in Great Britain by
TJ International Ltd, Padstow, Cornwall

Contents

Images

The author and publisher are grateful to all the institutions and individuals listed for permission to reproduce the materials in which they hold copyright. Every effort has been made to trace the copyright holders; apologies are offered for any omission, and the publisher will be pleased to add any necessary acknowledgement in subsequent editions.

Acknowledgements

For the research and writing of this book I received grants from the Arts and Humanities Research Council and the Central Research Fund of the University of London, several Department of Art Research Support Awards and an award from the International Fund, Goldsmiths, University of London.

The book would not have been possible without the gracious cooperation, compelling testimony, incisive commentary and kind assistance of: José Soares Acolette, Guilhermo Alfonso, Licínio Azevedo, João Azevedo, Brigitte Bagnol, Karen Boswell, João Paulo Borges Coelho, Simon Bright, José Luís Cabaço, Chico Caneiro, José Cardoso, Laura Cardoso, Sol de Carvalho, João Costa, Maria de Lourdes Torcato, Margaret Dickinson, Moira Forjaz, Pipas Forjaz, Polly Gaster, Ruy Guerra, Ophera Hallis, Lennart Malmer, Manuel Malo, Gabriel Mondlane, Oscar Monteiro, Isabel Noronha, Luís Carlos Patraquim, Pedro Pimenta, Jorge Rebelo, Luís Simão, Americo Soares, Camilo de Sousa, Felisbert Tinga and Ismael Vuvo. I owe huge thanks to those individuals who gave me permission to reproduce images, particularly Sara Mabombo who graces the cover of this book, and to those who read sections or the entirety of the manuscript and helped with fact checking: Pedro Pimenta, Margaret Dickinson, Ophera Hallis, Simon Bright, Polly Gaster and Gabriel Mondlane. I am grateful to numerous institutions and archives, including the Instituto Nacional de Audiovisual e Cinema (INAC), Maputo; the Arquivo Histórico de Moçambique, Maputo; the Arquivo Nacional da Image em Movimento (ANIM), Loures, Portugal; Filmske novosti, Belgrade; the British Film Institute, London; the Bishopsgate Institute, London; the Russian State Archive of Contemporary History, Moscow. I thank the following individuals in particular: Djalma Lorenço, director, and Ungulani Ba Ka Khosa, former director, of INAC; Tiago Baptista, director, and Joana Pimentel, researcher, at ANIM; and Stefan Dickers, archivist at the Bishopsgate Institute.

Over the many years that I have been conducting research towards this book, the field has expanded extensively. I am grateful for the scholarship and companionship of this transnational community of academics, artists and filmmakers that includes: Angela Ferreira, Mauro Pinto, Alda Costa, Robert Stock, Margarita Cardoso, Maria do Carmo Piçarra, Drew Thompson, Afonso Ramos, Catarina Simão, Guido Convents, José Filipe Costa, Teresa Castro, Olivier Hadouchi, Luís Trinidade, Ana Isabel Santos Strinberg, Susana Sousa Dias, Ansgar Schafer, Filipa César, Raquel Schefer, Ute Fendler, Maria Benedita Basto,

Ana Balona de Oliveira, Polly Savage, Nadine Siegert, Nicole Brenez, Diana Manhica, Vavy Pacheco Borges, Vanessa Vasic-Janekovic, Jeremy Hicks, Litheko Modisane and Aylin Basaran. During numerous visits to the Southern African region I have greatly appreciated the friendship and generosity of: François Belourgey, Jordane Bertrand, Severine Cachat, Zethu Matabene and Katja and Rodrigues José. In addition, certain artists, filmmakers, scholars and curators have been crucial to my intellectual formation; others have provided me with opportunities to participate in public events and publications: Irit Rogoff, Rob Stone, Mark Nash, Isaac Julien, Laura Mulvey, John Akomfrah, Kodwo Eshun, Angelika Sagar, Renée Green, Keith Shiri, George Shiri, Karen Alexander, Mark Sealey, Grant Watson, Nomusa Makubu, Tj Demos, Anthony Gardner, Françoise Vergès and Anna Collin.

I owe a huge debt of thanks to *African Articulations* Series Editors Stephanie Newell and Ranka Primorac, who understood exactly the kind of book I wanted to write and helped me to realise it. I am also grateful to Lynn Taylor at Boydell & Brewer for her advice and assistance with all aspects of the book's production and to Rohais Landon and Cecile Berbesi Rault for so expertly steering the book through its editorial stages. My thanks go to the anonymous peer reviewers who commented on the book proposal and manuscript. During the research and writing of this book I relied on a number of people who provided essential research assistance and help with transcription and translation: Raquel Jenkins, Alexandra Ezberova, Mark Brogan, Denis Fedorin, Arnold Chamunogwa and Sofia Saldanha. Sara Rodrigues, Wanderley Moreira and Dionea Rocha Watt played an equally important role in helping me to improve my Portuguese. Miriam Sampaio deserves special thanks for her generous help at a crucial moment. In recent years, I have been endlessly supported by some very special colleagues, some of whom read parts of my manuscript: Catherine Grant, Ian Hunt, Susan Kelly, Steven Morton, Shela Sheikh, Nicole Wolf, Wood Roberdeau and Kristen Krieder. I also thank those at Goldsmiths who helped to arrange release from teaching, namely Richard Noble, Stephen Johnstone, Suhail Malik and Edgar Schmitz. I am grateful for the technical assistance of Tolga Saygin, David Spraggs, Kevin Ward, Meg Ferguson and Ian Marsh, and for the administrative support provided by Ken Ross-Blundell, Angela Richards and Lydia Fernandes.

I thank all my family for their love and support, particularly my parents, Winifred and Patrick Gray, and my sisters Hazel Gray and Elizabeth Rumler. I am grateful to my uncle John Gray, in whose house I lived in Maputo in 2005. Lastly, with all my love, I thank my husband Luke and my children Tom and Jake.

Glossary

assembleias populares	Translates as 'popular assemblies'. These were the first democratically elected legislative bodies of Mozambique.
assimilados	The name given to the African subjects of the colonising Portuguese Empire from the 1910s to the 1960s who had reached a level of 'civilisation' according to Portuguese legal criteria. This theoretically qualified them for full rights as Portuguese citizens.
audiovisuais	Refers to photography, slide-shows and posters that might perform a supportive role in using the moving image for didactic purposes.
bairro	Translates as 'neighbourhood' or 'district' in a city or town.
barakalo	A secret language spoken by South African miners.
bantustans	A partially self-governing area set aside during the period of Apartheid for black inhabitants of South Africa and South-West Africa (now Namibia); a so-called 'homeland'.
cassava	A woody shrub cultivated in tropical and subtropical regions for its edible starchy tuberous root.
O Campo	A newspaper created by the Instituto de Comunicação Social (ICS) for rural communities.
chambas	Farms or agricultural land (see also *machambas*).
Changane	A tributary river to the Limpopo river which also forms a part of the Gaza province boundary.
Changana	A Bantu language spoken in southern regions of Mozambique, including Gaza, Inhambane and Maputo provinces.
chimbwido	Young people who assisted the ZANLA guerrillas.
chimurenga	Translates as 'revolutionary struggle' in the Shona language.
chitende	A traditional Mozambican stringed musical instrument played with a bow.

Chopi	A Mozambican ethnic group living in the Inhambane province, southern Mozambique.
cidade de caniço	Literally translates as 'reed city', referring to informal housing constructed around the European city centres.
cinema ambulante	A colonial mobile cinema conceived to promote consumer goods to the indigenous population.
cinema móvel	A post-colonial mobile cinema that went to rural sites to project films.
cipaio	A Mozambican recruited as a Portuguese soldier; also a lackey to the Portuguese.
continuadores	The youth wing of Frelimo.
cooperantes	Foreign development workers with a political commitment to the revolutionary project.
correspondentes populares	Reporters trained by the ICS to make video reports.
Estado Novo	Translates as the 'New State'. This was the corporatist authoritarian regime installed in Portugal in 1933 and overthrown in 1974. It was considered to be a fascist regime.
Fico	Translates literally as 'I am staying'. At Independence in Mozambique it was the name adopted by Portuguese settlers who agitated against Frelimo and briefly occupied areas of the capital.
grupo dinamizador	A dynamizing group.
indígenas	People originating in a country or region, but under Portuguese colonial law it referred to colonised populations who were not assimilated (see also *assimilados*).
Isitshikitsha	A Ndebele traditional ceremonial dance, historically performed for the king's pleasure.
Kipoko	A type of helmet mask carved from lightweight wood worn only by the chiefs in the community functions and dances of the Pende people of the Democratic Republic of Congo.
Kuxa Kanema	Translates as 'birth of cinema' and designates the national current events newsreel first produced in Mozambique in 1978.

latifundario	The agricultural estates owned by colonial settlers.
lojas do povo	Translates as 'peoples' shops'. These were cooperatively run grocery shops.
machambas	Farms or plots of agricultural land.
'Magaia'	A dissenting movement that emerged during the transition to independence from within the ranks of Frelimo's guerrilla forces. Named after Filipe Samuel Magaia, Frelimo's first commander, who was killed in 1966 by Lourenço Matola, a fellow guerrilla said to be in the employment of the Portuguese secret services.
Makonde	An ethnic group in northern Mozambique and southern Tanzania, whose culture developed on the Mueda Plateau.
Mapiko	The song and dance of the Makonde people from Tanzania and northern Mozambique, namely the Mueda Plateau, that was traditionally performed in secret to young men and boys at their initiation, in which the masked dancer represented the animal spirit of the clan. It was transformed and politicised during the armed struggle for independence.
Makwayela	A song and dance from southern Mozambique that developed as a cultural expression of resistance to conditions of labour experienced by Mozambican migrant workers in the South African mines.
Marrabenta	A type of music that developed in Lourenço Marques in the 1930s and 1940s, which fused Mozambican dance rhythms with Portuguese folk music.
marovo	An Angolan alcoholic drink fermented from the liquid extract from palm trees.
mestiço	Person of mixed heritage in the colonial period.
Msaho	A musical piece performed by groups of timbila players.
Muchongoya	A traditional dance from Zimbabwe identified especially with the Ndau people but to a lesser extent the Tsonga people. In Ndau it literally means stomping of the feet and was historically a war dance.
Ngalanga	A traditional Mozambican dance from Inhambane.
ngoma	a type of drum used by the Chopi people of the Inhambane province, southern Mozambique.

Nguinha	A dance and song from Inhambane associated with colonial labour.
O Povo	Translates as 'the people', but in Frelimo's discourse had shifting meanings, at times referring to the peasantry, at others to a broader concept of the 'masses', including the urban proletariat.
os comprometidos	Translates as 'the compromised', the name given to Mozambicans who were accused of collaboration with the colonial regime.
papabichas	The buses upon which many urban commuters depend.
palmatória	A perforated paddle that was used on the Portuguese plantations to inflict maximum scarring and pain upon forced labourers.
Resistência Moçambicana	Commando unit made of Portuguese armed forces and set up by the head of the Rhodesian Secret Service, Ken Flowers.
responsável	A leader, office holder, someone in charge.
Ronga	A south-eastern Bantu language spoken south of Maputo in Mozambique, extending into South Africa.
Sahwira	Translates as 'close bond' or 'recognised family best friend' in the Shona language.
Shimakonde (or Kimakonde)	The language spoken by the Makonde, an ethnic group in south-east Tanzania and northern Mozambique.
subúrbios	The peripheries or suburbs of the main cities.
timbila	Large wooden xylophones of the Chopi people of the Inhambane province.
ujamaa	Translates as 'familyhood' in Swahili and is the concept behind Julius Nyerere's social and economic development policies in Tanzania after it gained its independence from Britain in 1961.
uwavi	A form of sorcery or witchcraft practised by the Makonde residents of the Mueda Plateau in northern Mozambique.
ximbeca	A bamboo flute.

Abbreviations

AACC	Associação Africana de Cooperação Cinematográfica
ACOA	American Committee on Africa
ACTT	Association of Cinematograph, Television and Allied Technicians
AMOCINE	Associação Moçambicana de Cineastas
AMP	Associação dos Negros Moçambicanos
ANC	African National Congress
APIE	Administração do Parque Imobiliário do Estado
BBC	British Broadcasting Corporation
BIF	British Instructional Films
BSAP	British South African Police
CEA	Centro de Estudos Africanos
CEC	Centro de Estudos de Comunicão
CFMAG	Committee for Freedom in Mozambique, Angola and Guinea-Bissau
CFS	Centralni Filmski Studio Košutnjak
CIO	Rhodesia's (later Zimbabwe's) Central Intelligence Organisation
CONCP	Conference of Nationalist Organizations of the Portuguese Colonies
COREMO	Comité Revolucionário de Moçambique
DGS	Direccão Geral de Segurança
FACIM	Feira Agro-Pecuaria, Comercial e Industrial de Moçambique
FAM	Força Aérea de Moçambique
FPLM	Forças Populares de Libertação de Moçambique
Frelimo	Frente de Libertação de Moçambique
GAT	Grupo Amador de Teatro
GUMO	Grupo Unido de Moçambique
ICAIC	Instituto Cubano del Arte e Industria Cinematográficos
ICS	Instituto de Comunicação Social
IMF	International Monetary Fund
INAC	Instituto Nacional de Audiovisual e Cinema
INC	Instituto Nacional de Cinema
MANU	Moçambique African National Union
MFA	Movimento das Forças Armadas
MNR	Mozambican National Resistance

MPEA	Motion Picture Export Association
MPLA	Movimento Popular de Libertação de Angola
NATO	North Atlantic Treaty Organisation
NGO	Non-governmental organisation
OAU	Organisation of African Unity
ONU	Committee for the Coordination for the Liberation of Africa
PAIGC	Partido Africano da Independência da Guiné e Cabo Verde
PCI	Partido Comunista Italiano
PCP	Partido Comunista Português
PIC	Polícia de Investigação Criminal
PIDE	Polícia Internacional de Defesa do Estado
PPI	Plano Prospectivo Indicativo
Renamo	Resistência Nacional Moçambicana
RSA	Republic of South Africa
SADCC	Southern African Development Coordination Conference
SADF	South African Defence Force
SNCC	Student Non-Violent Coordinating Committee
SWAPO	South West African People's Organisation
TBARN	Técnicas Básicas de Aproveitamento de Recursos
TPA	Televisão Popular de Angola
TVE	Televisão Experimental
UANC	United African National Council
UDENAMO	União Democrática Nacional de Moçambique
UNAMI	União Nacional Africana de Moçambique Independente
UNESCO	United Nations Educational, Scientific and Cultural Organization
UNIPOMO	União dos Povos de Moçambique
UNITA	União Nacional Para a Independência Total de Angola
UPA	União dos Povos de Angola
USSR	Union of Soviet Socialist Republics
ZANLA	Zimbabwe African National Liberation Army
ZANU	Zimbabwe African National Union
ZAPU	Zimbabwe African People's Union
ZIPA	Zimbabwe People's Army
ZIPRA	Zimbabwe People's Revolutionary Army

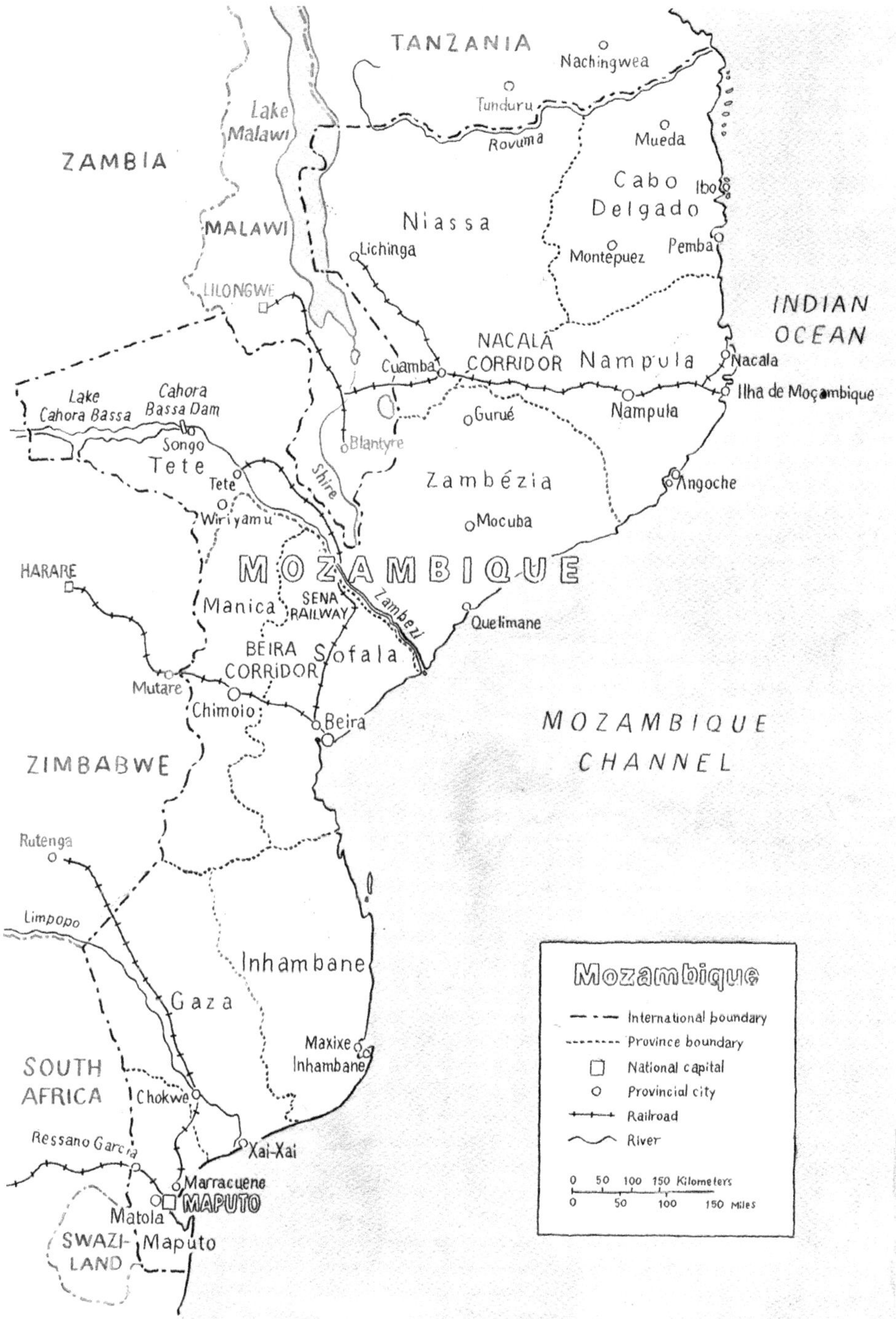
TANZANIA
Nachingwea
Tunduru
Rovuma
Mueda
Lake Malawi
ZAMBIA
Cabo Delgado
Ibo
Niassa
MALAWI
Lichinga
Pemba
Montepuez
LILONGWE
INDIAN OCEAN
NACALA CORRIDOR
Nampula
Nacala
Cuamba
Ilha de Moçambique
Lake Cahora Bassa
Cahora Bassa Dam
Gurué
Songo
Blantyre
Tete
Shire
Zambézia
Angoche
Wiriyamu
Mocuba
MOZAMBIQUE
HARARE
Manica
SENA RAILWAY
Zambezi
Quelimane
BEIRA CORRIDOR
Sofala
Mutare
Chimoio
Beira
MOZAMBIQUE CHANNEL
ZIMBABWE
Rutenga
Limpopo
Inhambane
Gaza
Maxixe
Inhambane
SOUTH AFRICA
Chokwe
Ressano Garcia
Xai-Xai
Marracuene
MAPUTO
Matola
SWAZILAND
Maputo
Mozambique
International boundary
Province boundary
National capital
Provincial city
Railroad
River
0 50 100 150 Kilometers
0 50 100 150 Miles

Introduction

I first visited the building that was once the Instituto Nacional de Cinema 'National Institute of Cinema' (INC) in Maputo in 2004, where I met Gabriel Mondlane, director of the Associação Moçambicana de Cineastes 'Mozambican Association of Filmmakers' (AMOCINE).[1] That occasion in 2004 was the first time that Mondlane recounted to me how he was picked out when he was still at school as one of a group of teenagers selected to receive training as filmmakers. The Frente de Libertação de Moçambique 'Mozambique Liberation Front' (Frelimo), which had led the armed struggle for independence, had in 1975 formed a government, taking control of a country in which most people had little experience of the moving image. In 1976, Frelimo set up the INC and decided that a new generation of Mozambicans – 'the children of workers and peasants' – should be trained as part of a wide-reaching revolutionary project of decolonisation that was intended to destroy the injustices and hierarchies established through colonial rule. Mondlane recounted to me that he discovered that this thing called 'cinema' was a whole world that produced the magic of moving images on the screen. This tantalising surface had been tightly guarded from the curious eyes of small boys like him, who would scuffle when the ushers refused to let them in. Bit by bit Mondlane learnt to use the mysterious buttons and machines in the sound room. In an edition of the INC's *Kuxa Kanema* newsreel from 1981 the young filmmaker is glimpsed at work.[2] A mobile cinema unit travels along a country road with people running behind in excitement. As the van enters the village, a loudspeaker announces that tonight there will be a projection of a film. 'You've heard of Internationalism, haven't you?' the speaker asks. 'This equipment is a gift from the people of the Soviet Union.' Children look on eagerly as the projectionist sets up the projector, and the newsreel cuts to an image of Mondlane inside the van adjusting the sound. Cinema is presented as the conduit and embodiment of socialist friendship and an agent of political

[1] AMOCINE was set up in 1991 to provide mutual assistance in a context in which state support for filmmaking had evaporated. Members included: Gabriel Mondlane, Camilo de Sousa, Isabel Noronha, Licínio Azevedo, João Ribeiro, Sol de Carvalho, Fatima Albuquerque, Ismael Vuvo, Jacinto Bai-Bai, Karl de Sousa and Karen Boswall. It is significant that the organisation is for filmmakers working in Mozambique rather than an association limited to those holding Mozambican nationality, which speaks to an enduring spirit of internationalism.

[2] *Kuxa Kanema*, episode 36, 21–28 December 1981.

mobilisation.[3] Mozambican filmmakers are shown bringing the moving image to the people and, in so doing, are connecting their own struggle to other revolutions around the world.

For more than a decade, the INC operated as the centre of moving-image production in the newly independent nation, and a radical cinema culture flourished despite considerable conditions of adversity. Mobile cinemas trundled across the country showing Mozambican people the new society that they themselves were in the process of constructing. The *Kuxa Kanema* newsreel (first produced in 1978 and 1979, then in a different format from 1981 to 1985) is animated by scenes of collective farms, dances outside factories, visits from foreign heads of state and speeches by President Samora Machel. Increasingly, the film cameras bore witness to the violence that seared across the country in the late 1970s and 1980s, when the government's stand against Apartheid and its commitment to socialist transformation came at a terrible price. White minority-ruled Rhodesia and then the South African Apartheid government sponsored the Mozambican National Resistance (later known by the Portuguese name Resistência Nacional Moçambicana, Renamo) to conduct a war of destabilisation so as to create a buffer zone against the processes of decolonisation and socialist revolution taking place across the African continent. This civil war, which was one of the most destructive conflicts through which the Cold War played out on African soil, tore Mozambican society apart. In Marxist theory, 'overdetermination' refers to a singular event that comes to eclipse all the multiple contradictions that precipitated it.[4] The collapse of the revolution and its dreams for cinema are punctuated by two such overdetermined moments: President Machel's death in a plane crash in 1986 and the devastation by fire of the INC in 1991.

By 1991, the same year as the dissolution of the Soviet Union, privatisation of the film industry was already underway as Mozambique began the transition from a Marxist–Leninist command economy to the free market and multi-party

[3] I first developed the notion of 'socialist friendship' in relation to filmmaking in Ros Gray (2012). 'Haven't you heard of internationalism? The Socialist Friendships of Mozambican Cinema', in Lars Kristensen (ed.) (2012). *Postcommunist Film – Russia, Eastern Europe and World Culture*. London and New York: Routledge.

[4] I will return to the ways in which the two conflagrations are 'overdetermined' in the conclusion. 'Overdetermination' has specific meanings in Freudian and Marxist thought. In *The Interpretation of Dreams*, Freud used the term to indicate the way in which singular effects in dreams were determined by multiple causes, each of which would in itself be enough to produce the effect, which in the dream comes to stand in for, displacing all of the determining causes. In Louis Althusser's reading, which draws on Freud, Marx and Mao, 'overdetermination' describes the way in which contradictions in a society may provoke a singular event, for instance a riot, which comes to displace the multiple causes of unrest. Sigmund Freud (1991). *The Interpretation of Dreams*. London: Penguin: Chapter 6; Louis Althussser (2005). *For Marx*. London: Verso: 87–128.

democracy. This radical shift in political direction paved the way for the 1992 peace settlement with Renamo, which ended sixteen years of civil war. Film production and distribution was privatised, and cinemas that had been run by the state were sold off. The films seemed to be, for the most part, inaccessible and it was not even clear which of the reels had survived the fire. Although a legacy of this period persisted in the pool of skilled professionals still dedicated to socially engaged film production, the revolution that had taken place in cinema in Mozambique was, it seemed, in ruins, scattered in fragments of personal memories, past hopes and present-day disappointments.

When Gabriel Mondlane showed me around the INC building in 2004, we stopped by the AMOCINE office, housed on the upper floor in a room that, unlike most of the second storey, had a roof. On the ground floor, aging Steenbeck editing machines warped and rusted, with parts precariously held together with duck-tape. Whatever film reels had survived the fire were now decaying in the heat and damp that seeped through the walls. Ascending the stairs again, we wandered into the bright sunshine that streamed through the remains of what had been the editing rooms. Mondlane told me that filmmakers now gathered under the stars at night to show each other work-in-progress projected onto the walls. The ghostly silhouettes of equipment and technical fixtures shadowed the concrete, which was pocketed with dents and holes. Mondlane raised his arm, gestured towards a charred wall and said: 'This is our screen.'

This book is woven out of such stories, gathered over more than a decade of work that has involved archival research at institutions and organisations in Mozambique and other parts of the world, and engagement with the growing field of scholarly writing, conferences and exhibitions on Mozambican revolutionary filmmaking and anti-colonial and internationalist cinema more broadly.[5] *Cinemas of the Mozambican Revolution: Anti-colonialism, Independence*

[5] Significant published research since the early 2000s, in chronological order, includes: Manthia Diawara (2003). 'Sonimage in Mozambique', in Gareth James and Florian Zeyfang (eds) (2003). *I Said I Love. That is the Promise. The Tvideo Politics of Jean-Luc Godard.* Berlin: b_books; Marcus Powers (2004). 'Post-colonial Cinema and the Re-configuration of Moçambicanidade'. *Lusotopie*: 261–278; Kodwo Eshun and Ros Gray (2011). *The Militant Image: A Ciné-geography*, special issue of *Third Text*, 1, 108, 25, January; Daniel Fairfax (2010). '*Birth (of the Image) of a Nation:* Jean-Luc Godard in Mozambique'. *Film and Media Studies* 3: 60; Guido Convents (2011). *Os Moçambicanos Perante o Cinema e o Audiovisual. Uma História Politica-Cultural do Moçambique Colonial até à República de Moçambique (1896–2010).* Maputo: CP; Alessandra Meleiro (2011). *Luso-African Cinema.* Special issue of the *Journal of African Cinemas*, 3, 2; Fernando Arenas (2011). *Lusophone Africa: Beyond Independence.* Minneapolis: University of Minnesota Press; Rui Assubuji, Paolo Israel and Drew Thompson (2013). *Notes on the Liberation Script in Mozambican History*, special issue of *Kronos: Southern African Histories*, 39, November; Angela Ferreira (2013). *Political Cameras.* Edinburgh: Stills

and Internationalism in Filmmaking, 1968–1991 is motivated by the desire to understand what was singular about this experiment with the moving image and how filmmaking made a crucial contribution to a nation-building project whose radicalism was grounded in socialist collectivisation, internationalism and decolonisation. It follows a body of work in filmmaking affiliated to a set of political aims and aspirations. It thus begins with the films made during Frelimo's armed struggle for independence (the first of which was made in 1968) and explores the efforts to harness cinema as an agent of social change both nationally and internationally in the context of a socialist revolution through to the Mozambican government's rejection of Marxist–Leninism and the fire that marked the end of the INC in 1991. *Cinemas of the Mozambican Revolution* frames this history and analysis in relation to the revolutionary politics of that radical moment, and in so doing departs from the categories of 'national cinemas' and 'world cinema' that tend to structure contemporary film studies. The radical 'moment' is understood here in the sense evoked in the writings of Henri Lefebvre.[6] It is not a linear measurement of duration but rather the radical moment reveals new possibilities that break through the barriers that limit emancipation. While it signifies a rupture, the radical moment also animates the dual meanings at play in the word 'revolution', which means both a break with the past and a cosmic cycle, and is, in Rob Shield's words, 'full of anticipation, insights into the future and déjà vu'.[7] The reading of the films in the broader context of their production and distribution offered in this book is intended to provide readers, who are for the most part unlikely to have easy access to the films themselves, an understanding of their aesthetic and historical

Scotland's Centre for Photography; Patricia Vieira (2013). *Portuguese Film, 1930–1960: The Staging of the New State Regime*. London: Bloomsbury; Ute Fendler (2014). 'Cinema in Mozambique: New Tendencies in a Complex Mediascape'. *Critical Interventions*, 8, 2: 246–260; Maria do Carmo Piçarra (2015). *Azuis Ultramarinos: Propaganda Colonial e Censura no Cinema do Estado Novo*. Lisbon: Edições 70; Robert Stock (2016). 'Cinema and Conflict in Postcolonial Mozambique: Archival Images as Illustration and Evidence in Estas São as Armas (1978). In Adriana Martins, Alexandra Lopes and Mónica Dias (eds) (2016). *Mediations of Disruption in Post-Conflict Cinema*. London: Palgrave Macmillan; Lúcia Ramos Monteiro (2016). *Africas: Cinema e Revolução*. São Paulo: Caixa Belas Artes; Maria do Carmo Piçarra and Teresa Castro (eds) (2017). *(Re)imagining African Independence: Film, Visual Arts and the Fall of the Portuguese Empire*. London: Peter Lang; Vavy Pacheco Borges (2017). *Ruy Guerra: Paixão Escancarada*. São Paulo: Boitempo; Frederico Lopes, Paulo Cunha and Manuela Penafria (2017). *Cinema em Português – X Jornadas*. Covilhã, Portugal: Universidade da Beira.

[6] As Rob Shields explains, the term 'moment' appears in numerous places in Lefebvre's writing, but rather than providing a precise definition, its significance must be gleaned through an interpretation of these passages. Rob Shields (1999). *Lefebvre, Love and Struggle: Spatial Dialectics*. Routledge: London and New York: 58–60.

[7] Shields (1999): 59.

significance and the ways in which they manifest the contradictions of that proleptic moment of decolonisation. My treatment of the films examines the new cinematic forms that emerged in dialogue both with vernacular culture and local imperatives, and with wider internationalist trajectories of militant filmmaking. I use the plural '*Cinemas*' to indicate that the collective experiences of the cinema screen and an understanding of its transformative potential was at the heart of multiple experiments with the moving image in the process of social change. As such, 'cinemas' includes not just production of film for projection in cinema theatres, but also works made on film and video for distribution via mobile cinema units and television broadcast. The INC developed a successful self-sustaining system of acquisition and distribution that funded production, and so this book situates film aesthetics within a wider history of production, distribution and exhibition that was part of an attempt to decolonise the film industry within Mozambique and in alliance with other decolonising countries. Scholarship on the development of the Hollywood studio system has demonstrated that technologies of the moving image are not neutral, but rather that they reflect the contradictions and injustices of the societies that produce them.[8] *Cinemas of the Mozambican Revolution* traces some of the debates that took place at the INC and other institutions as they appropriated technologies developed in industrialised societies for a country engaged in a process of decolonisation in conditions of scarcity. As television broadcast did not exist in Mozambique at independence in 1975, the revolution provided a unique opportunity to conduct research into ways in which a liberated national television service could be conceived and implemented, one that might avoid the alienating effects of commercial broadcasting in the West while contributing to a project of building national unity. *Cinemas of the Mozambican Revolution* explores one of the specific sites of revolutionary struggle from which films dedicated to African decolonisation made a planetary call for revolution to destroy imperialism. However, the book also investigates more vernacular approaches to film production and aesthetics that emerged in Mozambique that are less concerned with articulating an internationalist affiliation, but rather seek to explore the new revolutionary nationalist sentiments, local histories and forms of cultural expression in an attempt to build national unity across the fissures of race, class and ethnicity that structured colonial Mozambique.

The book begins by examining the films made by foreign filmmakers who came at Frelimo's invitation to document the armed struggle for independence that began in 1964. As explored in Chapter 1, 'We Will Win! Filming the Armed Struggle in Mozambique, 1968–1973', Frelimo lacked the resources to make its own films but collaborated with foreign filmmakers to produce documentaries.

[8] Richard Dyer (1997). *White: Essays on Race and Culture*. London: Routledge.

These were intended to break what Eduardo Mondlane, first President of Frelimo, called the 'curtain of silence' that hid the reality of Portuguese colonialism from the rest of the world and to demonstrate the new kind of society that Frelimo was starting to construct in the liberated zones.[9] From 1967, foreign filmmakers from Yugoslavia, Britain, China, the Soviet Union, Sweden, Italy and elsewhere made documentaries that were used as part of an intense diplomatic campaign in which Frelimo sought to destroy Portugal's claim that its colonial rule was a civilising mission, and attempted to present decolonisation in Mozambique as a humanitarian issue that cut across the polarities of the Cold War. Internal conflicts within Frelimo had erupted into violence in 1968. In 1969 Eduardo Mondlane was assassinated and a faction of Frelimo dedicated to socialist transformation became ascendant, led by Samora Machel.[10] The films made about the armed struggle by sympathetic filmmakers were important in terms of convincing supporters abroad that the Front was a unified organisation with firm control of its campaign, both in terms of military progress and social transformation in the areas it controlled. The chapter thus contextualises these film productions in relation to the first years of Frelimo, which saw the amalgamation in 1962 of regional nationalist movements, the setting up of headquarters in Dar es Salaam in Tanzania, the establishment of the Mozambique Institute, their military camps at Nachingwea and elsewhere in southern Tanzania and, following the launch of the armed struggle in 1964, the organisation of the liberated zones within Mozambique. During these years, Frelimo managed to form alliances that cut across Sino–Soviet tensions. It sought to build on the affiliations of the non-aligned movement, through which Third World countries attempted to foster cooperation so as to avoid dependency on the two superpowers of the Cold War. The armed struggle films were one of the ways through which Frelimo shaped the course of solidarity campaigns in Western Europe and North America. Crucially for the argument that the book makes about the proleptic function of the cinemas of the Mozambican Revolution, rather than the focus on images of combat, the films released between 1969 and 1973 portrayed the new kind of society that Frelimo was building in the liberated zones, through the creation of a new economic system, collectivisation of production, and by providing education, healthcare and opportunities for women. According to Frelimo, the liberated

[9] Eduardo Mondlane (1969). *Struggle for Mozambique*. Harmondsworth: Penguin.

[10] Although the culprit(s) have not been identified and it has been argued that both China and the Soviet Union may have had motivations for ordering Mondlane's assassination, the prevailing consensus is that the letter bomb that killed him was the work of Portuguese agents operating in Mozambique. George Roberts (2017). 'The Assassination of Eduardo Mondlane: Frelimo, Tanzania, and the politics of exile in Dar es Salaam'. *Cold War History*, 17, 1: 1–19.

zones were the precursor to the revolutionary nation that they would construct after independence. Chapter 1 attends to the varying ways in which the liberated zones were represented in these documentaries. While not initially intended for Mozambican audiences, the armed struggle films constitute a powerful image of Mozambican futurity that became foundational for Frelimo's post-independence revolutionary project and key to its claims for legitimacy. Crucially, the chapter studies how key flanks of Frelimo's ideology that were developed during these years are presented in the documentaries about the armed struggle, centred on a demand for disciplined militancy, the development of a decolonial pedagogy and cultural expressions of revolutionary nationalism, and the construction of national unity around an idea of dedication to *o Povo* 'the people'.

Chapter 2, 'From the Rovuma to the Maputo: Confluences of Independence, 1974–1975', focuses on filmmaking with Frelimo during the period of transition to independence. It examines the period from the Carnation Revolution when the Portuguese army overthrew the fascist colonial regime in Portugal in April 1974 to the declaration of independence in Mozambique in June 1975, and the following months, during which time plans were developed for a National Institute of Cinema, which would eventually open in 1976. This chapter examines the confluence of forces that inter-mingled for the first time at this moment and would have varying degrees of influence in shaping Mozambique's cinema culture in the years that followed. These include Frelimo, some of the foreign filmmakers who worked with them during the armed struggle, the cinephiles and amateur filmmakers of the colonial cinema clubs and filmmakers who had been in Portugal to participate in the Carnation Revolution and who, as that opportunity foreclosed, travelled to Mozambique to contribute to the new African nation. The chapter argues that the films made with Frelimo at independence reveal how the Front sought to present itself as a government-in-waiting and the only legitimate representative of the Mozambican people. It also examines the artistic cinema cultures that emerged from within settler society. In the years running up to independence, a number of experimental films were made (often in association with the colonial ciné-clubs) that expressed dissent, despite the oppressive nature of the regime and its extensive use of censorship. The chapter explores how, at independence in Mozambique, there were in fact different visions of what a 'Mozambican' or 'African' cinema might look like. Finally, the chapter examines how Frelimo responded to the need to keep the cinemas open and build film production despite the mass departure of Portuguese settlers, recruiting a team of intellectuals who had been involved with the ciné-clubs to devise a plan for a national film institute that would deliver a cinema of national unity. The films made by the INC would address the multilingual nation in the Portuguese language as means to promote a common revolutionary nationalist identity. They would teach *o Povo* the meaning of

'Independence', what it meant to be a Mozambican, and how the needs and energies of peasants and workers would dictate the revolution.

The following chapter, 'Birth (of the Image) of a Nation: Delivering Cinema to the People, 1976–1978', Chapter 3 studies the first few years of the setting up of the INC, which was established with a mission to 'deliver to the people an image of the people'. These initial years were a time of experimentation with, and conflict over, what it might mean to decolonise filmmaking and the wider system of film distribution and exhibition in a context of scarcity and a situation in which most of the population of Mozambique had little or no previous experience of the moving image. This chapter considers how Frelimo's policies to shape a Mozambican revolutionary nationalist cinema were implemented, the effort to train a new generation of Mozambican filmmakers and the impact of various foreign technicians and 'experts' who were invited to contribute as paid development workers known as *cooperantes*. The chapter explores how, alongside the seizure of equipment by Frelimo from the colonial film production houses, the INC provided opportunities for foreign filmmakers to relinquish their technological superiority through pedagogy, empowering a newly independent people by handing over knowledge of the means of production. Tensions at the INC between striving for technological perfection and exploring the emancipatory possibilities of other film formats more associated with amateur, artistic or militant film reflected debates that had been fomenting internationally. The chapter explores the internationalism of efforts to build a national cinema in Mozambique, both at the INC and at Eduardo Mondlane University, and how they were in dialogue with some of the most pressing discussions regarding militant filmmaking taking place around the world. Alongside the project to collectivise film production and open up the profession to people who were cut off from moving-image technology under colonialism, there was a concerted effort to take cinema to 'the people'. This involved not only the setting up of a network of distribution via mobile cinema units, but also experimentation with how to make films for this new audience that would further the revolution. The chapter surveys a number of experiments and proposals involving Super-8 and video and discusses the tensions that emerged between film's ethnographic capacity to capture scenes of everyday life, replete with contradictions and unscripted elements, and the imperative to use cinema to promote a clear political line defined by Frelimo.

Chapter 4, 'Who Exactly is the Party? Didacticism, the Battle of Information and the Vanguard Party, 1977–1979', addresses the didactic purpose of many of the INC's film productions, the role that cinema was understood to play in the 'battle of information' and the ways in which films made during these years address their audiences as people learning how to participate in the Mozambican Revolution. The chapter makes a detailed analysis of how short documentaries and the first version of the *Kuxa Kanema* newsreel that was produced in 1978 and 1979 answered to this demand, arguing that rather than assuming that these modes of communication are authoritarian, they may also be understood as anticipatory. The battle of information was motivated not only by the urgent need to disseminate information and mobilise the population, but also involved the crucial work that film could perform in terms of challenging the narratives about the region that were circulated by the white minority regimes in Rhodesia and South Africa. The chapter makes a reading of key documentaries made during these years that responded to attacks by the Rhodesian army on Mozambican territory, exploring works that provide a different model of didactic filmmaking based on emotive sensorial devices associated with propaganda and presenting a pedagogical approach to the reading of images, in which the viewer is instructed on how to make a decolonial interpretation of the colonial archive. In 1977, Frelimo announced that it was transforming into a vanguard Marxist–Leninist Party, aligning itself internationally more firmly with the Soviet Union and the Eastern Bloc. The chapter explores the implications that this pursuit of political purity had for filmmaking in the years that followed, through a close interpretation of the production history and aesthetics of Ruy Guerra's film *Mueda, Memória Massacre* 'Mueda, Memory and Massacre' (1979). The documentary revolves around a re-enactment of the massacre of civilians that took place in Mueda, Cabo Delgado, in 1960, an event that is credited with galvanising the independence struggle. Encompassing carnivalesque community theatre, eye-witness testimony and ethnographic scenes of everyday life in the revolution, *Mueda, Memória Massacre* presents a complex and self-reflexive interrogation of the making of the film itself as a moment in which collective memory articulated through performance is harnessed to the narrative of the nation-state.

At the onset of the 1980s, with the independence of Zimbabwe bringing attacks from Rhodesia to an end, Frelimo believed that Mozambique was poised to launch into a 'decade of development' that would involve a great leap forward in modernisation. Chapter 5, 'A New Symphony: Cinema and Television in the "Decade of Development", 1980–1984', examines film production in the early 1980s, which saw not only an expansion in the number of documentaries and newsreels made by the INC, but also a radical overhaul of the institution. The new Minister of Information José Luís Cabaço led this drive to increase professionalism and efficiency, which resulted in a re-launch of the *Kuxa Kanema* newsreel with a new, shorter format. The chapter focuses on efforts to harness documentary filmmaking to the projects of development, collectivisation and national unity and considers various attempts to develop filmmaking practices appropriate to the lived realities of Mozambicans and that would assist in the campaign against 'underdevelopment' in terms of literacy, health, agriculture, industrial production and female empowerment through the formation of cooperatives. The contestation between different approaches to revolutionary filmmaking continued, not only through the influence of foreign *cooperantes* and delegations from other socialist countries, but also through the varying approaches by Mozambican filmmakers themselves to the documentation of Mozambican cultural expression, particularly music and dance.

Explorations that began in the late 1970s into what technologies of the moving image would be appropriate to the Mozambican context continued, both through the launch of Televisão Experimental and in more marginal filmmaking projects hosted by Eduardo Mondlane University, which moved on from Super-8 to use video to support rural development. Aspects of the ambition to democratise production continued in the work of the Instituto de Communicão Social (ICS), which trained *correspondentes populares* 'people's reporters' to report on news stories affecting their communities. While Frelimo's public discourse continued to proclaim its adherence to Marxist–Leninism, the Mozambican government was beginning to court Western financial institutions and explore ways of opening up to the free market, as it sought to respond to the economic crisis that was engulfing the country. Chapter 5 describes the setting up of Kanemo, a private film production company established in collaboration with key figures in the Security Services as a means to interface with the free market. As the chapter explores, this took place in the context of a growing number of attacks by the MNR (known as Renamo after 1984) and anxiety about infiltration by the 'internal enemy'. The chapter examines some of the films that addressed how Frelimo dealt with 'counter-revolutionary' behaviour through both re-education and rituals of public confessions.

Chapter 6, 'Let Them Come! Filmmaking on the Frontline against Apartheid, 1980–1989', examines Mozambique's role in regional filmmaking collaborations in the 1980s, which sought to make an intervention against South Africa's campaign of destabilisation that targeted the independent nations around its border. It considers how a number of Southern African films attempted to shift global narratives about the region that privileged the perspectives of white minorities and former colonial powers, situating this work in relation to a wider discourse about neocolonial North–South power imbalances that continued to shape global media flows. The chapter makes a close analysis of *Pamberi ne Zimbabwe* 'Onwards Zimbabwe' (1980), a co-production between Angola and Mozambique made as a gift to the new nation; *Fronteiras de Sange* 'Borders of Blood' (1986), a Kanemo production directed by Mario Borgneth; and *Corridors of Freedom* (1987), directed by Zimbabwean Simon Bright with a crew from the Southern African region; among other documentaries and reports made by the INC about South African and Renamo attacks in Mozambique. It considers the way in which a number of documentaries present the significance of the Southern African Development Coordination Conference (SADCC), an organisation dedicated to regional cooperation to break economic dependency on Apartheid South Africa, which used economic coercion alongside military strategies to destabilise neighbouring states and bolster its dominance in the region. This international cooperation in film production is read as a continuation of earlier efforts at state level to re-organise the cinema industry at a regional level to support national film production in newly independent countries. While state institutions and socialist aspirations in Mozambique began to crumble under the pressure of the economic crisis and the devastation of the war, film cooperation on the frontline against Apartheid persisted. However, as the chapter argues, this was more a consequence of the commitment of individual filmmakers than the result of support from their governments, who stood to benefit from these regional cinematographic collaborations.

In 1984, Frelimo signed the Nkomati Accord with the South African government in a bid to halt the war of destabilisation, with Mozambique committing to end the sanctuary it provided for the African National Congress (ANC) and Pretoria agreeing to stop its support of Renamo. However, the Apartheid government failed to honour the terms of the agreement. Renamo stepped up its campaign to gain a firmer base within Mozambique and began developing a political platform of anti-communist defence of traditional cultures. Renamo was able to build on dissent from Frelimo, and by the mid-1980s the Mozambican government could only guarantee security in the large urban centres and along the coastline. Frelimo's campaign against the 'armed bandits' led the government to increase coercive tactics against its own population in an attempt to flush out the 'internal enemy'. Chapter 7 explores this as the context for three major feature-length fiction films that were made in the mid- to late 1980s. The first, Zdravko Velimrović's *O Tempo dos Leopardos* 'The Time of the Leopards' (1985), is examined as a last instance of cinematographic collaboration with the non-aligned nation of Yugoslavia. The socialist friendship with Yugoslavia had been manifested in filmmaking during the armed struggle and the transition to independence through documentary production, but the production history of *O Tempo dos Leopardos* reveals tensions between the desire for a war epic, drawing on the Yugoslav tradition of the Partisan film, and the attempt by Mozambican filmmakers to be truthful to the lived experience of the struggle. By contrast, *O Vento Sopre do Norte* 'The Wind Blows from the North' (1987) is a fiction feature scripted and directed by José Cardoso, made as a Mozambican production on 16mm black-and-white film so as to demonstrate the INC's capacity for independence. Cardoso's film denounced colonial society and drew attention to the way in which sexual violence towards women was a key aspect of fascist colonialism. In so doing, it offered another glimpse of what a Mozambican 'national cinema' could be, one in which history is filtered through the personal vision of the director. Production of Cardoso's film nearly halted when the country was thrown into disarray by the death of Machel in an aeroplane crash on South African territory in 1986. Machel's death marked a shift in Frelimo that had already been underway, to move from a socialist command economy to seek integration with Western financial institutions and the free market so as to secure much-needed loans. Frelimo's socialist project continued to wither away as the country was brought to its knees by famine and violence. The chapter describes the impact that this disintegration had on the INC, as its funds began to be reallocated by the government for other purposes and policy shifted direction towards initiating privatisation of the film industry. At this moment, Licínio Azevedo and Brigitte Bagnol directed *A Colheita do Diablo* 'The Devil's Harvest' (1988), a feature length fiction film shot on video that involved non-professional actors and a close attention to the lived realities of rural Mozambicans. While film production and cinema exhibition all but collapsed at the end of the 1980s even before the devastating fire of 1991, *A Colheita do Diablo* points towards the docu-drama. This hybrid mode of filmmaking emerged in the wake of the INC, offering a way in which Mozambican filmmakers could continue to make films that were socially engaged albeit in political circumstances that were radically different.

Cinemas of the Mozambican Revolution contributes to understanding the emergence of filmmaking dedicated to anti-colonialism, independence and internationalism, as part of a revolutionary project of decolonisation that began with the armed struggle and was foreclosed with the collapse of state socialism in the late 1980s. It argues that during these years Mozambique was a crucial site for experiments with ways in which the collective experience of the cinema screen could be harnessed for the purposes of radical social change. Looking beyond the two 'overdetermined' moments of Machel's death and the fire at the INC, the conclusion explores how some of the ambitions for cinema nurtured at the INC continued to be pursued in other guises after 1991, not least through a body of work produced by filmmakers formed through their experience at the INC who continue to make socially engaged films that cast a critical eye on the realities of the neoliberal present, as well as celebrating the diversity and resilience of Mozambican culture. In resisting the trope of disappointment that tends to cast revolutionary change as doomed to failure, this book retrieves the notion of the radical moment to understand the continuing affective charge of these films that anticipate a new society, even while fraught with the contradictions of the past and enduring forms of injustice. The book thus concludes by considering the ways in which some of the films analysed in this book have re-emerged in recent years, both through restoration projects that have re-circulated certain films, and through the way in which the films of the armed struggle and the INC have been incorporated into new works.

These phenomena are read here as 'afterlives' of the INC.[11] As such, this book seeks to make a contribution to scholarship on this unique moment of the Mozambican Revolution and its manifestation in, and through, sounds and images that announced the building of a new world.

[11] The work of Kristin Ross has been an important reference point. In particular, her books *May '68 and its Afterlives* and *Communal Luxury: The Political Imaginary of the Paris Commune*, which read historical revolts against the grain of the interpretations that came to dominate in the decades that followed those events. She emphasises the often overlooked anti-colonial and internationalist impulses at the heart of both, and her methodology involves engaging with the thinking and actions of key participants, who understood that they were involved in moments of historical significance. Kristin Ross (2002). *May '68 and its Afterlives*. Chicago: University of Chicago Press; Kristin Ross (2015). *Communal Luxury: The Political Imaginary of the Paris Commune*. London: Verso.

1 We Will Win! Filming the Armed Struggle in Mozambique, 1968–1973

By 1968 the Frente de Libertação de Moçambique (Frelimo) had been operating for six years. It had succeeded in combining regional anti-colonial organisations into a united front and had established headquarters in Dar es Salaam in Tanzania, where the Mozambique Institute provided housing and education for refugees fleeing colonial rule. Some refugees were settled in the south of Tanzania, where Frelimo set up a military training base at Nachingwea, a hospital at Mtwara and a children's education centre at Tunduru. The armed insurrection, which began in 1964, led to the capture of territory in the north of Mozambique, which Frelimo called 'the liberated zones'. The liberated zones are conjured in the films of the armed struggle made with Frelimo through images of guerrillas marching through the forest, columns of peasants carrying supplies, makeshift health clinics and schools comprising a blackboard hanging from a tree. Their meaning is conveyed in the faces and voices of men and women who describe how the armed struggle was transforming their lives. A new culture of revolutionary nationalism, the films argue, was being created in these sites through the collaboration between Frelimo and local peoples. The unity, discipline and cultural richness of this liberation movement are asserted in first-person accounts and scenes of everyday life, in dances, poetry, sculpture, speeches and songs.

During the armed struggle, filmmakers, photographers, journalists and activists from across the world were invited to see for themselves the base at Nachingwea in Tanzania and the liberated zones in the provinces of Cabo Delgado, Niassa and Tete. As documented in a regular column, 'Visitors in the Liberated Zones', in the Frelimo journal *Mozambican Revolution*, they came from Yugoslavia, the Soviet Union, China, Japan, Western and Eastern Europe, the United States, Algeria and Tanzania. This geographical range indicates the plural approach that Frelimo took during the armed struggle in cultivating alliances across the divisions of the Cold War and the Sino–Soviet split. Frelimo lacked the facilities to make its own films and it did not have the means to distribute and project films in the territories within Mozambique that it controlled. In the long history of revolutionary struggles in the twentieth century, this was not unusual. Frelimo was one of many revolutionary movements operating in conditions of scarcity, who drew on the commitment of militant filmmakers from elsewhere who had the knowledge, experience and access to a technology that was expensive and required skill.[1] In this tradition of militant filmmaking, pedagogy is a crucial component of a set of practices that seek to use cinema to make an intervention in situations of radical transformation. At this moment of filmmaking with Frelimo, however, the armed struggle films were not initially addressed to the Mozambican people, nor did the filmmakers who visited the liberated zones engage in training. Instead, the documentaries they made were intended to teach foreign audiences as part of an intense diplomatic campaign, in which Frelimo shaped the course of internationalist solidarity activism.

Frelimo's diplomatic campaign had three interconnected aims. First, it sought to break through the 'curtain of silence' in the West surrounding Portuguese oppression in Mozambique.[2] Putting the spotlight on atrocities such as the massacre of more than 500 civilian nationalist protestors at Mueda on 16 June 1960, it aimed to destroy Portugal's claim that its colonial rule was a civilizing mission and to make support for it by NATO members unacceptable. Second, it attempted to position decolonisation as a humanitarian issue that cut across the polarities of the Cold War.[3] Some of the films made with Frelimo were a means for delegations from socialist countries such as the Soviet Union and China to report back on an armed struggle that their governments were supporting by providing arms and military training. Others, crucially, were a way for Frelimo to reach out to potential sympathisers in the West who could provide humanitarian assistance and put pressure on their own governments to change their policies on Southern Africa and break ties with white minority and colonial regimes. Third, it aimed to tell the world about the new kind of society that Frelimo was building in the liberated zones, one that would 'end the exploitation

[1] The Dutch socialist filmmaker Joris Ivens (who participated through filmmaking in the Spanish Civil War and the Chinese struggle against the Japanese invasion, and trained cameramen to film the People's Militia during the Cuban revolution) is an emblematic example of this nomadic radicalism. According to Michael Chanan, Joris Ivens was a pivotal figure in the setting up of the Instituto Cubano del Arte e Industria Cinematográficos (ICAIC) in Cuba, and his pedagogical flair was given its greatest challenge when he took on the task of training military cameramen to film the People's Militia. They had only two months and had to learn from wooden models of cameras. Ivens's films were amongst those included in the first edition of FESPACO in Ouagadougou in 1969, which indicates how his work was recognised by the festival organisers as sharing similar revolutionary objectives to their own. See Michael Chanan (2003). *Cuban Cinema*. Minneapolis: University of Minnesota: 198 and Ros Gray (2007). 'Ambitions of Cinema: Revolution, Event, Screen'. PhD Dissertation, London: Goldsmiths, University of London: Chapter 6.

[2] Eduardo Mondlane (1969). *Struggle for Mozambique*. Harmondsworth: Penguin: 17.

[3] Sérgio Vieira interviewed by Tor Sellström. Tor Sellström (2002). *Liberation in Southern Africa – Regional and Swedish Voices*. Nordiska Afrikainstitutet, Uppsala: 54.

of man by man' through the creation of a new economic system, collectivising production, and the provision of education, healthcare and opportunities for women. According to Frelimo, the liberated zones were the precursor to the revolutionary nation that they would construct after independence.

Although filmmakers framed the armed struggle in ways that reflected the cultural and political contexts of the audiences they sought to address, Frelimo carefully orchestrated how its revolution was depicted on the screen. Beyond the significance of these films for Frelimo's international diplomatic campaign, this first phase of militant filmmaking is important for the powerful image of Mozambican futurity it produced. The liberated zones in the northern regions of Mozambique had a symbolic and metonymic significance beyond their military importance: they were sites where new modes of collective production were tested out. The liberated zones comprised small communities scattered over vast distances of rugged, forested terrain. Yet while they were vulnerable to Portuguese aerial bombardment and frequently had to be abandoned, these settlements function in the films as evidence that Frelimo was not, as Lisbon claimed, a mere 'terrorist' group.[4] Instead, the guerrillas and the communities they worked with are presented in the films as united in a principled organisation that was enacting a social revolution – creating a microcosm of the nation to come.

This image of Mozambican futurity was foundational for Frelimo's post-independence revolutionary project. In the years that followed, the liberated zones took on a status that has been described as 'mythic'.[5] In a special issue of the journal *Kronos* published in 2013, João Paulo Borges Coelho calls attention to the way in which the revolutionary reorganisation of everyday life in the context of the armed struggle was formulated into a 'Liberation Script', which came to function for Frelimo as a 'total historical explanation . . . located at the crossroads of power and knowledge'.[6] Its purpose in the new nation, Borges argues, was both to legitimate Frelimo as governing power and to act as a kind of 'navigation chart' to run the country:

[4] In 1968 Michael Sheppard directed a film shot in Guinea-Bissau about the Partido Africano para a Independência da Guiné e Cabo Verde 'African Party for the Independence of Guinea and Cape Verde' (PAIGC) for the ITN World in Action series called *A Group of Terrorists Attacked. . .* (1968). The title refers to a Portuguese newspaper article that is typical for the way in which Portuguese propaganda sought to dismiss the actions of the liberation movements challenging colonial rule. British anti-colonial historian Basil Davidson played a crucial role in the production.

[5] João Paulo Borges Coelho (2013). 'Politics and Contemporary History in Mozambique: A Set of Epistemological Notes'. *Notes on The Liberation Script in Mozambican History*, special issue of *Kronos*, 39, November: 13.

[6] Borges Coehlo (2013): 20.

> Working as a tangible piece of the future placed in the past, the liberated areas emerged therefore as a sort of 'fabricated reality' that tested and proved that the Front had the correct solutions to run the country.[7]

Borges' comment is understood here to refer to the way in which the revolutionary strategies and values that were developed by Frelimo during the armed struggle not only provided direction for government policy after independence, but also became the watchwords for a wide range social and behavioural change. The films analysed in this chapter are crucial to the construction of the cinematographic image of the liberated zones, and to understanding their proleptic power for imagining a socialist future for Mozambique. While the films were not exhibited in Mozambique during the armed struggle, they were a vital component of the cinema culture that was constructed after independence. Indeed, the documentaries made during the armed struggle were the first films projected as part of the independence celebrations in 1975, at a moment when Frelimo was suddenly faced with the task of convincing an entire nation of its legitimacy to govern. In the years that followed, they were frequently projected in cinemas, distributed across rural areas via the mobile cinema units, and later broadcast on television; sections of them were endlessly recycled in new films. The films of the armed struggle that were made during these intense few years were produced by foreigners, but they were made for Mozambique.

It is necessary to take some steps backwards so as to contextualise these film productions in relation to the first years of Frelimo, which saw the amalgamation in 1962 of regional nationalist movements, the setting up of headquarters in Dar es Salaam, the establishment of the Mozambique Institute, the camp at Nachingwea and, following the launch of the armed struggle in 1964, the organisation of the liberated zones within Mozambique. In the early years of the struggle, Frelimo forged socialist friendships that cut across Sino–Soviet tensions, drawing on Soviet and Chinese military assistance, while nurturing other connections within the non-aligned movement and with sympathisers within NATO. This chapter traces out Frelimo's direction of its international diplomatic campaign, including the recruitment of foreign activists to work for the Front in Tanzania, and how it oversaw the establishment of solidarity committees in Western Europe, Scandinavia and North America. In so doing, it examines the forms of socialist friendship and the solidarity work that led to the films that were produced between 1968 and 1973. As the struggle developed, tensions of class, ethnic rivalry and ideological difference emerged within Frelimo. These conflicts threatened to split the organisation, and there were eruptions of violence during the late 1960s that changed the organisation from a plural alliance to a revolutionary movement that prized discipline to the party

[7] Borges Coehlo (2013): 20.

line. Following the assassination of Frelimo's first president, Eduardo Mondlane, in 1969, this conflict, which has been described as the 'battle between the two lines', resulted in Frelimo's decisive turn to embrace Marxist–Leninism.[8] Thus one of the contradictions of the films produced from 1968 is that their insistence on the unity of Frelimo to reassure foreign supporters masked schisms that were to have enduring consequences.

This background of intense conflict, agitation and diplomacy is essential to understand how Frelimo sought to harness film to communicate its message to the world. It outlines the films' production histories and circuits of distribution, which form a cinematographic map of internationalist solidarity and socialist friendship. These include: *Venceremos* 'We Will Win' (1968), made by Yugoslav Dragutin Popović; *Behind the Lines* (1971) by British filmmaker Margaret Dickinson; *The People of Mozambique are Fighting On* (1971), directed by Chinese filmmaker Tan Qi; *Viva Frelimo!* (1971), made by a Soviet film crew and directed by Yuri Egorov and Leonid Maksimov; *I vårt land börjar kulorna blomma* 'In Our Country the Bullets Start to Blossom' (1971), by Swedish filmmakers Lennart Malmer and Ingela Romare;[9] *A Luta Continua* 'The Struggle Continues' (1971), by African-American civil right activist Robert van Lierop; *Dieci giorni con I guerriglieri nel Mozambico Livro* 'Ten Days with the Guerrillas in Free Mozambique' (1972), made by Italian Franco Cigarini, who was part of a delegation from the Communist municipality of Reggio Emilia. Finally the chapter considers *Étudier, Produire, Combattre* 'Study, Produce, Fight' (1973), made by the French collective Cinéthique with Frelimo, and the investigations of journalists such as the West Germans Reinhart Biermann and Ursula Pauli, who were among those who reported on the massacres of civilians by the Portuguese Army in Tete. These films reached out to communities with little knowledge about Mozambique or the realities of Portuguese colonialism. They sought to create new forms of identification, appealing to socialist solidarity but also to humanitarian values in countries whose governments would not be willing to consider military support to a movement that was increasingly orientated towards Marxist–Leninism.

Despite the wave of decolonisation that had swept across the Continent at the turn of the 1960s, the lusophone independence movements struggled against ignorance and indifference in the West regarding Portugal's use of mass violence, forced labour and discrimination in its African colonies. A rare foray into the realities of colonial Mozambique resulted in the 1959 article 'The dictatorship

[8] Aquino de Bragança and Jacques Depelchin (1988). 'From the Idealisation of Frelimo to the Understanding of Mozambique Recent History'. *Review (Fernand Braudel Center)*, 11, 1, Winter: 95–117.

[9] Dutch television crew from Kenmerk comprising Rob de Vries, Wim Louwrier and Henk Venema.

of Silence', written by Swedish journalist Per Wästberg. It denounced a country where:

> censorship, a well-trained state police and espionage keep criticism under lock and key. . . . Those who know most speak the least. . . . A triumphant curtain of silence which few foreigners manage to penetrate surrounds Mozambique. The whites keep silent about what they know. The authorities are unwilling to give actual information. . . . And the blacks do not have a voice. They are deliberately prevented from getting education [and] they are being cut off from news from the awakening Africa that surrounds them. At the least false step they risk corporal punishment and deportation. Nobody knows their thoughts and there is no one to give them expression.[10]

Eduardo Mondlane's book *Struggle for Mozambique* discusses the 'dearth of information' about the country and how this state of affairs was perpetuated by the Portuguese regime.[11] Ignorance helped the Portuguese regime to hide neglect, violent oppression and discrimination. NATO allies had vested interests in maintaining the status quo in Southern Africa; they continued to supply Portugal with arms, trained Portuguese soldiers in counter-insurgency combat and supported Portugal diplomatically. The Portuguese account of its empire as an anti-communist civilizing mission was accepted largely without question by countries whose vast wealth and global influence was built on centuries of colonial conquest and slavery.

Yet the tide of international opinion was turning, marked by the UN's adoption in 1960 of the Declaration on the Granting of Independence to Colonial Countries and Peoples, which rejected the legitimacy of colonial regimes. The following year, in February 1961, Mondlane, the first Mozambican to gain a PhD and an official to the UN, visited the country to assess the climate for a campaign against colonial rule.[12] The huge crowd that gathered to hear his necessarily restrained speech included Samora Machel and others who, within the next few years, would leave Mozambique to join Frelimo.[13] Already by the early 1960s, three regional nationalist movements had been established: the Mozambique African National Union (MANU), set up by Mozambican-born Makondes living in Tanganika (now Tanzania); the União Democrática Nacional de Moçambique (UDENAMO), which was formed in Bulawayo in

[10] Per Wästberg (1959). 'Tystnaden diktur' ('The Dictatorship of Silence'). *Dagens Nyheter*, 14 November; quoted in Tor Sellström (2002). *Sweden and National Liberation in Southern Africa Volume 1*. Uppsala: Nordiska Afrikainstitutet: 442.

[11] Mondlane (1969): 15.

[12] Sayaka Funada-Classen (2013). *The Origins of War in Mozambique: A History of Unity and Division*. Cape Town: African Minds: 224.

[13] As Funada-Classen points out, Mondlane was aware that PIDE agents would be among the audience. Funada-Classen (2013): 224.

Southern Rhodesia (now Zimbabwe) by Ndau from central Mozambique; and the União Nacional Africana de Moçambique Independente (UNAMI), which was set up in Nyasaland (now Malawi) by migrant workers and exiles from Tete. These three anti-colonial organisations recognised the need to unify into a single national liberation movement, as historical resistance to colonialism by Mozambicans never managed to transcend local struggles galvanised around individual figureheads.[14] The Conference of Nationalist Organisations of the Portuguese Colonies (CONCP) encouraged an alliance, as did President Kwame Nkumrah of Ghana and President Julius Nyerere of Tanzania. While Nkumrah and Nyerere had competing ideas about how a Mozambican independence movement should be directed, they shared a Pan-African vision of liberation and were concerned about the fragmentation of African independence movements, which, as in the Congo Crisis of 1960, had tended to serve neocolonial agendas.[15]

In 1962 Nyerere persuaded Eduardo Mondlane to become the leader of a movement that would unite MANU, UDENAMO and UNAMI, offering to host the headquarters in Dar es Salaam.[16] Mondlane was elected as Frelimo's first President, with the Presbyterian Minister Uria Simango, who had been the vice-president of UDENAMO, as his deputy. The fact that Mondlane was the most qualified and internationally connected was not his only advantage: having lived abroad for some years, he also benefitted from not being directly associated with any of the regional, and potentially rival, movements being brought under the umbrella of Frelimo. Mondlane's approach to leadership is described by Mustafah Dhada as 'charismatic pluralism': 'He was to deploy the force of his personality and his considerable persuasive skills to bring disparate nationalist forces to co-exist and thence work together towards one aim – a free Mozambique.'[17] At the First Congress of Frelimo, held in Dar es Salaam on 23 September 1962, solidarity and unity were recognised as the two

[14] It is noteworthy that all of these organisations included 'Mozambique' in their name, rather than the name of the region they hailed from – their ambitions were national rather than local.

[15] In 1960 Patrice Lumumba, the first elected president of the Republic of Congo, was challenged when the regions of Katanga and South Kasai seceded with support from the Belgian army and UN troops stationed in the Congo were ordered not to intervene. Lumumba appealed to the Soviet Union, who sent military assistance, but Joseph-Désiré Mobutu, who was in charge of the army, led a *coup d'état*, expelled the Soviet advisors and brought the government under his control. Lumumba was placed in captivity and shortly afterwards assassinated by Belgian agents. Godfrey Mwakikagile (2010). *Nyerere and Africa: End of an Era*. Pretoria and Dar es Salaam: New Africa Press.

[16] In 1961 Fanuel Mahluza, vice-president of UDENAMO, invited Mondlane to join their organisation, but he refused. According to Godfrey Mwakikagile, only Nyerere convinced him to leave New York and lead a united front. Mwakikagile (2010): 217.

[17] Mustafa Dhada (2016). *The Portuguese Massacre of Wiriyamu in Colonial Mozambique, 1964–2013*. London: Bloomsbury: 3.

fundamental weapons of struggle against colonialism and that it would be necessary to 'seek broad international support for the forthcoming struggle to liberate Mozambique'.[18] The gathering also recognised that, because of Lisbon's determination to hold on to its colonies, armed struggle was the only means by which independence could be achieved.

Initially, following the formation of Frelimo in 1962, a number of recruits were sent for military training to Algeria, which was becoming an important refuge for anti-colonial and Communist activists resisting fascism in Portugal.[19] However, Frelimo's leaders knew that further assistance would be needed. In 1961 Nikita Khrushchev had announced Soviet support for national liberation wars all over the world, re-animating Lenin's notion of 'World Revolution' that understood the colonies to be imperialism's 'weakest link' and that an alliance between the Soviet bloc and the colonised would make certain 'the final victory of socialism'.[20] While Frelimo began as a coalition of organisations with a range of political positions and influences, a powerful faction sought to shape the movement into a Marxist–Leninist party. The USSR came to see Frelimo as the only viable liberation movement capable of challenging Portuguese colonialism, despite initial concerns about Mondlane's connections with the United States.[21] In 1963 they began providing military training for Frelimo, increasing their assistance after the launch of the armed struggle in 1964.

Under Mondlane's leadership, Frelimo sought to avoid being perceived as taking sides in the Sino–Soviet split, unlike other liberation movements such as the ANC, and pursued a policy that the Frelimo president described as 'Panafrican neutralism in the Cold War'.[22] The Chinese government's support for Frelimo was helped by the fact that China already had a close relationship with Nyerere's government.[23] Nyerere made numerous visits to China in the 1960s and his *ujamaa* theory of African socialism was strongly influenced by Maoism.[24] Mao Tse-Tung himself received a delegation from Frelimo in 1963, and promises of military supplies followed.[25] According to Ian Taylor, when Frelimo launched its armed struggle in 1964, it was with Chinese-made

[18] John Marcum (1969). *The Angolan Revolution, Volume I: The Anatomy of an Explosion (1950–1962)*. Cambridge, MA, and London: The MIT Press: 284.

[19] Sellström, Volume 1 (2002): 447.

[20] Funada-Classen (2012): 207.

[21] Vladimir Shubin (2008). *The Hot 'Cold War': The USSR in Southern Africa*. Chicago: University of Chicago Press: 119–120.

[22] The ANC sided with Moscow.

[23] Shubin (2008): 129.

[24] James C. Scott (1999). *Seeing Like a State: How Certain Schemes to Improve the Human Condition Have Failed*. Boston: Yale University Press.

[25] Ian Taylor (2006). *China and Africa: Engagement and Compromise*. London and New York: Routledge: 93.

weapons.[26] From 1965 Frelimo fighters received instruction in Chinese guerrilla warfare at one side of the base at Nachingwea, while Soviet military personnel ran a training camp on the other. Chinese guerrilla warfare tactics enabled Frelimo to develop a campaign of attacks against the Portuguese army that were an effective strategy in rugged forested terrain.[27] Frelimo thus became the only African liberation movement that was able to receive sustained assistance from both Communist superpowers.[28]

Meanwhile, Frelimo also focused on civilian support and development, reaching out to potential sympathisers in the West. The centre of this effort was the Mozambique Institute, which was set up in 1963 with a grant from the Ford Foundation secured by Janet Mondlane, Eduardo Mondlane's American wife. Its objective was to provide education and teach nursing skills to Mozambican refugees in Tanzania, most of whom had an extremely low level of education. The teachers at the Mozambique Institute were aware that they were involved, as Jacinto Veloso recalls, in teaching 'something new, participating in the beginning stages of the education system of a country soon to be independent'.[29] They devised new courses in geography and history that focused on Mozambique rather than Portugal and taught techniques such as mapping, which might be useful for when the students joined the armed struggle.[30] The grant from the Ford Foundation provided the money to build a hostel for young Mozambicans, who were taught by senior Mozambicans and international volunteers. Frelimo recognised the acute shortage of educated Mozambicans who could take on leadership roles after independence, and the students at the Mozambique Institute were part of a small elite who had had some basic education in colonial schools.[31] The first students of the Mozambique Institute moved into the building at Kurasini outside Dar es Salaam in September 1964. However, as soon as Frelimo launched the armed struggle, the Ford Foundation withdrew its funding under pressure from Portugal. In response, Janet and Eduardo Mondlane turned their attention to Scandinavia.

[26] Taylor (2006): 94.

[27] Taylor (2006): 94.

[28] Bogdan Szajkowski (ed.) (1981). *Marxist Governments: A World Survey*. London: Palgrave Macmillan: 532.

[29] Jacinto Veloso (2012). *Memories at Low Altitude: The Autobiography of a Mozambican Security Chief*. Cape Town: Zebra Press.

[30] Veloso (2012).

[31] Joanna T. Tague (2015). 'Mozambican Refugee Settlement and Rural Development in Southern Tanzania, 1964–75', in Iris Berger, Tricia Redeker Hepner, Benjamin N. Lawrance, Joanna T. Tague, and Meredith Terretta (2015). *African Asylum at the Crossroads: Activism, Expert Testimony, and Refugee Rights*. Athens: Ohio University Press: 38–57, esp. 42.

Although Sweden had trade connections with Mozambique and made substantial use of the deep-water port of Lourenço Marques, the plight of Mozambicans was almost entirely unknown by the Swedes in the 1950s. This was to change during the 1960s thanks to the efforts of a number of highly committed journalists and activists, including Per Wästberg, author of the 1959 article, 'Dictatorship of Silence', cited above.[32] In 1961 the Swedish newspaper *Expressen* published a full-page article written by Marcelino dos Santos, and the same year the Mozambican poet and nationalist Noémia de Sousa wrote a militant 'Appeal', which was published in an anthology edited by Wästberg entitled *Africa Narrates* (1961). In 1962, just two months after the founding of Frelimo in Dar es Salaam, Joaquim Chissano attended the Afro-Scandinavian Youth Congress in Oslo, Norway, where he connected with Swedish representatives, and this was followed by intense diplomatic work by Eduardo and Janet Mondlane.[33] A Swedish Frelimo support group was set up in Uppsala in 1965, and in 1967 a parliamentary motion in favour of providing financial assistance to Frelimo was passed. With Swedish support, the Mozambique Institute was able to flourish for a number of years, becoming the centre of Frelimo's political and civilian activities and providing a formative experience for many teachers and students who would become future leaders in Mozambique.[34]

In 1964, the Mondlanes also visited the Netherlands and met with trade unions, activist organisations and churches, but not the government, which was an ally of Portugal. Some solidarity organisations in The Netherlands had already been set up in the 1950s to support the anti-colonial struggle in Algeria, and in the 1960s a circle of activists around Sietse Bosgra set up the Angola Committee to support liberation struggles in Southern Africa.[35] Subsequently, the Mondlanes, Oscar Monteiro and Dos Santos approached the Angola Committee with instructions to set up a solidarity organisation dedicated to Frelimo. In 1969 this was named the Eduardo Mondlane Foundation, and two Dutch activists, Jan and Frouke Draisma, went to teach at the Mozambique Institute.[36] Many of the activists in the Angola Committee were associated with the Pacifist Socialist Party and were hostile to their own government. Bosgra explains that Frelimo persuaded them to shift their approach:

> our attitude towards Dutch society was getting more constructive due to our talks with Frelimo. Until that time we had acted in 'protestish' ways . . . Frelimo taught

[32] Mondlane (1969): 15.

[33] Sellström, Volume 1 (2002): 448.

[34] Nadja Manghezi (2009). *The Maputo Connection: ANC Life in the World of Frelimo*. Johannesburg: Jacana Media: 18.

[35] Sietse Bosgra (2005). *Brothers in the West*. Amsterdam and Maputo: Netherlands Institute for Southern Africa and Arquivo Historico de Moçambique.

[36] Bosgra (2005): 32.

> us – it sometimes amounted to an instruction – to assess with more optimism the chances of getting things done for them in the Netherlands. We had to get over quite a few emotional scruples to be able to learn to see the Labour Party, let along the Christian parties, as our allies . . . We were quite impressed by the fact that Frelimo had severed its ties with a West German solidarity group that had refused to pursue broader links within civil society.[37]

In shaping the form of international solidarity, Frelimo was acutely aware of the power and potential of images to mobilise and inform communities. Frelimo was the only Southern African liberation movement to train its own photographers, and carefully controlled the production and circulation of the images they produced.[38] A number of guerrilla fighters, who included Colonel José Soares Acolette, Carlos Djambo, Simão Matias, Artur Torohate and Daniel Maquinasse, took photographs that were distributed by the Department of Information and Propaganda.[39] As Drew Thompson has analysed, the photographs were used in the liberated zones for the purposes of political education and to provide news of developments from different parts of the front.[40] Thompson emphasises the crucial but unstable role of photography in militating between different ethnic groups and political factions within Frelimo. As he points out, there were risks to Frelimo in visualising its armed struggle through the photographic image. An image could be a very effective propaganda tool in some contexts, but incendiary in others. For example, an image of deserters from the Portuguese army could be used as evidence that Frelimo's fight was against colonialism rather a campaign of vengeance against the Portuguese people. The same image might be greeted with dismay by some guerrillas, who saw Portuguese soldiers as enemies to be eliminated. The photographs were reproduced in Frelimo publications such as *Mozambican Revolution*, an English language journal primarily for foreign readers that was edited by Jorge Rebelo in Dar es Salaam. They also featured in Frelimo's Portuguese publications *Voz da Revolução* and *25 de Setembro*, which were produced at Nachingwea. An organisation of Finnish school students donated a printing press – a mark of how, by 1970, solidarity with Frelimo had become a popular cause across the Nordic countries.[41] Other Frelimo journals

[37] Bosgra (2005).
[38] Drew Thompson (2013). 'Visualising FRELIMO's Liberated Zones in Mozambique, 1962–1974.' *Social Dynamics: A Journal of African Studies*, 39, 1: 24–50.
[39] Thompson (2013).
[40] Thompson (2013).
[41] In an interview with Tor Sellström, Rebelo recalls:

> A very important contribution from the Nordic countries was the printing press that the Finnish students gave to Frelimo in 1970. It was installed in Dar es Salaam by Kid Ahlfors, who even went to the liberated areas inside Mozambique to see how the support was being used. This donation was really important. It brought about a big change in our information work, particularly concerning *Mozambique Revolution*. It was really

were shorter and did not include photographs because they were made with more basic printing methods, such as typewriters and stencils, though some did features drawings and cartoons.[42]

In the mid-1960s the USSR donated a Super-8 camera, and some Frelimo photographers began experimenting with taking footage, with the idea of making an archive of daily life in the liberated zones.[43] Frelimo did not have the trained personnel or the facilities to edit a film, but in 1967 an opportunity seemed to present itself. While in Cairo, Mondlane met Margaret Dickinson and Polly Gaster, two British women who were travelling through Egypt on their way to find work in the copper belt in Northern Rhodesia (now Zambia).[44] On discovering that Dickinson was a film editor and that Gaster's family were close to the British historians Thomas Hodgkin and Basil Davidson, Mondlane invited them to work with Frelimo in Tanzania.[45] Dickinson found the footage taken on the Super-8 camera to be inadequate for making a film and instead they took on roles in the Department of Information.

In 1968 discontent was growing among some students at the Mozambique Institute as some wanted to pursue academic studies abroad and resented

---

fantastic. We could put much more material in each bulletin and the quality improved dramatically. The printing press still works. We brought it from Dar es Salaam. It is in a printing unit now. It belonged to Frelimo, but we decided to make it a private company with links to the party.

TS: Did you also publish in Portuguese?

JR: Of course. In *A Voz da Revolução*. The nature of the articles was not exactly the same. For example, in English we would publish a long essay on the cotton regime. For the outside world that was important. But in Mozambique it was not so necessary, because the people knew about it.

Extract taken from Tor Sellström (2002). *Liberation in Southern Africa: Swedish and Regional Voices*. Uppsala: Nordiska Afrikainstitutet: 46. Available online http://www.liberationafrica.se/intervstories/interviews/rebelo/Rebelo.pdf.

42 *Jornal Semanal de Tunduru* and *Jornal do Centro* came out of the educational camps at Tunduru and Nachingwea, while *Rasgando as Trevas* and *O Camarada* were published at Frelimo schools near Dar es Salaam. The military bases within Mozambique also produced their own publications – *Os Heróicos*, made at the Cabo Delgado base, *A Luta Continua*, from Eastern Niassa, and *3 de Feveirio* from Tete – and a number of the films of the armed struggle feature scenes of their production. Maria Benedita Basto (2006). 'Who is Written? The Representation of the Other in Rewriting Experiments during the Portuguese Colonial War and the Mozambican Liberation Struggle'. *Italianistica Ultraiectina*, 1: 68–92; Eric Morier-Genoud (2012). *Sure Road? Nationalisms in Angola, Guinea-Bissau and Mozambique*. Leiden and Boston: Brill: 95.

43 Interview with Oscar Monteiro, Maputo, 2005.

44 Dickinson recounts that Mondlane struck up a conversation with them while they were in a queue wanting to change currency. Interview with Margaret Dickinson, London, 13 October 2005.

45 Interview with Margaret Dickinson, London, 13 October 2005.

having to participate in the armed struggle. There were also tensions driven by suspicions that leaders from the south of Mozambique were seeking to control Frelimo to the exclusion of other ethnic groups. Many of the refugees who fled Mozambique for Tanzania were Makonde from Cabo Delgado, and their leader Lázaro Nkavadame had allies in the Tanzanian government who were of the same ethnic group. Father Mateus Gwenjere, a teacher at the Mozambique Institute who was close to Simango and to these same factions within the Tanzanian government, incited students to accuse Eduardo and Janet Mondlane of being CIA agents and to criticise the presence of white Mozambicans and international teachers at the Mozambique Institute.[46] The Mozambique Institute exploded into violence on 6 March and 9 May 1968, leading to the death of one staff member and investigations by the Tanzanian authorities and the Organisation of African Unity.[47] During this period, a number of white people working with Frelimo were forced to leave Tanzania.[48] One of those expelled was Jacinto Veloso, a pilot who had defected from the Portuguese army by commandeering a plane and flying it to Tanzania to join Frelimo.[49] Veloso took refuge in Algeria, working from Frelimo's office in Algiers with solidarity groups in Europe, though he was also involved in clandestine and commercial activities on behalf of Frelimo and built connections with militant activists in Brazil that would become significant for filmmaking in Mozambique during the 1980s.[50] Dickinson and Gaster also had to leave Tanzania: Dickinson travelled to Nairobi, where she worked with Sérgio Vieira to finish Mondlane's book *Struggle for Mozambique*. Gaster was encouraged by Mondlane to return to Britain to set up a solidarity campaign.[51]

[46] According to Cabrita, Gwenjere had the ear of Tanzania's vice-president Abeid Karume, who favoured Simango over Mondlane as leader of Frelimo. João M. Cabrita (2000). *Mozambique: The Torturous Road to Democracy*. Basingstoke: Palgrave Macmillan: 54.

[47] Dhada (2016): 50.

[48] Conversation with Polly Gaster, Maputo, 27 July 2016. See also Sellström, Volume 1 (2002): 457.

[49] Veloso (2012).

[50] Of significance for later chapters in this book are the contacts Veloso made with members of the Brazilian urban guerilla group National Liberation Action (NLA) and the company SUDHEMIS, set up with Miguel Arreas de Alencar (the leader of NLA) and other Brazilian and French contacts, which was used to generate extra income for Frelimo. SUDHEMIS was the precursor to Socimo, the Mozambican Commercial and Industrial company set up after independence as the state's interface with the free market. For a time he also explored the idea of training as a filmmaker, pre-empting his later peripheral, though significant, involvement in film production in Mozambique after independence (see Chapters 5 and 6). See Veloso (2012).

[51] Gaster and Dickinson left in March 1968 because their visas were not renewed. A faction of the Tanzanian government was hostile to Frelimo's presence in Tanzania. The British women were particularly vulnerable because relations between Tanzania and the UK

The location of the Frelimo headquarters in Dar es Salaam, which by the late 1960s was hosting a number of African liberation movements, no doubt contributed to internal divisions, as the city had become a hotbed of Cold War espionage and geopolitical intrigue. However, the intensification of the armed struggle was also affecting how the internal contradictions within Frelimo played out. A new generation of young militant leaders were emerging who had been radicalised by their participation in the struggle.[52] This group included the Commander of Cabo Delgado Samora Machel and his wife Josina, who challenged the authority of traditional chiefs in the liberated zones and forged alliances with party ideologues such as Marcelino dos Santos. At the Second Congress in July 1968, a group of delegates from Cabo Delgado refused to attend. This faction, led by Lázaro Nkavadame, came to be characterised as 'traditionalists' who maintained 'a narrow nationalist posture with racialist and tribalist overtones'.[53] Nkavadame advocated a revival of 'Makonde consciousness' and rejected Frelimo's campaign as too ideologically driven.[54] Meanwhile, Mondlane accused Uria Simango of allying himself to China and conspiring to assassinate him. Simango accused Mondlane of being a puppet of the United States, while both Mondlane and Simango accused Father Gwenjere of treason. Amid the infighting, the Second Congress was held in the liberated zones within Mozambique for the first time. This congress affirmed the revolutionary line, declaring their war was essentially a political battle, and its direction was to be defined by the party. It consolidated Frelimo's move towards Communist Party forms of organisation, including a cell structure, democratic centralism, self-criticism sessions and the adoption of Marxist idiom.

On 3 February 1969, Mondlane was killed when he opened a parcel sent from West Germany that contained an explosive device. For some months Simango, dos Santos and Samora Machel led as a triumvirate, but on 3 November 1969 Simango distributed a pamphlet entitled 'A Gloomy Situation in Frelimo'.[55] It accused a group including dos Santos, Machel and Janet Mondlane of

---

were particularly poor at that point. Initially they both were advised to travel to Nairobi and wait until Mondlane could negotiate their return. When this proved impossible, Dickinson was asked to stay in Nairobi to finish *Struggle for Mozambique* with Vieira. Conversation with Polly Gaster, Maputo, 27 July 2016.

52 Carrie L. Manning (2002). *The Politics of Peace in Mozambique, 1992–2000*. Westport: Praeger: 46.

53 Allan Isaacman and Barbara Isaacman (1983). *Mozambique: From Colonialism to Revolution, 1900–1982*. Boulder: Westview Press: 97.

54 Zachary Kingdon (2002). *A Host of Devils: The History and Context of Making Makonde*. Abingdon: Routledge.

55 Uria T. Simango (1969), 'Gloomy Situation in Frelimo', 3 November, available at http://macua.blogs.com/moambique_para_todos/2010/01/suponho-nunca-ter-sido-tornado-publico-na-sua-totalidade-o-documento-apresentado-por-uria-simango-em-novembro-de-1969-e.html.

ordering the killing of Frelimo activist Silverio Rafael Nungu and of planning to assassinate Simango himself. The pamphlet advocated that Janet Mondlane be expelled as an agent of American imperialism.[56] Simango was expelled from the Central Committee and in 1970 he left for Egypt, where he and others set up a small rival independence movement called Coremo, which received support from China even while Chinese instructors continued to train Frelimo fighters.[57] In a meeting of the Central Committee held at Nachingwea between 4 and 14 May 1970, Samora Machel was declared Frelimo's new leader, with dos Santos as his deputy. This struggle, which became known as 'the battle between the two lines', resulted in victory for those wanting to carve out a socialist future for Mozambique.

It was in this tense context that the first film made with Frelimo about the armed struggle, *Venceremos* (1968) by the Yugoslav filmmaker Dragutin Popović, was made, with production beginning in the heady months leading up to Mondlane's assassination. Popović worked for Filmske novosti, a Yugoslav state-sponsored film production company set up after the Second World War that is credited with initiating a national tradition of documentary realism.[58] Filmske novosti primarily made upbeat, ten-minute propaganda newsreels that were the main source of audio-visual documentation of contemporary events until television became more commonplace in Yugoslavia in the 1960s. Filmske novosti made a considerable contribution to African liberation struggles, and Yugoslavian identification with African liberation struggles is not surprising: Yugoslav partisans had fought their own guerrilla war against German fascist occupation during the Second World War.[59] Their armed resistance was successful to an extent unparalleled elsewhere in Europe and it included the setting up of liberated zones that paved the way for Yugoslavia's later reconstitution, socialist statehood and autonomy from the Soviet bloc. Following its split from the Soviet Union in 1948 and its participation in the Bandung conference in 1955, Yugoslavia carved out a foreign policy of non-alignment, orientated towards cooperation with new nation-states in Africa and Asia. In 1961, the first conference of the non-aligned movement took place in Belgrade and one of the criteria for participating nations was that they support revolutionary national liberation

[56] Simango (1969).
[57] Taylor (2006): 95.
[58] Greg de Cuir (2016). 'Želimir Žilnik's Unemployed Bodies'. *Jump Cut: A Review of Contemporary Media*, 57. Available at https://www.ejumpcut.org/archive/jc57.2016/-DeCuirZilnic/text.html.
[59] Olivier Hadouchi (2016). *Images of Non-aligned and Tricontinental Struggles*. Belgrade: Museum of Contemporary Art: viii.

movements across the Third World.[60] Yugoslavia had supported the Algerian struggle for independence, providing arms and other supplies, and at the end of the 1950s Filmske novosti signed an agreement with the 'Picture and Sound' service of the Provincial Government of the Algerian Republic, promising to maintain a film archive of the Algerian struggle and to develop film stock in Belgrade. Photographers, camera operators and journalists worked with the Front de Libération Nationale (FLN), even helping to set up a filmmaking and photography school.[61] By the mid-1960s, the Yugoslavian camera operator Dragutin Popović and director Mića Zdravković were working with the Tanzanian Film Unit, which focused on the production of educational short information films. In October 1967 it was arranged that they would travel with Frelimo into the liberated zones in Mozambique.[62]

Venceremos was shot silent in black and white, with two different voiceover versions in English and French. The film begins with the title 'We Shall Win' displayed in English, followed by an image of a map of the world. The camera focuses on Mozambique, the voiceover declaring: 'There are big wars and there are small wars. There are wars that people talk about, and those that, due to circumstances and the forces of imperialism, are practically unknown.'[63] Over a panning shot of the forest, with view of the Cabo Delgado landscape, the voiceover continues: 'Our camera will inform the world about this liberation struggle, the struggle of a people to free themselves from colonial slavery.' *Venceremos* focuses on scenes of everyday life in the liberated zones, highlighting the work carried out by women living in the Frelimo bases and the medical centres set up in remote rural areas. Frelimo's leaders are depicted amongst their fellow guerrillas and local villagers: a shot of Samora Machel, then Commander of

[60] This was not a contradiction of the notion of peaceful co-existence that was central to the non-aligned movement. Rather, as Vijay Prashad argues, the notion of peaceful co-existence distinguished between armed struggle to eject colonialism and secure self-determination and the 'brinkmanship of nuclear warfare' that the rival superpowers were engaging in. Vijay Prashad (2007). *The Darker Nations: A People's History of the Third World*. New York: New Press: 103.

[61] Hadouchi (2016): xiv–xxv. See artist Milica Tomic's installation *Cinema School and the War of Independence* (2014–16). Various locations.

[62] N. R. (2011). 'Istorija u filmskim depoima' 'History in the Film Depots', *Politika*, 5 September. Available at http://www.politika.rs/sr/clanak/190228/Istorija-u-filmskim-depoima.

[63] Oscar Monteiro instigated the making of a 16mm version in Portuguese, for which he provided the translation and narration, so that the film could eventually be shown to Frelimo fighters and their sympathisers in Mozambique. He was surprised to receive a fee for this work, like any other employee of Filmske novosti, and he recounts that he used this to buy himself a 'nylon rain coat as well as a smart leather bag', which he carried into liberated Lourenço Marques when he returned in 1975 for independence. N. R. (2011).

Cabo Delgado, shows him marching within the line of soldiers moving through the forest. Much of the film is structured through a series of oppositions that emphasise that this struggle is bringing traditional ways of life into conjunction with modernity: 'News travels through different ways – by drum . . .', cue images of drumming, dancing and singing to greet the guerrillas, '. . . and by modern methods . . .', cue a shot of a radio. The military achievements of the guerrillas are balanced by an emphasis on Frelimo's other activities, which are geared towards social transformation and a future independent Mozambique. Shots of a blackboard hanging from a tree indicate that the struggle takes many forms, and is orientated towards developing peoples' potential and giving them political instruction. Over images of happy schoolchildren, the voiceover explains the central importance of education:

> Its also necessary to organise a new life in the liberated zones so that the people can have a better life than the one they had under colonialism. They need to create schools for the children. . . . Their nationalist consciousness needs to be constantly elevated. . . . Schools like these are found in nearly all the zones liberated by Frelimo.

The film shifts seamlessly between military and civilian elements, emphasising Frelimo's policy agreed in 1967 that the guerrilla army should be an extension of the Mozambican people: older children are shown in formation, doing their manoeuvres with sticks instead of guns. The voiceover explains: 'The children need to understand what the adults are doing so that they are ready at any moment to enter the lines [*filas*] of the combatants. Because the struggle will be long, and it will be difficult.'

Other sequences depict cultivation in the liberated zones. A panning shot of the forest concludes with women, some with infants on their backs, hoeing the soil. Whereas under the Portuguese, the voiceover argues, forced labour was common, in the liberated zones the people work for each other. Production in the liberated zones enables people to buy the goods they need at the lowest possible price: a bag of grain is weighed to secure a fair price, people peruse fabrics and clothes that are on sale. There is an intimacy to the scales of production, as goods pass between hands: a man uses a sewing machine to make clothes and gives the finished garment to a Makonde man, who is recognisable from his facial scarifications; an older villager greets arriving guerrillas with the gift of a chicken. 'Our camera films all this to show that in the areas controlled by Frelimo, life flows normally, life can be more prosperous for the Mozambican people.'

Venceremos emphasises the determination of those participating in the struggle, drawing attention to the challenges of coordinating an armed struggle in conditions of scarcity. Lack of transportation, for instance, means that all the materials needed for the struggle have to be carried by people travelling by foot and crossing the Rovuma river in canoes: 'There are no other means of transport.' The film reminds us that in this war there are 'shortages of everything', a point illustrated by scenes of basic health clinics and shots of people's feet – some without shoes. Yet still Frelimo continues its process of radical social transformation. A whole battalion of women is a sign of Frelimo's push for female emancipation. The film culminates in what the voiceover calls 'an incredible sight – 2,500 people gathered for a meeting to hear the leaders explain the plan for the liberation struggle.' At this special meeting, the leaders of the struggle in the province of Niassa give a report on their activities, including how many Portuguese planes have been downed. This gathering is presented in the film as evidence of an emerging mass movement and indeed, according to Boniface I Obichere, the purpose of holding the meeting in the liberated zones was to prove that Frelimo had liberated a significant proportion of the national territory.[64] On the one hand, while sympathetic journalists such as Basil Davidson and Anders Johansson applauded Frelimo's achievements, the problem of logistics meant that a lack of regular supplies was hampering the progress of the Front and leading to resentment towards the leadership in Dar es Salaam.[65] *Venceremos*, on the other, uses this moment to stress the importance of internationalist solidarity. Samora speaks to a huge crowd in the forest: 'All this isn't sufficient. We need friends to help us to win.'

After the footage was shot in Cabo Delgado, Eduardo Mondlane and his lawyer Oscar Monteiro travelled to Yugoslavia to view the film while it was being edited, Monteiro providing the voiceover for the speeches delivered by Samora Machel.[66] Mondlane was assassinated shortly after the film's completion, and so a preface was added that comments on this recent event. This additional sequence shows Mondlane standing before a map of the globe, then cuts to a scene in the liberated zones, where Samora and a group of guerrillas stand in the forest, saluting one another with fists raised and cries of 'Viva!'.[67] A camera captures Popović in the act of filming, then cuts to guerrillas marching through the forest, shot from below, so their bodies are silhouetted against the sky. Then follows footage of Eduardo and Janet Mondlane meeting with Filmske novosti editors, relaxed and in animated conversation, on the occasion of the film's premiere in Belgrade. Over these images, a voiceover speaking in Serbo-Croat reports on Mondlane's assassination, stressing that 'when Doctor Mondlane visited the editors of Filmske novosti, he expressed his desire to

[64] Boniface I. Obichere (1973). 'Eduardo Chivambo Mondlane and the Enigma of Revolutionary Leadership', *Ufahamu: A Journal of African Studies*, 4, 2: 170.

[65] Obichere (1973): 170.

[66] Interview with Oscar Monteiro, Maputo, 13 August 2005.

[67] According to an article published in the journal *Politika*, these images, which were shot in the hall of the Filmske novosti offices, are of historical significance because they are the only film footage of Mondlane. N. R. (2011).

expand the collaboration in the field of filming information on the struggle of the Mozambique Nationalist Front'.

After the death of Mondlane, Frelimo was keen to reassure its supporters abroad that the organisation was a united movement that had not been dealt a body blow, and this was one of the primary tasks of the documentaries made by foreign filmmakers in the months that followed.[68] Aside from his considerable charisma, powers of persuasion and rapport with the wider population, Machel had appeal because his ideological commitment was matched by his 'participation in the actual fighting'.[69] Certainly, the upheavals did not affect Frelimo's friendship with Yugoslavia in terms of cinematographic collaboration. Popović came to forge a relationship with Frelimo that lasted for the duration of the struggle for independence. As explored in Chapter 2, the films he made in the transition to independence depict the expansion of the political organisation into a party of the masses on a national scale. These films of the transition to independence would play a crucial role in legitimating Frelimo's claim that it answered to the revolutionary demands of *o Povo*. This claim depended on the cinematic representation of their armed struggle as a grassroots movement, rooted in the liberated zones.

Meanwhile in London, Margaret Dickinson had been raising the funds to make a documentary with Frelimo. The film was intended to contribute to the solidarity work of the Committee for Freedom in Mozambique, Angola and Guinea-Bissau (CFMAG), which was the solidarity organisation set up by Polly Gaster on her return from Tanzania. CFMAG was conceived as an organisation affiliated to the Anti-Apartheid Movement that would garner support for the liberation struggles in lusophone Africa.[70] Mondlane had already visited Britain, where he spoke at a meeting organised by the Movement for Colonial Freedom.[71]

[68] Interview with Joachim Chissano in Sellström (2002): 39.

[69] Obichere argues that the 'most successful struggles are those in which the ideological commitment of the leaders has been matched by their participation in the actual fighting; and one thinks of such leaders as Che Guevara, Ho Chi Min, Fidel Castro, Vu Ngen Giap, George Grivas, Houari Boumedienne and Mao Tse-tung.' Obichere (1973): 170.

[70] The Committee that Gaster formed included the historian Basil Davidson, Labour Lord Tony Gifford, Hilary Wainwright and Lord Kilbraken, who had been a journalist in Mozambique and had written articles denouncing forced labour, and it went on to play an important role in organising events and campaigning against Caetano's visit to London in 1973. Conversation with Polly Gaster, Maputo, 27 July 2016.

[71] The Movement for Colonial Freedom was an advocacy group set up in 1954 that had the support of leading figures in the Labour Party such as Harold Wilson, Barbara Castle and Tony Benn, as well as trade unions and rank-and-file members. They challenged the Labour Party's official position of not supporting independence movements. See Stephen Howe (1993). *Anticolonialism in British Politics: The Left and the End of Empire, 1918–1964*. Oxford: Oxford University Press: esp. Chapter 6.

Britain and Portugal had an alliance that dated back to the signing of the Treaty of Windsor in 1386, and the British government had cordial relations with the Salazar regime.[72] Mondlane recognised that this historic relationship and the UK's prominent role in NATO meant that London was a key site from which to run a solidarity campaign. The organisation was kept small, those involved deciding not to seek mass membership so as to avoid the risk of it being hijacked by other factions within the nationalist movement, as Mondlane was already aware of a possible challenge to his leadership.[73]

Although the CFMAG had some high profile supporters on the left, financing a feature-length documentary about an armed struggle against Portuguese colonial rule was no easy task. Dickinson was not well known as a director, nor did she have a famous journalist to anchor the film.[74] Dickinson eventually secured the support of the film distributor Charles Cooper. Cooper was a member of the Communist Party and since the 1930s had been involved with the Kino Group, who circumvented British film censorship to organise projections of Soviet films such as Sergei Eisenstein's *Battleship Potemkin* (1925) for trade unions and Soviet friendship societies. In the 1960s, his film distribution company, Contemporary Films, helped launch artistically and politically significant films such as those of the Czech and French New Wave and the work of directors such as Satyajit Ray from India and Luis Buñuel from Mexico.[75] Contemporary Films guaranteed Dickinson cinema distribution, and Cooper helped Dickinson to fund raise from left-wing sympathisers so that she could return with a camera operator to Tanzania. Finally, in 1970 Dickinson and John Fletcher crossed over the border into Mozambique to shoot the first armed struggle documentary to be made in colour and with synchronised sound.

Dickinson intended to return to Frelimo's original concept of creating an archive of everyday life in the liberated zones by making a kind of in-depth ethnography of radical change. This would require spending an extended period with a community so as to film how the struggle was transforming their lives.

[72] The Anglo-Portuguese Alliance was ratified at the Treaty of Windsor in 1386.

[73] Polly Gaster recalls that the last time she met Mondlane on a visit to London he was 'very anxious' about the threat posed by Simango, but pleased that a younger generation of leaders such as Samora Machel were rising through the ranks thanks to their participation in the armed struggle. Conversation with Polly Gaster, Maputo, 29 July 2016.

[74] By contrast, Michael Sheppard's *A Group of Terrorists Attacked. . .* benefitted from the support of anti-colonial historian Basil Davidson, who was well respected within the media establishment. The practice of lending weight to a subject through the use of famous journalists was beginning to be critiqued by a rising Leftist movement that eventually helped shape the more radical practice of early Channel 4. Conversation with Margaret Dickinson, 20 February 2019.

[75] Ian Christie (2001). 'Charles Cooper: Obituary'. *Guardian*, 4 December.

She originally negotiated with Jorge Rebelo to make a trip of six weeks, with the proviso that it would include a prolonged stay within a community. However, circumstances on the ground meant that their time in the liberated zones was reduced to two weeks, making such an approach impossible. Dickinson's crew arrived in Niassa just after the Portuguese launched the offensive 'Gordian Knot' on 10 June 1970, which was conceived by General Kaúla de Arriaga. Arriaga was a newly appointed commander who was a specialist in counter-insurgency methods, particularly American military strategy in Vietnam.[76] Unlike the United States army, however, Arriaga did not have to worry about public opinion – he had *carte blanche* from Lisbon to carry out the mass bombings of Frelimo bases and civilian targets, using scorched-earth tactics to try to break Frelimo's supply chains.[77] Combining aerial bombardment, paratroopers, commando, naval and specialist units, the Gordian Knot campaign was intended recapture the region and defeat the guerrillas once and for all. While Gordian Knot did succeed in destroying a network of 165 camps and over forty tonnes of war material, Frelimo was able to retreat and regroup from the Western flank, preparing to launch a new front in the north-western province of Tete while Portuguese troops were still engaged in combat in Niassa and Cabo Delgado.[78]

The onset of Gordian Knot meant that filming had to be done at daybreak, the team in a continual state of exhaustion because of being constantly on the move to avoid attacks.[79] Dickinson had hoped to take enough footage to make a film in the observational manner of direct cinema, and so avoided relying on an overbearing voiceover to expound the argument.[80] However, she found that the brief interviews and scenes of schooling, medical clinics and political meetings that they managed to capture were inadequate to unfold a narrative in themselves. Thus a voiceover is used through most of the film, which, in the absence of Frelimo activists who spoke English, was provided by the British actor Clive Swift, who offered his services for free. The aesthetic form of the film, as manifest through its interplay of sound and image, was shaped by the constraints of war and scarcity, pushing the director's vision away from testimonies that would speak with greater autonomy and towards more explicatory formats.

Behind the Lines opens with Makonde sculptures that illustrate the exploitative relation between coloniser and colonised – people bound and in chains, a white baby being carried by black servants – but also figures of guerrillas who bear arms. The decision to begin the film with images of Makonde sculptures was

[76] Dhada (2016): 54.
[77] Dhada (2016): 55.
[78] Dhada (2016): 55.
[79] Interview with Dickinson, London, 2005.
[80] Interview with Dickinson, London, 2005.

significant.[81] Traditionally these wooden sculptures were made for spiritual purposes within small communities and featured complex representations combining multiple different human, animal and spirit figures carved out of a single piece of wood. The Makonde were the last of the indigenous populations of Mozambique to be 'pacified' by the Portuguese, in a battle on the Makonde plateau in 1917 in which warriors led by Mbavala were defeated by Portuguese and Nyassa Company forces.[82] In the decades after this defeat, as Zachary Kingdon explains, the Makonde resisted enforced cotton production through all means possible, including sabotage, arson, insurrection and flight.[83] Cotton production was a poor source of income, due in part to the heavy taxes imposed by the colonial authorities, and carving sculptures became a means of providing extra resources for farming families. It also became a way of expressing anger and despair, as carvers turned to making melancholy skeletal figures or sometimes even satirical depictions of colonial administrators, engorged with food and holding implements of torture. Although relations between the Makonde chiefs and the Frelimo leadership were not without strife, activists from the province played an important role in collectivisation in the liberated zones because they had extensive experience of forming cooperatives.[84] As well as establishing agricultural cooperatives, Makonde carvers set up sculpture workshop collectives. Frelimo encouraged them to develop new themes, and as well as figures that illustrated colonial oppression or satirised colonial administrators, carvers devised new forms such as the 'unity of the people' genre that symbolised the aspirations of the liberation struggle.[85]The voiceover in *Behind the Lines* gives a historical introduction to the armed insurrection that situates it geopolitically as part of a struggle against capitalist Apartheid. It makes the point that without the white minority regimes of South Africa and Rhodesia and the support of NATO countries such as Britain, the Portuguese regime would not be able to hold on to her African colonies.[86] In the absence of visual evidence of atrocities committed in Mozambique by the colonial regime, Dickinson's film includes close-ups of a gruesome trophy photograph, one of a number taken by Portuguese soldiers involved in mass killings in Angola

[81] Mondlane's book *Struggle for Mozambique* discusses how Makonde's carving practices had responded to colonial oppression.
[82] Kingdon (2002): 24
[83] Kingdon (2002).
[84] Kingdon (2002): 27.
[85] Kingdon (2002).
[86] Dickinson managed to get hold of footage of the Portuguese army by swopping some of the film of Frelimo with a filmmaker who was making a documentary about the colonial war from the perspective of the Portuguese for Scottish television.

in 1961.[87] *Behind the Lines* personalises the armed struggle with a number of interviews with Frelimo guerrillas who give first-hand accounts of how participation in the struggle was transforming their lives. The first dialogue is with Alberto Joaquim Chipande, who recounts how he led the attack that began Frelimo's armed struggle. Pedro Juma describes his work organising the agricultural cooperatives, while Wills Kadawele, who had previously worked within the colonial administration, describes his job as First Secretary for Niassa in charge of the civilian population.[88] Later in the film, three women – Monica Chitupila, who was responsible for political education and mobilisation, her assistant 'Mary' (Amelia Omar) and a younger woman called Maria Sulila, who studied at the Frelimo secondary school in Tanzania, describe how joining Frelimo opened up possibilities for education that were not available to them under colonialism. They discuss their work as soldiers, as translators and as political educators, and the difficulties of being away from their families. While the people interviewed in *Behind the Lines* hold positions of responsibility, they are rank-and-file rather than the party leadership. Dickinson, of course, would have had access to Frelimo's leaders had she so wished, but that was not the kind of documentary she wanted to make. The film documents a political meeting in which Frelimo activists explain the struggle to local people with translation provided by interpreters, in contrast to the mass meeting featured in *Venceremos*. Frelimo is depicted as a movement that is diverse and that offers opportunities for people from all walks of life to fulfil their potential.

The sequence when people are shown arriving at this gathering is one of the crucial moments of the film. Photographs are hung on strings tied to trees, pre-empting the *jornais do povo* 'people's newspapers', which after independence were made up of a montage of news images pinned up onto walls. While photographs of the Mozambique Institute, the training of guerrillas, agricultural production, medical care and schools were important tools for

[87] Afonso Ramos explains that, in the wake of the massacre of white settlers and black communities in the north of Angola on 15 March 1961 by the União dos Povos de Angola (UPA, later FNLA), distressing images of the victims were circulated and exhibited by the Estado Novo as part of an international propaganda campaign that justified Portugal's continued presence in Africa as part of a civilizing mission. Portuguese soldiers were shown the photographs, and rumors that guerrillas had committed acts of cannibalism were used to encourage brutal retaliation. The photographs of beheaded guerrillas were taken as trophies by Portuguese soldiers, but they were leaked to journalists sympathetic to the cause of decolonisation and eventually were printed in newspapers internationally. Margaret Dickinson recalled to me that she thought she had first seen them printed in the British newspaper *The Morning Star*. Afonso Ramos (2014). 'Angola 1961, o Horror das Imagens', in Filipa Lowndes Vicente (2014). *O Império da Visão: Fotografia no Contexto Colonial português (1860–1960)*. Coimbra: Edições 70: 397–432.

[88] Shortly after the shooting of *Behind the Lines*, Wills Kadawele defected to the Portuguese.

Frelimo's diplomatic campaign abroad, here we see them being used within the liberated areas in Mozambique for the purposes of mobilisation and for countering colonial propaganda. Many rural communities that Frelimo needed to win over were accustomed to speeches and debates, but, as the voiceover points out, communication through images was something new. Photographs enabled knowledge about, and contact with, a wider world beyond their immediate communities. Images were beginning to create visual connections to other people, who like them, were now to be called 'Mozambicans', and to struggles far away that resonated with their own.

Another key moment of the film, in terms of its articulation of the new revolutionary culture emerging in the liberated zones, shows Frelimo cadres teaching each other the dances and songs from their different regions across Mozambique. The use of traditional Mozambican music and songs in the soundtrack of *Behind the Lines* underlines the fact that full independence required transformations more profound that military successes. For Frelimo, the project of decolonising Mozambican culture was not about hankering after an idealised past, but about creating a new national culture orientated towards the future. While traditional Mozambican music was permitted in some colonial contexts, it was forbidden in the Catholic Church. European forms of music were taught to Mozambicans in colonial schools, churches and the military as part of the wider project of assimilating a small indigenous elite. Conversely, from the late 1950s the Catholic Church began translating Christian hymns into Mozambican indigenous languages so as to extend its influence to a wider proportion of the population.[89] As Paulo Soares explains, however, during the armed struggle these traditions of Christian and military choral music were adapted in the composition of new revolutionary songs, which blended Mozambican melodic structures and rhythms with Western vocal techniques and harmonies.[90] These rousing songs were intended to unify all the different ethnic groups of Mozambique within a frame of revolutionary nationhood. Armed struggle, *Behind the Lines* proposes, is the alchemy that fuses a new culture out of the best elements of indigenous ways of life and forms of expression. It is a national culture that promises to cut across ethnic divisions and social inequalities after independence.

Some months later, while *Behind the Lines* was still in post-production, a Chinese film crew was assembled to make a documentary with Frelimo. China already had a strong alliance with Tanzania, and the Chinese collectivisation of rural life had profoundly influenced Nyerere's agricultural policy. By 1970,

[89] Paulo Soares (1980). 'A Valorização da Musica e Cancão Tradicional em Moçambique', in Ministério da Educação e Cultura (1980). *Música Tradicional em Moçambique*. Maputo: Ministério da Educação e Cultura: 14–15.

[90] Soares (1980): 15.

Chinese assistance in Africa, animated by the spirit of mobilisation that drove the Cultural Revolution, found its 'zenith' in the audacious Tazara Railway project.[91] The Tazara Railway was intended to serve an anti-imperialist agenda as it would connect the Zambian copperbelt to the Tanzanian coast, facilitating economic development and breaking the region's dependency on white minority-ruled South Africa and Rhodesia.[92] Nyerere had solicited Chinese support for the project in 1965, and the vast and treacherous construction work began in 1970 with China providing interest-free loans, technical guidance and tens of thousands of labourers.[93] Priya Lal points out that the Chinese made substantial use of film, as well as radio and printed matter, to 'advertise the depths of the Sino-African relationship and extol the benefits of Maoism', the Chinese Embassy in Dar es Salaam even applying to build a cinema adjoining their ambassador's house.[94] Film director YuBen Wang and cinematographer LeGuan Yu were already in Tanzania shooting a documentary entitled *Tazara Railway* when they received an order from the Chinese ambassador to Tanzania, Zong Xi Dong, to assemble a press corps with military trainer Nan Feng Fang and two translators LiZhao Ju and ChaoQin Zhan.[95] They were to journey to the liberated areas in Mozambique, their task being 'to create a research report and a documentary film, so that our nation could support the rebellion of the Mozambican people.'[96]According to Guido Convents, the film they made, entitled *The People of Mozambique are Fighting On* (1970), is 'less interested in Frelimo's preoccupation with healthcare, education and economic development, and more interested in methods and tactics used by the guerrillas against a

[91] Deborah Brautigam (2009). *The Dragon's Gift: The Real Story of China in Africa*. Oxford: Oxford University Press: 40.

[92] According to Deborah Brautigam, it was Cecil Rhodes who first proposed the construction of the Tazara Railway. However, when Kenneth Kaunda raised the possibility of re-animating the project, the World Bank rejected the idea as unfeasible. Brautigam (2009): 40.

[93] Some 50,000 Chinese technical personnel worked on the project. Lu Rucai (2016). 'Du Jian: Witness to the Birth of the TAZARA'. China.org.cn, 12 January. Available at http://www.chinatoday.com.cn/english/report/2015-12/29/content_710567.htm.

[94] Priya Lal (2014). 'Maoism in Tanzania: Material Connections and Shared Imaginaries', in Alexander C. Cook (ed.) (2014). *Mao's Little Red Book: A Global History*. Cambridge: Cambridge University Press: 109.

[95] The Tazara Railway links the Zambian copper belt to the coast through Tanzania. Nyerere first solicited the Chinese government for assistance with the project in 1965, and construction began in 1970. It was China's biggest overseas development project at the time and involved interest-free loans, technical advice and labour.

[96] Tan Qi (2009). 'A Personal Memoir of Shooting *The People of Mozambique are Fighting On*'. *Popular Cinema*, 12.

Western (colonial) army'.[97] It is an approach that perhaps reflects the fact that Chinese support for Frelimo was military rather than humanitarian. Chinese military training was considered to be appropriate because it was focused on guerrilla tactics against an enemy with superior weapons technology. An article in the Chinese film journal *Popular Cinema* gives an account of the filmmaking process that emphasises the Afro-Asian solidarity forged between the Chinese film crew and Mozambican guerrillas during the month-long visit to the liberated zones.[98] YuBen Wang recounts how they crossed enemy lines accompanied by three guerrilla battalions. His narrative stresses the Maoist themes of humbleness, revolutionary sacrifice and the toughness of the Chinese film crew, mentioning scarcity of food; long marches across rugged terrain, dense forests and rivers; and the ever-present danger of aerial bombardment and landmines.[99] These hardships are contrasted by anecdotes of everyday heroism, resourcefulness and the warm welcome they receive from orphaned children who perform a 'traditional dance' on their arrival, which is documented for the film.[100] The trip culminates with a farewell party in which Mozambican and Chinese comrades hold hands and sing *The East is Red* and *No More Portuguese Devils*. Tan Qi's article reports that YuBen Wang gave Samora Machel his own kettle as a souvenir gift, to replace the broken one owned by Machel. According to the film director, Machel was greatly pleased with *The People of Mozambique are Fighting On* and took it with him on his trips abroad, though the film was only shown in China after Mozambique gained independence in 1975.[101]

Shortly afterwards, the Soviet Union sent journalists and filmmakers to make a film about Frelimo. The Soviet film *Viva Frelimo!* (1971), by Yuri Egorov, Leonid Maksimov and *Pravda* correspondent Oleg Ignatyev, who co-wrote the

[97] Guido Convents (2010). *Os Moçambicanos perante o Cinema e o Audiovisual: Uma História Política-Cultural do Moçambique Colonial até à República de Moçambique (1896–2000)*. Maputo: CP: 349.

[98] Qi (2009).

[99] According to Brautigam, rather than seeking to impose Maoism on newly independent African governments, Chinese advisors attempted to lead by example and had gained a reputation for their dedication and willingness to work alongside African peasants rather than addressing themselves to local chiefs. 'The Maoist model had a different impact of China's aid [than Nyerere's project of collectivising farming] . . . through the example set by Chinese aid workers and some of the choices. In Maoist China, as researcher Jonathan Unger reported: "the politically moral man or woman was supposed to remain behind to finish up work in the dark even if no one were around to notice it." In their African projects, the Chinese tried to encourage Ministry of Agriculture technicians to disregard their fixed ideas about work they considered beneath them. Chinese experts jumped into the muddy rice paddies beside local farmers, and took turns scaring away birds, an activity normally done by children.' Brautigam (2009): 39.

[100] Qi (2009).

[101] Qi (2009).

script, displays high production values and is coloured by Soviet cinematic representations of military history. Similarly to *The People of Mozambique are Fighting On*, the Soviet film privileges the figure of Samora Machel. Egorov was a graduate of the VGIK film school. In the late 1960s he worked with the Partido Africano da Independência da Guiné e Cabo Verde 'African Party for the Independence of Guinea and Cape Verde' (PAIGC) in Guinea-Bissau, where he made *The March of Freedom* (1968), and in 1970 he filmed with the Movimento Popular de Libertação de Angola 'People's Movement for the Liberation of Angola' (MPLA) in Angola, participating in the assault on the Portuguese fort at Kayanda.[102] While the Yugoslav and Chinese films were shot in Cabo Delgado where the armed struggle began, and Dickinson's film was shot in Niassa, for the making of *Viva Frelimo!* the filmmakers travelled to Tete, where Frelimo were opening up a new front. The independence of Zambia in 1964 provided Frelimo with the possibility of infiltrating Tete from across the Zambian border, entry to the province being otherwise blocked by Malawi, which under President Banda pursued a foreign policy of cooperation with white minority regimes in Southern Africa. After some initial forays and retreats, in 1968 Frelimo renewed their attacks in the province.[103] The Tete offensive was a particular challenge for Frelimo. In 1969 the Portuguese had begun work on the Cahora Bassa dam. This vast project was the centrepiece of Lisbon's plan to 'buttress the war through economic and infrastructure initiatives'.[104] This was intended to counter accusations that Portugal neglected to develop its colonies and was an extension of the policy that began in the 1950s of encouraging mass migration of settlers to Mozambique and Angola. Funded by a consortium of Portuguese, German, British and South African companies, the dam was chiefly intended to produce electricity for South Africa. The location of the filming of *Viva Frelimo!* was thus highly significant, enabling the filmmakers to depict anti-colonial struggle as a battle for sovereignty over natural resources.

Viva Frelimo! opens with footage of Dar es Salaam, almost in the mode of a city symphony film, with jaunty music typical of Soviet documentary reportage over elevated urban views, shots of cargo ships in the port and street scenes. A voiceover in Russian announces:

> The port of Dar es Salaam is the gateway to the world, the image of Tanzania itself. From here, we will start our story. Today the African states of Tanzania and Zambia . . . are paths to the people of Africa who are fighting for their independence and

[102] P. Mikhalev (1971). 'Angola, Your Son!', ВОКРУТ СВЕТА, 1 March. Available at http://www.vokrugsveta.ru/vs/article/4525/.

[103] Funada-Klassen (2012): 262.

[104] Dhada (2016): 54.

> the valuable priceless cargo of this port is the aid from France, from the Soviets and other socialist countries for whom the word freedom is sacred.

As the soundtrack takes on a sinister tone, the film reports on the assassination of Mondlane, noting that Western newspapers seized on this news to declare that Frelimo was finished. However, the film cuts immediately to a scene of Samora Machel in the midst of a crowd of guerrillas who shout out '*Viva Frelimo!*' – Frelimo lives on with a leader who is at one with the fighters for a free Mozambique. The filmmakers are shown being briefed by Machel, who talks about the importance of documenting the Tete offensive, the alliance of 'Portuguese colonialists and Rhodesian and South African racists', the destruction and atrocities the filmmakers will witness, and the significance of the Cahora Bassa dam. As Machel speaks, the camera lingers on the faces of the guerrillas – an older man, a woman, an adolescent boy in uniform and a young woman – who sit listening to him, attentive and serious.

The next images show engineering plans relating to Cahora Bassa seized by Frelimo, with guerrillas pouring over them. 'Why', the voiceover asks, 'are these neutral drawings being read as a strategic map? Because now the map of Africa has become the topography for narrating the struggle for freedom.' The film cuts to images of a topographical map of Africa, showing the natural features of the terrain rather than national borders, and zooms in on Mozambique to show the three provinces – Cabo Delgado, Niassa and Tete – where the armed struggle is playing out, and the site of the Cahora Bassa dam. 'Remember these lines,' the voiceover instructs, as arrows pointing South show the expropriation of Mozambique's natural resources to Rhodesia and South Africa. Sublime images follow of the Zambezi river and Victoria Falls, the music on the soundtrack subsumed by the sound of crashing water. The Zambezi is a natural flow of water that, the voiceover comments, the Portuguese have not yet 'enslaved'. The metaphor continues: while Lisbon, Pretoria and Salisbury plan the electricity lines along which millions of white settlers will be housed, Frelimo is the force of nature that will break down their walls.

As Mustafa Dhada explains, water did actually play a crucial role in shaping the armed struggle in Tete.[105] The Cahora Bassa dam not only promised to elevate Portugal in the eyes of the international community, but would also flood a huge area and thus cut off a route for Frelimo to enter Mozambique from Zambia. Portugal's objective in Tete was to prevent Frelimo from reaching the central province of Manica-e-Sofala, which would threaten the city of Beira, a key port for Rhodesia's access to the Indian Ocean. With construction of the damn underway, Frelimo sought to penetrate south as quickly as possible from Unkanha in northern Tete, which they were able to access from Zambia. As the

[105] Dhada (2016): 56.

Portuguese started forcibly removing people from villages in the North in an attempt to stop Frelimo from gaining their support, Frelimo 'loaded its activists on the military trucks disguised as Unkanha residents . . ., thus gaining in a fell swoop a political foothold near Lundo, Buxo and Mucumbura, where they regrouped to politicise the local population.'[106] Once their logistical structures and food supplies were in place, Frelimo guerrillas were able to launch attacks in the south of Tete. Armindo Martins Videira, the Portuguese commander in Tete, had been selected by de Arriaga and shared his approach to counter-insurgency. Videira responded to Frelimo's infiltration of Tete with offensives that failed to eradicate Frelimo but were devastatingly brutal.[107]

Over images that show Portuguese soldiers picking their way through minefields, *Viva Frelimo!* explains that while Frelimo had the advantage on the ground, the Portuguese army controlled the skies. A key scene depicts Samora Machel arriving at a village that had been destroyed in an aerial bombardment. Villagers stand in silence as if frozen to the spot, gazing at their burning houses, and the soundtrack is again overtaken, this time by the sound of the forest burning. A Soviet cameraman is shown filming, and the voiceover recalls Machel's words at their initial briefing: 'Tell the truth about it!' The camera circles around Machel as he picks up a crying baby and addresses the children who stand on the ashes of their homes. So it is, the voiceover explains, that the Portuguese attempt to terrorise the local populations, but the people of Mozambique continue to support Frelimo. A column of women carrying supplies on their heads as they walk through the forest testifies to their defiance.

The second half of *Viva Frelimo!* adopts a lyrical tone that recalls romantic depictions of Soviet military history.[108] The music in the soundtrack softens as the film documents daily life in the liberated zones, including the organisation of collective work, with some of the images showing people carving in unison. The film crew follow the guerrillas on their marches, passing through the site of a ruined Portuguese army base, and witness a sixteen-year-old fighter named Jacinta Ana reuniting with her elderly mother whom she has not seen for many months. The guerrillas are also seen at rest, reading *Voz da revoluçao*, one of the guerrillas sporting a small Soviet badge on his shirt – a small five-pointed star with a picture of Lenin as a child in the centre – the emblem of the Communist pioneers. The final sequence shows a great stone in the shape

[106] Dhada (2016): 58.

[107] Dhada comments that Videira viewed the colonial war as winnable – 'all you needed was to have your wits about you, be on high alert at all times, unbridled force, and an arsenal of weapons at your beck and call!' Dhada (2016): 58.

[108] For example, Vladimir Motyl's depiction of Red Army heroism during the Russian Civil War in *White Sun of the Desert* (1970), one of the most popular Soviet films ever made, which is screened to cosmonauts before most space launches as a good luck ritual.

of Mozambique, with lines painted on it that mark out the boundaries of the provinces. Around this great stone schoolchildren are receiving a geography lesson from their teacher, who is a former guerrilla and thus 'is also a part of this history.' Just as the stone map represents the entirety of Mozambique so too the guerrilla army includes people from every province. 'Where are you from?' the guerrillas are asked: 'From Nampula', 'Niassa', 'Cabo Delgado', 'Manica-Sofala', 'Tete', 'Zambezia', 'Lourenço Marques', 'Gaza', 'Inhambane' . . . The film concludes with the raising of the Mozambican flag, and the guerrillas raise their guns and cry out: 'Down with colonialism! Down with imperialism! A luta continua! Viva Frelimo!'

Viva Frelimo! conveys pathos using a soundtrack familiar to Soviet audiences. It provides emotive cues that punctuate the scenes of suffering, consolation and camaraderie, in which Samora Machel performs as an exemplary heroic revolutionary leader. In the same year a quite different kind of film was made by the Swedish filmmakers Lennart Malmer and Ingela Romare, who needed to reach out to a public that might be hostile to military action supported by the Soviet Union and who were mostly unaware of Sweden's economic entanglement with white minority and colonial regimes in Southern Africa. Their documentary, called *I vårt land börjar kulorna blomma* 'In Our Country the Bullets Start to Blossom', marks a departure from previous approaches in that it focuses on the guerrillas as poets and analysts of their own struggle. *I vårt land börjar kulorna blomma* was in fact one of a number that Malmer and Romare made with lusophone liberation movements in the late 1960s and early 1970s. In 1969 Social Democrat Olaf Palme became Prime Minister of Sweden. A staunch supporter of Frelimo, Palme sought to develop a foreign policy based on non-alignment and humanitarian 'non-lethal' assistance for anti-colonial organisations.[109] That same year, Malmer and Romare made their first visit to Mozambique, travelling to Beira to try to make a television programme about the Portuguese colonial system.[110] They were expelled after four days when the Polícia Internacional e de Defesa do Estado 'International and State Defence Police' (PIDE) got wind of their intentions.[111] That same year they made *Southern Africa: Another Vietnam?* (1969) and *We Love Freedom More Than Peace* (1969), which introduced the ANC, the South West Africa People's Organisation (SWAPO) and Frelimo's liberation struggles to the Swedish public.

[109] As Jorge Rebelo, then Frelimo's secretary for information, has stated about Swedish assistance: 'all the support was non-lethal – as it was called at the time – or humanitarian, in the fields of education, health and to a certain extent information.' Sellström (2002).

[110] They had already made the film *En Nations Födelse* with PAIGC in Guinea-Bissau in 1968.

[111] Lennart Malmer and Ingela Romare (1971). 'Filming the New Society'. *Mozambican Revolution*, 49: 19.

Another documentary, *Mozambique is Our Country*, further familiarised the Swedish audiences with the cause of Mozambican independence.

In 1971 the Swedish filmmakers spent 'about two weeks' with Joaquim Chissano in Cabo Delgado taking the footage for *I vårt land börjar kulorna blomma*.[112] In an article reporting on that visit for *Mozambican Revolution*, Malmer and Romare state:

> As far as possible we wanted to get the possibility of identification with the Mozambican people, a possibility to identify the circumstances the people are facing, well aware about the wall in between their reality and that of the Swedish and western TV-audience. We wanted to break through the strange surface and the constant mistrust most people have towards everything that they feel as (or consider as) propaganda, dogmatic or not.[113]

The way in which Malmer and Romare set about to break this 'strange surface', formed both by ignorance about a situation on the other side of the world and by suspicion about overtly partisan filmmaking, is unique among the documentaries made about Frelimo at this time. *I vårt land börjar kulorna blomma* is distinctive in featuring guerrillas reciting Frelimo poetry, as well as participants in the struggle speaking directly to camera to reflect on their situation and their aspirations for the future. It is also divided into chapters with titles that quote from the poetry and prose of Frelimo, a practice that aligns the documentary to the genres of the essay-film and the ciné-pamphlet. Such critically reflective modes of filmmaking tend to revolve around a set of ideas rather than a necessarily linear plot and can involve polemical denunciations of oppression by exposing the social contradictions in the juxtaposition of image, sound, voice and text.[114] The film's title, too, comes from a poem that was written by Jorge Rebelo, though at the time it was published under the collective rubric of 'the poetry of Frelimo' in the anthology *Poesia de Combate* (1971), one of the first of the books published by Frelimo with the aid of the printing machine donated by Finnish school students.[115] The poem calls for a poetry of combat that would 'forge simple words that even children can understand':

> Come, tell me all this, brother.
> After, I will forge simple words
> That even children can understand,
> Words that will enter every house like the wind,

[112] Malmer and Romare (1971): 18.
[113] Malmer and Romare (1971): 18.
[114] Nicole Brenez (2005). 'A Propos de Nice and the Extremely Necessary, Permanent Invention of the Ciné-pamphlet', Rouge. Available at http://www.rouge.com.au/7/propos_de_nice.html.
[115] Frelimo (1971). *Poesia de Combate*. Dar es Salaam: Frelimo.

> Words that will fall like red-hot embers
> Into the soul of our people.
> In our country the bullets start to blossom.

Like songs and slogans, poetry was recognised as a necessary part of the political movement, one that rendered the ideas animating the struggle into forms of words that were memorable and seductive. For those leaders who were part of the small elite who had studied in Portugal and later been associated with the Paris-based publishing house Présence Africaine, writing poetry had been an important stage of politicisation – a way of re-connecting with an indigenous culture that they had been cut off from through assimilation, albeit expressed in the Portuguese language. As the war developed, poems were written about many aspects of the armed struggle. Themes included the suffering that motivates the struggle, as in José Craveirinha's 'Grito Negro', the determination and heroism of the Frelimo guerrilla, exemplified by Armando Guebuza's 'If You Ask Me Who I Am', the loss of comrades, for example Machel's 'Josina, You Are Not Dead', written after the death of his wife Josina Machel in 1971, and poems in anticipation of freedom and independence. As Robbie Shilliam notes, the poetry of combat articulated Frelimo's particular approach to, for example, internationalist solidarity, as in Rebelo's poem 'Brothers in the West' (1972).[116] The publication of the anthology *Poesia de Combate* marked the beginning of the formation of a literary canon that expressed an idea of revolutionary nationalism through poetry of combat. The poems gave voice to the emerging subjectivity of the committed militant, and while some articulated sentiments such as longing or grief, revolutionary determination ruled over ambivalence or doubt.[117]

I vårt land börjar kulorna blomma begins with inter-titles that explain where Mozambique is, its size – equivalent to Sweden and Norway combined – and gives details about Portuguese exploitation and neglect: just one doctor for every 25,000 people, restrictions on freedom of movement, forced labour, deportations to the mines in South Africa, taxes and massacres of civilians. Photographs illustrate this suffering, some of which had already been used in Dickinson's *Behind the Lines*, including images of forced labour and barbarities carried out by the Portuguese. Yet while *I vårt land börjar kulorna blomma*

[116] Robbie Shilliam (2011). *International Relations and Non-Western Thought: Imperialism, Colonialism and Investigations of Global Modernity*. London: Routledge.

[117] Maria Benedita Basto argues that the literary manifestation of Frelimo's project came increasingly ossified into what she calls 'ready-made ideas'. She looks to the more marginal poetry printed in the more basic Frelimo journals published at education camps and in the liberated zones rather than Dar es Salaam for works that demonstrate more complex performative inhabitations of the 'imperial library' of Portuguese literature. Basto (2006): 97.

includes some moments of didactic factual and historical exposition, the film circles around the voices and faces of those participating in the struggle, and indeed the subtitle 'Images of a Freedom Struggle' suggests precisely this collage of an idea of Frelimo. The next section features a prolonged shot in which a Frelimo soldier looks directly at the camera. At the same time, a woman's voice reads the poem that is here translated as 'In Our Country Bullets Blossom', including these lines of invitation to reveal the embodied experience of revolt:[118]

> Come, my friend, tell me about your struggle.
> Show me the body where the enemy sowed revolt.

A Frelimo fighter addresses a seemingly improvised speech to the camera, explaining the conditions of repression in everyday life under Portuguese colonialism, and how this has motivated people to join the liberation struggle. A Makonde woman speaks in Shimakonde about her experience of colonialism and how the war has impacted the lives of villagers. Armando Guebuza, who joined Frelimo's struggle in 1963 at the age of 23, recites his poem 'If You Ask Me Who I Am':

> If you ask me
> Who I am
> I will tell you nothing.
> I will tell you nothing.
> I'll show you the scars of centuries
> Which furrow my black back
> I'll look at you with eyes of hatred
> Shot red with blood
> Shed through the years . . .I'll tell you nothing
> But you will know why I fight.

While the camera hovers just above head level of a column of guerrillas moving along a narrow path cut through the vegetation, a voiceover recounts the massacre at Mueda, the beginnings of Frelimo and the launch of the armed struggle. It recounts Frelimo's successes: that a quarter of the country is liberated, how they have opened schools and hospitals, but also that the problems are enormous: there is widespread illiteracy and the problem of working between different languages. 'There are no roads in the liberated zones, everything has to be carried.' At the sound of a helicopter overhead, all the fighters stand and listen as the threat of aerial attack approaches.

[118] In Margaret Dickinson's translation, the title of the poem is 'In Our Country the Bullets Start to Flower'. Margaret Dickinson (1972). *When Bullets Begin to Flower*. Nairobi: East African Educational Publishers.

An inter-title, 'And the Comrades come with words like grenades', insists that words are also weapons in this struggle, in terms of communication with the world outside, Frelimo's constant effort to woo the people to the cause of anti-colonial resistance, and for the guerrillas to fortify themselves. With the help of an interpreter, Chissano gives a rallying speech, advocating death rather than submission to the Portuguese. 'Frelimo with the people', Chissano echoes Mao's famous revolutionary slogan, 'is like fish in water – that is why the Portuguese are targeting the people.' Words are also weapons used by the enemy. Frelimo cadres (including Chissano) sit at a table in a wooden hut without walls and discuss the psychological warfare waged by the Portuguese against the people. The terror takes the form of not only napalm bombing (dropped by the Fiat G.91 planes supplied by NATO), but also intimidation in terms of constantly circulating planes that drop pamphlets and agents who are sent to infiltrate the local people. But the film also shows the counter-offensive in this war of words. As guerrillas listen to a broadcast of *Voz de Moçambique*, the camera focuses in on a copy of a book in Spanish entitled *Por qué triumfa el Viet-Cong*, testifying to the process of cross-fertilisation of revolutionary practices and ideas through the circulation of texts along the networks of Tricontinentalism.[119] A section of the film includes interviews with the editors of a Frelimo journal: one man operates a printer by hand, while another talks about the importance of publishing to provide news of the struggle. Another guerrilla reflects:

> When the Portuguese came, they set about stopping the future of our people, because a people without a culture don't have any value in this society, in modern life. So from when the struggle started, one of Frelimo's preoccupations was unifying the culture of the Mozambican people.

As the camera moves upwards to focus on a photograph of Eduardo Mondlane that hangs from a branch overhead, the voiceover reads a text that argues that in the revolutionary struggle that is unfolding the union between the intellect and the hand will create a 'New Man'. While the contours of Frelimo's conception of the 'New Man' would harden in the months and years to follow, the film presents a lyrical utopia of poetic expression. The following inter-title reads: 'The world that I am fighting for is beautiful as a dream'. Over images of women rhythmically pounding grain, the voiceover reads a poem that offers this vision of emancipation to a loved one.

The dream that is conjured is proleptic, nurturing and generative. The section titled 'We must sow the future for those who come' features scenes of education

[119] For an analysis of the international circulation of key texts of militant filmmaking and the work of translation, see Jonathan Buchsbaum (2011). 'One, Two, Third Cinemas', in Kodwo Eshun and Ros Gray (2011). 'The Militant Image: A Ciné-geography', special issue of *Third Text*, 108, 25: 13–28.

in the liberated zones, while in the chapter: 'I want to be a doctor so that I can serve my people' Simão Ilias talks about his desire to train as a doctor so that he can make a contribution to the Mozambican nation of the future. Romare asks him when Mozambique will be free, to which he replies: 'No one knows when Mozambique will be free.' The camera lingers on his face as he averts his gaze and stares sadly at the ground. As in *Behind the Lines*, *In Our Country* compares the determination and clarity of the guerrillas with the Portuguese soldiers, many of whom were illiterate or had little knowledge of Mozambique. One of the combatants argues: 'We are fighting in our own country.' Their combat is a popular struggle not a war of aggression, not targeted at Portuguese people, but rather aimed at self-determination for their country. To illustrate his point he reads the Frelimo poem 'The Guerilla'. The film ends with the drumming of the Mapiko, a frenetic dance that was traditionally performed in secret to young men and boys at their initiation, in which the masked dancer represented the animal spirit of the clan. The voiceover reads the poem 'We are Freedom, Comrade'. This utopian future is the seed that has already taken root in the liberated zones – manifested in bodies working together, voices and words.

Although different in approach to the Soviet film, *In Our Country* sets up a relation between Swedish viewers and Frelimo that is essentially romantic. It is, for instance, uncontaminated by reminders of Swedish investments in Southern Africa, such as the Cahora Bassa dam. Malmer and Romare's documentary was broadcast in early 1972 on Swedish television and, according to Tor Sellström, it played an extraordinarily important role in the formation of Swedish public opinion.[120] Focusing on the poetry of the armed struggle, *In Our Country* succeeded in humanising the guerrilla movement. It opened up a space of identification in a liberal democracy whose support for Frelimo was conditional on the Swedish government maintaining a distance between humanitarian support and the lethal business of armed insurrection.[121]

Another documentary filmed in 1971, *A Luta Continua* (1972), directed by the African-American civil rights lawyer Robert van Lierop, sought to extend Frelimo's networks of solidarity across the Atlantic. Van Lierop was one of many African-American activists who had campaigned against imperialist violence such as the war in Vietnam alongside Civil Rights work. During the 1960s Van Lierop met Eduardo Mondlane while he was in the United States,

[120] Tor Sellström (2002). *Sweden and National Liberation in Southern Africa Volume 2*. Uppsala: Nordiska Afrikainstitutet: 94.

[121] Chissano recalls the difficulty Frelimo had with Sweden's requirement that even its medical supplies should not be used by combatants. 'They gave us medicines to treat civilians, but we said that humanitarianism means that a man with a gun also has a right to life and to be treated when he is wounded. A wounded civilian could come to the hospital for treatment, but a soldier could not be treated with the same medicine. This was shocking to us and on that point we had to be sharp.' Sellström (2002): 40.

and when Sharfudine Khan arrived in New York to represent Frelimo at the UN they discussed how they could increase support for Frelimo. 'The idea of a complete media treatment came up,' Van Lierop recalls, 'articles, photos, even a film documenting the struggle.'[122] As Komozi Woodard points out, the political establishment in the United States had long attempted to intimidate and condition black leaders to think of foreign affairs as the exclusive domain of the White House.[123] Meanwhile, the CIA recruited a number of African-American agents to infiltrate and disrupt Frelimo.[124] Yet as R. Joseph Parrott argues, the 'new militant race consciousness of Black Nationalism meant that the lusophone African liberation struggles were important symbols of resistance and self-determination.'[125] Black radicals came to understand their own oppressed communities as an 'internal colony' of the United States, and anti-colonial writers helped them to analyse these conditions and point to ways of organising resistance.[126]

Van Lierop wanted to use film to extend this 'fictive kinship' with the Third World for a two-fold purpose: to support Frelimo's international diplomatic campaign and to strengthen the activism he was involved with in the United States.[127] He believed that Frelimo demonstrated the importance

[122] William Minter, Gail Hovey and Charles Cobb Jr. (eds) (2008). *No Easy Victories: African Liberation and American Activists over a Half Century, 1950–2000*. Trenton: Africa World Press: 142; R. Joseph Parrott (2015). '*A Luta Continua*: Radical Filmmaking, Pan-African Liberation and Communal Empowerment', *Race and Class*, 57, 1, July–September: 20–38.

[123] Mainstream media pundits propounded the patronising view that they would be 'confused' by events in Africa and vulnerable to manipulation by 'bigots' who would assert racial identification above duties of citizenship. Woodard here quotes from an article published in *The Washington Post* that warned Civil Rights activists against seeking out international relations. Komozi Woodard (2006). 'Amiri Baraka, the Congress of African People and Black Power Politics from the 1961 United Nations Protest to the 1972 Gary Convention', in Peniel E. Joseph (ed.) (2006). *The Black Power Movement: Rethinking the Civil Rights–Black Power Era*. London: Routledge: 57.

[124] Leo Aldridge pretended to be Mozambican in order to infiltrate Frelimo, where he caused considerable disruption before being expelled. Leo Milas infiltrated Frelimo in the early 1960s and later was one of the founding members of Renamo. The CIA also targeted Mozambicans educated in the United States, such as José Massinga who admitted in the 1980s that he had been a CIA agent and Luís Serapiao who was a professor at Howard University in Washington as well as a founder of Renamo. Serapiao focused his attacks on questions of race within Frelimo, targeting Janet Mondlane particularly, and collaborated closely with the Rhodesian army. Gerard Horne (2002). 'Reflecting Black: Zimbabwe and US Black Nationalism', in Eddie S. Glaude (2002). *Is it Nation Time? Contemporary Essays on Black Power and Black Nationalism*. Chicago: University of Chicago Press: 95.

[125] Parrott (2015): 23.

[126] Woodard (2006): 69.

[127] Woodard (2006): 62.

of collective organisation and of understanding revolution as a social process of transformation that would need to take place alongside self-defence. In an article for *Mozambican Revolution*, Van Lierop stresses that:

> The revolution in Mozambique is a process and not an event. Every single day small steps are taken to prepare the way for the next generation which must continue the struggle begun by the comrades of this generation. Sensational events or individual have no place in this revolutionary process. This struggle is something akin to a long distance relay race which requires – patience, teamwork, coordination, stamina and determination . . . People in America who profess to be revolutionaries but who deliver simplified messages of quick non-ideological struggles could learn much from the people of Mozambique who are in the front line of the world-wide struggle against imperialism, colonialism and racism.[128]

Reaching a far wider audience than the books of political theory written by the leaders of the lusophone independence movements, *A Luta Continua* explained Frelimo's socialist ideology through practical examples and focused on social cooperation and transformation rather than military achievements.

Van Lierop financed the film by reaching out to progressive organisations and churches associated with the American Committee on Africa (ACOA), an organisation that Van Lierop had helped to lead.[129] Significant financial backers included the radical philanthropist and anti-Vietnam War campaigner Carol Ferry (whose husband W. H. 'Ping' Ferry worked for the Ford Foundation) and Peter and Cora Weiss, who were friends of Eduardo Mondlane.[130] As Van Lierop had no experience as a filmmaker, he recruited the photographer Robert Fletcher to travel with him to Mozambique as cinematographer. Bob Fletcher had begun his work documenting African-American communities and the civil rights movement as a student in 1963, and in 1964 he worked for SNCC Photos, which was the media arm of the Student Non-Violent Coordinating Committee (SNCC). Although Fletcher's experience was predominantly in photography, from 1965 to 1968 he had worked for the Southern Visual Education Service, a SNCC project that produced grassroots educational films, such as *If You Farm, You Can Vote*, which aimed to encourage rural workers to register to vote and educate others about the benefits of cooperative farming. In 1968 he attended the Congress for Writers, Artists and Intellectuals in Havana, Cuba, as a delegate of the SNCC. The theme of the congress was 'The Problems of the Third World' and it was here that Fletcher met members of Frelimo and became

128 Robert van Lierop (1971). 'The Revolution Lives in the Hearts of the People', *Mozambican Revolution*, 49: 16–17.

129 According to R. Joseph Parrott, the ACOA had difficulty in overcoming the suspicions of black communities because of its predominantly white leadership. Parrott (2015): 14.

130 Minter, Hovey and Cobb Jr. (eds) (2008): 142.

interested in African liberation struggles. Van Lierop and Fletcher arrived in Tanzania in late 1971, from whence they travelled to the liberated zone of Niassa to spend five and a half weeks filming.[131] Their original plans for the film were compromised, however, when they lost some of their equipment while crossing the Rovuma river. They were forced to use a 16mm spring-wound Bolex camera, which meant they were limited to very short takes and syncing the sound in the editing process.[132] Thus, as in *Behind the Lines*, Van Lierop's voiceover in *A Luta Continua* is essential to the unfolding of the film's argument. Van Lierop's commentary presents a unified popular revolutionary nationalist movement and emphasises that the struggle is part of a global anti-imperialist movement. *A Luta Continua* opens with a travelling shot across the Niassa landscape and the sound of birdsong, cutting to footage of Frelimo guerrillas crossing a tree-truck bridge. The soundtrack then flits between different items on a Radio RSA broadcast from South Africa, creating a set of connections between the struggles against colonialism and Apartheid in Southern Africa and racial conflict in the United States: President Nixon's decision to quell the revolt at Attica prison, a South African response to the Mogadishu Declaration, which claims that poor blacks will be taxed more heavily to pay for the quelling of 'pleasure-loving terrorists' living outside South Africa's borders.[133] Finally another voice, speaking in English but with a Mozambican accent, addresses all Mozambican people to announce the beginning of Frelimo's armed insurrection against Portuguese colonialism on 25 September 1964. Van Lierop's own voice then contextualises Frelimo's struggle, locating Mozambique on a map of Southern Africa and highlighting the area now controlled by Frelimo. A section on Mozambique's colonial history then explains the Portuguese exploitation of Mozambicans as slaves and its historical attempts to crush local resistance, which only succeeded in 1918. The film lays out Mozambique's significance to the white minority regimes in the region and the nature of Portugal's fascist government, 'which seeks to export its class contradictions to the colonies' while being itself a 'neocolony' of richer capitalist nations. Portugal is provided with military and economic aid by NATO powers, easing the burden of its colonial wars. They do so because 'Portugal is their agent' in Southern Africa – a poster of the African continent includes the logos of multinational corporations that exploit this relationship to access Mozambique's extensive mineral resources.

131 Bob Fletcher and Robert van Lierop (1973). 'The Quiet War in Mozambique'. *Ebony*, February: 93.

132 Van Lierop recalls that film editor Richard Skinner had fortunately experience of editing television commercials, which meant he was skilled in editing with quick cuts. Minter, Hovey and Cobb Jr. (eds) (2008): 143.

133 The Mogadishu Declaration of 1971 asserted that Pretoria's refusal to negotiate meant that black South Africans could only be freed through an armed struggle and that no African state should initiate contact with the Apartheid government.

The Cahora Bassa dam, which is financed by an international consortium of business interests, is planned to supply most of the energy it produces to South Africa, and Portugal plans to settle large numbers of its citizens in the area of the dam as a 'second line of defence' against Frelimo, while over 25,000 Africans have been forcibly removed.

Van Lierop then describes the founding of Frelimo in 1962. What they established, the voiceover claims, was not just a military and political organisation, but also an educational, health and social services institution, and through the armed struggle it has become a 'revolutionary party of the masses of Mozambicans'. Over footage of Frelimo soldiers doing drills in the forest and cadres carrying out paperwork, Van Lierop explains that Frelimo's organisation is founded on a notion of responsibility rather than hierarchy – the leaders are called '*responsaveis*' – the responsibles. The film claims that the struggle has taught people to suppress their own egos for a common goal, and people are often called upon to do tasks that cut across traditional ideas of gender or age. Van Lierop asserts that it is thus the 'people of Mozambique' who are the main weapons in this struggle, 'their unity and their political consciousness'. *A Luta Continua* highlights the role of Frelimo's armed struggle in overturning traditional and colonial hierarchies that kept women in subservient positions. According to the film, both men and women in Frelimo now fight, teach, cook and perform other housekeeping chores. Images show soldiers in uniform talking with civilian women and passing a baby between them. The film admits that Mozambican society has 'a way to go' in terms of women's liberation, but it asserts that revolution must be seen as a dynamic process of transformation – 'just like a mango seed undergoes a change from seed to tree, becoming stronger and more firmly rooted in the process so too grows the revolution in Mozambique'. Mingling with the voiceover are the sounds of women singing, which come together with the images of the dance that it accompanies.

Cultivation and nurturing are powerful metaphors for Frelimo's socialist project: the film shows images of young women attending school – a blackboard hung from a tree – many for the first time. In *A Luta Continua*, the words of Eduardo Mondlane explains why Frelimo attached such great importance to education: first, because as people become better informed their support for Frelimo grows, and second, because a future independent Mozambique will be in 'grave need' of educated citizens to 'lead the way in development'. Van Lierop's voiceover continues, education is not a way to achieve 'upward mobility' or to 'isolate themselves as an intellectual elite', nor is it a meaningless abstraction that leads to dependency on external economic conditions', instead in education there is a future promise that is shaping the future of Mozambique and of Africa. After lessons, teachers do not retreat to 'exclusive suburbs' while the pupils 'retreat further into the ghettos'. Rather, they are part of the same movement, living and working alongside their pupils. Frelimo's establishment of health centres is compared with Portuguese neglect of rural populations, and the way in which colonial agricultural policy were led meant that peasants were more vulnerable to disease because of malnutrition. Footage shows cadres with medical training administering care to people with gunshot wounds, napalm burns, parasites, as well as giving vaccinations.

Van Lierop points out that in rural Mozambique there are 'no grocery stores – everyone must be able to live off the land.' Archive images illustrate how many Mozambicans were forced by the colonial regime to grow cash crops such as cotton or coffee rather than food. Released from this enforced labour, the people are able to devote their energies to subsistence farming. The film shows scenes of farming in the liberated zones and discusses the creation of agricultural cooperatives and Frelimo's constant drive to increase production. Indeed, at the beginning of the growing season of 1971 to 1972, Samora Machel issued directives 'concerning the way production must be organised, its importance from the economic and social point of view, and its role in the political formation of the militants'. Entitled 'Sowing the Seeds of Liberation', these directives, which were widely circulated and published in *Mozambican Revolution*, propose that, for the practice of revolutionary agricultural production to be properly transformative, it should have a symbiotic relation to study, involving the sharing of knowledge and the building of national unity. In the 'enemy zone', Machel argues, where workers are exploited by capitalist colonialism, manual labour is 'thought dishonourable, shameful, low'. By contrast, in the liberated zones participation in agricultural production is a collective endeavour that everyone should participate in as means to self-sufficiency. Collective agricultural work is what enables militants to overcome their differences and to cement national unity.[134] Crucially, it builds resilience and provides opportunities for militants both to learn from and to teach the masses:

> Production is a school because it is one of the sources of our knowledge, and it is through production that we correct our mistakes. It is by going to the people, that we both learn and teach the people. If our army did not produce, how would we have grown cassava in Tete, when the people had no knowledge of cassava? If we had contented ourselves with making speeches about cassava, would the cassava have grown? What better way of defending our production in Tete against bombing

[134] 'If I am a Nyanja, and cultivate the land alongside an Ngoni, I sweat with him, learn with him, appreciating his efforts, and I feel united with him. . . . With him I am destroying tribal, religious and linguistic prejudices, all that is secondary and divides us. Unity grows with the growing plant, with the sweat and intelligence we both mingle with the soil.' Samora Machel (1971). 'Sowing the Seeds of Liberation'. *Mozambican Revolution*, 49: 21.

raids, chemical weapons and enemy incursions than diversification of production, introduction of new crops and crops which are resistant to enemy action.[135]

The scenes of collective farming segue into images of devastation, demonstrating how agricultural production is often targeted by Portuguese army assaults by air. The footage of combat seen here, in which Frelimo fighters shoot back at Portuguese aircraft, was extremely rare, in contrast to the quantity of war footage from the perspective of Portuguese soldiers. *A Luta Continua* is in fact the only film about Frelimo's armed struggle that has actual battle scenes, because the crew were accidentally caught up in a surprise attack.[136]

Van Lierop argues that, as with American troops in Vietnam, as soon as Portuguese troops hit the ground they are disadvantaged, so that while their command of the air enables them to seize small areas they are usually driven out again within a few weeks. The film shows footage of wounded Portuguese soldiers being airlifted away and then the same horrific photographs of victims of the massacres used in the British and Swedish films. The aim of the Portuguese offensive is threefold: to destroy the people's food, to terrorise the local population in the liberated areas so that they come to feel that Frelimo cannot protect them, and to destroy the 'institutions of national reconstruction' – the clinics, schools and nurseries built by Frelimo in the forest. Such destruction, however, fails to destroy these institutions, because 'they are carried in the hearts and souls of the people' rather than in the temporary structures that house them. Thus activities such as teaching continue even in the midst of fierce military assaults. 'The Struggle Continues', Van Lierop explains, are the words that Eduardo Mondlane used to sign off his letters. In the armed struggle this phrase takes on heightened significance, signifying the multiple ways in which 'the struggle continues' in every aspect of daily life. The weapons of war are thus just one of the tools of revolution – they enabled Frelimo to create the liberated zones free from Portuguese control. Frelimo aims at changing patterns of life, and so, the voiceover asserts, it 'is like a farmer nurturing seeds, transplanting these seeds so as to produce stronger trees that will be the foundation of the new society'. A nursery named after Josina Machel serves as an example of this process – an institution that was only available for the rich under colonialism.

135 Machel (1971): 22.

136 The attack woke the film crew and soldiers who were accompanying them. Frelimo photographer Simão Matias later recalled that, as the film crew began documenting the attack, he picked up his camera rather than his gun to photograph his fellow guerrillas: 'when I was firing my camera, in the middle of the rumble, the whistles of bullets, I started to feel equal with good friends, the soldiers of the base that were shooting their guns.' A. Naroromele (1985). 'Fui Sempre Jornalista e Quero Continuar a Ser' [I have always been a journalist and forever I want to be one]. *Domingo*, November 3: 3; cited in Thompson (2013).

In the armed struggle the nursery is the place where Frelimo can take care of children whose parents are not there for them, either because they are fighting for Frelimo or because they have been killed in the war. 'It's the place where we plant the seeds, so that later we can plant them into bigger *chambas* [agricultural land].' Here, children can learn what their role will be in the future society – they are the true *continuadores* (youth wing of Frelimo).

The film concludes with a section dedicated to revolutionary nationalism, communicated through images of people moving in unison. As in *Behind the Lines*, *A Luta Continua* describes how Frelimo is composed out of people from different tribes across the country brought together through the armed struggle, a process summed up in the slogan 'To die a tribe, to be born a nation'. The guerillas learn dances from other regions, as well as songs and dances that have become part of a national heritage rather than belonging to a single ethnicity. 'The guerilla army makes this a living concept as it transplants the culture of the people of Mozambique throughout the country.' Van Lierop quotes from Samora Machel while the film cuts to footage of guerillas marching:

> When we march we feel stimulated and content, because during the march we learn about ourselves and we resolve any individual problems. During the march we perspire together and each drop of sweat fertilizes our soil and consolidates our unity.

These agricultural metaphors – of propagation, nurturing seeds, transplantation of seedlings and fertilizing the soil – evoke forms of life that are vigorous but still young. The scale of this revolutionary cultivation is, for now, that of a newly established *machamba*. Yet the setting of the sun that concludes the film, with shouts from the guerillas of 'Viva Frelimo! A Luta Continua!', promises that this cycle of life, in which Frelimo is embedded and through which it extends its roots across the liberated zones, will begin again with each new day.

A Luta Continua was distributed through networks of activists in North America, who organised projections in colleges and universities, and by solidarity committees in Britain and Scandinavia, who ensured its wide circulation across Europe. Van Lierop recalls that the film was even smuggled into South Africa, where it was shown in Soweto before the uprising: 'The title of the film, *A Luta Continua*, began to appear scrawled on Soweto walls.'[137] At these gatherings, the film projection was usually accompanied by presentations by activists. These increased the effectiveness of the film as a tool of mobilising support and inspiring activism in the United States, for which it offered examples for replication. Discussions were supported by an accompanying pamphlet that recommended forms of action such as organising boycotts of southern African goods, initiating educational campaigns and engaging in 'mass political actions

[137] Minter, Hovey and Cobb Jr. (eds) (2009): 143.

against identifiable imperialist targets (e.g. corporations with investments in Southern Africa; communications outlets that have failed to report on the wars of national liberation)'.[138] Van Lierop's interpretation of Frelimo's version of socialism spoke to the aspirations of African-American activists concerned with communal control of resources, racial equality and internationalist solidarity. As R. Joseph Parrott comments, in *A Luta Continua* Frelimo's specific struggle to liberate Mozambique is transformed into 'a universal narrative of resistance and self-determination'.[139]

In 1972 Frelimo received a delegation from the Communist municipality of Reggio Emilia in Italy, and this visit resulted in the documentary *Dieci giorni con I guerriglieri nel Mozambico Livro*, directed by Franco Cigarini. While other films made in the liberated zones with Frelimo were intended to reach out to new sympathisers, *Dieci giorni con I guerriglieri nel Mozambico Livro* was a report back to a community who had been offering material support to Frelimo for some time. Italy had no historical relationship with Southern Africa. Its colonial exploits in Eritrea, Somalia and Libya were relatively short-lived and the Italian government did not succeed in maintaining strong ties with its former colonies.[140] The particular relationship that developed between Italy and Mozambique was driven instead by grassroots activism and shaped by the way in which socialists worked with progressive Catholics to build popular democracy and anti-colonial solidarity.[141] This decentralised cooperation between Mozambique and Italy was nurtured by left-wing parties that had connections both with central government and with the so-called 'Red Towns', which had left-wing local governments. The Catholic Church was also able

[138] Africa Information Service (1973). 'A Discussion Guide for the Film *A Luta Continua*.' New York: Africa Information Service.

[139] Parrott (2015).

[140] Luca Bussotti, Antonella de Muti (2013). 'Italy and Mozambique: Science, Economy & Society within a History of an Anomalous Cooperation'. *Advances in Historical Studies*, 12, 4: 186.

[141] Bussotti and Muti quote Cabaço: 'It is not possible to understand the cooperation between Italy and Mozambique if we do not remember the peculiarity of the Italian democracy in the post war period, its partisan tradition and, in particular, the dream of a historic compromise between the Catholic and socialist positions as regards social justice. With the beginning of the anti-colonial struggle, the means of communication between our two peoples expanded the missionary experience, incorporating components of political identity which took off from the hands of the Portuguese colonial government its control on this relationship. This space opened the way to the first interventions of a Catholic Church committed to the destiny and the aspirations of colonised people... Also the role played by the political left winged forces on the issue of the Third World grew.' José Luís Cabaço (2003). *La Polvere e la pioggia*. Maputo: Ambasciata d'Italia–Ufficio per la Cooperazione allo Sviluppo. In Bussotti and Muti (2013): 189.

to influence the Central Democratic Party, who was in government, and they supported relations with Mozambique through a parallel network of NGOs.

In 1962, two years before the beginning of the armed struggle, Marcelino dos Santos contacted Dina Forti, who was the point of contact for the Partito Comunista Italiano 'Italian Communist Party '(PCI) for liberation movements in developing countries. Through Forti, dos Santos was able to arrange a meeting with Giancarlo Pajetta, head of the International Department of the PCI. When Frelimo began the armed struggle in 1964, the Communist-controlled municipality of Reggio Emilia sent a message of support. The Italian connection strengthened further in 1966, when Frelimo activist José Luís Cabaço came to Italy with two objectives: to study sociology and to build a network in Italy to support the struggle against Portuguese colonialism. The Rome Conference, which took place from 24 to 26 June 1970, was an important event for legitimising the independence movements, much to the fury of the Portuguese regime. Agostinho Neto, Amilcar Cabral and Marcelino dos Santos were received as representatives of their respective countries rather than as colonial subjects of Portugal. The conference announced the adoption of a policy of nurturing solidarity by twinning African nations to particular Communist municipalities in Italy. Angola was linked to Prato, Guinea-Bissau and Cape Verde to Arezzo, and Mozambique to Reggio Emilia. Giuseppe Soncini, director of Santa Maria Nuova Hospital, was approached by the Communist Party to lead the Reggio Emilia twinning with Mozambique. Soncini set up a partnership between the Reggio Emilia hospital and a medical clinic in Cabo Delgado, which consisted of just a few huts. In 1972, Frelimo organised an expedition for an Italian delegation led by Soncini to enable them to cross the border of Tanzania into liberated zones in northern Mozambique. The delegation included Lanfranco Turci, who was head of the Department of Health of the Emilia Romagna region, Angelo Pisi, vice mayor of Reggio Emilia, journalist Marisa Musu and Franco Cigarini, a photographer and documentary filmmaker commissioned by the Reggio Emilia city council to document the expedition.

Made as an audio-visual report of the delegation's visit to Cabo Delgado, *Dieci giorni con I guerriglieri nel Mozambico Livro* features an animated voiceover and dynamic camera shots. The film describes the liberated zones as a 'laboratory' in which young and old Mozambicans, intellectuals, functionaries and even deserters from the Portuguese army are working together to create a new society. *Ten Days* sketches out the history of the armed struggle, the sequence culminating in footage of people running into an underground shelter from an air raid, rapid montage of images of bombs falling, a child crying, guerrillas running through the forest, guns at the ready, and finally slows to images of people mutilated and crippled by the bombs. There are scenes of schooling, cultivation, Makonde sculpture workshops, the printing of Frelimo newsletters and images of the Frelimo school at Bagamoyo. In a dramatic close-up, Samora

Machel speaks directly to the camera, asserting the legitimacy of the armed struggle against Portuguese colonialism and imperialism and explaining that their campaign is part of a wider battle against poverty and ignorance. Working to construct 'a new mentality in our people', Machel claims, 'Our struggle is against tribalism and racism.' It is not directed against the Portuguese people, but rather 'Our struggle is on behalf of the world.'

Beside the triumphalist tone, the film also details the difficulties Frelimo faces, in terms of the transportation of goods through the liberated zones, sanitation and the scale of illiteracy. Armado Guebuza, who is depicted giving a lesson to children using a blackboard hanging from a tree, discusses the role of education in communicating 'the story of our country and our culture'. Heroic shots of female guerrillas and children performing manoeuvres emphasise that this is a people's war – the entire population are involved in the armed struggle. The film culminates with images from a public meeting, in which Frelimo leaders and members of the Italian delegation address a large crowd and celebrate solidarity between the peoples of Italy and Mozambique. Finally, a female guerrilla speaks about the problems facing the people, and the film closes with a rendition of the Frelimo anthem.

As Frelimo continued to resist the onslaught of Operation Gordian Knot in Niassa and Cabo Delgado, the guerrillas pushed down through the western province of Tete. By June 1972 Portuguese commanders were convinced that Frelimo had infiltrated communities within the area known as the 'Wiriyamu Triangle', a clutter of villages located on a plateau near the Zambezi river close to the border with the central province of Sofala. A number of successful attacks by Frelimo enraged the Portuguese, and after an ambush of heavily armed commandos resulted in severe casualties, the surviving commandos swore to get their revenge.[142] On 16 December 1972 Portuguese soldiers supported by officers from the Direcção Geral de Segurança 'Directorate of Security' (DGS) began their attack. They were under orders to 'clean up' Wiriyamu, patchy intelligence having failed to reveal that Frelimo operations had in fact by then moved further south. The soldiers headed to the villages of Chaworha, Wiriyamu, Juawu and Djemusse, where they herded villagers into their huts, hurling in grenades and firing on escapees.[143] More than 385 people were killed, a total amounting to nearly a third of the entire population of the Wiriyamu Triangle.[144]

[142] Dhada (2016): 67.

[143] For a detailed anatomy of how the massacres unfolded, see Dhada (2016): 159–172.

[144] According to Dhada, the total number of victims is '385 named dead', a tally that excludes casualties during the three-day manhunt for escapees that followed, those whose names cannot be recalled by surviving villagers due to memory loss and victims brought to the DGS headquarters for interrogation. Dhada (2016): 171.

While the Portuguese army committed numerous mass killings of civilians during the armed struggle, news of the Wiriyamu massacre did finally get out.[145] On 10 July 1973, *The Times* carried an article titled 'Portuguese massacre reported by priests' that gave an account of the killings.[146] The article was published on the eve of an official visit to London by Marcelo Caetano, who became prime minister of Portugal after the death of Salazar, and instead of the visit furthering Portugal's relations with the British government, he was met with protests coordinated by CFMAG and calls from the Labour Party for the invitation to be cancelled. The Portuguese government responded by trying to discredit the report, claiming that the massacres had not happened because Wiriyamu did not exist! The British newspaper *Sunday Times* sent its reporter Peter Pringle to Mozambique, and he managed to interview and photograph a fifteen-year-old boy named António Mixone, who had survived the massacre at Chaworha. Frelimo facilitated further visits by journalists from East Germany, Algeria and Italy, who also reported on atrocities committed by the Portuguese. In 1973 the West German journalists Reinhard Biermann and Ursula Pauli spent five weeks in Tete, staying at a Frelimo base on the banks of the Zambezi, and visiting orphanages, schools, medical posts and agricultural cooperatives. On 22 May they filmed the aerial bombardment of the village of Luiva.[147] Their article for *Mozambican Revolution* comments on the presence of white Rhodesian soldiers in Tete and their reputation for being 'even more cruel than the white Portuguese troops.'[148] During the visit they made a 16mm film in colour, for distribution to European TV stations, and the material and testimonies they gathered provided evidence of further massacres and the extent of civilian suffering. An article in the Wisconsin newspaper, *La Crosse Tribune*, comments: 'although they were not looking for atrocity stories, almost every one of the 50 interviews they recorded in Mozambique contains accounts by people who suffered beatings and torture, or who witnessed massacres and murders.'[149] While the Lisbon government continued to enjoy the support of the United States and NATO, and persisted in

[145] Massacres by the Portuguese army in Mozambique during the armed struggle included: Chai as a revenge for the first attack by Frelimo ('Chai: O Massacre que os colonialistas esconderam', *Tempo*, 364: 35); the week after the attack on Chai, Portuguese troops went on a four-day rampage through the villages of Biamualo, Malani, Limba/Erimba and Napandika, killing around 700 people; Inhaminga as part of Operation Gordian Knot (Fathers J. Martens, A. Verdaasdonk, J. van Rijen, A.van Kampen and J. Tielemans (1974). 'Diary of Inhaminga'. *Issue: A Journal of Opinion*, 4, 2: 62–73); in 1971 in the Mukumbura region of Tete province in reprisal for the death of three Rhodesian soldiers ('A Priest Describes Portuguese Butcher', *Mozambican Revolution*, 50, January–March 1972: 10).

[146] It was Father Adrian Hastings, a missionary who was in touch with priests based in the Wiriyamu area, who had initially smuggled their reports on the massacre to Rome.

[147] 'Orphans Tell of New Atrocities', *The Age*, 23 July 1973: 5.

[148] Frelimo (1973). 'Visitors in Free Mozambique'. *Mozambican Revolution*, 55: 9–10.

[149] *La Crosse Tribune*, 24 July 1973: 37.

issuing denials and disinformation, the flow of reports of indiscriminate violence meant that the tide was turning inexorably against the fascist colonial regime.

One of the final documentaries made with Frelimo during the armed struggle was by the French film collective Cinéthique in 1973 at the Frelimo school in Bagamoyo, Tanzania. The title of the film, *Étudier, Produire, Combattre*, was based on a slogan that communicated Frelimo's new decolonial pedagogy, one that would cultivate symbiotic relationships between study and physical labour, theory and practice, and ideology and combat.[150] Cinéthique began as a film journal of the same name that was set up by Marcel Hanoun, Gérard Leblanc and Jean-Paul Fargier, among others, and was influenced by Jean-Luc Godard and the avant-garde literary magazine *Tel Quel*. Perhaps one of the most theoretically orientated of the film collectives that emerged in France in the wake of the worker and student protests of 1968, Cinéthique increasingly identified with Marxist–Leninism and sought to address questions of the relation between theory and practice through experimentation with film form, particularly the use of inter-titles and *détournement*.[151] As Paul Grant explains, 'The collective's hope for the film was that it would open up a discussion about revolutionary education, and they set among its intentions the struggle for women's liberation, the struggle against elitism and the uniting of the people "to conquer the enemy . . . and produce an original national culture".'[152]

The conflicts around class, ethnicity and political line that had erupted into student revolt and led to the closure of the Mozambique Institute in 1968 convinced Frelimo that elitism needed to be nipped in the bud. The education centre at Tunduru and makeshift 'class-rooms' in the liberated zones taught to primary level, but in addition Frelimo set up new headquarters and a secondary school at Bagamoyo, close to Dar es Salaam. The Bagamoyo school became the laboratory for Frelimo's educational policies and its attempt to build a decolonial alternative to colonial pedagogy, continuing the work that had begun at the Mozambique Institute. The student revolt at the Mozambique Institute was interpreted by Frelimo's ideologues as evidence of the dangers of petty-bourgeois individualism to the revolutionary project, and they saw it as essential to transform education so that schools would serve the purpose of training up dedicated revolutionary cadres rather than self-serving elites who might become the puppets of neocolonialism.

Frelimo's pedagogical strategy was consolidated at the second Conference of Education and Culture held in 1970. Drawing on the experience of social

150 Michael Cross (2011). *An Unfulfilled Promise: Schools in Mozambique*. Addis Ababa: Organisation for Social Science Research in Eastern and Southern Africa: 54.

151 Paul Douglas Grant (2016). *Cinéma Militant: Political Filmmaking and May 68*. New York and Chichester: Wallflower Press: 152–153.

152 Grant (2016).

transformation in the liberated zones, education was to be understood as a tool for serving *o Povo* rather than for enabling individuals to pursue personal ambitions. Refusing colonial hierarchies between mental and physical work, students were taught the value of self-sufficiency and self-criticism. Pedagogical methods were geared at replacing the individualist mentalities of colonial capitalism and developing in its place a new revolutionary subjectivity produced through collective work, sharing of resources and knowledge, democratic participation and the forging of new kinds of social relations.

Étudier, Produire, Combattre includes footage taken at the Bagamoyo school and drawings that provide further illustration.[153] As well as scenes of lessons, the film shows pupils tending the school garden, making bricks and sewing clothes. A voiceover explains that children are taught self-sufficiency and learn to 'bind themselves to the masses'. The revolution is not about a 'return to source', but rather education offers an escape from superstition and tribalism, while not neglecting the 'empirical knowledges of the people', from which the young militants can learn. Students also need to transform their own relations with one another and work towards the emancipation of women (here the camera lingers on a journal illustrated with a photograph of Josina Machel). Images follow of the pupils in their simple dormitories, which have running water and comfortable beds. While these lodgings may seem modest, the voiceover points out, Frelimo is keen that pupils be aware that they are relatively privileged. The emphasis on political education is 'the principle guarantee against the reproduction of the elitist tendencies'. It is these 'elitist tendencies', the film argues, that characterised the 'reactionary minority' of students who revolted in 1968 – young people who were told that they would administrate the country after independence and that they should not 'dirty their hands with agricultural work'. As a result, admission to the secondary school is conditional on pupils demonstrating their political commitment. After nine months of school, the voiceover explains, the pupils take 'holidays' in the liberated zones, during which they contribute to the struggle by carrying goods and helping with healthcare and agricultural production. In the final sequence of the film, the voice of Samora Machel summarises the priorities of education as a revolutionary task, one that must be combined with production and armed struggle. As he speaks the words 'Study', 'Produce', and 'Fight' appear, interspersed with shots of a hand writing, a hand hammering a nail, and finally shots of school children as they quickly disperse. 'He who studies', concludes Machel, 'should be the spark that lights the flame that is the people.' While the primary function of most armed struggle films was to galvanise material assistance and ideological support for

[153] According to Gerard Leblanc, the film is now lost, but a detailed scene-by-scene description of *Study, Produce, Fight* was published in a dossier on liberation movements in *Cinéthique*, 25/26 (1980).

Frelimo internationally, this is a film about militant education in the Bagamoyo school that itself has a function to teach, bringing back to Europe methods by which the Mozambican revolution was shaping a new vanguard through its radical pedagogy.

While Frelimo began as a front comprising diverse factions, ten years of armed struggle and internal conflicts had produced a model of a new revolutionary subjectivity. This subjectivity was theorised through the figure of the 'New Man', which defined a specifically 'Mozambican personality' that was forged out of the experience of the armed struggle and involved the eradication of values, ways of life and systems of belief that did not comply with Frelimo's political line. New ideas and comportments would form the basis of social relations to replace those that existed under the colonial system. This included aspects of 'traditional' Mozambican society, which Frelimo saw as being mired in exploitation, corruption, sexism, racism, obscurantism, tribalism and alienation from African roots. The comportment of Samora and Josina Machel demonstrated the kind of discipline and selflessness that Frelimo demanded of its guerrillas. The transformation of each individual's consciousness was seen as an essential component of the revolutionary struggle, as Machel pointed out: 'Even when the systems of exploitation have been destroyed, if we do not fight the mentality underlying them, then sooner or later, slowly or rapidly, the system will spring up from its ashes again, nourished by the negative values preserved within us.'[154] While the 'New Man' resonates with Fanon's assertion that decolonisation would produce a new kind of humanity separate from the murderous 'humanity' of colonial Europe, it is worth noting that the propaganda discourses of the fascist regime in Portugal also featured a 'New Man' who embodied spiritual purity and dedication to the New State.[155] The 'New Man' is a modernist invention. Like 'the people' and 'the masses', the 'New Man' is an empty signifier that holds together a political identity.[156] The task of the 'New Man', therefore, is to sweep away all that is counter to the construction of the nation-state.

The films of the armed struggle, in varying ways, personalise their narratives of national becoming. Some, such as *Behind the Lines* and *I vårt land börjar kulorna blomma*, include first-person accounts by people who describe how the struggle was transforming their lives and how they wished to contribute to

[154] Samora Machel (1979). 'Fazer da Escola uma Base para o Povo Tomar o Poder', in Departamento do ideológia da Frelimo (1979). *Estudos e Orientações*, 6, July 1979: 23

[155] Patricia Vieira (2013). *Portuguese Film, 1930–1960: The Staging of the New State Regime*. London: Bloomsbury: 31 and 58.

[156] Paulo Israel locates Frelimo's politics as a form of populism, drawing on the argument in Ernesto Laclau (2005). *Critique of Populist Reason*. London: Verso. Paulo Israel (2010). 'The Formulaic Revolution: Song and the "Collective Memory" of the Mozambican War of Independence. *Cahiers d'Études Africaine*, 1, 197: 181–216.

an independent Mozambique. Others, such as *Viva Frelimo!* and *The People of Mozambique are Fighting On*, revolve around Samora Machel as heroic leader who serves as both example and metonym for the entire movement. The films visualise the guerrilla movement through a certain bodily intimacy: images that tend to be shot at head height show guerrillas and peasants march together along pathways cut through the forest. They greet each other with salutes, handshakes, embraces and gifts of appreciation. *Venceremos*, *Viva Frelimo!* and *Dieci giorni con I guerriglieri nel Mozambico Livro* show the movement's political leaders, its doctors, nurses and journalists at work – in discussion with cadres, explaining the purpose of the struggle to remote rural communities, administering medical care and teaching adults and children. The people of Frelimo are also the peasants, who cultivate the crops and carry supplies. The material infrastructures may be fragile – health clinics made from sticks in temporary clearings, pictures hang from pieces of string, blackboards attached to trees – and they are ready to be disassembled at any moment. This very poverty of materials emphasises that the strength of the moment lies in its participants – in their determination, vision and flexibility. Different kinds of voice and song populate the armed struggle films. They demonstrate an emerging revolutionary national culture that has regional variations at the moment in which these cultural forms are captured in the process of being, in Paulo Israel's phrase, 're-organised around socialism's nodes of meaning'.[157] Indigenous dances and songs were being wrenched to the task of a new kind of revolutionary realism.[158] Choral hymns express the unison sought by Frelimo in its relation with *o Povo*. Poetry written in Portuguese is dedicated to exalting Frelimo's project and to revealing the subjectivity of the combatants. The films present a utopian vision of a society in a process of transformation, in terms that are small-scale, fragile, intimate and yet powerful. Frelimo's liberated zones, its schools and camps are depicted as the laboratories of experimentation in which new social relations were being constructed. By the mid-1970s, the 'New Man' was being consolidated as a model for replication that would be launched across the nation at independence. The wistful Simão of *I vårt land börjar kulorna blomma*, who yearns to serve Mozambique as a doctor in the future, says that he imagines the liberation struggle will take a long time. However, within a few years independence would come with startling rapidity. The revolutionary nation being fabricated in the liberated zones and on celluloid would come crashing into the unwilling mechanisms of the colonial state.

157 Paulo Israel (2009). 'Utopia Live: Singing the Mozambican Struggle for National Liberation'. *Kronos*, 35, 1: 100.

158 Joana Makai, a practitioner of Mapiko interviewed by Paulo Israel, describes the revolutionary songs dedicated to Frelimo's political project as 'songs where we sing what happened. And things that existed, that we see with our eyes'. Israel (2009): 99.

From the Rovuma to the Maputo: Confluences of Independence 1974–1975

2

Within a year of the 1973 revelations of the Wiriyamu massacre (see Chapter 1), the Carnation Revolution in Portugal toppled the New State and Frelimo was catapulted into the position of being able to demand independence for Mozambique. As Rui Assubuji and Patricia Hayes recount, in November 1974, shortly after the signing of the Lusaka Accord that brokered independence, Samora Machel was flown from the Zambian capital to Nachingwea, the Frelimo military base in Southern Tanzania close to the border with Mozambique. With him were Frelimo officials and journalists from Lourenço Marques who had taken the inaugural flight from the Mozambican capital to Dar es Salaam on a new route that opened following the Carnation Revolution; from Dar they travelled to join Machel in Zambia.[1] Journalist Migueis Junior published a series of accounts of this trip in the newspaper *Notícias*, recalling that he and his colleagues looked down from the plane, searching 'down on the ground for the key that would perhaps open for us the secret, the magic of Frelimo's most famous political-military centre.'[2] This vertical perspective onto the territory was one that had, during the armed struggle, only been available to those operating on the side of the Portuguese army. Now that Frelimo was poised to take over the government of Mozambique, it was they who could command this view from the skies, and this too signals a shift in orientation of the films made with Frelimo away from addressing only international audiences to capturing the hearts and minds of the people of Mozambique.

Back in Tanzania for the occasion was Yugoslav camera operator Dragutin Popović, who had made *Venceremos* with the liberation movement (see

[1] Rui Assubuji and Patricia Hayes (2013). 'The Political Sublime: Reading Kok Nam, Mozambican Photographer (1939–2012)', in Rui Assubuji, Paolo Israel and Drew Thompson (ed.) (2013). *Notes on The Liberation Script in Mozambican History*, special issue of *Kronos: Southern African Histories*, 39, November: 70.

[2] Migueis L. Junior (1974). 'Visit to Some Courses of the Revolution', 'Nachingwea: Behind the Northern Border – A Little of New Mozambique' and 'Nachingwea: The Land of Men in an Act of Liberation'. *Notícias*, 22 November; cited in Assubuji and Hayes (2013): 70.

Chapter 1).[3] Between 1974 and 1975 Popović made two more documentaries that captured crucial moments in the transition and gave cinematic form to key claims that Frelimo sought to make about its legitimacy to take control of the nation-state. The first, *Nachingwea: A intelligência e a mão* 'Nachingwea: Intelligence and the Hand' (1975), harnessed the myth of Frelimo's famous military camp for the purposes of propaganda, presenting it as a microcosm of the nation to come. The second film, *Do Rovuma ao Maputo* 'From the Rovuma to the Maputo' (1975), follows Machel's month-long 'triumphant and symbolic presidential journey' from the Rovuma river, which constitutes the northern border with Tanzania, to the capital of Lourenço Marques, which at independence was renamed after the Maputo river, part of which forms the southern border with the South African province of Kwa-Zulu Natal. The film culminates in the proclamation of independence on 25 June 1975, where at his investiture Machel declared that 'the decisive factor for our success is the unity of our people from the Rovuma to the Maputo.'[4] Spanning the entire territory of the nation, the journey comes to signify Frelimo's symbiosis with the desires of the people. While in previous films made with Frelimo, Mozambicans are represented by individuals and small groups, in these two films an image of the people as a mass is first glimpsed, in a state of rapture at Frelimo's victory. Machel, more often now dressed in a presidential suit rather than military uniform, is seen addressing and mingling with huge numbers of people who flocked to greet him. Between each of the stopovers, the film shows Machel seated in an aeroplane or looking down from the window of a helicopter at the landscape below, the new president's ascent to the air symbolising Frelimo's command of the territory.

The phrase 'from the Rovuma to the Maputo' encapsulates the idea of national unity as the 'overriding political virtue in post-independence Mozambique'.[5] National unity, it was hoped, would subsume the divisions that the Portuguese regime had sought to sow between the different ethnicities and tribal groupings within the nation.[6] Furthermore, it would provide the strength to face the vast challenges of decolonisation and national reconstruction. Mozambique's

[3] According to a 'Request for Technical Assistance – Newsreels and Documentaries, 1967/68' sent by the Tanzanian Ministry of Information and Tourism to the Danish government, Popović and Zd.'s contract to work at the Tanzanian Film Unit ended on 30 June 1967. 104.P.3.TANZANIA.68_Audiovisuelt Projekt_1968–1969, Danish National Archive. I am grateful to Aylin Basaran for drawing my attention to this document.

[4] Frelimo (1975c). 'The President's Message to the Nation on Independence Day'. *Mozambique Revolution*, 61, 25 June: 21–23.

[5] Colin Darch and David Hedges (2013). 'Political Rhetoric in the Transition to Mozambican Independence: Samora Machel in Beira, June 1975', in Assubuji, Israel and Thompson (2013): 38.

[6] Darch and Hedges (2013): 38.

long border exposed the new nation to Rhodesia on the western flank and to South Africa to the south, and both these white minority-ruled countries had substantial military resources that they could channel to support a Portuguese settler-led counter-revolution, should they so wish. Against these threats, as Colin Darch and David Hedges point out, Frelimo saw its most powerful weapon as being persuasion.[7] They needed to unite the diverse colonised peoples of Mozambique behind the idea of independence and their project of radical social transformation. The armed struggle had taught Frelimo that people in Mozambique had no inherent loyalty to an abstract notion of the nation-state whose borders were based on the arbitrary divisions agreed between European colonial powers at the Conference of Berlin. Moreover, when the Carnation Revolution suddenly opened up the period of transition, Frelimo was an unknown entity to the majority of Mozambicans. While Frelimo had cultivated a broad solidarity network abroad, within Mozambique Machel was still a shadowy figure. To a population largely unaccustomed to images, let alone the dynamic animation of film, the moving image had huge potential for mobilisation.

This chapter focuses on filmmaking with Frelimo during the period of transition to independence, between the Carnation Revolution in April 1974 and the Declaration of Independence in June 1975, and the following months, during which time plans were developed for a National Institute of Cinema, which would eventually open in 1976. It thus examines the confluence of forces that inter-mingled for the first time at this moment and would have varying degrees of influence in shaping Mozambique's cinema culture in the years that followed. These include Frelimo, the foreign filmmakers who worked with them during the armed struggle, the cinephiles and amateur filmmakers of the colonial cinema clubs, and filmmakers who had come to Portugal to participate in the Carnation Revolution and who, as that opportunity for radical change foreclosed, travelled to Mozambique to contribute to the new nation. In the process, they expanded the range of experimentation with form through which the films of the transition responded to, and intervened within, the unfolding scene of revolution.

The films made with Frelimo at independence reveal how the Front sought to present itself as a government-in-waiting and the only legitimate representative of the Mozambican people. Frelimo's experience of organising the liberated zones would provide a model for mass participation in a project of radical change towards decolonisation, a task requiring political education and mobilisation on a vast scale. Alongside these exhortations, the films identify specific challenges and counter-revolutionary elements that persist despite the

[7] Darch and Hedges (2013): 38.

demise of colonialism. Crucial to the rhetoric of the films made with Frelimo at the tense moment of independence, this chapter argues, is an elision between the 'we' of Frelimo and the 'we' of the people. At stake is the weaving together of a new revolutionary nationalist culture based on a shared history of resistance to colonialism, now extended from the militants of the movement to the entire population of Mozambique.

While the films made at independence with Frelimo assert the experience of the liberated zones as a blueprint for the new nation, this was not the only form of filmmaking taking place in Mozambique. As well as a small number of colonial production houses set up during the 1960s, whose output chiefly comprised newsreel, some fiction films and, by the early 1970s, pornography, there was also a cinema culture of dissent that was nurtured by left-wing intellectuals in the urban centres of Lourenço Marques, Beira and Nampula. A number of filmmakers associated with the cinema clubs made amateur and independent films that offered less flattering perspectives on life in the colony. Although these were subjected to heavy censorship by the regime, they offer alternative visions of 'Mozambican' or 'African' cinema expressing a politics that ranged from reformist to revolutionary. The Carnation Revolution led to the lifting of film censorship across the Portuguese empire and as a result the commercial cinema screens were flooded with films that gestured towards competing versions of what freedom might mean. These ranged from cinemas antagonistic to mainstream commercial film – the individualist artistic rebellion of European auteurs, the heroic depictions of class struggle in Soviet film and the collective articulations of liberation and decolonisation of Third Cinema – to more reactionary kinds of film production, including pornography, which for Frelimo was part of the history of sexual exploitation in colonial Mozambique and symptomatic of capitalist decadence and corruption.

Frelimo responded to this situation by recruiting a team of intellectuals who had been involved with the colonial ciné-clubs to devise a plan for a National Institute of Cinema (INC). Their agenda was to create a national cinema funded through transforming and connecting the system of production, exhibition and distribution so that film could function as an agent of social transformation and nation-building. Among the individuals who contributed to the conception of the INC, there were contrasting, and even contradictory, notions of cinema and what it could achieve in the revolution. For the urban elite who frequented the colonial ciné-clubs, the screen was a site of artistic and intellectual engagement. By contrast, Frelimo's interest in cinema was primarily instrumentalist. Early on in the struggle, Frelimo realised the importance of producing information and propaganda, as it was necessary to convince Mozambicans to support the armed insurrection as well as to garner support abroad. Dispersed peasant communities had to be shown how their difficulties were compounded by colonial exploitation and persuaded that fighting for independence could improve their lives. Rural populations divided by culture and language, with little frame of reference outside their immediate worlds, had no inherent nationalist commitment to abstract notions of independence, revolution or the nation-state.[8] By 1975 Frelimo was convinced that cinema could teach 'the people' the meaning of independence, what it meant to be Mozambican and could show how the needs and energies of the peasants and workers would dictate the revolution. Despite the contradictions and conflicts between those formulating what a Mozambican cinema might be, the phrase 'From the Rovuma to the Maputo' encapsulated the national unity that film would embody and encourage.

By 1974, Portugal's determination to keep hold of its empire at any cost, whether socially or economically, had stripped the state of internal and international credibility and support. Colonial wars in Mozambique, Angola and Guinea-Bissau were consuming forty per cent of Portugal's national budget.[9] The financial and human burden of fighting three wars on the African continent led the New State to pursue a policy of 'Africanisation' of the Portuguese army, as well as the formation of local African militias as a further counter-insurgency force.[10] In the final months of the war approximately fifty per cent of soldiers fighting on the colonial side were in fact Africans.[11] At the same time, the

[8] Looking back at this period, the Resolutions to the first Frelimo Conference of Information and Propaganda in 1975 conclude that during the struggle: 'in zones where it was possible to carry out intense activity in information and propaganda before beginning the armed struggle, [these campaigns] had immediate success. On the contrary, in places where that wasn't possible, our soldiers often came face to face with indifference and even hostility from populations who had for centuries been submitted to intense colonialist propaganda.' 'nas zonas em que foi possível realizar uma actividade intensa de informação e propaganda antes de começar a luta armada, esta conheceu sucessos imediatos. Pelo contrário, onde e quando tal nao foi possível, os nossos combatentes tiveram muitas vezes de enfrentar a indiferença e mesmo a hostilidade da população que durante séculos esteve submetida a uma intensa propaganda colonialista.' 'Mensagem do Departamento de Informação e propaganda da província de Cabo Delgado à Conferência Nacional do Departamento de Informaçao e Propaganda da Frelimo', in Frelimo (1975a). *Documentos da Conferência Nacional do Departamento de Informação e Propaganda da Frelimo*, Macomia, 26–30 November: 10.

[9] Stewart Lloyd-Jones (2002). 'An End or a Beginning for Portugal? Some Notes on the Legacy of 25 April 1974'. *Lusotopie*, 2002/2: 144.

[10] João Paulo Borges Coelho (2002). 'African Troops in the Portuguese Colonial Army, 1961–1974: Angola, Guinea-Bissau and Mozambique'. *Portuguese Studies Review*, 10, 1: 137.

[11] The Portuguese had recruited Africans into its forces since the 'pacification campaigns' of the late nineteenth century, and indeed historians have argued that up to ninety per cent of the Portuguese troops fighting for the Portuguese in the battle for the Zambezi valley were African. However, the extent to which Africans participated in Portugal's military apparatus varied considerably at different historical moments. At the beginning

Portuguese army ramped up the intensity of its counter-insurgency tactics, attempting to hide and deny news of mass killings that were starting to leak out, to outcry from the international community. Even the military elite was divided, with figures such as General Spínola, who led the counter-insurgency campaign in Guinea Bissau, recognising that Portugal could not win its colonial wars militarily. Spínola began to argue that reforms would be needed to win over the colonised populations and maintain Portuguese dominance through a devolved neocolonial arrangement. Under Marcelo Caetano, the New State's last prime minister who came to power after the death of Salazar in 1968, there was an effort to promote a small number of colonised peoples into the colonial administration, but as an attempt to block the progress of the liberation movements, it came too little and too late.

As early as 1970, Frelimo was in contact with anti-fascist activists arriving in Algiers who told them of a movement in Portugal called the Revolutionary Brigades, which was breaking line with the Communist Party and drawing up plans to overthrow the New State, in 'solidarity with the struggles of peoples of the colonies'.[12] Through its networks in Lisbon, Paris and Algiers, Frelimo followed the development of a group of army officers who in 1973 formed what became known as the Movimento dos Capitães, the 'Captains' Movement'[13] The Captains' Movement, evolving into the Movimento das Forças Armadas, the 'Armed Forces Movement' (MFA), came to recognise the hopelessness of the colonial wars and began plotting to remove the Caetano regime, to end the colonial wars and to retreat from the territories of Angola, Guinea-Bissau and Mozambique. By 1974, Frelimo had a significant presence in four out of nine provinces, controlling large areas in Cabo Delgado, Niassa, Tete and Nampula.[14]

---

of the armed struggles top-ranking Portuguese generals, including Kaúlza de Arriaga, argued strongly against increasing the numbers of African soldiers because they believed they were 'little less than potential terrorists.' The integration of Africans into Portuguese fighting forces occurred much later in Mozambique than in Angola and Guinea-Bissau, in part due to the fact that this was Kaúlza de Arriaga's field of control. They only started to operate on the ground in Mozambique in 1974, after Kaúlza de Arriaga had been dismissed by Caetano. Borges Coelho (2002): 132–135 and 145–146.

[12] The Revolutionary Brigades were founded in 1970 by Isabel do Carmo, Carlos Antunes and Pedro Goulart, who advocated armed struggle against the regime. Jacinto Veloso (2012). *Memories at Low Attitude: The Autobiography of a Mozambican Security Chief.* Cape Town: Zebra Press: 23.

[13] This was not initially an inherently radical organisation. It was set up to protect the interests of the officers' corps who felt threatened by new regulations instituted that year which gave soldiers with combat experience the chance of accelerated promotion – hardly a revolutionary or democratic aim. Lloyd-Jones (2002): 144.

[14] The tenth province of Mozambique was only formed after independence. Barry Munslow (1984). 'State Intervention in Agriculture: The Mozambican Experience', *Journal of Modern African Studies*, 22: 204.

Armed with foreknowledge that a coup was imminent, Frelimo intensified its attacks in the south of Mozambique, preparing to occupy areas including Manica, Inhambane and Gaza.[15]

Meanwhile, in the early hours of 25 April 1974, Zeca Afonso's rebel song 'Grândola, Vila Morena' was broadcast on the radio in Portugal, a signal to troops who had the night before begun a silent, simultaneous advance on Lisbon, Mafra, Tomar, Figueira da Foz, and other cities. With this signal, they began seizing key targets, one of the most critical being the occupation of Rádio Clube Português in Lisbon. The first of a series of broadcasts broke the news that the army was rising up against the government to liberate Portugal. They stated their purpose: 'the armed forces began a series of operations at dawn today with the aim of liberating the country from the regime that has ruled for so long.'[16] As day broke, crowds joined the sieges of governmental buildings, euphorically claiming their freedom with slogans of 'The People United Will Never be Defeated!', 'Death to PIDE' and 'Freedom for Political Prisoners'. Flower-sellers in Chiado released carnations to the crowd, and young soldiers in dishevelled uniforms unbuttoned their shirts and unlaced their boots to signify their overthrow of authority. Notably, in this mass protest barely contained by the armed forces, only four people were killed when PIDE officers, surrounded at their headquarters, opened fire on the crowd outside. Having initially evaded capture by escaping from the Ministry of Marine Affairs through a hole in the wall, Caetano finally gave himself up when the young captains of the MFA agreed to allow Spínola to parlay his surrender.[17] While elements of PIDE and the National Guard resisted, the armed forces subdued them and many of the political prisoners were released in the early hours of the following day.[18] Portugal's revolution had begun, but the full independence of the African colonies was not yet certain.

At 1.26 am on 26 April, General Spínola unexpectedly found himself President of the Junta for National Salvation and made a television statement naming the senior officers in charge.[19] These officers, who had all overseen

15 Veloso (2012).

16 Cited in Afonso Praça, Albertino Antunes, António Amorim, Cesário Borga and Fernando Cascais (1974). *25 de Abril: Documentos*. Lisbon: Casaviva: 11–12.

17 Lloyd-Jones (2002): 143.

18 Praça *et al.* (1974): 32.

19 General Spínola was governor and commander-in-chief of the armed forces in Guinea; General Francisco da Costa Gomes, former deputy secretary of state for the army and former commander-in-chief of the armed forces in Angola; Captain José Baptista Pinheiro Azevedo, professor of the naval school and veteran of various missions in Africa and member of NATO; Captain of the Fregate António Alva Rosa Coutinho, former provincial director of Marine Services of Mozambique; Brigadier Jaime Silvério Marques, former governor of Macau, commissioner to NATO; General of Aeronautics

colonial repression and military campaigns on the three African fronts of Guinea-Bissau, Angola and Mozambique, were now steering the Junta for National Salvation. The readiness with which the MFA handed power over to the establishment is perhaps not surprising given that its roots were reformist rather than revolutionary.[20] But beneath Spínola, there were more radical factions within the MFA from different traditions of political activism.[21] The mastermind of the coup, Otelo de Carvalho, was an officer born in Mozambique who rose through the army ranks while serving in Guinea-Bissau and Angola, and he was one of a number of Communists. Such figures would shortly become driving forces of the revolution. They strongly favoured an immediate withdrawal of Portuguese troops from all African territories and sympathised with those liberation movements orientated towards socialism.

By May 1974, while the fighting continued, Frelimo had begun negotiations with the provisional government of Portugal to bring colonial rule to an end. On 7 September 1974 Machel signed the Lusaka Accord with a delegation from the Portuguese provisional government led by Minister without Portfolio Ernesto Augusto Melo Antunes. The Accord granted the people of Mozambique their right to independence and self-determination by the date of 25 June 1975. In the meantime a number of new political parties sprang up in Mozambique to contest Frelimo's claim to represent the people, adding to the organisations that had been established during the armed struggle by Frelimo dissidents such as Uria Simango, Adelino Gwambe, Father Gwendjere and David Mabunda (see Chapter 1). These anti-Frelimo organisations included the Mozambique United Group (GUMO), led by Joana Simão, the União dos Povos de Moçambique 'Union of Peoples of Mozambique' (UNIPOMO) and the Mozambique Revolutionary Committee (COREMO). The centre for these dissident groupings was the city of Beira. Beira had been the centre of operations for entrepreneur and former government minister Jorge Jardim, who was also a close friend of

---

Diogo Neto, former commander of the aerial zone of Cape Verde and Guinea; Colonel of Aeronautics Carlos Galvão de Melo. Praça *et al.* (1974): 33–34.

20 As Stewart Lloyd-Jones points out, the fallen regime was in no position to argue, suggesting that the myth of the MFA's revolutionary fervour perhaps masks more contradictory and conservative motives for the rebellion. Lloyd-Jones (2002).

21 Botelho Moniz and Humberto Delgado are two of the most important figures that exemplify this progressive tendency within the Portuguese armed forces. Delgado was a general in the air force who challenged Salazar by standing for presidential elections in 1959, following which he was suspended from the armed forces and was forced to seek refuge in the Brazilian embassy from where he escaped to exile in Algeria. In Algeria he sought the support of Ben Bella, the PCP and the *lusophone* liberation movements but was assassinated by PIDE in 1965. In March 1961 Moniz, who was a general and the Minister of Defence, wrote to Salazar following the beginning of the armed struggle in Angola, calling for reforms in colonial policies. His recommendations were rejected and in April that same year he led an attempted coup against Salazar.

Prime Minister of Rhodesia Ian Smith. From this key city in the colonial regime's infrastructure, Jardim had sought to stoke African opposition to Frelimo that could be manipulated in the interests of maintaining Portugal's dominance in a new neocolonial configuration. Frelimo saw these organisations as being the puppets of PIDE and the Rhodesian Secret Service – intended to agitate against Frelimo under the pretext of calls for multiparty democracy.

On 7 September 1974, the very day the Lusaka Accord was signed, a group of Portuguese settlers called the Dragões da Morte 'Dragons of Death' or Moçambique Livre 'Free Mozambique' attempted a coup in Lourenço Marques. Although they managed to occupy the offices of Radio Moçambique for a time, Mozambicans from the city's peripheries streamed into the European centre, and with Frelimo's support, the Portuguese army regained control.[22] The European centre of the city they occupied was already riddled with deserted spaces. A mass exodus of the Portuguese population began in the last years of the colonial war, gained momentum following the toppling of the fascist regime in Lisbon and increased dramatically after the failed coup of 7 September and the violence that followed.[23] Many returned to Portugal, while others moved to South Africa or to Rhodesia, where some of the Africans conscripted into the Portuguese army also fled. The latter constituted a pool of fighters opposed to Frelimo who would shortly be shaped into an opposition force by the Rhodesian secret service. Over a period of eighteen months, nearly ninety per cent of the Portuguese population left Mozambique. At independence new Minister of the Interior Armando Guebuza announced that any settlers who did not support Frelimo had twenty-four hours to leave the country with only twenty kilos of luggage, an order that became known as the law of '24/20'.[24] More settlers were expelled by the new government because they were considered 'economic saboteurs'. Frelimo was also challenged from within its own ranks. In December 1975, a mutiny broke out at the Machava barracks when soldiers from the newly formed Mozambican army marched on Maputo. Sympathisers of a shadowy movement known as 'Magaia' were said to be prominent in this rebellion.[25] The uprising took some three days to suppress, and, according to Stephen Weigert,

[22] Jacinto Veloso recalls in his memoirs: 'When we arrived in Lourenço Marques that night, we were accommodated at the military air base because the city was totally barricaded in response to the revolt of the settlers, dubbed *Ficos*. There were barriers, obstacles, people on the lookout – a countless number of defensive precautions taken by the people of the city against the far-right settler putsch.' Veloso (2012).

[23] On 20 and 21 October 1974 Portuguese commandos opened fire, causing 35 deaths.

[24] Paul Fauvet and Marcelo Mosse (2003). *Carlos Cardoso e a Revolução Moçambicana*. Maputo: Ndjira: 49.

[25] The movement was named after Felipe Samuel Magaia, Frelimo's first military commander who was killed in 1966. Although most attributed Magaia's death to Portuguese agents, some dissenters blamed Frelimo's own insurgents for his death. Stephen Weigert (1996).

'suspected "Magaia" members were said to have been purged from the ranks of the military in subsequent months.'[26]

In the face of this uncertainty, Frelimo was keen to harness film to the task of presenting its own account of the transition to independence that would leave no doubt about its legitimacy. Frelimo turned to filmmakers with whom they had already worked during the armed struggle, including the Yugoslavian Dragutin Popović, the African Americans Robert van Lierop and Bob Fletcher and, in the year following independence, the Soviet Yuri Egorov. The first of these films, Popović's *Nachingwea: A intelligência e a mao*, represents the history of Frelimo through the story of the camp. The subtitle, which translates literally as 'intelligence and the hand', refers to the ideological approach that Frelimo developed following the internal conflicts of the late 1960s, in which manual work was placed on a par with intellectual endeavours and revolutionary theory was supposed to derive from practice and the lived experiences of Mozambican workers and peasants. This piece of land allocated to Frelimo by the Tanzanian government in 1965 in an act of Pan-African solidarity becomes the central metaphor for the film. Nachingwea begins as an area that is 'dry, arid and denuded of vegetation' and is transformed by Frelimo militants into a verdant and productive zone, as trees are cleared to make way for cultivation, make-shift tents become houses, workshops and schools made of bricks and mortar.[27] The camp achieved self-sufficiency in food and even produced an income that contributed towards medical expenses and the acquisition of communication systems.[28] While conditions in Frelimo's rural camps were difficult, the party elite prided itself on the discipline the organisation enforced on combatants, in contrast to other liberation movements that Tanzania hosted.[29] As such, it functioned as a 'rehearsal' for how Frelimo planned to integrate rural communities into their revolutionary nationalist project.[30] Cultivation of the fields runs parallel to the awakening of political consciousness through education and military training. Frelimo is thus the mechanism that brings together militants with 'the people' to fight for independence against the enemies of the 'exploited classes'.[31] In Nachingwea's transformation into fertile land, the base becomes a zone in which

Traditional Religion and Guerrilla Warfare in Modern Africa. Basingstoke: Palgrave Macmillan: 71.

26 Weigert (1996): 71.

27 Instituto Nacional de Cinema (1982). *Retrospectiva do cinema Moçambicana*. Maputo: INC: 11.

28 Assubuji and Hayes (2013): 70.

29 Pamela dos Santos gives an account of the Frelimo camps in Tanzania and how Frelimo viewed other liberation movements such as the ANC in Nadja Mangezi's 2009 book *The Maputo Connection: ANC Life in the World of Frelimo*. Cape Town: Jacana Media: 21–25.

30 Assubuji and Hayes (2013): 71.

31 Instituto Nacional de Cinema (1982).

people realise their productive potential, suggesting that Frelimo was poised to carry out the same task across the whole of Mozambique.

The intimacy and bodily scale of Popović's earlier armed struggle film *Venceremos* contrasts starkly to *Nachingwea*. The only aerial shots available to filmmakers sympathetic to Frelimo during the armed struggle had to be acquired from films made with the Portuguese army, who conducted most of their assaults from the air. The opening moments of *Nachingwea*, however, features a shot from a plane that sweeps over the territory of the camp. There follows a shot of dry cracked earth, devoid of vegetation. Thenceforth, the film moves to scenes of collective work, as earth is transformed into bricks and the soil is turned into cultivated fields. Featuring a voiceover and musical soundtrack that mainly comprises jaunty orchestral military music, *Nachingwea* suggests a formula for imagining the birth of a nation through armed struggle. In this film we see the emergence of an image of the masses through collective work – bodies are locked in syncopated action, with eyes lowered or turned away from the camera, fully engaged in hoeing the fields, harvesting corn and performing military exercises. Along with this depersonalisation of national allegory, there is a sense of vast proliferation in production – of crops, of chickens, goats, ducks, and of increased numbers of people working in unison. From these scenes of collective production, the film moves on to a sequence of military displays. Military training at Nachingwea was divided between Chinese and Soviet instructors, who occupied two different sides of the camp. Both the Maoist guerrilla tactics advocated by the Chinese and the Soviet focus on conventional warfare are visible in the manoeuvres performed for the camera. The exercises of the Frelimo combatants include martial arts, but as the film moves on, the soldiers are seen operating anti-aircraft guns and other increasingly heavy-duty weapons. Some hundred or so guerrillas in uniform are seen receiving political instruction as a core part of the education offered at the camp. This is a key part, the voiceover points out, of 'the process of the transformation of man'.

If the camp, as James C. Scott argues, is the apogee of the state's drive for disciplined administration and control of both people and natural resources, its power derives from its scalability.[32] As discussed in Chapter 1, the forms of cultivation organised by the guerrillas during the armed struggle involved transplanting different people, plants and techniques into new territories. Frelimo advocated learning from local practices but sought to rationalise, improve and expand them to increase food production. Agricultural techniques also served as a key metaphor for Frelimo's political work of cultivating a new 'Mozambican personality', a revolutionary subjectivity embodied by the figure of the 'New Man'. Despite Frelimo's injunctions to 'learn' from the peasants, its

[32] James C. Scott (1998). *Seeing Like a State: How Certain Schemes to Improve the Human Condition Have Failed*. Boston: Yale University Press.

agricultural policy in the years that followed independence was marked by a failure to give adequate support to small-scale local cooperatives and family farms.[33] Instead, Frelimo privileged large state farms that were formed out of abandoned colonial plantations and were dependent on heavy machinery and migrant labour. Boaventura de Sousa Santos, João Arriscado Nunes and Maria Paula Meneses point out that the questioning by African nationalist movements of colonialist forms of knowledge soon withered away after independence, as '"defeating underdevelopment" became the new rallying call'.[34] These sequences in *Nachingwea* are in contrast to the small scale of Frelimo's ground operations in the liberated zones. The camp of Nachingwea is a 'machine of replication', presented in the film as a utopian microcosm that can be transplanted and expanded across the territory of Mozambique.[35]

Machel attended two mass meetings that took place at Nachingwea during the transition.[36] The first was in November 1974, after the signing of the Lusaka Accord, and the second in May 1975, before he began his triumphal journey from the Rovuma river to Maputo. At the gathering at Nachingwea in May 1975, some 240 prisoners described as 'reactionary agents and traitors to the Mozambican people' were brought before Frelimo guerrillas, officials and invited guests. In the film, the voiceover introduces this scene by saying that political education includes learning about the 'criminals' who threaten 'our people'. Prisoners in uniforms are marched past, followed by leaders of the opposition in civilian clothes. Joana Simão, Simango, Kavandame, Basílio Banda and Verónica Anyayiva (Namiva) are paraded in front of Frelimo cadres, who laugh and jeer at them. These people, the voiceover claims, 'constitute an authentic living museum of crime and reaction'. These black Mozambicans who have betrayed their own people demonstrate that 'colonialism has no colour, capitalism has no race, and imperialism has no fatherland.' A recently declassified document citing an 'eye-witness' account of this ceremony describes an 'impressive if degrading spectacle lasting some seven hours', in which:

> main offenders were required to read aloud long and detailed confessions of their crimes, culminating in what Samora Machel called his 'Christmas turkey', Uria

[33] Barry Munslow (1984). 'State Intervention in Agriculture: the Mozambican Experience'. *Journal of Modern African Studies*, 22: 199–221.

[34] Boaventura de Sousa Santos, João Arriscado Nunes and Maria Paula Meneses (2008). 'Opening up the Canon of Knowledge and Recognition of Difference', in Boaventura de Sousa Santos (ed.) (2008). *Beyond Northern Epistemologies: Another Knowledge is Possible*. London: Verso: xxxvii.

[35] Anna Tsing (2016). 'Earth Stalked by Man', *The Cambridge Journal of Anthropology*, 34, 1: 2–16.

[36] Assubuji and Hayes (2013): 70.

> Simango . . . After each confession the reader was told to ask the crowd what punishment he deserved, with crowd generally loudly demanding hanging.[37]

However, the film assures its audience that Frelimo's approach is not to kill them, but to learn from their example that 'renegades and criminals are weaker than the people'. Samora Machel is shown addressing the crowd, and the voiceover continues with a series of slogans that present Frelimo as a force of nature: 'The Revolution is a powerful river' or 'The people are always victorious'.

The final section of *Nachingwea* is dedicated to depicting visits from Frelimo's closest allies: Agostinho Neto of the MPLA, Oliver Tambo of the ANC, Ndabaningi Sithole of the Zimbabwe African National Union (ZANU) Party, Joshua Nkomo of the Zimbabwe African People's Union (ZAPU) Party, and finally Kenneth Kaunda of Zambia. Nachingwea is thus not only 'the centre of our struggle' but 'the centre of our internationalism', a project that will continue into the future as Frelimo assures the ANC and ZANU of its ongoing support. Scenes of a football match and a performance of the Kipoko traditional dance unfold with the soundtrack of a Frelimo hymn, emblems of national identity brought together under Frelimo's flag, which is now the flag of Mozambique. Yet in *Nachingwea*, the symbiosis of Frelimo with the people also involves the identification of 'enemies of the people'. Following the violent upheavals within the movement in the late 1960s, Frelimo had expanded its objectives. In 1970 the Central Committee declared that Frelimo's struggle was no longer merely anti-colonial, defining the enemy as 'whoever at a certain moment practices exploitation of man by man, whatever the methods and forms that exploitation takes'.[38] Despite the assurances of clemency offered in the film, the leaders of the opposition paraded here would all, some years later in unknown locations, be executed – a decision that Marcelino dos Santos later defended as an act of 'revolutionary justice'.[39] In contrast to *Venceremos*, which is characterised by a determined hope of eventual victory and an effort to smooth over the internal divisions that then threatened to tear Frelimo apart, *Nachingwea* presents Frelimo's victory over its enemies, who are not only the Portuguese colonial

[37] US Department of State (1975). 'Frelimo Pardons 240 "Traitors"', Wikileaks Public Library of US Diplomacy (Tanzania Dar es Salaam, March 18) Available at https://www.wikileaks.org/plusd/cables/1975DARES00806_b.html; cited in Polly Savage (2017). 'Os Bolseiros: Ideology, Internationalism and the Artist in Cold War Era Mozambique'. PhD Thesis. London: Royal College of Art.

[38] Frelimo (1970). *Mozambican Revolution*, 43, April–June; cited by Munslow (1984): 206–207.

[39] On 29 July 1980 Jacinto Veloso signed the *Ordem de Acção* no.5/80 for the execution of seven dissidents, including Uria Simango, Lázaro Nkavadane and Joana Simão. Carrie L. Manning (2002). *The Politics of Peace in Mozambique, 1992–2000*. Westport: Praege: 45. Benedito Tomás Mulanga (1995). 'As Mortes de Simango, Gwenjere e Outras', *Savana*, 10 May.

regime but also the enemies within – who now are named and will face the consequences.

Popović continued to be Frelimo's preferred point of contact with Tito's regime in negotiating further assistance in the field of film production. However, by 1975 relations between Frelimo and the Yugoslavian government were deteriorating. A report on the journey to Tanzania and Mozambique, dated 25 April 1975 and written by Popović's director Mića Zdravković, recounts that when the film crew arrived in Dar es Salaam they heard from their ambassador that a Yugoslav television crew had been denied an interview with Machel.[40] Machel told Popović and Zdravković that he was unhappy that promises of weapons, food and support 'in terms of film' from the Yugoslavian government had not been forthcoming, blaming this on 'bureaucracy' and a failing of Yugoslav diplomats rather than 'politics'.[41] Machel requested that they should accompany him from Dar es Salaam to Lourenço Marques to make a feature-length film about this triumphal journey.[42] With tensions mounting between the Yugoslavian government and Frelimo due to production costs that repeatedly stretched beyond Filmske Novosti's budget, *Do Rovuma ao Maputo* would be the last film made as a collaboration between Mozambique and Yugoslavia for a decade.

Do Rovuma ao Maputo follows Samora Machel's month-long 'triumphant and symbolic presidential journey' from the Rovuma river to Maputo that culminated in the proclamation of independence on 25 June 1975. The film, which is in black and white, records Machel giving speeches and the elated reception he received from the masses of people who flocked to catch a glimpse of him. Machel travelled extensively during the months of the transition, making visits to the German Democratic Republic, Bulgaria and Romania, who had all supported the armed struggle, and to Frelimo's neighbouring African allies, Tanzania and Zambia, who had crucially allowed the Front to launch its offensives into Cabo Delgado, Niassa and Tete from across their borders. This particular journey, spanning the totality of the territory now under Frelimo's

[40] Popović was employed by Filmske novosti as a camera operator, though he is credited as director of *Venceremos* and *Nachingwea*. Mića Zdravković and Dragutin Popović (1975). 'Izvestaj sa Puta u Tanzaniju I Mozambik' ['Report on the journey to Tanzania and Mozambique']. 25 April. Belgrade: Filmske Novosti Archive.

[41] Zdravković and Popović (1975).

[42] The report concludes with a list of works in progress that require urgent attention: the completion of a film entitled *Message from the President of Frelimo*, including thirteen sound copies on 35mm and one on 16mm by 15 May 1975; the development of the feature film *Camp in Nachingwea*, plus a short film of 15 minutes on the same subject. The final task listed is to accompany the 'President of Frelimo on the journey through Mozambique and the arrival on the ceremony of independence in Lourenço Marques, as well as the developing of the film of these events'. Zdravković and Popović (1975).

control, asserts the figure of Machel as presidential statesman. Machel made over thirty speeches during this triumphal journey.[43] In the film, Machel is seen arriving by plane in Mueda on 24 May, and significantly here, as in other towns and cities, he is wearing a suit rather than military uniform. Marcelino dos Santos and Joaquim Chissano accompany him as he greets people and addresses a crowd. From Mueda he toured Frelimo bases in the liberated zones, going to villages such as Ibo, Angoche, Morrumbala and Wiriyamu. Machel is seen leading large groups of people to visit significant landmarks, such as the Cahora Bassa dam and the site of a memorial at Wiriyamu, where Machel inspects human remains from the massacres carried out by the Portuguese army in 1972. In these scenes, Machel is presented alternately as relaxed, serious, warm in his interactions, and, perhaps most importantly, as a charismatic speaker and statesman.

Crucially, the tour included provincial capitals such as Lichinga, Pemba, Nampula, Quelimane, Tete and Beira, where Frelimo had no public presence during the armed struggle. Beira in particular was foreign territory for Frelimo. The port-city was the lynchpin to Portugal's economic and political plans to shore up its alliances across the Southern Africa region, and during the 1960s Beira was a key location for mass settlement and the development of infrastructures, as well as the centre of military and intelligence operations.[44] Politically, too, Beira was seen as antagonistic to Frelimo because it was here that Jorge Jardim had, with the approval of the last Portuguese Minister for Overseas Territories, Rebelo de Sousa, supported the establishment of anti-Frelimo African political groups that were intended to prove that Frelimo did not represent the majority of Mozambicans and to propose alternative scenarios to full independence.[45] At this tense moment of transition, the mass meetings that were held as Machel swept down south across the country were crucial for Frelimo to communicate its message to a population that had little access to news and current affairs – there was no television broadcast in Mozambique, newspapers published in Portuguese were limited in circulation and the content of commercial cinema and radio was tightly controlled.

Darch and Hedges's detailed analysis of the speech Machel gave in Beira reveals the extent to which Frelimo recognised the urgent need to recruit supporters in these strongholds of Portuguese colonialism, where they expected to meet counter-revolutionary resistance.[46] Although Machel's speeches are

[43] Darch and Hedges (2013): 38.
[44] Darch and Hedges (2013): 42.
[45] GUMO's political activity began shortly after the 25 April *coup d'état* in Portugal, on 11 and 12 May 1974. Paul Fauvet (1984). 'Roots of the Counter-Revolution: The "Mozambique National Resistance"'. *Review of African Political Economy*, 29, July 1984: 110–111.
[46] Darch and Hedges (2013): 34.

not audible in *Do Rovuma ao Maputo*, except for a few seconds of his address at the ceremony of independence, Darch and Hedges's commentary on Machel's rhetoric and use of Mozambican Portuguese is extremely useful for understanding his huge appeal and why the films of the Mozambican Revolution so often focused on his speeches and the rapport he built with his audiences. During the triumphal journey, Machel made expressive use of Mozambican Portuguese, a vernacular oral form distinct from the normative standard that was based on educated European speech.[47] The speeches feature short phrases and sentences in repetitive patterns, a simplified grammar and limited lexis. Technical political vocabulary such as 'communism' and 'Marxist–Leninism' is absent from the Beira speech, and instead Machel addresses the social contradictions of colonial society. He denounces those groups that benefitted from assimilation, who are described as 'thieves' or 'puppets', or are characterised with dismissive diminutives, as when Machel refers to 'o pretinho assimilado' 'the assimilated little black man'. These enemies of the people are compared to a 'we' that carefully elides the distinction between the 'we' of Frelimo and the 'we' of Mozambicans.[48] Machel frequently asks his audience to affirm whether or not he is expressing their view, saying 'Ouviram?' 'Do you hear?', 'É ou não é?' 'Is it or isn't it?' or 'Certo?' 'Correct?' There are also long variations on formulaic phrases that produce a crescendo of responses and function as disciplinary devices. To 'Viva o povo moçambicano unido do Rovuma ao Maputo!' 'Viva the united people of Mozambique from the Rovuma to Maputo', the audiences respond 'Viva!' To 'Independência ou morte!' 'Independence or death!' the crowd replies 'Venceremos!' 'We Will Win!' As Darch and Hedges point out, in making the correct response, the crowd demonstrates their commitment to Frelimo's project.[49]

There were practical arguments for the use of Mozambican Portuguese in addressing mass audiences as it was more easily understood by large parts of the population for whom Portuguese was a second language.[50] The choice for Machel to speak in Mozambican Portuguese also contributed to the task of creating political unity centred on Frelimo's revolutionary nationalism. As Christopher Stroud explains, 'immediately after independence, the revolutionary government sought to further its popular legitimacy by appealing to vernacular, or non-standard forms of Portuguese in a rhetoric of political

[47] Darch and Hedges (2013): 35.
[48] Darch and Hedges (2013): 61.
[49] Darch and Hedges (2013): 58.
[50] The Rádio Moçambique conference held between 26 and 30 November 1975 under Frelimo's ideological tutelage argued that the use of Mozambican Portuguese as the common language was preferable because most listeners did not easily understand European Portuguese. *Tempo*, 271, 1975: 60–1.

mobilisation and authority.'[51] The use of Mozambican Portuguese had a potent political affect. Unlike standard Portuguese, which was the language of mastery used only by European settlers and the tiny number of assimilated Africans, Mozambican Portuguese was understood to be a more 'horizontal' means of communication, suggesting a language shared between people in conditions of equality committed to a radically egalitarian politics.[52] Indeed, the form of Portuguese spoken by Mozambicans as the revolution unfolded was a subject of debate throughout the 1970s, Machel even suggesting on one occasion that the 'clear ideas, clear content, clear objects' of a revolutionary people would 'cultivate' a better, more 'enriched' Portuguese.[53] Machel makes theatrical use of Mozambican Portuguese to interpellate his audiences as a new collective subject – that of patriotic Mozambicans mobilised to overthrow colonialism and together build a new society.

Significantly, the camera, often slightly raised above the crowd, includes white people who are shown at ease with thousands of jubilant black Mozambicans. They proudly raise their fists in identification with Frelimo as the legitimate force to lead the new nation. These scenes affirm Frelimo's claim to embody a modernist politics that was anti-racist and anti-tribal, open to everyone who wanted to join its project of revolutionary transformation. The final sections of the film show the approach to Lourenço Marques, following the advance of the runners who bear a torch with which to light an eternal flame, representing the unity of Mozambique. Machel arrived on 23 June, *Mozambique Revolution* reporting that 'half a million people lined the route from the airport to the presidential residence to witness the occasion.'[54] *Do Rovuma ao Maputo* then switches to footage of the moment of independence: at midnight on 24 June at Machava Stadium, the flag of Portugal is lowered and replaced with that of Mozambique. This footage with synced sound is the only part of the film where Machel's words are not summarised by the voiceover, and it includes a few seconds of his speech proclaiming independence.

[51] Christopher Stroud (2002). 'Framing Bourdieu Socio-Culturally: Alternative Forms of Linguistic Legitimacy in Postcolonial Mozambique', *Multilingua: Journal of Cross-Cultural and Interlanguage Communication*, 21, 2–3: 254.

[52] J. Katupha (1994). 'Language and Problems of Technical and Cultural Development in Latin Africa: the Mozambican Case', in M'hammed Sabour (ed.) (1994). *African Perspectives in Development: Voices from the South*. Joensuu: Joensuu University Press: 57.

[53] Mia Couto (1981). 'Ainda o Problema da Linga: Submissão Cultura?', *Tempo*, 536, 18 January: 11; Christopher Stroud (1999). 'Portuguese as Ideology and Politics in Mozambique: Semiotic (Re)Constructions of a Postcolony', in Jan Blommaert (ed.) (1999). *Language Ideological Debates*. Berlin and New York: De Greyter Mouton: 343–380.

[54] Frelimo (1975b). 'The Nation Celebrates Independence', *Mozambique Revolution*, Independence Issue, 61, 25 June.

Across Mozambique, the days from 21 to 29 June were dedicated to celebrations. Buildings and streets were decorated with banners and posters with slogans hailing independence. There were displays of revolutionary dramas and songs, sporting events, a festival of youth, and performances of traditional dances and music, which under colonial rule had been restricted (see Chapter 1). The capital was a site of gathering for hundreds of foreign delegations from sympathetic nations and from solidarity organisations that had supported Frelimo during the struggle. Polly Gaster brought from London eight films about the armed struggle that were in the collection of the Committee for Freedom in Mozambique, Angola and Guiné (CFMAG). A programme of projections of these films was organised by Frelimo member Luís Simão, with help from the ciné-club of Lourenço Marques.[55] This formed the material for the 'revolutionary spectacles' that were held in the city's cinemas.[56] On the first day of independence, the vice-president of Frelimo Marcelino dos Santos announced at a ceremony held at the Town Hall that Comrade Samora Machel was entrusted as the first president of Mozambique.[57] That afternoon some 15,000 Mozambicans participated in a parade, in which 200 vehicles were decorated to represent 'various aspects of the exploitation and oppression of our People under Portuguese colonialism'.[58] The finale was a march-past by regular forces, artillery and guerrilla units of the newly formed Forças Populares de Libertação de Moçambique 'People's Forces of Liberation of Mozambique' (FPLM), the women's detachment and members of the naval wing.

Robert van Lierop and Bob Fletcher were among the foreign activists and filmmakers who had worked with Frelimo during the armed struggle who returned to Mozambique at independence to make *O Povo Organizado* 'The People Organised' (1975). After making *A Luta Continua* (see Chapter 1), Van Lierop had given up his law practice and dedicated himself to the Mozambique Film Project. To continue this work, he established in late 1972 the Africa Information Service (AIS) with Prexy Nesbitt, an African-American anti-Apartheid activist who had assisted Jorge Rebelo in editing the journal *Mozambican Revolution* in Dar es Salaam.[59] The AIS distributed books such as

[55] Conversation with Luís Simão, Maputo, 5 August 2016.

[56] Frelimo (1975b).

[57] Frelimo (1975b).

[58] Frelimo (1975b).

[59] Nesbitt and Van Lierop first met in 1968 when Van Lierop, a lawyer at the time, defended him and a group of students from Columbia University who were protesting against the university's expansion into Harlem. William Minter, Gail Hovey and Charles Cobb, Jr. (2008). *No Easy Victories: African Liberation and American Activists over a Half Century, 1950–2000*. Trenton, NJ, and Asmara: African World Press: 93.

Amílcar Cabral's *Return to Source*, which, along with the two films Van Lierop made with Frelimo, had a profound influence on activists in the United States.[60]

Conceived as a sequel to *A Luta Continua*, *O Povo Organizado* was intended to be the second in a trilogy dedicated to Mozambican liberation. Shot in colour like Van Lierop's previous film made with Frelimo, the documentary weaves between scenes from the independence celebrations, a mass rally and other documentary footage, providing insight into how Frelimo understood the political challenges they faced in enacting a revolutionary project in a country devastated by centuries of colonial misrule, the destruction of war and stark divisions between the segregated cities and impoverished rural communities. The film begins on the eve of independence, with Joachim Chissano, the prime minister of the transitional government of Mozambique, greeting foreign dignitaries. *O Povo Organizado* then cuts to the lowering of the Portuguese flag at Machava Stadium and the raising of the Mozambican flag. As the multitude dances in the falling rain, the camera cuts to Machel on the podium as he embraces Prime Minister Gonçalves of Portugal.

O Povo Organizado had a didactic purpose, which is evident in the potted history it gives of the 'long and difficult' armed struggle 'against a military power far superior in numbers and arms'. While Frelimo did not have weapons like tanks and planes with which to fight a modern war, they managed to liberate a third of the country, the voiceover arguing that 'everything was due to determination, discipline and the people of Mozambique.' This section, which makes clear that the human consequences of the war were felt on both sides, concludes with a description of the implosion of the Portuguese empire amid images of a sabotaged train and other damaged infrastructures. British newspaper headlines and news footage depict the Carnation Revolution, and the film identifies certain key moments of the transition: the signing of the Lusaka Accord, the revolt of the settlers and the release of Portuguese soldiers by Frelimo, who are seen boarding ships in huge numbers to return to Europe.

Repeatedly, particular sounds or music provide a segue between different scenes, marking transitions to the next theme, and here the new national anthem 'Viva Frelimo' leads into images of the independence day parade.[61] The

[60] William Minter, Gail Hovey and Charles Cobb Jr., *No Easy Victories* Interview: Robert van Lierop. http://www.noeasyvictories.org/interviews/into7_vanlierop.php

[61] *O Povo Organizado* was edited by Paul Evans, who, according to Lierop, had a gift for working with sound and music in the editing process. 'Paul apprenticed as an editor on *Midnight Cowboy*. He had an uncanny ability to work with music and sound in the editing process, and that's why you'll notice in that film, the second film, *O Povo Organizado*, that the music plays such a crucial part in moving the film forward and telling the story. The music plays a role in cutting from scene to scene. That was one of Paul Evans' real strengths as an editor.' *No Easy Victories* Interview: Robert van Lierop. http://www.noeasyvictories.org/interviews/into7_vanlierop.php

continuadores, children of the youth wing of Frelimo, are seen leading the march, followed by members of the armed forces, workers with gun and plough insignia, and women's groups. The floats depict scenes of colonial life and Mozambican resistance. However, the voiceover points out, 'the end of the armed struggle doesn't signify the end of the revolution, but rather the transition to a new phase of the revolutionary process.' With this phrase, the images shift to village scenes, though unlike the scenes of collective work seen in *Nachingwea*, here there is only ever one figure in the frame. Solitary individuals are depicted grinding grain, working the soil and caring for children, demonstrating how rural communities were fragmented and isolated under colonial rule. Frelimo has inherited a country where there is 'constant struggle against drought and hunger'.

O Povo Organizado presents Frelimo's proposed solution to this rural crisis as being centred on the creation of collective villages. Strategic hamlets set up during the colonial war, the voiceover explains, will be transformed into a new social system, with crèches, clinics and schools built in the villages as part of this social transformation. In its plan to collectivise village life, Frelimo not only drew heavily on Nyerere's *ujamaa* experiment in Tanzania (see Chapter 1), but also built on the re-organisation of rural areas by the colonial authorities. Borges Coelho argues that the strategy of 'villagisation' was a crucial part of the Portuguese counter-insurgency campaign.[62] Villagisation began in 1964 and continued until 1971. It involved the enforced resettlement of rural communities in strategic hamlets (also called 'protected villages') so as to isolate them from the guerrillas. As such, they sought to prevent Frelimo from living among the peasants as 'the fish swims in water' – a slogan of Mao Tse-Tung that Frelimo leaders were fond of repeating. This left large areas of the countryside vacant, and the Portuguese army took advantage of that to engage in brutal scorched-earth operations, such as burning crops to 'destroy the means of life'.[63] Protected villages, which, unlike traditional small scattered settlements had facilities such as schools and sanitation, were also intended to operate as part of the counter-insurgency campaign by winning over the 'hearts and minds' of the peasants so that they would be less tempted to give their support to Frelimo.[64] Certain

[62] João Paulo Borges Coelho (1993). 'Protected Villages and Communal Villages'. PhD Thesis, University of Bradford: 203.

[63] Borges Coelho (1993): 203.

[64] One of the ironies of Frelimo's agricultural policy is that it initially made the same mistake as the colonial regime, by failing to adequately take account of local perspectives in its villagisation programme. As Borges Coelho points out: 'both attempted, through villagisation, to achieve local political and administrative control; both failed to base this profound change on the transformation of slash and burn agriculture which had characterised community economy until then. While the colonial state did not even attempt such as transformation, the independent one did not achieve it.' Borges Coelho (1993): 3.

strategic hamlets were built in cement and provided with good amenities to serve as showpieces for international propaganda.[65]

A striking aspect of *O Povo Organizado* is the contrast it depicts between rural and urban lives. The film shifts to a panoramic shot of Maputo, the voiceover asserting that Frelimo intends to tackle the inequalities between the city and the countryside. Frelimo saw the colonial cities as sites of segregation and inequality, as well as a potential source of counter-revolutionary activity. In contrast to Marx and Engels, who in *The Communist Manifesto* claim the city is a place where peasant populations could be rescued from 'the idiocy of rural life', Samora Machel in his investiture speech on 25 June presented the colonial cities as 'centres of vice and corruption and of alienating foreign influence'.[66] As Darch and Hedges point out, in his speeches Machel reserved particular scorn for figures such as *o pretinho assimilado*, the assimilated elites who considered themselves superior to other Mozambicans because they were able to affect European manners. Although the colonial system is 'finished', the voiceover points out, it is here in the city that the 'contradictions of colonial society persist'. In the colonial period Lourenço Marques grew around the port infrastructure and the railway, serving the mining economy of neighbouring countries, and developed a hierarchical structure in which the services were located in the centre where the white settlers lived. Beyond the margins of the 'concrete city', large informal neighbourhoods were constructed, designated the *cidade de caniço* 'reed city', because most of the walls were made from this material.[67] Over a travelling shot of boutique shop windows, the voiceover proclaims: 'Maputo, formerly Lourenço Marques, is a paradigm example of the contradictions and paradoxes that Frelimo faces. This is where Frelimo will confront the greatest obstacles to the revolutionary process.' As the travelling shot moves over the modernist houses of central Maputo, the voiceover continues: 'The colonialists created two societies – the centre, urbanised, where all the services were laid on for European inhabitants.'

An image of a train moving along the railway line that cuts through the fabric of Maputo to the port is pierced by the sound of the train whistle, and the film moves to the other side of the city. Here in the *barrios*, the film demonstrates, there are 'practically no services, no electricity, no water supplies to the huts'. Instead women and children are shown collecting water from a tap in the street. While life is hard, there is camaraderie in evidence that contrasts with the individualist consumerism of the city centre – a man comes to help a woman as

65 Borges Coelho (1993): 205.

66 Cited in Thomas H. Henriksen (1978). 'Marxism and Mozambique'. African Affairs, 77, 309, October: 452.

67 Carlos Nunes Silva (2015). *Urban Planning in Lusophone African Countries*. London: Routledge.

she lifts a heavy bucket of water from her head. To address the poverty, illiteracy and illness that 'service the forces of capitalism and colonialism', the film asserts, it is necessary to 'eliminate individualist attitudes'. In contrast to liberal democracies, where political parties vie to represent particular constituencies, *O Povo Organizado* suggests that there is, in fact, no gap between Frelimo and the people of Mozambique. The voiceover concludes this section with the statement: 'Frelimo insists upon the participation of the masses in the political process and that the government is, in fact, the people mobilised.' A scene of such mobilisation is presented next, with images of a presidential cavalcade surrounded by motorbikes arriving at Machava Stadium for a mass rally held one month after independence. Machel, wearing a suit, mounts to the podium and addresses the audience of 100,000 people, who 'were mobilized to attend this rally on very short notice'.[68] Along with a stream of slogans – 'Long Live the Popular Republic of Mozambique', 'Down with colonialism', 'Down with reactionaryism', 'Down with racism' – Machel gives a speech that denounces colonial capitalism. Close-ups of faces in the crowd show the urban audience listening, laughing and applauding. As Machel addresses the need to 'eliminate the *latifundios*' 'large estates', the film shifts to images of work on the sugar plantations.

Replacing the plantation system was a crucial part of Frelimo's agricultural reforms. An aerial shot of the huge offices of Sena Sugar Estates fills the screen. Sena Sugar's operations were exemplary of the way in which Portuguese colonialism served as a 'labour-selling enterprise' to international corporations.[69] This British-owned company controlled the cultivation and refining of sugar cane across the province of Zambezia, and the colonial system allowed it to profit by using seasonal migrant labour that was paid well below its value.[70] Under Salazar, the administration of the agricultural sector was 'rationalised' for the purposes of more effective exploitation through the imposition of taxes, pass laws and a network of local chiefs appointed by the Portuguese.[71] This controlled the movements of the rural workforce and compelled them to provide their labour for six months of the year. Frelimo's agricultural reforms, the voiceover explains, are needed to end 'starvation wages' and the dominance of foreign companies who control agricultural production.[72] *O Povo Organizado* connects

[68] The Mozambique Film Project, *A Discussion Guide for the Film* O Povo Organizado *(The People Organized)*. New York: African Information Service: 5.

[69] Judith Head (1980). 'Sena Sugar Estates and Migrant Labour', in *Mozambican Studies*, 1: 53–54.

[70] Head describes how Sena Sugar resisted wage increases and made use of child labour. Head (1980): 58–62.

[71] Head (1980): 53–54.

[72] Munslow argues, however, that in the first five years of independence the Mozambican government continued to favour large state farms created out of those that had been

these contemporary forms of exploitation, in which the colonial state served the interests of corporate capitalism, with the long history of foreign powers exploiting Mozambique's people and natural resources. A drawing depicts slaves in shackles being loaded onto ships, while a satirical cartoon shows an imperialist in a top hat with a vacuum cleaner hovering up the natural resources of the African continent.

The film then shifts to consider the state of Mozambican industry. Here too, migrant labour has a crucial impact on the national economy. The voiceover explains that, because the country lacks sufficient jobs in industry, it is hoped that workers will continue to be able to travel to South Africa to find work in the mines. Frelimo was in fact committed to ending migrant labour but recognised that the system of exporting mine labour to South Africa was so embedded within Mozambique's economic system that it needed to continue in the immediate future.[73] Ruth First argues in *Black Gold: Mozambican Miner, Proletarian and Peasant* that this pattern of labour migration could not be combatted by ideology alone but would involve the reintegration within a reformed agricultural sector of this formerly exported labour.[74] Images of cotton, drinks-bottling and cashew-processing factories follow. The film points out that these conditions, while fraught with contradictions, also open up possibilities for new kinds of solidarity.

While a global perspective is necessary to understanding how imperialism skewers the national economy, 'a vital part of the socialist project in Mozambique is that Frelimo wants to work with other African countries who have supported liberation, rather than just with Portugal and South Africa.' Of the strong alliances Frelimo forged with neighbouring progressive African states, none was more emblematic of Pan-African solidarity than their friendship with President Julius Nyerere of Tanzania. A scene at the airport depicts Nyerere's arrival on 30 August 1975. The first state dignitary to be received by President Machel, he is greeted with a military band, canon fire and performances of traditional dances, followed by talks on education, economy, transport, communications

abandoned by or seized from the plantation owners. These were dependent on heavy machinery, skilled managers and migrant labour. Despite these drawbacks, they were privileged to the expense of other more grass roots models of agricultural production. Munslow (1984).

73 Ruth First points out: 'Migrant labour was part of the penetration of the money economy, when the social formations of Mozambique were subordinated to the purposes of the spread of capitalism. This penetration left no corner of rural agriculture untouched. The coercion of the colonial state undermined the reproductive base of the rural economy. Eight decades of the system of migrant labour made it a structural necessity for rural producers living under colonialism.' Ruth First (1983). *Black Gold: Mozambican Miner, Proletarian and Peasant*. Brighton: Harvester Press: 3–4.

74 First (1983): 4.

sectors. The voiceover quotes a speech by Nyerere in which he states that the 'Mozambican people had opened the doors of their prison, and now constituted a free nation, ready for economic liberation.'

Weaving back to the challenge of agricultural production, the film then turns to the role of the army because, as well as the crucial task of defending Mozambique's long border with Rhodesia, this is an 'army of the people' and therefore: 'It is a force for production, for mobilisation, and for education.' In contrast to the earlier images of isolated villagers, here soldiers are seen working alongside peasants, thus demonstrating 'the value of productive work'. Over scenes of people hoeing the fields in syncopated rhythm, with close-ups of smiling faces, the voiceover proclaims: 'All the population participates in the development of the country' – even government officials who 'work long hours organising programmes of work' also engage in the growing of food. The experience of collectivisation in the liberated zones, where manual labour was elevated, and militants and school students were expected to participate in cultivation, clearly provides the model that Frelimo intended to expand across the new nation.

Similarly the *lojas do povo* 'people's shops', which are pictured in the next scene, were first experimented with in the liberated zones. As people at this *loja do povo* are shown weighing out grain, the voiceover argues that these institutions reflect a new economic system in which cooperatives eliminate the need for exploitative middlemen and make basic goods more affordable to the peasants. In fact, the departure of traders who constituted a crucial part of Mozambique's commercial network contributed to the country's economic crisis in the years that followed.[75] Small family producers, a sector almost completely overlooked in Frelimo's early agricultural policies, were suddenly left bereft of the means to sell their surpluses. *O Povo Organizado* thus reflects a moment of great optimism that the solutions that Frelimo had developed during the armed struggle to address constant food shortages and logistical problems could be rolled out on a national scale, and that these would overcome the difficulties caused by the destruction of infrastructures during the war and the mass departure of skilled technicians and managers.

A sequence follows that shows the Cahora Bassa dam, the building of which Frelimo's guerrilla campaign in Tete had sought to disrupt because it was in part intended to cut off their access to the south (see Chapter 1). In this film, it stands as an example of how 'colonial projects were never intended to benefit the

[75] As Munslow explains, by the early 1980s Frelimo was forced to reassess its agricultural policy in the face of the failure to return agricultural production to pre-Independence levels. Large state farms were recognised to be too dependent on expensive technology requiring skilled workers that Mozambique did not have, and Frelimo started to give greater support to small-scale cooperatives. Munslow (1984).

Mozambican people'. Shots of the electricity lines that took the energy generated by the dam to South Africa demonstrate how Mozambique's natural resources were misappropriated in the interest of foreign powers. Next the film shows scenes of ruined buildings and infrastructures, the voiceover commenting that the Portuguese encouraged the departing settlers to destroy as much as possible before they crossed the border into South Africa. Destruction of property, however, is nothing compared to the destruction of lives in the rural areas during the war. An illustration shows Portuguese soldiers attacking villages, followed by a shot of a dead tree silhouetted against the sky and household objects scattered over the ground. These stand in for the atrocities committed by the colonial army in the Wiriyamu triangle in the last years of the armed struggle. Yet, the voiceover reassures, those who were injured 'will not be sent back to their huts and hidden away.' Images of amputees walking together and attending adult education classes demonstrate that Frelimo intends that the injured will be cared for at centres of rehabilitation, where they can 'regain their dignity by participating in the revolutionary process'. These centres include political education, depicted through a scene in which a Frelimo cadre stands in the middle of a small circle of adults and children. Speaking in Portuguese, which is translated by an interpreter, he gives a lecture on the evils of colonialism and the importance of independence.

This scene marks a shift in the film to a focus on health, education and culture, in which the new institutions being created by Frelimo are compared to their colonial counter-parts. The expertise and equipment available at Maputo Central Hospital demonstrates how services under colonialism were only well developed for the settlers – by contrast, the voiceover points out, most people in the country have never seen a doctor. Frelimo intends that the kinds of small-scale medical centres that were set up in the liberated zones will be extended across the nation. Health workers based in their own communities are at the forefront of Frelimo's health campaigns against cholera and other diseases. The Escola Primaria in the Polana district of Maputo stands as an example of how colonial education was narrow, expensive and exclusionary. The secondary school students who attended this formerly elitist educational establishment now join in with their new fellow students in agricultural work as well as lessons in class. Black and white pupils are seen walking into the fields together with a soundtrack of children singing a Frelimo song about Chissano. Reflecting the radical decolonial pedagogy that Frelimo developed at its school in Bagamoyo (see Chapter 1), the voiceover proclaims: 'In the new Mozambique, science is a collective work that reflects the whole of society. Manual and intellectual labour is considered equal. Students and their teachers participate in production.' Furthermore:

> Today education is based on the Mozambican personality. The creation of a new society involves the destruction of the old one and its corrupt values. It is necessary to create a new culture capable of negating the thinking of traditional society and the colonial capitalist system.

In 1976 Graça Simbine, the new minster of culture and wife to the president, defined the creation of a 'Mozambican personality' that would forge new social relations.[76] It involved bringing into being a 'New Man, the Socialist Man, the man free from all superstitious and obscurantist subservience'.[77] This New Man adhered to the watchwords of 'Unity, Work and Vigilance' and displayed the 'values of the working and peasant class'.[78] The sequence concludes with a scene in Tete Province of teachers and children walking through the fields, together singing and clapping.

Finally, *O Povo Organizado* presents manifestations of Mozambique's revolutionary nationalist culture. Unlike colonial art that is isolated in museums or commercial galleries, Mozambique's new revolutionary nationalist culture 'emerges from the people' and is embedded in everyday life – whether it is in the form of traditional dances such as the Kipoko or women plaiting each other's hair. The reality of the formation of this revolutionary nationalist culture was, of course, far less organic than the film implies. Frelimo had already during the armed struggle started to privilege certain kinds of cultural expression as more 'authentically' Mozambican and through the publication of anthologies was forming a nationalist canon. Nevertheless, one of the notable features of *O Povo Organizado* is the highly effective way in which it uses popular songs in the soundtrack to convey that Frelimo's revolutionary nationalism is a vital and collective project that unifies the people of Mozambique and builds on a shared history of resistance to colonialism. For example, in the scene in which school children are seen leaving the fields, they sing together 'Tiyende Pamodzi' 'Let's Go Together', a song that originated in the Zambian liberation struggle and known throughout East Africa to stress unity and working together in order to achieve victory.[79] The film concludes with a montage of paintings, sculptures and photographs of Josina Machel and Eduardo Mondlane, two icons of revolutionary sacrifice that mingle with depictions of 'Mozambican history as seen through the eyes of its people'.[80]

As with Van Lierop's earlier film *A Luta Continua*, for *O Povo Organizado* the Mozambique Film Project produced an educational booklet with factual

[76] Graça Simbine (1976). 'New Social Relations in Mozambique'. *Ikwezi*, II, IV, December: 50.
[77] Simbine (1976): 50.
[78] Simbine (1976): 50.
[79] Mozambique Film Project (1975): 8.
[80] Mozambique Film Project (1975): 8.

information and directions on how to guide discussions at projections of the film.[81] Funds raised at the screenings of *O Povo Organizado* in the United States enabled Van Lierop in 1977 to present Machel with a cheque to cover the costs of building a health clinic in rural Niassa. Both Van Lierop's films now also had a second life in Mozambique, where they became resources for Frelimo in the fields of education and mobilisation. Frelimo favoured these films by filmmakers such as Popović and Van Lierop for the purposes of propaganda. In contrast to the radical experimentations with form emerging in situations of revolutionary change at the time (which sought to challenge the viewer to make new connections through bombastic montage or symbolism, as in the work of Solanas and Getino or Santiago Álvarez), Popović and Lierop made use of conventional documentary camerawork and didactic voiceover. However, at independence there was in fact a range of ways in which the recurrent themes, tropes and narratives of Mozambican resistance to colonialism were treated, some more experimental and expressive. Indeed, in the context of colonial rule, ciné-clubs functioned as spaces of dissent from the regime in which various cinematographic experiments emerged that attempted to speak to the lived realities of Mozambique.

In the mid-1960s, the armed insurrection had only just begun, and independence was unimaginable to most Mozambicans, particularly in the south. Censorship of the press and lack of channels through which information could travel across the vast territory meant that the processes of decolonisation occurring across the continent in the early 1960s barely registered in public consciousness. Maria de Lourdes Torcato, then a journalist at the newspaper *Notícias*, explained to me that in colonial Mozambique little was known of the independence of most African nation-states and the experiments with 'African Socialism' unfolding elsewhere.[82] As Eduardo Geada argues, the cinema was an important site for affirming Portuguese patriotism and naturalising the social hierarchies and ideology that the New State depended on, hiding 'the violent reality of the dictator, of capitalist exploitation and of colonialism'.[83] Legislation in 1953 decreed that all the overseas provinces should establish local delegations of the National Cinema Censure Commission to ensure that Portuguese values and language would be promoted in the cinema theatres in the colonies. Most of

[81] Mozambique Film Project (1975).

[82] Maria de Lourdes Torcato wrote the first article published in a Mozambican newspaper about an African country achieving independence, which appeared in *Notícias* in 1974. Taking advantage of a new South African air route via Mozambique to Madagascar, which was set up by the Apartheid regime for commercial reasons, she was able to research and write about Madagascar's independence in 1960, which had a big impact in radicalising the political consciousness of an educated urban readership. Interview with Maria de Lourdes Torcato, Maputo, 2005.

[83] Eduardo Geada (1977), 'O Imperialismo e o Fascismo no cinema'. Lisbon: Morães: 74

the forty-two cinema theatres in Mozambique were owned by one family, that of Manuel Rodrigues and his sons, who maintained them as spaces that were, in the words of Marcus Powers, 'profoundly racialised and exclusive'.[84] Even if by the early 1970s assimilated Africans could in theory enter, they might not feel at ease among audiences that were predominantly white.[85]

From 1961, Portuguese proprietors began setting up a small number of production houses that competed against each other for commissions from the Centro de Informação e Turismo, the state organ responsible for propaganda about the colonies. The chief output of these Mozambican production houses was newsreel. *Actualidades de Moçambique*, produced by Antonio Melo Pereira, *Visor Moçambicano*, made by Courinha Ramos of Somar Filmes, and *Imagem de Moçambique*, produced by Eurico Ferreira on behalf of Rádio e Televisão de Portugal (RTP), regularly reported on visits by officials to the 'overseas province', highlighting the benefits of colonial rule and the bravery of the Portuguese soldier defending 'Portugal' against 'the enemy'.[86] A. G. Dagron suggests that the fact that this 'enemy' was never named in the films led to the impression that the colonial army was fighting *fantasmas* 'ghosts', an unsettling affect given that the purpose of the newsreels was to reassure settlers of the permanence of the Portuguese presence in Africa even while this was being challenged by anti-colonial incursions.[87] Only a few of the people working at the film production companies were black, and these employees were kept in subservient roles.[88] According to João Costa, as the armed struggle intensified in the early 1970s opportunities for non-white camera operators increased as they were seen as being able to travel into the conflict zones more easily than their white peers.[89]

Under colonial rule the film clubs that were set up by left-wing cinephiles within settler society became important sites of political as well as artistic engagement. In the context of colonial rule, when Mozambique was subject to the double censorship of Portuguese fascism and South African Apartheid, this creation of a social sphere of progressive critical interaction was a political act even when the material was not overtly political, and their projections

[84] Marcus Power (2004). 'Post-colonial Cinema and the Re-configuration of Moçambicanidade'. *Lusotopie*: 264.

[85] Maria de Lourdes Torcato recounted to me the experience of going to the cinema in Lourenço Marques with a *mestiço* friend from Cape Verde. Her friend felt uncomfortable being the only non-white person in the audience, and they left the screening. Interview with Maria de Lourdes Torcato, Maputo, 2005.

[86] Power (2004): 266.

[87] A. G. Dagron (1978). 'Africa: El cine em Moçambique', *Film/Historia*, 1 March: 44–56; cited in Powers (2004): 267.

[88] Interviews with Manuel Malo and João Costa, Maputo, 2005.

[89] Interview with João Costa, Maputo, 2005.

sometimes included films that could not be seen in Portugal.[90] The ciné-club of Lourenço Marques, for example, which was set up in 1957, featured projections of such films as Vitorio de Sica's *The Bicycle Thief* (1948) and Tony Richardson's *The Loneliness of the Long Distance Runner* (1962), which addressed social inequality. De Lourdes Torcato, then a journalist at *Notícias*, recalled to me that films such as these played a crucial role in her politicisation.[91]

In 1961, members of the Lourenço Marques ciné-club José Almeida and Manuel Faria de Almeida established a 'commission of cinema enthusiasts' to promote the production of experimental film, and it was in these attempts at aesthetic freedom, in contrast to the commercial films of the period that tended to function as propaganda for the New State, that critiques of the regime first emerged from within settler colonialism. Noticeably, however, they focused on white settler protagonists and were concerned with the constraints and injustices they experienced rather than the violence, forced labour and poverty suffered by most African Mozambicans. The Beira ciné-club similarly provided a space for projections and discussion of José Cardoso's amateur films. Cardoso worked as a pharmacist, and during the 1960s he used the chemicals he had access to through his employment to process his 8mm films.[92] Made with his wife and their circle of friends, the films voiced criticism of the regime by presenting life in the 'overseas province' as shabby and rife with poverty, repression and despair, combining realism with inventive forms of symbolism that make reference to the claustrophobia and violence of everyday life under the New State.

O Anúncio 'The Advertisement' (1961) tells the story of a young homeless white man played by Cardoso who responds to a job advertisement and experiences discrimination. At one point in his ramblings he enters a party in a bar, where a group of revellers in fancy dress invite him to share a beer. His desperation is encapsulated in a moment when he steals some boiled eggs. He drops one on the dance floor, whereupon he scrambles on his knees between the legs of the dancers to pick it up, only to see it crushed underfoot. The morning after he awakes alone with the detritus of the party all around him, and he is left with nothing to do but continue his lonely wandering through the streets. The film garnered Cardoso attention both within Mozambique and abroad and was included in a festival of amateur film in Italy. *Raizes* 'Roots' (1968) begins with a sequence that cuts between scenes of the beach, a young boy who is slapped, a middle-aged man (again played by Cardoso) who laughs manically, and a man's body washed up on the beach. Young people play cards, a girl weeps, young people dance to rock and roll, and a man lusts after images of scantily clad women. There are scenes of a couple pre- and post-coital. The

90 Interview with Maria de Lourdes Torcato, Maputo 2005.
91 Interview with Maria de Lourdes Tocato, Maputo, 2005.
92 Interview with José Cardoso, Maputo, 2005.

film culminates with sad young boy who looks on at other children playing at shooting each other with guns. An adult hands him a shotgun, and he shoots the other children dead. Cardoso's final amateur film *O Pesadelo* 'The Nightmare' (1969) similarly addresses the violence at the heart of colonial society. It depicts children catapulting stones at marching boots. Despite its symbolic approach, *O Pesadelo* was banned for its critique of militarism.

Manuel Faria de Almeida's *Catembe – 7 dias em Lourenço Marques* 'Catembe – 7 days in Lourenço Marques' (1964) was another film that fell foul of the censor for depicting the realities of racial segregation and discrimination in the colonial capital. Entering *The Guinness Book of Records* as the film that received the most cuts ever in the history of censorship, *Catembe* was left, according to the filmmaker, 'without sequence, without rhythm, without sense'.[93] *Catembe* was made after Faria de Almeida had studied filmmaking in London, where he had been influenced by the Free Cinema movement to make *Streets of Early Sorrow* (1963). The Free Cinema movement, whose leading figures included Tony Richardson, Lindsay Anderson, Lorenza Mazzetti and Karel Reisz, strove to create a new kind of filmmaking that would open up a space of freedom between the pressures of the commercial film industry on the one hand and the expectations of more propagandistic political filmmaking on the other. *Streets of Early Sorrow* offers a powerful depiction of the psychological damage of racist violence. The South African actor Lionel Nkagane plays an exile in London who is traumatised by the Sharpeville massacre, when on 21 March 1960 police opened fire on a demonstration against the Pass Laws, killing sixty-nine people. With a jazz soundtrack that dramatises the mental torment of the survivor, the protagonist is thrown into crisis by seeing school children playing 'Ring a Ring o' Roses' in their school playground. Nkagane began his career as assistant director to Zoltan Korda, working on the seminal anti-Apartheid film *Cry the Beloved Country* (1951), following which he was forced into exile in London. Some years after acting in *Streets of Early Sorrow*, Nkagane directed his own short film *Jemima and Johnny* (1966). Interestingly, Nkagane's film also filters the effects of racism through a story centred on two children, but more optimistically their friendship enables them to overcome the prejudices of the white boy's father when they narrowly escape their own tragedy.

Faria de Almeida returned to Mozambique with a desire to use film to cast a light on the realities of life in the colonial capital. Significantly, the very title of the film signals that this is a portrait of a divided city, as it contains the name of the capital in the subtitle, but forefronts Catembe, the beach on the other side of the bay that overlooks the dazzling skyline of the European city centre. Although

[93] Faria de Almeida quoted by Maria do Carmo Piçarra, who notes that the film was cut in 103 places. Maria do Carmo Piçarra (2015). *Azuis Ultramarinos: Propaganda Colonial e Censura no Cinema do Estado Novo*. Lisbon: Edições 70: 242.

Catembe's butchering by the censors makes it hard to assess how successful the intended film would have been, what survives defies genre. It recalls the city-symphony films of the early twentieth century that portrayed particular cities, often over the course of a day, focusing on quotidian activities of different social classes. *Catembe* depicts scenes of everyday life in the capital, with short vignettes satirising bourgeois domesticity and predatory forms of masculine sexuality, as well as questions put to passers-by and a more extensive interview with journalist Fernando Carneiro, who is critical of the complacency of local politics. The film varies in tone from playful to slapstick, to moments of clichéd romanticism, to the powerful scenes of waves crashing on Catembe beach as the fishermen haul in their catch, their poverty and hard labour contrasting starkly to the consumerism and luxury enjoyed by whites over the water. Crucially, as well as shots of the 'reed city' and black people walking the streets without shoes, a substantial part that is missing from the film due to censorship is an entire section centred on a young *mestiço* woman called 'Catembe', whose narrative was intended to be at the heart of the film's critique of segregation. Faria de Almeida reports that the letter he received from the censor finished by saying: 'in the film there were two distinct societies, entirely separated one from the other: the white and the black.'[94]

Yet the opening of *Catembe* leaves no doubt that the film is also a retort to Metropolitan condescension towards the 'overseas provinces'. The director is seen stopping passers-by in Lisbon and asking them if they have ever been to Mozambique. This sequence was cut in numerous places when respondents answered with phrases such as 'Lisbon, in Portugal', or 'I returned to Portugal', because this was seen as presenting Mozambique as a separate country rather than an overseas province. In fact, in Lourenço Marques, white settlers enjoyed a degree more freedom than was possible in Portugal. The city, with its small number of *assimilados*, its substantial Indian and Chinese populations and regular influx of South African tourists, was arguably a far more cosmopolitan place than Lisbon. The aesthetic innovation evident in *Catembe* disrupts the conventional narrative that has been told about the emergence of the experimental film movement *Cinema novo* in Portugal, which is an account that has centred almost entirely on Lisbon and the influence of the French *Nouvelle vague*. *Catembe* has a different relational geography somewhat detached from the metropole of the Portuguese colonial regime, which in Eurocentric accounts is understood as the centre of innovation that eventually trickles down to the peripheries of the empire. *Catembe* may be understood as an attempt at freedom in that it uses experimentation with form to express criticism of the colonial regime, even if its position is reformist rather than revolutionary. This reformist

[94] Piçarra (2015): 241.

position was soon to be foreclosed. In London the Free Cinema movement and the communities of African exiles seems to have provided an artistic and political context that Faria de Almeida was able to participate in. Following the banning of *Catembe*, however, he became an isolated figure, caught in the atmosphere of fear that predominated under fascist rule in Portugal, and this lead to his work being completely overlooked and forgotten even after the Carnation Revolution that brought fascism and colonialism to an end.[95] At independence, Faria de Almeida returned to Portugal, foregoing the opportunity that might have emerged to contribute to a new kind of cinema in Mozambique.

Some years later, one film was produced within settler society that made a bolder critique of the colonial system. By then, Frelimo's armed struggle had liberated parts of northern and central Mozambique, Joaquim Lopes Barbosa made the fiction film *Deixem-me ao menos subir as palmeiras* 'Let me at least sit down under the palm trees' (1972), which showed the brutality of forced labour on a sisal plantation. Lopes Barbosa was another filmmaker whose entry into cinema at an early age was through a film club, this time that of Porto in Portugal. During his military service, he worked for the Department of Cinematography of the Cartographic Services of the Army, and following that in the late 1960s he embedded himself in the colonial film culture of Angola, before moving to Mozambique in 1970. Lopes Barbosa was invited to come and work in Mozambique by film director Eurico Ferreira and producer Courinha Ramos, who were in Angola for the projection of *Zé do Burro* 'Donkey Joe' (1971). [96] The first feature film produced entirely in Mozambique, *Zé do Burro* is a comedy about a rural Portuguese man and his donkey making a new life in a remote part in the north of the country. His tenacity and capacity for hard work show him in a heroic light in comparison to local black Mozambicans who are presented as lazy and work-shy, and attacks by marauding Chinese communists put his strengths into further relief. While Lopes Barbosa was appalled at the 'burlesque artificiality' of *Zé do Burro*, he was impressed that the colony had adequate laboratories and equipment for making films, facilities that were then lacking in Angola.[97]

In contrast to the sentimentalising of colonial occupation in *Zé do Burro*, Lopes Barbosa was determined to use cinema to communicate what he called 'African themes and aesthetics' and to make a film for African audiences.[98] *Deixem-me ao menos subir as palmeiras* offers a different meaning to the idea of a national cinema that was conceived within the framework of the INC. Lopes

[95] The efforts of film scholar Piçarra have been instrumental in bringing the film to greater attention in Portugal in recent years.

[96] Piçarra (2015): 262.

[97] Piçarra (2015): 265.

[98] Lopes Barbosa interviewed in Piçarra (2015): 265.

Barbosa took the decision that the film's African protagonists would speak the local language of Ronga rather than Portuguese, the language that was privileged both under the colonial rule and by Frelimo, who favoured it as a *lingua franca* that would transcend ethnic differences. Even the speech of the white settler characters was dubbed into English in the soundtrack, which was an effort to bypass the censors that did not pay off.[99] An interview with Lopes Barbosa by Maria do Carmo Piçarra reveals the extent to which the filmmaker was motivated by the fact that while there was an abundance of literature that expressed Mozambican perspectives, in the realm of the moving images there was 'absolute silence'.[100] The director recruited non-professional actors with the help of artist Malangatana Valente, who had been imprisoned by the Portuguese authorities because of his connections with Frelimo and nationalist sympathies.[101] Lopes Barbosa drew on both Angolan and Mozambican literary influences. The title cites a line from the poem *Monangambe* by the Angolan poet António Jacinto, which conveys the brutal conditions of African workers: 'Ah, let me at a least sit down under the palm trees/ Let me drink marovo, marovo/ and forget diluted in my drunkenness.' This poem resonated for Lopes Barbosa with the violence conveyed in the short story 'Lunchtime' published in the collection *We Killed the Mangy Dog* by Mozambican author Luís Bernando Honwana, and it was this work that Lopes Barbosa adapted for the cinema screen.[102]

Honwana's short story tells of an old man named Madala who has to work under the regime of a cruel foreman. Madala receives a visit from his daughter Maria, who is set to marry Djima. Maria and the foreman enter into conversation and agree to meet that night, but shortly afterwards he sexually assaults her in the long grass in broad daylight. Maria is overcome with shame that her father knows about the assault, and when the foreman learns that she is Madala's daughter he offers the old man money and drink as compensation. Lopes Barbosa's film includes a number of elements that are different to the short story. Though the decision to make the foreman in the film a black Mozambican rather than a white settler could be seen as an attempt to avoid censorship, other aspects are far more confrontational. While the short story concludes with the workers returning to their labour, in the film Maria's sexual assault and the mistreatment by the foreman that leads to Madala's death precipitates a workers' revolt. After the confrontation, Djima leaves the sisal plantation, suitcase in hand, his flight from the scene of oppression constituting an act of anti-colonial resistance. The final sequence of the funeral marks a shift from narrative to a more symbolic register that speaks to the wider historical moment

99 Piçarra (2015): 271.
100 Piçarra (2015): 270–271.
101 Savage (2017).
102 Luís Bernardo Honwana (1969). *We Killed the Mangy Dog*, London: Heinemann.

of decolonisation. As well as the group of mourners, whose members include Maria and Djima, around twelve white people stand in a line confrontationally, some even wearing hats recalling cowboys. Lopes Barbosa explains that this:

> symbolises colonial society, represented by its fundamental structures: power, represented by the ministry: the clergy, the priest, PIDE, by the two police officers in civil clothing who wear dark glasses; civil society… [including] women and men as representing the colonial nuclear family.[103]

A guerrilla, played by Malangatana, is also seen in the landscape. With the sun rising behind him, the film acknowledges that the armed struggle is already underway.

Lopes Barbosa's association with Courinha Ramos, who never actually read the script, led the authorities to expect nothing too controversial from *Deixem-me ao menos subir as palmeiras*, though when they heard of Malangatana's involvement the artist was brought in for questioning about the film. However, when the film was projected to the authorities they were incensed. Lopes Barbosa lost his job at Courinha Ramos's production company Somar Filmes in July 1973 and three months later, fearing for his safety, left Mozambique.[104] After the Carnation Revolution, Courinha Ramos had copies of the film made in Lisbon.[105] But in the midst of the heated tensions of the transition, Lopes Barbosa was not able to get the film projected in Mozambique because the producer was fearful that its subject matter would be incendiary.

The kinds of restrictions and censorship that filmmakers such as Barbosa faced abruptly came to an end in 1974, with the toppling of the New State regime. The Carnation Revolution brought a wave of new kinds of films to Portugal and its African colonies that previously had been banned. In Portugal the Carnation Revolution led to radical upheavals in the film industry as filmmakers seized control of commissioning, production and distribution and demanded an end to censorship and protection for the national archives at the Cinemateca.[106] This held vital historical evidence, which they feared remaining fascist elements might try to destroy. The films censored under fascist rule ranged from Charlie Chaplin's film *The Great Dictator* (1940), which was only shown publicly in Portugal in 1974, to Bertolucci's *Last Tango in Paris* (1972). The lifting of censorship opened the floodgates to films of all kinds, including overtly

[103] Lopes Barbosa quoted in Piçarra (2015): 286.
[104] Piçarra (2015): 272.
[105] Piçarra (2015): 294.
[106] Dossier 'Cinema: Não à censura', *Cinéfilo*, 31, 4 May 1974. Reprinted in Maria João Madeira (1999). *25 de Abril no Cinema: Antologia de Textos*, Lisbon: Cinemateca Portuguesa-Museu de Cinema: 24–25.

political realist films, sexually explicit artistic films and pornography.[107] As well as commercial cinema, different modes and traditions of radical filmmaking came out into the open, from Soviet montage, through narratives of African liberation, to the provocations of the European avant-garde.

Militant filmmakers and photographers from across the world flocked to Portugal to document and participate in the revolution. The Cinemateca Portuguesa acted to put fascism into reverse by inviting filmmakers from Portugal and abroad to appropriate the national archive so as to make films that would reveal and denounce the crimes of fascist colonialism and tell new stories of class struggle and collective action.[108] When Mozambique became independent, a number of filmmakers who had been in Portugal to participate in the Carnation Revolution travelled to Maputo, recognising that the tremors that had begun in Lisbon were producing potentially more radical and enduring changes in the former colonies. One group that accompanied the German filmmaker Thomas Harlan had made the film *Torre Bela* (1975), a documentary about the occupation of a rural estate by local peasants, who transform it into a cooperative. A crucial aspect of the period known as the *Processo revolucionario em curso* 'Ongoing revolutionary process' (PREC), which followed the Carnation Revolution and lasted until November 1975, was that efforts to collectivise and form cooperatives constituted perhaps the most significant questioning of the very notion of private property in Western Europe in the late twentieth century. The film *Torre Bela* had a huge impact in terms of its unique representation of a collective action. Unlike most militant films that tended to rely on voiceover to spell out a clear political message, *Torre Bela* featured very long takes that allowed interactions between protagonists to unfold. The camerawork was undertaken over a period of months by American cameraman Russell Parker, who was much more present at the collective than Harlan. These documented rhythms of collective labour, jubilant and emotive meetings, and the emergence of certain figures as revolutionary leaders. Rather than showing the occupiers in a heroic light, the film depicts fierce and often drunken debates between the participants about how to enact a revolution, in which their role as actors and Harlan's interventions as director had a decisive effect, leading José Filipe Costa to argue that the making of the film 'forged the event'.[109] What kind of film Harlan would have made about the Mozambican

[107] Teresa Barreto Borges, 'Exibição em Portugal 15 de Abril de 1974–30 de Setembro de 1976', in Madeira (1999): 66–77.

[108] Ros Gray (2006), 'Ambitions of Cinema: Revolution, Event, Screen', PhD Thesis, University of London.

[109] José Filipe Costa (2011). 'When Cinema Forges the Event: The Case of Torre Bela', in Kodwo Eshun and Ros Gray (2011). 'The Militant Image: A Ciné-geography'. *Third Text*, 25, 1, January: 105–116.

Revolution cannot be known, as Frelimo officials seized their footage after a scuffle in a restaurant and its whereabouts remains unknown.[110] However, while Harlan left Mozambique, Russell Parker and João Azevedo, who were among the crew, came to play an important role some years later in Mozambique, with a project to use filmmaking to make an intervention in encouraging the setting up of rural cooperatives (see Chapter 4).

Another group of filmmakers who came from Portugal to Mozambique to film independence were the Brazilians José Celso and Celso Luccas, of the radical theatre group Oficina Samba.[111] Celso and Luccas had left Brazil, which was then under military dictatorship, and, arriving in Portugal at the time of the Carnation Revolution, made the film *O Parto* 'The Delivery' (1974), a compilation film made from footage from the Cinemateca Portuguesa. Opening with a graphic scene of childbirth, *O Parto* charts the fall of the Salazar regime, the Carnation Revolution, the independence of Portugal's African colonies and the ascendancy of left-leaning leaders to the provisional government, who, it is supposed, will facilitate the birth of a new socialist society. Realising that Mozambican independence was imminent, Celso and Luccas approached a Portuguese television company with a proposal to film the liberation of this former colony.

The film '25' (1975) that Celso and Luccas succeeded in making achieves a strange fusion of divergent tendencies, being about Mozambican independence but also expressing a global political imagination that suggests that this specific struggle is part of a culture of revolution beyond borders that has an almost mystical dimension. The title refers to 25 June 1962, the date of the foundation of Frelimo; 25 September 1964, the 'Day of Resistance' that began the armed struggle; 25 April 1974, when the Carnation Revolution toppled fascism in Portugal, and 25 June 1975, the day Mozambique became an independent country. The film begins and ends with images of a blackboard in one of the liberated zones. On this blackboard various people spell out '*re - vo - lu - cão*'. This alphabet of Revolution is the new language the colonised are learning so as to liberate themselves. The filmmakers claimed that '25' is about 'revolutionary love', just as Hollywood makes romantic movies, but here transformed into something that transcends the individual in the event of liberation through the birth of a new shared political consciousness.[112]

An early sequence plays on the dual sense of the word 'revolution' both as the historical break constituted by the radical emergence of the new and as cosmic cycle that animates the universe. The camera pans out from an image of

[110] I am grateful to José Filipe Costa who uncovered this information during the research and interviews with Thomas Harlan for his film *Red Line* (2012).

[111] Oficina Samba was the title of the collective from 1973 to 1979.

[112] '25', *Tempo*, 365, 2nd Trimester, 1977: 51.

an antique gyroscope, an instrument of navigation in which a globe is mounted in such a way that it can spin in all directions, while a voiceover proclaims:

> For four hundred years or more Portugal believed itself to be the centre of the world. Around the metropole, a galaxy was formed out of a vast empire: the overseas. Until we discovered that there is no centre, no fixed point in the universe. And yet it turns, everything turns.

The image of the gyroscope segues into close-up circling shots of Celso and Luccas, with film cameras at their eyes, and then to an image of a Steenbeck editing machine with its multiple reels and rotating rollers, the slider controlled by the hand of a young black boy. The word 'revolution', as Hannah Arendt explains, has a dual meaning, indicating both cyclical rotation and the birth of the new, and this sequence plays on both significations.[113] The voiceover continues: 'Revolution is the end of slavery, the destruction of the master, the liberation of the slave, a long struggle of those below against those above.' Over an image of a white man and white woman sitting with the black child at the Steenbeck, the film declares that '25' is 'a film made by Mozambicans, Brazilians and Portuguese'. Birth had already featured in *O Parto* as a key metaphor for the emergence of the new through revolutionary change, and in '25' infants and children become a symbol for the new nation of Mozambique. However, if revolution is the 'new alphabet' that the colonised must learn in order to liberate themselves, it is arguable that the young child included here as a symbol of the new nation infantilises the Mozambicans who are claimed as collaborators in the film's production. The paternalism apparent in this image indicates one of the contradictions that persists in the midst of this radical moment.

If the thread of this film is the circulation of 'revolutionary love', it strings together a curious menagerie of sounds and images. '25' combines footage of the liberated zones, work in communal villages, celebrations of independence and grassroots theatrical re-enactments of colonial injustice performed at the Saint Sebastian Fortress in Ilha de Moçambique. Inter-titles flash up keywords – '*De - co - lo - ni - za - ção*' 'decolonisation' – broken into syllables as if to facilitate learning. Allusions to racial conflict in the USA are made through footage of civil rights protests, Black Panther demonstrations and Ku Klux Klan lynchings, overlaid with the sound of Billie Holiday's 'Strange Fruit'. Across a film lasting, in its longest version, over three hours, these images and sounds suggest a common culture of revolutionary struggle, liberation and political consciousness reaching out across time and space.

The section titled 'Period of Transition' reveals the class contradictions still in evidence on the streets of Lourenço Marques in these 'last hours of a city'.

[113] Hannah Arendt (1963). *On Revolution*. Harmondsworth: Penguin.

A black man using crutches and another who sits on the ground begging are juxtaposed to white settlers who lounge and gorge themselves in restaurants. A poster for Bertolucci's *Last Tango in Paris*, a film that was only distributed in Mozambique following the lifting of censorship that came with the Carnation Revolution, stands in for urban decadence and futility, as the voiceover announces 'Lourenço Marques, your days are numbered.' The tone veers into farce, garish funeral music accompanying the camera as it closes in on the shop window of a staid funeral parlour called *Funeraria Ultramar* 'Overseas Funeral'.

The next section, titled 'The Mine', begins its denunciation of colonial conquest with superimposed images: the word 'INVASION', piles of coins, and banknotes fluttering across the screen, with whispering voices asking 'Where are the mines? Where are the mines? The mines of King Solomon!' The questions refer to H. Rider Haggard's *King Solomon's Mines* (1885), a novel about European adventurers seeking vast riches in an 'unexplored' region of Southern Africa, which inspired numerous feature films. Gunshots puncture a map of the continent of Africa, showing the route that the Portuguese took around southern cape to reach Mozambique. A series of paintings and statues of Portuguese explorers culminate in an image of a black man who looks fiercely at the camera. As the camera closes in on a black man's injured back, a voice responds: 'The mines are here.' What follows is a montage of archival photographs and drawings, interspersed with images from Jorge Brum do Canto's film *Chaimite* (1953), to depict four hundred years of exploitation and resistance.

The inclusion of sequences from *Chaimite* is significant in that the historical fiction film is a repository for a set of claims about the Portuguese colonial occupation of Mozambique. Set in nineteenth-century Mozambique, it depicts the war between the Portuguese and the Gaza empire, which at its height in the 1860s stretched across southern Mozambique, southeastern Zimbabwe and parts of South Africa. The film focuses on particular families of Portuguese settlers of varying social classes, who contribute within the framework of a peaceful hierarchy to the cultivation of Mozambique, in contrast to the marauding masses of violent Africans who revolt against them. *Chaimite* thus represents the transplantation of the Portuguese rural ethos, which Brum do Canto had romanticised in his earlier film *A Canção da Terra* 'The Song of the Earth' (1938), to Africa, and the extension of the Portuguese nation across African territory.[114] It also depicts actual historical military leaders, including Mouzinho de Albuquerque, Paiva Couceira and Caldas Xavier, who were Portuguese commanders, and Ngungunhane, the chief of Gaza, who was eventually captured by the Portuguese and then paraded with his family through

[114] Hilary Owen and Anna Klobucka (2014). *Gender, Empire and Postcolony: Luso-African-Brazilian Intersections*. New York: Palgrave Macmillan: 72.

the streets of Lisbon before being exiled on the Azores. Celso and Luccas extract *Chaimite*'s emotional climax – Ngungunhane's defeat, which is depicted through the moment of his arrest when his attempt to meet the gaze of Mouzinho de Albuquerque fails and he lowers his eyes in submission. While these historical African resistance fighters were defeated despite their superior numbers because of military technology, in *Chaimite*, as Patricia Vieira points out, these victories are interpreted as miracles that 'attest to the divine mandate that the colonisers have to govern the native population'.[115]

In '25', however, such narratives of white supremacy are shattered into fragments and reassembled into a collage in which images of the black labour that sustained the colonial regime are juxtaposed with scenes of white settler luxury. The voiceover, interspersed with snatches of speeches by Samora Machel and testimonies from cotton workers, explains that in fact three corporations – the Mozambique Company, the Niassa Company and the Zambezia Company – controlled the territory and its people, and oversaw the transportation of raw materials from the colonies to the metropole. Images of opium smoking from Barbosa's *Deixem-me ao menos subir as palmeiras* suggest the suffering of the exploited, a point reinforced by a Makonde sculpture of a figure engaged in the same form of escape.

The film accelerates through a sequence of images in a kaleidoscopic denunciation: hunting scenes from *Chaimite*, the butchering of animals by white tourists on safari, Martin Luther King, police violence against civil rights activists, protestors in South Africa, as well as images of Pinochet with his generals, through which '25' recalls the massacres of leftists that followed the coup in Chile in 1973.[116] Reactionary forces are shown 'everywhere when the masses revolt without arms, without organisation'. The sequence culminates in the moment from *Birth of a Nation* when the Ku Klux Klan sweeps through the town and leaves the body of a murdered black man on a doorstep. As Ella Shohat and Robert Stam argue, white supremacist films such as *Chaimite* and *Birth of a Nation* offered white viewers the possibility of being sutured to 'the omniscient cosmic perspective of the European master-subject'. [117] However, here this position of privilege is shattered. This avalanche of images of white violence is followed by an abrupt shift into a slower rhythm of images accompanied by a sombre soundtrack, which gives an account of the beginnings of Frelimo. Over

[115] Patricia Vieira (2013), *Portuguese Film, 1930–1960: The Staging of the New State Regime*, London: Bloomsbury: 82 and 212.

[116] The sequence recalls a final section of Fernando Solanas and Octavio Getino's *La Hora de las Hornos* 'The Hour of the Furnaces' (1968), which culminates in the iconic still image of the face of Ernesto Che Guevara, taken after he was killed in Bolivia.

[117] Ella Shohat and Robert Stam (1994). *Unthinking Eurocentricism: Multiculturalism and the Media*. London: Routledge: 105.

scenes of Frelimo guerrillas practicing their manoeuvres, '25' tells the story of how Mondlane succeeded in uniting regional independence so as to organise resistance to colonialism. The preceding images of colonial violence serve to justify the necessity and righteousness of Frelimo's armed struggle. Now is the time when the colonial statues have fallen – it is time to 'sweep away the old images' in order to usher in the new. Here it is symbolised by a little girl who stands with her fist raised in a gesture of victorious resistance.

Later in the film, Machel discusses the need for education and political mobilisation for a campaign against hunger and poverty, his monologue intercut with the images and sounds of a rousing performance of the Makwayela. This song and dance has its origins in the south of Mozambique, where it developed as a form of cultural resistance to the punishing conditions that many Mozambican migrant workers suffered in the South African mines. Here, however, '25' shows the Makwayela re-invented at independence to celebrate Frelimo's victory. Indeed, from 1973 onwards the Makwayela had become the predominant cultural activity in Frelimo schools, its modality of choral singing with vocal exclamations being ideally suited to political lyrics intended to teach and reinforce Frelimo ideology.[118] At this moment of independence, the Makwayela became a national form. Machel is asked about the people of Portugal, and he responds by pointing out the way in which they too suffered under the Salazar regime – they too are afflicted with problems of hunger, neglect and illiteracy. Unlike in Mozambique, Machel comments, the people of Portugal 'haven't yet found the correct political line'. At the moment of this statement, the film cuts briefly to a still photograph of two impoverished Portuguese women, whose bodies are confined within a narrow alleyway of shacks.[119] A single still image, in the midst of this euphoric expression of Mozambican cultural strength and political certainty, emphasises how the armed struggle, by precipitating the Carnation Revolution, also liberated the people of Portugal.

While in '25' the words of Machel summarise many of Frelimo's positions, the significance of independence is also communicated through symbolic gestures that proliferate across different sections of the film. For instance, in the depictions of celebrations of independence, one of the dancers stands with a piece of cloth draped over his face. Shortly after a close-up shows a boy's face, eyes closed, followed by a group of men and boys who hide themselves behind

[118] Paulo Israel (2014). *In Step with the Times: Mapiko Masquerades of Mozambique*. Athens: University of Ohio Press: 157.

[119] Although it has not been possible to identify the provenance of this particular image, it is worth noting that at the time of the Carnation Revolution, a number of documents of shanty town conditions were made to expose the plight of impoverished Portuguese communities by photographers such as the Chilean Gerard Bloncourt and filmmakers such as Eduardo Geada, who made *Lisboa, o Direito à Cidade* 'Lisbon, the Right to the City' (1974).

tribal masks. The opening of eyes and the removal of masks indicates that the dawning of independence in this new revolutionary nation means the people of Mozambique will free themselves from superstition and the divisions of tribalism that were fostered by the Portuguese – finally they can see. A similar but more sinister tableau comes later in the film, following a section that depicts the Portuguese counter-offence, including the Cahora Bassa dam, the arrival of General Kaúlza de Arriaga to Beira in 1970, napalm bombing during the Gordian Knot offensive and finally the massacre at Wiriyamu on 16 December 1974. Small groups of people stand on platforms and present to the camera human remains.

On their arrival in Mozambique, Celso and Luccas gathered over eight hours of footage and decided to make one long film instead of the seven shorts originally planned.[120] The Portuguese television company who originally commissioned them rejected this proposal, but instead they got support from the Serviço Nacional de Cinema 'National Cinema Service', who ended up producing it as their first film, made as a celebration of independence. Significantly, however, it would seem that Frelimo didn't know quite what to make of '25'; though it was screened at Cannes, shown on French television and widely distributed through activist circuits in Europe and South America. A 16mm copy of '25' was sent clandestinely from France to Brazil, which was still under military dictatorship.[121] According to the filmmakers, its call for decolonisation and liberation was experienced by Brazilian audiences as 'a "wind" from the lands of Africa, a breathe of fresh air after years of suffocation' that showed 'light at the end of the tunnel'.[122] But while the film clearly had considerable impact in Brazil, '25' quickly slipped into obscurity in Mozambique.[123] Instead, *Do Rovuma ao Maputo*, which is far more orthodox, became the film most widely distributed across the country through the mobile cinemas. The very length and exuberance of '25' could be understood as an expression of freedom liberated from the demands of both commercialism and propaganda.

Other aspects, however, militated against its adoption by Frelimo. In one sequence, '25' switches repeatedly from the state celebrations of independence in Maputo, with flags raised, military salutes and politicians embracing each other, to a scene on the beach where people gather 'around the furnace that is Frelimo' to celebrate independence in another way. A huge crowd forms a circle

[120] Israel (2014): 52.

[121] Celso Luccas (2016). 'Blecaute na Censura: Sobre 25, de José Celso Martinez Corrêa e Celso Luccas', in Lúcia Ramos Monteiro (2016). *Africas: Cinema e Revolução*, São Paulo: Caixa Belas Artes: 88.

[122] Luccas (2016): 88.

[123] As discussed by Pedro Pimenta in his introduction to the screening of '25' at Encontros – Maputo: Festival de Cinema Documentário, 29 September 2005.

around a fire, and, as the sun rises and waves crash on the beach, they dance and sing in a ritual imbued with mysticism. The film thus refuse to represent Mozambican identity as a single entity, or to elide the Frelimo elite with 'the people', here signified as a more mysterious multitude of bodies who, it seems, are somewhere else, with their own signs and modes of expression that cannot be contained or represented by the symbols and rhetoric of official politics.

In the wake of the Carnation Revolution in 1974 the colonial film clubs in Mozambique were able to declare their political affiliations more openly. As censorship ended, they turned their attention to the radical filmmaking of the Tricontinental. For instance, an edition of the journal *Objectiva* produced by the Lourenço Marques film club in July 1974 includes articles on '25 April and the Film Clubs', Sarah Maldoror's *Sambizanga* (1972), the role of cinema in politics, Chilean cinema, as well as excerpts from the writings of Aimé Césaire and Mao Tse-Tung, a translation of Solanas and Gettino's article 'Towards a Third Cinema' and the poem 'The Guerrilla' by Damião Cosme, one of the poets included in the Frelimo anthology *Poesia de Combate*.[124]

However, not all the cinema cultures that emerged in this new space of freedom were so in tune with the politics of Frelimo. The impact of sexual liberation spurred on by youth movements in consumer societies abroad was felt within colonial society in Mozambique, and had been addressed in some of the films made by José Cardoso and Manuel Faria de Almeida during the 1960s. During the transition to independence, most of the films projected in the cinemas in Mozambique featured explicit sex scenes. When Bertolucci's *Last Tango in Paris* was projected in Mozambique in 1974, it provoked polemical responses, though Guido Convents reports that the journal *Tempo* included a more tempered debate about whether paternalistic censorship of sexually explicit films was really an appropriate revolutionary response.[125] In the same year, Fernando Silva and Courinha Ramos made the sex comedy *O Vendedor* 'The Salesman' (1974) about a Maputo businessman who sells mattresses and is compelled to demonstrate the effectiveness of his merchandise with various female customers.[126] Intended as a parody of pornographic films, *O Vendedor* draws attention to the seedy side of the colonial city. The Baixa area of Lourenço Marques was a centre for prostitution, as documented by photographer Ricardo Rangel, who created iconic images of white South African men mingling with

[124] Ciné-Clube de Lourenço Marques, *Objectiva*, July 1974. I am grateful to Guilherme Afonso for giving me access to his archive of documents from the Lourenço Marques and Maputo film clubs.

[125] Guido Convents (2010). *Os Moçambicanos perante o cinema e o audiovisual: Uma história Politica-cultural do Moçambique Colonial até à República de Moçambique (1896–2010)*. Maputo: CP: 382–3.38

[126] José de Matos Cruz (1999).'Cinema Luso-Moçambicano', *Revista Camões*, 6: 40.

black women in the red light district.[127] In the early 1970s Lourenço Marques became a centre for the production of porn films destined for the South African market, and by 1973 Mozambique was actually making more feature films than Portugal due to the output of porn by Somar Filmes and the production house of Antonio Melo Pereira.[128] The arrival of Frelimo brought the influx of sex tourists from South Africa to an abrupt halt; the market for prostitution collapsed and women in the Baixa district who were thought to be sex workers were gathered up and sent to re-education camps.[129] Although Fernando Silva would go on to play an important role in the INC's early years and Eurico Ferreira assisted in the making of *O Povo Organizado*, Courinha Ramos's affiliations were firmly with the colonial regime. The next film that he produced was Viriato Barret's *Moçambique, Documento vivo* (1975), which according to a description of the film in *Notícias*, 'ridiculed Samora Machel with the voice of Mickey Mouse' and included a defence of the Portuguese occupation of Mozambique by General Kaúlza de Arriaga, architect of the Gordian Knot offensive that was launched against Frelimo in 1970.[130]

In November 1975 Frelimo established a National Cinema Service so as to keep the cinemas in the cities running in the chaos that followed the mass departure of the Portuguese.[131] The National Cinema Service also supported the production of films that were sympathetic to Frelimo and would present the new government in a favourable light. The first films released by the Service were those made to document the transition to independence. They included Popović's films *Nachingwea* and *Do Rovuma ao Maputo* and Celso and Luccas's '25'. However, the service was only a temporary measure to fill the gap while a more substantial institution could be set up, one that would push forward transformations in the film industry in line with Frelimo's radical programme of decolonisation, nationalisation and redistribution.

The first Conferência Nacional de Departamento de Informação, held in Macomia from 26 to 30 November 1975, attempted to mark out Frelimo's ideological strategy in relation to its political aims for independence. The *Documentos* state:

[127] Ricardo Rangel (2002). *Illuminando Vidas: Ricardo Rangel and the Mozambican Photography*. Christoph Merian Verlag.

[128] Power (2004): 263.

[129] 'Mulheres desejam mudar de vida. Desferido golpe eficaz na prostituição e intermediários. Encerrados os cabarés da Rua Major Araújo'. *Notícias*, 10 June 1974. See the conclusion of the present volume for a discussion of Licínio Azevedo's *Virgim Margarida*, a fiction film based on the testimonies of some of these women.

[130] The Notícias article is cited in João Matos-Cruz (1981). O Cais do Olhar: Fonocinema português. Lisbon: Cinemateca Portuguesa: 151.

[131] See the interview with Margaret Dickinson, London, 2005.

> At the price of much blood, the liberated zones were taken in the face of colonialist aggression, establishing a new type of relations between men and serving as an experimental laboratory for the society we intend to construct.[132]

Resolutions laid out the various means through which the revolutionary process was to be communicated to the people so that the new kind of society begun in the liberated zones could be extended across the country and into the cities. The role of information and propaganda in the construction of this new power was defined at the conference as empowering 'the people' individually and collectively by building political consciousness about their 'rights and needs, the tasks that have to be realised, pride in their culture and personality, and awareness of their sovereignty'.[133]

The First National Conference further clarified Frelimo's objectives for cinema. At this stage, Jorge Rebelo, Mozambique's first Minister for Information who had edited the Frelimo journal *Mozambican Revolution* from Dar es Salaam, viewed film as secondary in effectiveness to the radio in its capacity to reach 'the masses' of Mozambicans who did not have access to the cinema.[134] However, the Resolution on Cinema, Books and Records highlights three fronts through which filmmaking and distribution would be transformed. First, it condemned 'the projection of films based on themes that negate the realities of Mozambicans, namely the exhibition of films that are pornographic, include gratuitous violence or markedly reactionary ideologies'.[135] Concerned that some foreign films had the effect of alienating Mozambican audiences from their own cultures, Frelimo saw its role as protecting people from films that were contrary to their values, and the discussions at the conference took no account of the possibility that films could be read against the grain of the director's intentions. Minutes to a meeting held on 12 November 1975 show Frelimo's concern about the quantity of films that had unacceptable levels of 'pornography and gratuitous violence' that had flooded into Mozambique from 1974, because of the lifting of censorship during the Carnation Revolution.[136] Frelimo announced that it would nationalise all channels of distribution into Mozambique and set up a Comissão de Exame e Classificação de Espectáculos to control exhibition and define 'rigorous criteria' for the classification of films. Second, it stated the necessity to create 'a truly Mozambican cinema', recommending the production

132 Frelimo (1975a): 3.
133 Frelimo (1975a): 11–12.
134 Interview with Jorge Rebelo, Maputo, 2005.
135 Frelimo (2005). *Documentos da Conferência Nacional do Departamento de Informação e Propaganda da FRELIMO*. Macomia, 26 to 30 November 1975.
136 'Acta de uma reunião onde se discutiram questões relacionadas com o cinema no período imediatament posterior à independência', 12 November 1975. Jorge Rebelo kindly provided a transcript of this document.

of films about the armed struggle, colonialism and 'the various phases of revolution in our country'.[137] This would involve the construction of systems of distribution that would take cinema to Mozambicans across the country, emphasising the importance of mobile cinemas for education in the collective villages, specifically though documentaries that would be commissioned by the Department of Information. Third, it addressed the need to set up film circuits with other socialist countries. As well as combating the neocolonisation of the cinema industry, this would give Mozambicans access to 'films that testify to the struggles of other Peoples of the World against oppression and exploitation, on the struggle of the working classes, films of a political, educational and informative nature, recreational but not in ways that mitigate against our cultural values and ideological principles'.[138]

Frelimo's idea of the role that cinema could play in independent Mozambique was based on the way in which film had been used during the armed struggle for the purposes of propaganda and mobilisation. Cinema fell under the aegis of the Ministry of Information, thus classifying film as a different category from literature, music and other arts that were the responsibility of the Ministry of Culture. However, the people that Rebelo called upon to devise a plan for a national institute of cinema were intellectuals, mostly from Lourenço Marques, who had been involved in the colonial ciné-clubs. Their cinephilia militated against a notion of film being limited to its use as a political tool. The group comprised Americo Soares, Luís Carlos Patraquim, Mota Lopes, Maria de Lourdes Torcato, Julius Kazembe, Maria Amelia and Luís Simão. Soares and the poet, playwright and journalist Patraquim had been involved in a left-wing group in Lourenço Marques and had fled to Sweden as refugees in 1973, only returning to Mozambique in 1975. Lopes and Torcato were journalists who worked for the newspaper *Notícias*; Kazembe, a poet. Maria Amelia worked for the film distributor Mundo Films; and Simão had been involved in the ciné-club of Nampula from 1970 to 1971.[139] Soares and Patraquim knew Torcato from their involvement with the Associação Nacional de Moçambique, which gathered white settlers who were democrats and pro-independence. The Associações were an important part of intellectual life in Lourenço Marques, and they included the Centro Associativo dos Negros, which was a group of assimilated black intellectuals, and the Associação Africana, which were another elite of mixed-race writers and journalists, such as the poet Noemia de Sousa. When the group met at the home of Americo Soares in 1975, the cinemas had already been nationalised and Jorge Rebelo gave them a *carte blanche* to organise the

[137] 'Resolução Sobre': 79.
[138] 'Resolução Sobre': 78–79.
[139] Conversation with Luís Simão, Maputo, August 2016.

Instituto National de Cinema as they saw fit.[140] Americo Soares had a vision of what the INC could be: they would take control of the management of distribution, and with the revenue they would build a Mozambican cinema that was more than propaganda. The films made at the INC would be in Portuguese to avoid privileging any particular ethnic grouping, and their aim would be to promote national unity, represent Mozambican realities and use mobile cinema units to take films beyond the confines of the cities so that it could reach all Mozambicans 'from the Rovuma to the Maputo'.[141]

In the two years spanning the fall of the fascist colonial regime in 1974 to the months following independence in 1975, the cinema screens in Mozambique were flooded with new kinds of images that expressed conflicting ideas about what freedom might mean. In the midst of the chaos of the transition, however, the films made with Frelimo show the emergence of a new cinematic figure – that of the Mozambican people in the process of liberating themselves through participation in the fields of agricultural production, education and healthcare. Films made with Frelimo at this moment tell new narratives of national becoming that presume a shared history of resistance to colonialism, in which the camp at Nachingwea and the experience of organising agriculture, cooperative trade and healthcare in liberated zones are presented as a blueprint that will be rolled out across the new nation. The topos of the city enters into films made with Frelimo as sites still structured by the colonial policies of segregation and a potential source of counter-revolutionary threat. For the first time, the Mozambican 'people' are depicted as a mass, joined in syncopated gestures of labour, in song, and united as they joyfully greet their new president, Samora Machel. While voiceover is often still used to convey a coherent argument about Frelimo's strategies and the challenges that the country faced, increasingly the cameras focused on Machel, whose powerful rhetoric is turned to the task of cajoling his audiences to recognise the crimes of colonialism and to identify themselves as proud Mozambicans. The powerful image of Samora Machel surging across the country 'from the Rovuma to the Maputo' is a symbol of Frelimo as a force of nature, suggesting certainty of victory and confidence that the Front had the correct strategies and an unquestionable legitimacy to govern.

Yet, as this chapter has explored, Frelimo in fact faced vast challenges at independence, with the threat of invasion by Rhodesia and South Africa, infrastructures in a state of ruin and the mass exodus of colonial administrators, technicians and traders. While the films made with Frelimo at independence suggest that Machel's reception by the people of Mozambique was uniformly rapturous, and indeed it is the case that they enjoyed broad support from wide sections of the population, the new government also met resistance

[140] Conversation with Maria de Lourdes Torcato, Maputo, 9 August 2016.
[141] Conversation with Maria de Lourdes Torcato, Maputo, 9 August 2016.

from within white settler communities, from African opposition movements and from within its own ranks. Frelimo set out to transform society not only through nationalisation and redistribution, but also by destroying both colonialist and tribalist mentalities that they saw as threatening to undermine their revolutionary project. In 1976 an article in *Tempo* reported that some 3,000 people had been sent to re-education camps, for crimes including theft, prostitution, smuggling and political dissent.[142] In this context, film had a crucial role to play in mobilisation and political education. Whatever the contradictions present in Mozambique at independence, the INC's mission was clear. Its task was to invent a revolutionary nationalist cinema for Mozambique, one that would reflect Mozambican realities and that would promote national unity through films in Portuguese. For the first time, the technology of film would make a universal address to all Mozambicans, uniting the people from the Rovuma to the Maputo.

[142] *Tempo*, 28 March 1976, cited in Henriksen (1978): 457.

3 Birth (of the Image) of a Nation: Delivering Cinema to the People, 1976–1978

On 4 March 1976, the Instituto Nacional de Cinema (INC) opened on 946 Avenida Agostinho Neto. In an interview in 2005, Manuel Malo recounted to me the story of how it was that he came to work for the INC some weeks later. Malo had been employed at the colonial production house owned by Antonio Melo Pereira, whose output prior to independence included the newsreel *Actualidades de Moçambique* 'news of Mozambique' and pornographic films destined for the South African market.[1] Malo recalled that:

> In the company where I worked . . . everything stopped when the coup happened in Portugal on 25 April 1974. . . . During that time the 'nationalisations' happened, in which abandoned businesses were taken. But in the case of Melo Pereira's laboratory, it hadn't been abandoned. He had only made a trip to Portugal when his laboratory and equipment was seized. I was the only Mozambican working for Melo Pereira's company, up until 1976. Before there had been a few other Mozambicans, but they were older than me and had been conscripted into the military. From 25 April, the only Mozambican working there was me. The others were three Portuguese, and they soon went back to Portugal because Melo Pereira said he didn't have the money to continue paying them whereas I received much less money. . . . So from 1974 to 1976 I kept hold of the key to the studios, and every day I went there, opened the doors, cleaned the equipment, and stayed there waiting. . . . Then one Monday morning when I arrived there was a man in a suit standing at the door. I had no idea who he was. I took the keys from my bag, went to open the door, but the man told me to wait, saying: 'Don't open the door.' I was astonished and asked him who he was, to which he replied: 'I have orders not to let anyone enter this building.' Finally he identified himself, saying he was from the Polícia de Investigação Criminal (PIC). . . . I collected the few personal things I had and he took the key, even though I was scared to hand it over to him. . . . I made my way to the Centro de Informação e Turismo, which paid for all the documentaries Melo Pereira made, to inform them what happened. . . . And so that was how the laboratory of Melo Pereira . . . fell

[1] Marcus Power (2004). 'Post-colonial Cinema and the Re-configuration of Moçambicanidade.' *Lusotopie*: 263.

> into the hands of the INC. He had known about the setting up of the INC, but I had no idea. After two weeks he packed his bags and he and his wife left for South Africa . . . he got onto the train with tears in his eyes, crying right in front of me. Shortly afterwards I presented myself at the INC and was given work there. I continued working at the INC, where the same machines I had worked on before had been transferred – to this very building.[2]

During the revolution, Malo rose from being the loyal under-paid servant of Melo Pereira to the position of Head of the Laboratory at the INC, which he continued to run, often in conditions of adversity, until 1991. He described to me how he and his fellow technicians worked day and night to process the INC's flagship production, the *Kuxa Kanema* newsreel, but were never mentioned by name on the credits of the film reels that travelled across the country. A combination of continued deference to his colonial master and consciousness of racial injustice, of dedication to his work at the INC and an awareness of its significance makes this an ambivalent testimony. In addition to the technology seized from the colonial production houses, countries of the Soviet bloc provided equipment, while other essential items were purchased, on some occasions by international *cooperantes* who could source certain items abroad. This process whereby technologies developed in the West were appropriated to the cause of decolonisation raised debates about how and in what forms cinema could make a social intervention. In the Mozambican Revolution, cinema expressed some of the most radical hopes of the new nation. It was the means through which new revolutionary subjectivities were actualised through technologies that were simultaneously new and nearly out of date.

The first few years of the INC were a time of experimentation with, and conflict over, what it might mean to decolonise and democratise filmmaking. This chapter considers how Frelimo's policies to shape a Mozambican revolutionary nationalist cinema were implemented, the effort to train up a new generation of Mozambican filmmakers and the impact of various foreign technicians and consultants. Class and race played out in arguments over political priorities and the allocation of resources, underpinning heated debates over what technologies and techniques were appropriate for a country going through a rapid and tumultuous process of decolonisation.

In this sense, Maputo was at the heart of debates that had been rumbling across the Tricontinental over what should constitute a revolutionary cinema. The conflict between striving for technological perfection and the emancipatory possibilities of other formats that were associated with amateur, artistic, ethnographic or militant film reflected debates that had begun at the Instituto Cubano del Arte e Industria Cinégraficos (ICAIC) in the late 1960s, when Julio

[2] Interview with Manuel Malo, Maputo, 18 May 2005.

García Espinosa, then director of ICAIC, published the essay 'For an Imperfect Cinema'.[3] Written at a time when ICAIC was within reach of Hollywood standards of technological perfection, Espinosa warned against taking this as an absolute measure of quality. The task was rather for filmmakers to work out how best to insert themselves into the revolutionary situation that was unfolding, with whatever means were available to them. The project of building a national cinema in Mozambique was thus also profoundly internationalist, and in dialogue with the most important discussions regarding militant filmmaking taking place around the world. The INC set out not only to promote a revolutionary agenda to the Mozambican people, but also to construct systems of acquisition, distribution and production and foster international collaboration in ways intended to challenge the capitalist structure of the film industry through regional solidarity and collaboration.

In Mozambique, the birth of the revolutionary state coincided with an attempt to build a national cinema that would reach a new mass audience with no prior experience of the moving image. Alongside the effort to collectivise film production and open up the profession to people who were cut off from the technology under colonialism, there was a concerted effort to take cinema to 'the people'. The possibility of engaging with audiences that had no previous experience of cinema intrigued a number of filmmakers who came to Mozambique in the late 1970s. One of the tropes of colonial 'first contact' narratives is a replaying of what Michael Taussig calls the 'shock waves of surprise' when audiences experience mechanical reproduction for the first time, a kind of 'magic' that was repeatedly reanimated 'in frontier rituals of technological supremacy'.[4] If the colonial situation is about this moment of power, the Mozambican Revolution produced opportunities for foreign filmmakers to relinquish this technological superiority through pedagogy, empowering a newly independent people by handing over the means of production. The Carnation Revolution in Portugal had unleashed a desire among radical filmmakers to bring cinema and filmmaking to the impoverished rural populations who had been cut off from modernity through the neglect of the Salazar regime.[5] A number of filmmakers who had been involved in projects such as these came to Mozambique after independence and were interested, once again, in placing filmmaking into situations of radical change. Tensions emerged between the film's ethnographic capacity to capture scenes of everyday

[3] Julio García Espinosa, translated by Julianne Burton (1979). 'For an Imperfect Cinema'. *Jump Cut*, 20: 24–26.

[4] Michael Taussig (1993). *Mimesis and Alterity: A Particular History of the Senses*. New York: Routledge: 207–208.

[5] See José Filipe Costa (2002). *O Cinema ao Poder: a revolução do 25 de Abril e as políticas de cinema entre 1974–1976: os grupos, instituições, experiências e projectos*. Lisbon: Hugin.

life, replete with contradictions and unscripted elements, and the imperative to use cinema to promote a clear political line defined by Frelimo.

Projects conceived in Mozambique during these years sought to experiment with how to democratise production and exhibition of the moving image so that it could make an intervention in the process of radical decolonisation and revolution, though not always in ways that Frelimo was open to. Crucial to these projects was an awareness of the impact and importance to people of seeing images they could identify with on the cinema screen. While the INC was the centre of film production nationally, Eduardo Mondlane University was also a pivotal site for experimentation with different film formats and production methods. As well as the question of *how* and *by what means* films should contribute to the Mozambican Revolution, these more marginal experiments also reflected key questions being addressed at the INC about *who* should be empowered to make films. This chapter examines to what extent and by what means filmmaking was transformed by ambitions to decolonise the film industry and create an image of change.

In 1975 Jorge Rebelo had tasked a small circle of cinephiles associated with the ciné-clubs to devise a plan for setting up the INC (see Chapter 2), and in 1976 Americo Soares was appointed as director. The INC was housed in a building that was converted from its previous use as a restaurant by the architect José Forjaz, and it was here that the filmmaker and technician Eurico Ferreira installed the INC's first equipment for processing 35mm and 16mm films.[6] The renovation of this building for the INC was part of sweeping changes taking place across the capital. Forjaz had been appointed to direct Frelimo's effort to redistribute private properties that had been abandoned by departing Portuguese settlers and to rename streets and buildings. Under colonial rule street names in Lourenço Marques were chosen to consolidate foreign domination, imposing on the Mozambican people the values, history and culture of the Portuguese colonisers. With its ascent to power, Frelimo decreed new names that were intended to 'reflect the values and traditions of the new Mozambican society'.[7] The city was remapped with liberation movements, socialist heroes and moments of revolutionary victory. Avenida 24 de Julho, Eduardo Mondlane, Salvadore Allende, Amílcar Cabral, Ho Chi Minh, Vladimir Lenin, Karl Marx, Praça da Independência – the names marked the city as the space of revolution. In 1976 all rented property was nationalised, and this was the single event that most transformed the racial demographics of the city, dismantling the segregation

[6] Guido Convents (2011). *Os Moçambicanos Perante o Cinema e o Audiovisual: Uma História Politico-cultural do Moçambique Colonial até à República de Moçambique (1896–2010)*. Maputo: CP: 437.

[7] 'Maputo: Alterada a Toponímia'. *Tempo*, 306, 1976: 4.

imposed through colonialism.[8] Businesses abandoned by their Portuguese owners that were seized and nationalised included the colonial film production houses, complete with their archives and equipment. By 1978, the forty-two cinemas in Mozambique's cities, which had been maintained as the preserve of the settler elite by Manuel Rodrigues and his family (see Chapter 2), were taken into the hands of the state.

The INC eventually comprised a few editing suites, a sound mixing studio, a projection space, an archive for Mozambican productions and another for international films, and a laboratory for developing black and white film. Urgent tasks in the INC's first years were to organise and plan a national film service to manage the cinemas that had been abandoned by Portuguese owners, to set up a national distribution service and to develop a production unit. The national distribution service involved establishing delegations in the different provinces of Mozambique. From 1976 to 1978, José Cardoso, as Director of the INC 'delegation' in Beira, managed film distribution to the cinemas and trained up projectionists. In an interview with me in 2016, Laura Cardoso described how she and her husband started what she called a 'cinema school' in Beira, which involved projections of films translated into local languages, indicating the enthusiasm with which the cinephiles and amateur filmmakers of the ciné-clubs set about the task of making film more widely available.[9] Camilo de Sousa, who had been a political refugee in Sweden before joining Frelimo in Tanzania and training as an explosives expert during the armed struggle, was employed by the Department of Information and Propaganda in the northern province of Cabo Delgado to organise film distribution orientated towards political mobilisation.[10] In 1978, Luísa Lourenço was made responsible for training projectionists at the INC in Maputo, developing a programme along the lines that Cardoso had in Beira.[11] José Passe was one of the projectionists who took film reels, a projector and a generator to rural areas, at first sometimes having to take the train or hitch a lift.[12] Eventually the INC built up a fleet of mobile cinema units so that by 1978/1979,

[8] Property was restricted to no more than one house or apartment in the city and another in the countryside for every family. All other houses released in this process were handed over to the Administração do Parque Imobiliário do Estado (APIE), which was the organisation set up to re-allocate and manage state buildings so that Mozambicans of all origins could occupy the vacated dwellings.

[9] Conversation with Laura Cardoso, Maputo, 7 August 2016.

[10] José Luís Cabaço (2016). 'Ruy Guerra num Breve Panorama do Cinema Moçambicano no Seculo XX'. La Furia Umana. Available http://www.lafuriaumana.it/index.php/63-archive/lfu-30/662-jose-luis-cabaco-ruy-guerra-num-breve-panorama-do-cinema-mocambicano-no-seculo-xx.

[11] Convents (2011): 424.

[12] Teresa Sá Nogueira (1986). 'Cinema Moçambicano (VI) Cinema Móvel'. *Tempo*, 17 August: 48.

when the department for Mobile Cinema received ten vans from the Soviet Union and a vehicle from East Germany, they had a total of thirty-five vehicles.[13]

In the wake of independence, Frelimo faced an acute shortage of skilled workers and managers across all sectors of the economy, due to the mass departure of Portuguese settlers.[14] While the INC had managed to recruit some ciné-club members and employees of the colonial production houses who were sympathetic to Frelimo, their numbers were inadequate to the task ahead. Rebelo first turned for assistance to allies who had assisted Frelimo during the armed struggle. In 1976, the government of Yugoslavia sent a film crew that included Popović and Zdravković to Mozambique on a 'consultancy mission' for a period of several months. Correspondence between Rebelo and Sima Karaglanović, the general manager of Filmske Novosti, reveals that his delegation visited the INC building on 30 June 1976 to inspect the building works and installation of equipment. Karaglanović advised Rebelo to put in a request to the Yugoslav government for funding to send a film crew to work at the INC for a period of two years, suggesting that they would produce regular newsreels, information films, documentary films and film documents for later use, and that part of their remit would be to train up Mozambican filmmakers.[15] He recommended that while black-and-white film could be processed and finalised in Maputo, if the film crew were to shoot in colour, this could only be done with Kodak colour negative, which would have to be processed in Belgrade.[16] However, by 1976 Yugoslav assistance to Frelimo in the area of film production had repeatedly pushed Filmske Novosti over its budget. These financial constraints meant that the INC was forced to look to other allies to get its operations off the ground.[17]

13 Convents (2011): 424.

14 Most of the minority Chinese and Indian populations also left at independence, resulting in the collapse of the country's trade network as they had owned many of the small trading businesses, which family farms depended on for getting their produce to market.

15 The letter recommends that the 'experts' should include a director/editor, one or two camera operators, chief of lab (light grading expert), one picture and music editor and a sound engineer. It also insists that 'a must for immediate production and training' is 'one editing table for 35 and 16mm films, 6 plates made by Officine Prevost', 'one editing table for 35 and 16mm films with 4 plates', 'one NAGRA taperecorder', 'one synchronizer for Nagra', and 'lighting equipment (at least 4 Bolex Lites with stands of 2KW)'. Letter to Jorge Rebelo, Minister of Information, from Sima Karaoglanović, General Manager, Filmske Novosti, Maputo, 2 July 1976. Archive of Filmske Novosti, Begrade, Yugoslavia.

16 Letter to Jorge Rebelo (1976).

17 Notes from a meeting on 27 January 1976 at Savezni Zavod za Medjunardonu Naućnu, Prosvetno-Kulturnu (Allied Institute for International Scientific, Education-Cultural and Technical Co-operation). Present were: head of the Savezni Zavod, head of Filmske Novosti Sima Karaoglanović, SSIP The Department for International Affairs (responsible for film distribution), and representatives from government departments. Filmske Novosti archive, Belgrade.

While the INC received delegations of filmmakers from other socialist countries such as Cuba and North Korea in the 1970s and 1980s, the most sustained involvement in setting up the organisation came in the form of foreign development workers who were known as *cooperantes*. These individuals were sought out for their professional skills, though it was also important that they had a political commitment to the revolutionary project.[18] The *cooperantes* who came to work at the INC for periods of one to two years at a time brought knowledge and experience that had considerable impact on the organisation. *Cooperantes* received a modest salary from the Mozambican government that allowed them to live in relative comfort in the centre of Maputo.

Margaret Dickinson, who made the film *Behind the Lines* during the armed struggle (see Chapter 1), was one of the first foreign filmmakers to be invited to work as a *cooperante* at the INC. As she was committed elsewhere until the following year, Dickinson recommended the filmmaker, theorist and activist Simon Hartog.[19] Hartog was a significant figure in the London experimental film scene, his work straddling both alternative cinema and mainstream television broadcasting. He was one of the founders of the London Film Co-op, which was the main association for underground and artist-filmmakers, and he also worked on the BBC's flagship current affairs programme *Panorama*. One of his *Panorama* programmes reported on the events of May 1968 in Paris, and Hartog followed with interest the setting up of the États Généraux du Cinéma by activist filmmakers to think through how to organise a national film industry that would challenge the 'colonisation' of French cinema screens by American films.[20] This metaphor of colonisation created a conduit for First World filmmakers resisting American capitalist hegemony to identify with Third World filmmakers who were struggling against imperialism, which opened up opportunities for learning from each other's strategies and experiences. Calls to nationalise the film industry were also stirring in the United Kingdom, as the Association of Cinematograph, Television and Allied Technicians (ACTT),

[18] ANC activist Nadja Manghezi recalls that during the late 1970s 'Maputo was full of *cooperantes*, the internationalists who had come to show their solidarity with the anti-colonial struggle and help Frelimo achieve its socialist goals. They were dedicated to the cause and had given up their own aspirations at home, for some years at least. They loved all that Frelimo stood for and hated everything that stood in the way of development and freedom.' Nadja Manghezi (2009). *The Maputo Connection: ANC Life in the World of Frelimo*. Jacana: 124.

[19] Margaret Dickinson (2011). 'Flashbacks from a Continuing Struggle', in Kodwo Eshun and Ros Gray (2011). 'The Militant Image: A Ciné-geography'. *Third Text*, 108, 25, 1: 133.

[20] Simon Hartog (1972). 'Les États Généraux du Cinéma: The Nationalisation of the Cinema'. *Cinema Rising*, 1, reprinted in Margaret Dickinson (1999). *Rogue Reels: Oppositional Film in Britain 1945–90*. London: British Film Institute; Dickinson (2011): 133: 109.

the filmmakers' and broadcasters' trade union, responded to the dominance of American studios. In 1971 Hartog was commissioned to write a report exploring the possibilities for nationalising the British film industry. Published in 1973 under the title *Nationalising the Film Industry*, the ACTT report drew on the debates in Paris that he had observed in 1968.[21]

Another formative experience came in 1973, when Hartog attended the Meeting of Third World Filmmakers in Algiers.[22] This gathering drew seminal anti-colonial filmmakers including the Senegalese Ousmane Sembene, the Mauritanian Med Hondo, Flora Gomes from Guinea-Bissau, who had recently returned from training as a filmmaker in Cuba, and Cuban Santiago Álvarez. It articulated a set of ambitions to decolonise cinema and define liberationist aesthetics and modes of practice.[23] Filmmakers debated how to construct cinema industries that would produce films that reflected the realities of Third World peoples' lives, supported by the framework of the revolutionary nation-state and autonomous from the film distribution networks that were dominated by American corporations. In this context, delegates looked beyond the debates of the États Généraux du Cinéma to existing national film institutes from the socialist Third World, such as those of Cuba and Algeria.

Hartog's focus on 16mm film production rather than 35mm was not his only contribution to the INC. He also assisted Americo Soares in devising a new system of acquisition and distribution. Instead of renting films from distributors, the INC set out to build an archive of world cinema by negotiating the rights to buy copies of films outright. Cinema ticket receipts were then ploughed back into the INC to fund filmmaking, making the relationship between consumption and production reciprocal, and the film copies were added to the INC's international archive. Initially, the INC relied heavily on material donated by the Soviet Union and other countries in the Eastern Bloc in an effort to gain autonomy from Portuguese distributors who claimed they had no choice but to provide the Mozambican cinema circuit with Motion Picture Export Association (MPEA) titles. The INC objected to this as it would have meant paying royalties for films that were considered not suitable by the Comissão de Exame e Classificação de Espectáculos (CECE).

The CECE answered to the Ministry of Information and had two main objectives, which had been defined at the First National Conference of the Department of Information and Propaganda of Frelimo held in 1975 (see

[21] Simon Hartog (1973). *Nationalising the Film Industry*. London: ACTT Publications.

[22] Hartog is listed in the 'Resolutions of the Third World Filmmakers Meeting in Algiers, 1973' as an observer representing the British Filmmakers' Union. Teshome Gabriel (1982). *Third Cinema in the Third World: The Aesthetics of Liberation*. Ann Arbor: UMI Research Press: 107.

[23] Gabriel (1982).

Chapter 2). This meeting condemned films 'based on themes that negate the realities of Mozambicans' and insisted that cinema should promote the 'cultural values and ideological principles' of Frelimo.[24] Frelimo was in part responding to the influx of films they deemed to be pornographic during the transition period, which included hard-core pornography as well as films of artistic significance that had some explicit sexual content. However, it was also intent on harnessing the power of the moving image to the task of ideological work – to assert the legitimacy of Frelimo to govern the country and to instruct audiences on how to participate correctly in its revolutionary project. Creating the 'New Man' and 'New Woman' of the Mozambican Revolution meant not only destroying tribal loyalties and obscurantist practices, but also challenging the reactionary and racist imperialism promoted in many Hollywood films.

In May 1977, an INC delegation comprising Americo Soares, Simon Hartog and Luís Simão met with the MPEA in London. The MPEA executives made it clear to them that the market for film distribution in the former Portuguese territories was so small that dealing directly with Mozambique 'would not suffice to pay for our cigars'.[25] Pedro Pimenta recounted to me that this situation forced the acquisition department to acquire American titles from the independent sector, which meant that some seminal works, such as Barbara Kopple's *Harlan County USA* (1976), Charles Burnett's *Killer of Sheep* (1978) and Haile Gerima's *Harvest: 3000 Years* (1976), were projected in Mozambique.[26] In addition, through the late 1970s INC staff in acquisition, including Pimenta, Torcato and Hartog, travelled widely to festivals abroad to procure films to put before the CECE. Eventually, the INC learnt that the MPEA had 'authorised' Portuguese distributors to select films for distribution in Mozambique, and thereafter, once a year Pimenta would travel to Lisbon to review a pre-selected list of Hollywood films for Mozambique, which included fiction features that depicted the souring of the American dream, such as Martin Scorsese's *Taxi Driver* (1976) and Francis Ford Coppola's *Apocalypse Now* (1979). Only a limited number of such films were shown in Mozambique due to budgetary constraints.

While initially the predominance of Soviet propaganda films led to a slump in cinema-going, in the years that followed films from socialist countries of the Eastern Bloc continued to feature prominently. These were shown alongside special film seasons that demonstrate the INC's alignment with liberationist films that were then emerging across the African continent and the Third

24 'Resolução Sobre o Cinema, o Livro e o Disco', in Frelimo (2005). *Documentos da Conferência Nacional do Departamento de Informação e Propaganda da FRELIMO*. Macomia, 26 to 30 November 1975: 79.

25 Email correspondence with Pedro Pimenta, 1 April 2019.

26 Email correspondence with Pedro Pimenta, 1 April 2019.

World.[27] In 1976 the INC programmed its first festival of Cuban cinema with films supplied by a delegation of filmmakers from the ICAIC led by Santiago Álvarez. While in Maputo, Álvarez made the film *Maputo: Meridiano novo* 'New Meridian' (1976), which used archive footage to tell the story of the armed struggle and its culmination in the proclamation of independence. This was one of a series of films that Álvarez directed between 1975 and 1978 that address Cuban internationalism and solidarity with Africa and the first of two that he would make in Mozambique.[28] The visit from the ICAIC delegation to the INC thus had geopolitical significance. On 7 November 1975, just days before Angola's declaration of independence on 11 November, Cuban forces had launched Operation Carlota, a massive military campaign to defend the Movimento Popular de Libertação de Angola 'People's Movement for the Liberation of Angola' (MPLA) government from South African troops that were marching on Luanda. In his speech announcing Operation Carlota to the Cuban Communist Party Congress, Fidel Castro made a series of claims about Cuba's African heritage that marked a new departure for Cuban internationalism, recentring the nation's revolutionary identity around the island's African heritage to justify military intervention on an unprecedented scale.[29] In support of this re-orientation of Cuban foreign policy, the ICAIC produced a number of films in the mid- to late 1970s dedicated to Cuban solidarity with the newly independent nations of Angola, Guinea-Bissau and Mozambique.[30] While most of these documentaries, unsurprisingly, focused on Angola, the visit of the delegation of ICAIC filmmakers enabled Álvarez and his team to make a film that would, in the words of crewmember Rebecca Chávez, 'provoke a genuine emotion and identification with the people of Mozambique'.[31] The 'meridian' of

[27] Guido Convents reports that three-quarters of the films projected in Mozambique between 1975 and 1981 were from the Soviet Union, Bulgaria, Yugoslavia, Poland, East Germany and Cuba. Convents (2011).

[28] Ros Gray (2017). 'Clear Lines on an Internationalist Map: Foreign Filmmakers in Angola at Independence', in Maria do Carmo Piçarra and Teresa Castro (eds) (2017). *(Re)imagining African Independence: Film, Visual Arts and the Fall of the Portuguese Empire*. London: Peter Lang: 71–73.

[29] The day 7 November marked the 132nd anniversary of the slave rebellion on the Triumvirato sugar plantation in Cuba, which was led by an enslaved woman named Carlota. The military operation in Angola named after her thus evoked both a spirit of insurrection that was claimed for Cuban nationalism and an idea of solidarity and sacrifice. Gray (2017): 70–71.

[30] *Luanda ya no es de San Pablo* 'Luanda Doesn't Belong to Saint Paul Anymore' (1976), directed by Santiago Álvarez; *Angola: Victoria de Esperanza* 'Angola: Victory of Hope' (1976), directed by José Massip; *Cabinda* (1977), directed by Fernando Pérez; and *Guerra en Angola* 'War in Angola' (1978), directed by Miguel Fleitas. Gray (2017): 69–76.

[31] Rebecca Chavez (1978). 'El internacionalismo en la obra de Santiago Álvarez', *Cine Cubano*, 91–92: 129.

the film's title not only refers to geographical measurement, but is also extended to indicate a realignment of the axes of anti-capitalist, socialist struggle. In her *Cine Cubano* article Chávez commented on *Maputo: Meridiano novo* that 'the structuring of information allows not only an approach to a changing reality, but also warns of the fascist dangers in other latitudes,' the other latitudes referring to the axis of white minority regimes that constituted a threat to Mozambican sovereignty and its revolution.[32] *Maputo: Meridiano novo* combines archival material with footage taken on the streets of Maputo by ICAIC cinematographer Julia Simoneau, and the tension between these elements is accentuated through inventive use of colour tints and extra-diegetic music that together suggest that the challenges facing Frelimo not only are external threats to the nation, but rather include the persisting contradictions that are the legacy of colonialism.

Meridiano novo opens with images of the official ceremony of independence on the night of 25 June, but this is followed by footage taken at dawn in the centre of Maputo in a section titled '*Maputo Moderno*' 'Modern Maputo'. The tall concrete buildings, cars, neon lights, a Christian church and statues of Portuguese explorers still standing in the European city centre even after the official announcement of independence present a stark contrast to the '*Maputo do Tereiro Mundo*' 'Maputo of the Third World', depicted through images of people living in the *cidade de caniço*, which lack basic infrastructures such as pavements. This contradiction is further underlined through the disjuncture between the images and the soundtrack. Accompanying the images of the city centre is a jazz version of the musical theme of Stanley Kubrick's *2001: Space Odyssey* (1968), composed by Alex North. While Kubrick's film juxtaposes a future space age with prehistoric scenes, *Maputo: Meridiano novo* contrasts the 'ultramodernity' of colonial city centre with the poverty of the *bairros*, an obscene segregation that persists in independent Mozambique. By contrast, the Samba that accompanies the images of the 'Maputo of the Third World' is a musical genre created mainly by black inhabitants of the peripheries of Rio de Janeiro, these sounds from elsewhere creating another axis of identification – a new latitude of solidarity constituted through sound and image.

Colour also plays a crucial role in the way in which the film structures its disparate elements, chromatic differences indicating conflicting ideologies and historical moments, or alternatively creating a connection between different times and places. Thus, for example, images tinted green of Samora Machel in civilian clothes addressing a mass rally are juxtaposed with scenes with the same tonal hue from the liberated zones in which he addresses Frelimo guerrillas, underlining the genesis of independent Mozambique in the armed struggle, during which the correct revolutionary line was identified and confirmed. By

[32] Chavez (1978): 128–129.

contrast, archival images in the film that are tinted yellow catalogue abuses of segregation in Southern Africa, as documented by the international press. This section connects the South African tourist industry, which during Portuguese rule exploited Mozambique as a destination for sex tourism, with the exploitation of Mozambican labour and natural resources. Indeed, a highly ironic shot of the publication *The Banker* focuses on an article titled 'South Africa: a survey'; it introduces the film's own survey of the white capitalism of Apartheid. Scenes of people boarding a crowded train at the Ressano Garcia train station in Maputo, the customs at the border, the Cahora Basa dam built by the Portuguese to supply South Africa with electricity, along with images of gold and diamonds juxtaposed with young black children, reference the flows of people and resources out of Mozambique to feed South African dominance in the region.

The final section of *Maputo: Meridiano novo* is notable for its focus on the figure of Josina Machel as an exemplary revolutionary icon. The film concludes with footage shot in the streets of Maputo that follows a group of women wearing headscarves and *capulanas*, some carrying babies, one eating an ice cream. This relaxed scene of everyday life cuts to an image of Josina Machel in uniform, carrying a gun. The contrast makes a revolutionary demand: to confront the social inequalities that persist in independent Mozambique and the ongoing threats from South Africa and Rhodesia with the same revolutionary determination that drove the armed struggle.

In addition to the programme of Cuban films, a festival of African films was organised in 1977, and there were regular screenings of Algerian, Bulgarian, Romanian, Italian and Soviet films in the late 1970s and early 1980s. Maria de Lourdes Torcato explained to me that the primary aim of the acquisition team was to buy the rights to films that appealed intellectually, aesthetically and politically.[33] However, they also tried to source films that had mass appeal by tapping into local tastes for specific genres, catering to the demand for the rural romances of Indian musicals and the action sequences of kung fu and karate films, which had always been more popular in Mozambique than the Westerns.[34] During the Mozambican Revolution there was an effort by intellectuals to understand the appeal of certain forms of popular culture. An article in *Tempo* by Sol de Carvalho, for instance, seeks to understand the huge popularity of kung fu films to the *lumpenproletariat*, suggesting that Mozambicans identified with the non-Western hero who fights off his enemies with his hands rather than with guns, kung fu being a skill that, in

[33] Interview with Maria de Lourdes Tocato, Maputo, 2005.

[34] This was not the case in other African countries. For instance, the Western genre has a long history of popularity in Burkina Faso, to the extent that it has become a theme in contemporary films.

theory, anyone can learn.[35] As Vijay Prashad argues, it is clear that such cinematic identifications, involving Afro–Asian exchange of symbols and narratives of resistance, are emancipatory in that they bypass both Western models and dogmas of cultural purity.[36] The INC also sought to educate audiences through debates at screenings, critical literature and the library known as the Serviço de Documentação, which was set up in the INC building by Pedro Pimenta.[37] Thus certain currents of cinephilia at the INC enabled cinematic pleasure to extend beyond Frelimo's narrower understanding of the usefulness of film for the purposes of propaganda.

The INC also opened the possibility of Mozambique becoming a key site for film production in southern Africa, as well as building on links with socialist countries and networks across a South–South axis, particularly with Cuba and Brazil. Maputo attracted filmmakers involved in decolonising the field of the moving image across the African continent, including Med Hondo, who had attended the Meeting of Third World Filmmakers and visited the INC in 1976.[38] What distinguished the politics of the screen emanating from Maputo, however, was the extent of its ambition and that its project of decolonisation was seen as viable because it had the backing of the Mozambican state.[39] The Conferência Africana de Cooperação Cinematográfica, held in Maputo between 21 and 24 February 1977, was a crucial moment in the crystallisation of hopes to create regional infrastructures through which to break dependency and challenge the economic and cultural hegemony of the West. The conference launched the Associação Africana de Cooperação Cinematográfica (AACC), which was the first attempt to re-organise the cinema industry at governmental level between multilingual African nation-states.[40] The speech by Jorge Rebelo that opened the conference laid out a vision of how this constituted a 'new front of combat against imperialism'.[41] The battle for the 'cultural liberation of Africa' was not

[35] Sol de Carvalho (1980). 'Cinema Kung-Fu: Violência gratuita ou Ideologia da violênia?' *Tempo* dossier, 2 November: 21–33.

[36] Vijay Prashad (2002). *Everybody was Kung-Fu Fighting: Afro-Asian Connections and the Myth of Cultural Purity*. Boston: Beacon Press.

[37] Interview with Pedro Pimenta, Johannesburg, 2005.

[38] Articles about Hondo appeared in *Tempo*. See 'Abid Hondo: Fazer com si um cinema descolonizado "Cinema de Luta"'. *Tempo*, 316, 1976: 58–59.

[39] Some years later in Burkina Faso, when Thomas Sankara came to power in 1983, there was a similar overlap of gatherings and organisations of filmmakers concerned with developing revolutionary cinema and a political leadership eager to support them. See Chapter 6 in Ros Gray (2007). 'Ambitions of Cinema: Revolution, Event, Screen', PhD Thesis, University of London.

[40] Present at the Conference were delegations from Tanzania, Zambia, Congo, Guinea, Madagascar, Angola, Guinea-Bissau, Cabo Verde, S. Tomé and Príncipe.

[41] Speech by Jorge Rebelo at the Conferência Africana de Cooperação Cinematográfica, 21 February 1977. Reprinted in *Retrospectiva do Cinema Moçambicana*, Instituto Nacional de Cinema, Maputo, June 1982.

merely a question of aesthetics, as in the 'reactionary ideology' of *Negritude*, but demanded the creation of political and economic spheres autonomous from those structured by neocolonialism:

> Our objectives are not only, therefore, to combat and neutralise the enemy cinema in our countries. They are also to produce, exhibit and develop truly revolutionary cinema, a cinema that participates and is capable of pushing forward revolutionary transformation. In order to do this, we must establish a gradual rupture with economic and technological dependency in the sectors of production, distribution and cinema exhibition. The combat on this front is even more decisive when the cinema that dominates our countries, as still is the case in most of the world, is that which is directly controlled by a complex network of international monopolies.[42]

The AACC would be open to all African countries and would seek to cooperate with other organisations with the same objectives, calling on all member states to follow Guinea-Conakry in nationalising their cinema industries and aligning itself with the Organisation of African Unity (OAU).[43] However, this primary

[42] 'Os nossos objectivos não são apenas, portanto, o de combatermos e neutralizarmos o cinema inimigo nos nossos países. São também os de produzirmos, exibirmos e desenvolvermos o cinema verdadeiramente revolucionário. Para isto teremos que estabelecer uma ruptura gradual com a dependência económica e tecnológica nos sectores da produção, distribução e exibição cinematográficas. O combate nesta frente é tanto mais decisivo quanto o cinema dominante nos nossos países, como ainda na maior parte do mundo, é aquele que se encontra directamente controlado pela complexa rede dos monopólios internacionais'. Speech by Jorge Rebelo at the Conferência Africana de Cooperação Cinematográfica, 21 February 1977.

[43] Specifically, the Conference resolved that the AACC would: (1) decide on common policies with regard to production, acquisition, importation and distribution of films; (2) establish a film import and distribution community, embracing all the cinema circuits of member states; (3) coordinate the development of cinema production and contribute to its promotion, build up or develop basic infrastructures, promote the distribution and exhibition of films produced or co-produced by member states within and beyond the Association; (4) initiate, encourage and support activities involving the development of consciousness about the political function of the culture of the people through cinema, within and between member states, without prejudice towards the initiatives of respective national cinema organisations; (5) assure the training and employment of technicians; (6) cooperate with, participate in, or become members of other international organisations with the same or similar objectives; (7) establish a fund for the realisation of these objectives. Immediate tasks included securing ratification for these plans by each member government, setting up financial and organisational plans and protocols, and establishing regional bases for the Association. The Acting Secretary also declared the AACC's intention to make a study of the possibilities for translating films into different languages; preserve copies of films in a regional archive to ensure accessibility between member states; set up an itinerant film festival that would focus on films by member states and publish a trimestral bulletin to provide information on the AACC's activities. 'Conferência Africana de Cooperação Cinematográfica'. *Tempo*, 335: 63–64.

objective of displacing foreign distribution monopolies by regional intra-African distribution circuits failed due to lack of political commitment by many of the participating countries. Later collaborations with Angola, Zimbabwe and Tanzania in the field of film production were more successful (see Chapter 5). These built on Frelimo's alliances with other liberation movements during the armed struggle and the need to form a united front against white supremacy in the region.

No less urgent than the acquisition of foreign films and the administration of distribution was the production of films in Mozambique that would, in the words of the INC's slogan, 'deliver to the people an image of the people'. As decreed in the Resolutions on the Cinema, Books and Records, the INC's task was to create a 'truly Mozambican cinema' that would feature films about the armed struggle, colonialism and 'the various states of revolution in our country.'[44] This national cinema was intended to support the emergence of a new subjectivity produced through participation in the Mozambican Revolution. During the armed struggle the desired revolutionary subjectivity, the 'New Man' or 'New Woman' of the Mozambican Revolution, had been constructed around the figure of the guerrilla as a model of disciplined militancy. In Frelimo's discourse, the term '*o Povo*' referred to the peasantry, who in the films about the armed struggle are presented as the beneficiaries of, and willing participants in, Frelimo's effort to organise a new society in the liberated zones (see Chapter 1). During the transition to independence, *o Povo* initially took cinematic form in the vast crowds of people who flocked to welcome Samora Machel in *Do Rovuma ao Maputo*. *O Povo* is more differentiated in *O Povo Organizado*, following closely Frelimo's analysis of class in which rural populations are seen as having greater revolutionary potential than city-dwellers, understood to be corrupted by colonial mentalities. The figure of *o Povo* is more ambivalent in '25', where it takes on a cosmic resonance that threatens to detach itself from Frelimo's instrumentalist agenda (see Chapter 2). By the time the INC was established in 1976, the roles that cinema would play in the Mozambican Revolution were beginning to be defined. Certain social groups were still more closely associated with *O Povo*, but the term also operated as an invitation to identify with the national collective – the masses that the leadership sought to enthral through charismatic appeal. Along with the figures of the 'New Man' and the 'New Woman', the term '*o Povo*' acted an interpellation aimed at every individual, maintaining a state of vigilance about whether they were participating in the Mozambican Revolution in the correct way. Beyond this, however, what emerged in these early years of the Mozambican Revolution on the cinema screens are images and sounds of a people engaged in a process of

[44] 'Resolução Sobre o Cinema, o Livro e o Disco': 79.

liberation and national development. This new political constituency faced an image of itself for the first time and formed an identity as a people through their own cinematic image.

An urgent question facing the INC was not only *how* the films of this 'truly Mozambican cinema' would 'deliver to the people an image of the people', but *who* would make them. This was a question that potentially had profound consequences for the task of dismantling colonial hierarchies that existed within the film industry and across Mozambique. The INC's first film made by a Mozambican filmmaker was Fernando Silva's *Ano 1 da Independência* 'Year 1 of Independence' (1976), which documented the key events of the first year of the new nation. Fernando Silva had started making films as a teenager in Lourenço Marques using an 8mm camera, and he was one of the few who had worked in the colonial film production houses that had stayed opened after independence.[45] These production houses, which included Somar Filmes, where Silva worked, were small-scale operations. Not only were the staff that remained after independence too few to meet the needs of building a new national cinema, but those who had professional skills in filmmaking were white. Under colonial rule, the black Mozambicans who had managed to secure work in the film industry were confined to menial roles.

In 1976 Americo Soares and Simon Hartog planned a training programme for production staff and, with the help of the first director of production, Polly Gaster, they purchased equipment and recruited students. Gaster received instructions from the Ministry of Information that the students for this programme should be 'the children of workers and peasants'.[46] In fact, the trainees were for the most part the children of the urban lower-middle class, though their number included young people who had been involved in the armed struggle, such as the young women Lídia Muianga, Antonia Machado and Clara Macia. Nevertheless, the decision to recruit young black Mozambicans signalled a desire to break from the colonial past and address the forms of segregation that persisted in terms of education and professional skills. That same year, a group of young Mozambicans who were still at school were selected through the Ministry of Labour for training in different aspects of filmmaking. This 'opportunity' involved a certain degree of compulsion. Being 'picked out' at a time when Rhodesian forces were attacking Mozambique was for some a source of huge anxiety. In an interview with me in 2005 Gabriel Mondlane, who became Mozambique's leading sound engineer, recalled:

> At that time we were all so involved in what was going on that there was this feeling that if there was any kind of situation . . . we might be conscripted . . .

[45] Convents (2011): 437.
[46] Conversation with Polly Gaster, Maputo, September 2010.

> Mozambique was then at war with Rhodesia and at the same time there was the possibility of some Mozambicans going to study in Cuba and East Germany . . . On this particular day I was at school having my normal lessons with the teacher, when three people came into the class. They asked the teacher to show them the book with our marks, and all the students' reports . . . They made me and some of my classmates stand up, they looked at us, but they didn't even ask any questions . . . We didn't know what was going to happen. In fact that was terrible to think about – we thought we were going to be sent to the army . . . The people came back and said to a few of us: 'You're not coming to school from tomorrow, bring your pen and go to the Ministry of Labour.' Just that – no more details . . . So we went to the Ministry the following day, though one boy didn't come. I think he ran away because he was way too scared . . . but I was eager to know why we'd been called there. . . . We were given puzzles and tests . . . I passed through various stages . . . When those of us who were left got to the last stage we were told: 'You're going to work in cinema'. I didn't really understand what that meant . . . Previously when I had tried to go to the cinema with my friends the ushers would throw us out . . . But in those days, when you were told you had to go because there was no way to escape. What could I do? It was the time of revolution, and people had to occupy their assigned roles. Finally, we were brought to the INC. We weren't asked what we wanted to do . . . but I was sent to the sound department . . . Later on when I saw all the buttons in the sound room I never thought I'd be allowed to touch those things and manage to work them . . . But very soon I was learning how to use them, and . . . my teacher could see I could handle those techniques by myself.[47]

Dickinson returned to Mozambique in 1977, having been recruited to train seven editors in nine months.[48] Dickinson pointed out in an article for the ACTT journal *Film and Television Technician*, written shortly after her return from Mozambique, that most of her trainees were school leavers 'with only one or two years of secondary school who had never seen a piece of film in their lives before and had not even watched many movies'.[49] As a result, part of the teaching involved weekly projections of films from the collection that the INC had inherited. In an interview with me in 2005, Dickinson described the INC's film archive as 'eclectic': it included colonial newsreels, Soviet and British documentaries such as Mikhail Romm and Dimitry Vasilev's *Lenin in October* (1937) and Humphrey Jenning's *Listen to Britain* (1942), as well as popular genres such as Indian musicals, which the young Mozambicans felt more of an affinity for because they featured stories that were closer to their lives.[50]

[47] Interview with Gabriel Mondlane. Maputo, 14 September 2005.
[48] Margaret Dickinson (early 1980s). 'An Editor in Mozambique', in Eshun and Gray (2011): 136.
[49] Dickinson (early 1980s), in Eshun and Gray (2011): 136.
[50] Interview with Margaret Dickinson. London, 13 October 2005.

The practice of filmmaking was learnt mainly on the job and trainees were quickly launched straight into making films that were destined for the public. Dickinson's article for *Film and Television Technician* recounts:

> It sounds like a recipe for chaos and certainly in my own department the first month was rather like a slapstick comedy on cutting-room accidents. Apart from the predictable crop of dropped centres, shorts were joined upside down, back to front, out of rack, cans lay around unlabelled and trims turned up in odd places hopefully labelled 'trim'. Fortunately I did not have to watch what went on elsewhere, but the lab delivered us a few howlers – and as for the shooting crews, anguished comments on the track told their own story. Nevertheless after a while life began to feel a little more normal: cans began to acquire labels, rushes began appearing in sync, trims found their way into the right bundles and even reappeared when required. This was lucky since we could not afford too many mistakes.[51]

The training programme included tasks that involved trainees working more autonomously in small groups so as to get experience of every aspect of film production, with the expectation that those with an aptitude for taking on directorial responsibilities would emerge, despite the fact that they had not had the advantage of coming from a highly educated background. In this respect, the INC training programme was innovative for its time and pushed against the elitism that structured the film industry. One of their projects was to work with a sponsor to make three instructional films that would test out different methods of influencing behaviour. The trainees worked with the world-renowned British dental health expert Martin Hobdell, who was then working as a *cooperante* in Mozambique. The short films they produced attracted the attention of global dental health organisations as they were the first to give as much details on the best ways to use *mulalas* – the traditional toothbrushes used in Mozambique that are made from sticks taken from the *Euclea Natalensis* bush – as they did on Western, plastic toothbrushes. The trainees were also given the opportunity to devise their own short films in groups, from concept through to scriptwriting and direction. These ranged in topic from a documentary about a newly established children's nursery, a subject much favoured by Frelimo, to a portrait of an eccentric individual who lived alone on the beach. As well as making films themselves, the trainees learnt by observing and assisting the other professional filmmakers who were employed by the INC. According to Dickinson, this sometimes led to tensions with other *cooperantes*, who were housed in the city centre, whereas most of the trainees had to travel long distances to get home, and thus could not stay late into the night to assist editors who preferred to work after-hours.[52] Even in the context of efforts to address

[51] Dickinson (early 1980s), in Eshun and Gray (2011): 136.

[52] Conversation with Margaret Dickinson, London, 19 November 2015.

the impact of colonial segregation, subtle forms of discrimination continued to operate, with privileges of race and class re-asserting themselves through the logistics of everyday life and access to technology.

By 1977, Frelimo had recruited more *cooperantes* from Brazil and Canada. Brazilian Murilo Salles began working as a photographer and cinematographer in Brazil and came to Mozambique via Europe with the Mozambican-born director Ruy Guerra, who was already known for his films that were central to the *Cinema novo* movement in Brazil.[53] Although Salles intended only to stay in Mozambique for a few weeks, after giving some classes on photography in cinema he was asked to join the INC and ended up staying for two years, working as an editor, a director and a teacher of camera. Guerra began writing film reviews at the age of seventeen in Lourenço Marques, before training as a filmmaker in France at the prestigious Paris film school IDHEC, and then moving to Brazil. There, he made a key contribution to the *Cinema novo* movement in Brazil, working as a director, editor and cinematographer. While Guerra's best-known films made in Brazil, such as *Os Fuzis* 'The Guns' (1964), feature worker protagonists and address urban class struggle, other films, such as *Os Deuses e os Mortos* 'Of Gods and the Undead' (1970), are more allegorical and fuse elements of the mythic and the revolutionary in rural Brazil. Like many militants of his generation, Guerra was forced to leave Brazil because of the military dictatorship. Beyond his work as an individual filmmaker, Guerra was interested in how filmmaking, distribution and exhibition might be transformed into an effective anti-imperialist system.[54] The Mozambican Revolution enabled him to extend his influence beyond that of an individual militant to contribute to a more ambitious decolonisation of cinema.

Guerra returned to Mozambique for Frelimo's Third Congress in 1977 and acted as a consultant for the INC in the late 1970s and 1980s. Although he held no formal public position, he had a decisive influence on the vision and policies of the INC and was at the heart of the debates that raged at the INC over what technologies were appropriate for making films in Mozambique and how to

[53] Murilo Salles (1988). 'Eu Tinha Que Fazer Um Filme Sobre a Geração 68'. *Filme Cultura: Directores estreantes – 27 depoimentos sobre a experiência de realizar a primeira longa-metragem*, available http://www.murilosalles.com/film/cl_no1.htm.

[54] 'I don't deny the necessity to make political cinema, in a certain context, with effective possibilities, nearly a didactic cinema at a certain level; I think that is entirely valid. But within the actual context of cinema, the traditional structures of distribution are obeyed, and it doesn't interest me to make political cinema with these types of limitations. For this reason, I've looked to open an historic discourse, that effectively opens up to more wide-reaching trajectories.' Interview with Ruy Guerra (1974). 'Cinema Novo, Análise Histórica, o Golpe de Estado do 25 de Abril, Moçambique, Cinema e Independência'. *Cinéfilo*, 37, 22 June, republished in Maria João Madeira (ed.) (1999). *25 de Abril no Cinema: Antologia de Textos*. Lisbon: Cinemateca Portuguesa–Museu de Cinema: 37.

push forward an agenda of increasing efficiency and professionalisation. The year he directed *Operação Búfalo* 'Operation Buffalo' (1978), a documentary about the slaughter of buffalos in Gorongosa National Park that tracks the buffalo from its natural habitat to the shop windows where its hide and horns are sold as commodities. Other documentaries and the 'fiction' film *Mueda, Memória e Massacre* 'Mueda, Memory and Massacre' (1979) followed, which made a decisive contribution to expanding the cinemas of the Mozambican Revolution (see Chapters 4, 5 and 6).

The first Canadian filmmaker to arrive in Mozambique was Madeleine Taylor, who made the film *Year III: Communal Village* (1981) about the process of collectivising agricultural production. With her came sound engineer Glen Hodges who recommended Ron Hallis as someone who could process film.[55] Following Hodges's recommendation, the Hallis couple were recruited after Américo Soares and Luís Simão saw Gilles Carle's *L'Ange et la Femme* (1977) at the Cannes Film Festival.[56] The film had been edited by Ophera Hallis, but crucially for the Mozambicans it was filmed on 16mm and then blown up by Ron Hallis to a 35mm version for projection.[57] The INC had the equipment for making films on 35mm, and this was the format needed for projections in the cinemas. However, Soares and his team knew that shooting on 16mm was much cheaper and the equipment less bulky and intrusive, so it would be the better option for shooting newsreel and documentaries in a situation where there was no television broadcast. What impressed them about *L'Ange et la Femme* was that the 35mm projection was of a high quality, despite the fact that the film had been blown up from 16mm. Ron Hallis had a reputation for being a 'jack-of-all-trades', as in Montreal he had set up his own equipment and laboratory to shoot, develop and print his own film stock, and to record and transfer sound.[58] In the early 1970s the couple had made a series of independent films on 16mm, some of which they processed entirely by themselves. The fact that one of their independent films was *Toni, Randy and Marie* (1971), a portrait of a transsexual dancer, suggests that, despite Frelimo's reputation for being somewhat puritanical, the ideological vetting of *cooperantes* was, at this point at least, carried out with a light touch if at all. Ron Hallis made an initial visit to Mozambique in 1977. Ophera Hallis recalled to me that he was given a cheque for US$35,000 to purchase blow up equipment in North America.[59] The couple bought a printer and a blow up machine in New York, which were transported to Mozambique when they came together in 1978. This equipment

[55] Ron Hallis (1980). 'Movie Magic in Mozambique'. *Cinema Canada*, February: 19.
[56] Convents (2011): 461.
[57] Hallis (1980): 19.
[58] Lois Siegel (1978). 'Montreal Cowboy'. *Cinema Canada*, 44 February: 17.
[59] Skype conversation with Ophera Hallis, 21 March 2019.

enabled the INC to shoot on 16mm and transfer to 35mm. The achievement of this was, as Convents points out, something of a coup for the INC.[60] Raquel Schefer and Catarina Simão follow Guerra in theorising the INC's competence in processing and printing 35mm and 16mm film as a 'tropicalisation' of these formats, a conceptual move that honours the successful adaptation of a Western technology to the Mozambican context.[61] However, also at stake in this unique historical conjuncture is a set of manoeuvres and exchanges between the ad hoc world of independent filmmaking in Western Europe and North America and the needs and desires of this new African nation. Here 16mm, which in the West was becoming the poetic medium of artist-filmmakers, became crucial to the task of producing a national newsreel that would be the precursor to television.[62]

Towards the end of their first year working at the INC, Ron and Ophera Hallis made a number of their own documentaries in the communal village of Omm near Xai-Xai. The making of these films followed an encounter that Ron Hallis had with a Makwayela dance group who were performing outside a café in Maputo. Hallis recalls being struck by the leader of the group, Antonio Matusse, who was dressed in white colonial military uniform adorned with Frelimo colours and an MPLA button, along with white gloves and a traffic controller's armband. A passer-by explained the meaning of the song by saying 'He is telephoning Salazar, telling him he will never again touch this earth.'[63] The couple befriended Matusse, who invited them to the Omm communal village near Xai-Xai, which had been established following the devastating floods of 1977. Enchanted by the 'spirit of the village', they returned in the months that followed to make a number of documentaries and to organise projections of the films.[64] The documentaries by Ron and Ophera Hallis made during this period were *Colonialism Has Fallen* (1979) and *A Revolução La Famba* (1979). These were distributed throughout North America and showed a different perspective on Mozambique than the image that was presented by the mainstream media. Indeed, the Canadian Department of External Affairs monitored the couple

60 Convents (2011): 461–462.

61 Raquel Schefer (2018). 'Ruy Guerra's *Mueda, memória e Massacre*: The missing images'. *The Journal of African Cinemas*, 10, 3: 205–223.

62 Eastman Kodak introduced 16mm as a more affordable format than 35mm for amateur filmmakers. However, in the 1930s it came to be used for educational films, and large numbers of professional 16mm filmmakers emerged in the 1950s and 1960s, who generally produced information films for industry and government. The demand for newsreel for television increased the use of 16mm because the equipment was far more portable than 35mm. For a discussion of the significance of 16mm and 8mm to independent artist-filmmakers in Western Europe and North America, see Erika Balsom (2017). *After Uniqueness: A History of Film and Video Art in Circulation*. New York: Columbia University Press.

63 Balsom (2017): 20.

64 Balsom (2017): 23.

and accused them of promoting communism.[65] While the Hallis couple were invited to work at the INC in part because of what they could teach Mozambican trainee filmmakers, this independent filmmaking that they carried out on their own initiative undertook a vital didactic purpose of teaching Canadians about the revolution unfolding in Mozambique.

The fascination with bringing cinema to 'the people' was a powerful experience for filmmakers in Mozambique, and it propelled a number of projects that were more marginal to the INC's core operations. This experience of delight in sharing the 'magic' of cinema had already prompted José Celso and Celso Luccas to propose a project, following on the making of their film '25' during the transition to independence (see Chapter 2). The filmmakers were greatly impressed by the first projection of '25' at the Scala cinema in Maputo, as for most of the audience this was their first experience of seeing a film. The experience convinced Celso and Luccas that 'Africa has as much need for images as it does for proteins'.[66] Celso and Luccas documented scenes of people queuing to go to the cinema for the first time in their lives, to see '25'. These scenes were the focus of Celso and Luccas's next short film *As Bichas* 'The Queues'. The film '25' was also taken by mobile cinema turbo vans for projections in villages, where it served a didactic purpose, opening up discussions about Mozambican history.[67] Celso and Luccas became intrigued by the idea of setting up a project in which local people in villages and *bairros* would be taught to make their own films through decentralised information units. These would coordinate not only film and video production, but also distribution of these and other archival films, thus connecting isolated communities through the moving image. Celso and Luccas returned to Brazil in 1977 but although this project was not realised in Mozambique, their thinking about it informed a later project in Amazonia entitled 'Video in the Villages'.

Within the INC, the question of what technologies were appropriate to the context of the Mozambican Revolution was addressed primarily in relation to what formats of film should be used for different productions, as staff grappled with what equipment was available to them and how it could be appropriated to the needs of a national cinema. By the mid-1970s, a series of technological shifts were taking place across different fields of moving-image production. New film and video formats were becoming more widely available, though these were still something of an unknown quantity, while other technologies were facing obsolescence. Film industry standards in North America, Western Europe

65 Skype conversation with Ophera Hallis, 21 March 2019.

66 Cited in Isabela Oliveira Pereira da Silva (2010). '"Babaros Tecnizados": Cinema no Teatro Oficina'. MA dissertation, Faculdade de Filosofia Letras e Ciênias Humanas, Universidade de São Paulo: 81.

67 Silva (2010): 83.

and the Eastern Bloc privileged 35mm, though 16mm was still widely used for information and ethnographic films, as well as for newsreel footage intended for television broadcast. During the 1960s in North America and Europe, 16mm had come to be thought of as a poetic medium, and it offered autonomy for those who did not want to work within the commercial studio system. In 1965, Eastman Kodak launched the Super-8 format, which was largely marketed to amateurs for home-movie making, but was also used by some artists who appreciated its imperfections and capacity for colour saturation as aesthetic qualities. In 1971, Sony began selling videocassette recorder (VCR) decks and tapes, bringing to a mass market a technology that had first been developed for capturing live images from television cameras on magnetic videotape. The foreign filmmakers who arrived in Mozambique as the INC was being set up thus came with their own sets of ideas, equipment and expertise, and entered into this highly politicised debate.

Jean Rouch arrived in Maputo in September 1977 at the invitation of Jacques d'Arthuys, the then French cultural attaché to Mozambique, who had previously been posted in Chile before the coup that destroyed Salvador Allende's government in 1973. Rouch had been filming in Africa since 1941, and his ethnographic films and works such as *Moi, un Noir* (1959), which featured African protagonists telling their own stories, were at the centre of controversy around questions of representation and authenticity. In his famous confrontation with Ousmane Sembène in 1965, the Senegalese director had applauded *Moi, un Noir* but accused Rouch of 'looking at black men as if they were insects' in his ethnographic films.[68] By the mid-1970s, Rouch was a key figure in international debates relating to the use of audio-visual technology for the documentation and study of oral traditions in Africa, but his filmmaking was also crucial to the development of the *Nouvelle vague* in France.[69] Rouch coined the phrase *cinéma vérité* 'truthful cinema' to describe an observational mode of filmmaking exemplified by *Chronique d'un Été* (1961), a film he made with Edgar Morin that captures tensions on the streets of Paris at a moment of decolonisation. *Chronique d'un Été* blurs fact and fiction, using non-professional actors who improvise and sometimes engage with the film crew on camera, creating moments of self-reflection and provocation to pose the possibility of cinematic truth as a question.

[68] Jean Rouch and Ousmane Sembène (1982). 'Jean Rouch–Sembène Ousmane: "Comme des insectes"' *CinémAction*, 17, February: 77–8.

[69] Jean Rouch (1969). 'Utilisation des techniques audio-visuelles pour la collecte et l'étude des traditions orales en Afrique.' UNESCO colloquium, November. Dahomey (now Benin): Porto Novo: 14–20; Jean Rouch (1974). 'The camera and the Man'. *Studies in Anthropology of Visual Communications*, I, 1; Jean Rouch (1975). 'Situation and Tendencies of the Cinema in Africa'. *Studies in the Anthropology of Visual Communication*, 2/1.

During this initial visit Rouch made the short film *Makwayela* (1977) using 16mm colour film with a number of trainees. In an interview in the United States the following year, he recalled that the group included 'some people who had escaped from Brazil, from Portugal, and so on; and they were trying to find their own revolution in Mozambique'.[70] The footage for this film was gathered during a visit to a glass-bottling factory. After a brief sequence that shows the production of drinks bottles inside the factory, the film moves to the courtyard outside, where ten or so workers dance the Makwayela. They then explain the significance of the dance and how it originated in the experience of harsh labour in the South African mines. Traditionally the song is sung in Fanagalo, the Bantu-based Pidgin English spoken by miners as a lingua franca. As Simon Gikandi notes, switching between Pidgin and the colonial language can involve acts of recoding and assertions of authority that are contingent on the interlocutor and the circumstances.[71] Here, the song in Portuguese denounces imperialism and Apartheid. At this moment of the Mozambican Revolution, the Makwayela is transformed into a hymn to internationalism sung in Portuguese.

D'Arthuys and Rouch were keen to tap into French government money that was available for cultural projects even though the French state was not prepared to give other forms of financial support to a Marxist African country.[72] In particular, Rouch wanted to experiment with what could be done with Super-8 in the context of revolutionary decolonisation. He proposed training people to make film 'postcards' in Super-8, because it was much cheaper, lighter and faster to develop than other kinds of film. With this technology, films could be shot during the day, processed chemically in a small machine, then edited and projected the same evening so that the people who had filmed and been filmed could comment on the images. The INC had already embarked on filming with 16 and 35mm film and considered Super-8 to be an amateur format. During this first trip, however, Rouch turned to Fernando Ganhão, the Rector of Eduardo Mondlane University, who put him in contact with various departments, and it was there that he put forward his idea that Super-8 was a film format ideally suited to a 'developing' country.

[70] John Adams (1978). 'Jean Rouch Talks about his Films to John Marshall and John W. Adams (September 14th and 15th, 1977)'. *American Anthropologist*, New Series, 80, 4: 1005–1020, transcript available at http://www.der.org/resources/jean-rouch/jean-rouch-interview.html.

[71] Simon Gikandi (2016). *The Oxford History of the Novel in English, Volume Eleven: The Novel in Africa and the Caribbean since 1950*. Oxford: Oxford University Press: 490.

[72] Manthia Diawara (2013). 'Sonimage in Mozambique', in Gareth Jones and Florian Zeyfang (eds) (2003). *I said I Love. That is the Promise. The Tvideo Politics of Jean-Luc Godard*. Berlin: b_books: 113–115.

In the 1970s and 1980s, Eduardo Mondlane University was an important centre for scholarship dedicated to emancipatory political struggle across Southern Africa, despite the fact that most Portuguese staff and students left after 1975 and in the first three years of independence the number of lecturers dropped to fewer than ten.[73] The academics at Eduardo Mondlane University had the urgent task of providing accelerated training to address the desperate shortage of rural teachers. Frelimo also directed the university to establish social sciences based on Marxist analysis not only to produce knowledge about the history and present conditions of Mozambique, but also to create a critical voice from within the Mozambican Revolution. The Centro do Estudos Africanos (CEA), which was directed by Aquino de Bragança, was at the vanguard of this effort. De Bragança modelled the CEA on the Centro do Estudos Africanos in Lisbon, which had been crucial to the development of nationalist thought in the Portuguese colonies in the 1940s and 1950s. It drew sociologists, anthropologists, political scientists, legal scholars and economists from across Southern Africa and beyond, including ANC activists such as Ruth First and Albie Sachs, British archivist Colin Darch, Mozambicans Teresa Cruz e Silva, Luís Brito and Yussef Adam, and Jacques Depelchin from Congo.[74]

As well as the CEA, Rouch set up long-standing relations with two other sections at the university. One of those was the project Técnicas Básicas de Aproveitamento de Recursos 'Basic Techniques for Harnessing Natural Resources' (TBARN), whose team included João Paulo Borges Coelho. Its remit was to establish communication with rural areas and identify and harness local technical knowledge for development in the context of collectivising agricultural production. The other was the Centro do Estudos de Comunicão (CEC), led by Bento Sitoi, where Jorge Constante Pereira and João Azevedo, among others, used silk screen prints and photography to carry out communication work and produce pedagogical materials with TBARN. In the wake of the Carnation Revolution in Portugal, Azevedo had assisted the cooperative that was set up by peasant occupiers of the rural estate of Torre Bela, and so had been involved in the making of Harlan's film of the same name (see Chapter 2). Russell Parker, who operated the camera for *Torre Bela* and worked on Rui Simões' film *Bom Povo Portugues* 'Good People of Portugal' (1981), also

[73] Carlos Fernandes (2013). 'History Writing and State Legitimisation in Postcolonial Mozambique: The Case of the History Workshop, Centre for African Studies, 1980–1986'. *Kronos*, 39: 132.

[74] Aquino de Bragança, a confident of Samora Machel and Marcelino dos Santos, was one of the founders of CONCP in Casablanca in 1962, and had been an editor of the leftist magazine *Afrique-Asie* in Algeria during the armed struggle. Ruth First was one of a number of leading ANC figures living in exile in Mozambique, including her husband Joe Slovo, who was commander of the ANC military wing Umkhonto we Sizwe, and she was appointed Director of Research at the Centre for African Studies at Eduardo Mondlane University in 1978.

came to work at CEC. Their personal trajectories were thus connected more with political activism than ethnography, Mozambique offering revolutionary possibilities that had been cut short in Portugal.

Rouch was invited to lead a series of workshops that took place at Eduardo Mondlane University in 1978. The Super-8 workshops were conducted with colleagues from the Université de Paris X–Nanterre, where he taught ethnographic filmmaking. The campus had been a centre of student radicalism during the events of 1968, and Miguel Alencar, Jacques d'Arthuys, Philippe Costantini and Nadine Wanono were all linked to the Comité du film ethnographique and the Section de cinéma de l'Université de Paris X–Nanterre. Like João Azevedo, Costantini had been in Portugal during the Carnation Revolution and had been involved with militant filmmaking in rural areas. The workshop project involved setting up a laboratory for processing Super-8 film with sync sound at Eduardo Mondlane University. Rouch and his colleagues made arrangements for importing a Kodak Supermatic S8 Processor. The French government paid for the equipment, which had to be transported into Mozambique from South Africa. This raised the suspicions of the Mozambican authorities, who were wary of the purpose the equipment would serve, though the system was of great interest to filmmakers in Maputo because it meant that they would no longer have to rely on South African facilities for processing Super-8.[75]

The Nanterre filmmakers were aware that they would be training young people unfamiliar with the language of film, and began by showing Eisenstein's *The Battleship Potemkin*, because it was thought to be more straightforward to introduce cinema with a silent movie.[76] The first films they made with their trainees were twenty to forty minutes long, each made within the space of two weeks and shot in various locations in Maputo using material supplied by the French embassy.[77] Their focus was on everyday scenes far from the choreographed political rituals of public life. The French filmmakers argued that Eduardo Mondlane University was not subjected to the same level of scrutiny as the INC, in terms of whether its film productions conformed to the requirements of the Ministry of Information and the Department of Ideological Work, though other filmmakers who worked at the INC at the time report that they did not feel overtly controlled in terms of their cinematic output. One

[75] Super-8 had been a popular amateur format widely used by settlers prior to independence. Drew Thompson, presentation at Symposia International, Eduardo Mondlane University, 2010. Convents (2011): 450.

[76] A roundtable discussion with participants in the project, including Jacques d'Arthuys, Nadine Wanono, Miguel Alencar and Philippe Costantini, convened by Jean-Pierre Oudart and Dominique Terres. Jean-Pierre Oudart and Dominique Terres (1979). 'Une Expérience de Super 8 au Mozambique'. *Cahiers du Cinéma*, 246: 54.

[77] Sites included the Hospital Central, the Chiango school, the Museu de Arte Popular and the Escola de Formação de Quadros de Educação. 'Super 8'. *Tempo*, 406, 1978: 13.

of the effects of these experiments was that some of the films were used to advocate for changes at a micro-political level. For example, in the hospital in Maputo students shot scenes of patients gathering on the veranda; the images showed women doing each other's hair as they would in their own homes. D'Arthuys recounts how the authorities wanted those images cut because it was thought they promoted behaviour that was unhygienic and inappropriate to a hospital.[78] The filmmakers argued that the patients were addressing social and psychological needs that were not being met in their treatment, which kept them in an alien environment for long periods. As a result, room was provided in the hospital for this purpose, making a change in the functioning of the institution. Nadine Wanono recalls that this method of filmmaking, which was very close to lived realities, sometimes 'did not correspond totally to the Frelimo line' but instead 'raised contradictions'.[79] 'Some students simply wanted to delete the "non-conformist" sequences, while others wanted to keep the controversial elements so as to fuel a healthy debate.'[80] According to Wanono, therefore, capturing the quotidian risked being interpreted as a dissenting gesture.

According to Convents, the workshop films were contentious because they featured people speaking in indigenous languages at a time when the government was promoting Portuguese for the purposes of national unity.[81] To avoid the accusation that the films were promoting 'tribalism', Rouch provided copies of each film with a narration in Portuguese, which would be used whenever the films were shown outside their local community. Costantini has claimed that ethnographic documentation risked conflict with Frelimo's desire to present a unified nation of people committed to collectivisation, citing the example of a film about a collective village that began as a proposal by the National Museum to make a comparison between a traditional Marave village in Tete and a new collective village.[82] According to Costantini, the students decided to change the brief and focused only on life in the collective village so as not to conflict with Frelimo's battle against tribalism, meaning that even before the cameras started rolling, self-censorship worked to tailor the image to an idea of what Frelimo wanted for Mozambican reality.

Manthia Diawara argues that the very characteristic that Rouch perceived to be the advantage of Super-8 – its disposability – meant that his project

78 Oudart and Terres (1979): 56.

79 Nadine Wanono (2007). 'Fragmentos da história de Moçambique em Super 8mm'. *Notícias*, 5 September, cited in Convents (2011): 451.

80 Convents (2011): 451.

81 Convents (2011): 451.

82 Jean-Pierre Oudart, Serge Daney and Dominique Terres (1979). 'Enquête: Super-8 au Mozambique'. *Cahiers du Cinéma*, 296, January: 54–59.

in Mozambique was of little interest to the INC.[83] Super-8 was prone to deterioration, meaning that it would have to be saved onto other mediums to be kept, a factor that was an important consideration for an institution whose remit was to create a national cinema. According to Convents, when the films were projected, there were complaints about the poor quality of the medium.[84] Although the INC was not interested in taking up Rouch's approach to filmmaking with Super-8, a few filmmakers who went on to work at the INC undertook some training with him.[85] The experience of running the workshops convinced Rouch and his associates to set up Ateliers Varan, an organisation established in 1981 that is dedicated to teaching documentary filmmaking in countries lacking the resources to fund grassroots moving-image production.

The Super-8 laboratory set up at Eduardo Mondlane University and run by Arlindo Mulhovo was used by TBARN and CEC from 1978 through to the early 1980s and Rouch's ideas informed their experiments with how filmmaking with communities and the projection of films could assist rural development, particularly in the setting up of rural cooperatives. Since the beginning of the effort to set up collective villages after independence, films from the armed struggle such as Popović's *Nachingwea* had been shown as a model of Frelimo's socialist transformation.[86] In contrast to these more ideological images of collectivisation, those working at TBARN and CEC were interested in filming processes of social change so as to provide remote communities with examples of transformation taking place elsewhere. Crucially, they wanted to embed local indigenous techniques within pedagogy so that communities could be proud of the knowledge that they had as well as that which was being instructed to them by the new authorities.[87] In the late 1970s, a number of films were made on Super-8 in the southern region around Maputo.

[83] According to Diawara, Godard was able to assist Rouch by making transfers to video. This was the first time Godard and Rouch met. See Diawara (2013): 103.

[84] Convents (2011): 450.

[85] Among the trainees who learnt how to make Super-8 films with Rouch at Eduardo Mondlane University were Mulhovo, José Negrão, João Paulo Borges Coelho, Stella Malta, José Baptista and Moira Forjaz. Moira Forjaz and João Paulo Borges Coelho informed me about their participation in interviews that I carried out with them in 2005 in Lisbon and Maputo. By the late 1970s Baptista, Forjaz and [first name] Langa (who had worked at CEC making silk screen posters) were involved in filmmaking at the INC, and in the 1980s Mulhovo went on working for Televisão de Moçambique. Other names listed here are mentioned by Angela Ferreira. Ferreira interviewed João Paulo Borges Coelho for the research she conducted into Rouch's activities in Mozambique for her exhibition *Political Cameras (For Mozambique Series)*. Angela Ferreira (2013). *Political Cameras*. Edinburgh: Stills Scotland's Centre for Photography: 17. Interview with Moira Forjaz, Lisbon, 19 October 2005.

[86] Interview with João Azevedo, Lisbon, 3 December 2016.

[87] Interview with João Azevedo, Lisbon, 3 December 2016.

Tijolos 'Bricks' (1978) was an hour-long film that was accompanied by a publication, which outlined a project to incorporate traditional knowledge into an accelerated adult education programme. Over a period of five months the team made regular visits to the Magude district near the border with South Africa, where the Centro Inter-provincial de Formação Acelerada de Adultos 'Inter-provincial Centre for Accelerated Adult Education' was located. The people being trained were party chiefs of new villages, grassroots leaders, women from the National Women's Organisation and locally elected judges who served in the people's tribunals. The participants in the project were in the process of undertaking a year's training that was the equivalent of basic schooling and that comprised literacy, accountancy and history. The role of CEC and TBARN was to carry out research into improving life conditions and to help the participants take concrete actions in a context of scarce resources. The researchers and filmmakers were also undergoing a pedagogical experience, in terms of learning local techniques and honing their filmmaking skills, as Russell Parker trained Mulhovo and Langa through the making of *Tijolos*. Magude had a history of brick production as there were still the remains of a brick-making factory, which one of the participants had worked at. An old man from the area showed the participants how to make brick moulds so that they could produce bricks by hand. The team experimented at a small carpentry workshop until they managed to make a design of their own that resembled the model in the engineering books at the university. They constructed a clay oven and tried out different mixtures of clay and sand to make good quality bricks. The film shows a huge party of some 250 people who gathered for the firing of the bricks and performed songs and dances from different provinces of Gaza, Inhambane and Maputo. Once the bricks were fired they took them to the Engineering Faculty to test for strength, discovering that they could be used to construct buildings of up to three storeys. Participants used these bricks to build a refectory and a residential building that were more permanent than wattle and daub.

A number of other Super-8 films were made by CEC and TBARN in the late 1970s. Bento Sitoe directed *Tracção Animal* 'Animal Traction' (1978), which depicted donkey owners who were so poor that they were forced to feed their animals with copies of the *Notícias* newspaper. In the same year, as recounted to me by João Azevedo, Robert Mugabe's aide Edson Zvobgo put in a request for filmmaking training to be provided for ZANU guerrillas.[88] Parker began working on a daily basis with a group of young Zimbabweans so that they could contribute to film and television production in Zimbabwe after independence.[89]

[88] Interview with João Azevedo, Lisbon, 3 December 2016.

[89] I am grateful to José Filipe Costa for providing me with a copy of Russell Parker's curriculum vitae, which contains the following note: 'In my role as Professor of Communications, Eduardo Mondlane University, Peoples Republic of Mozambique, I

However, from 1978 to 1979, Mozambique came under repeated attack by the Rhodesian army and the young people Parker worked with were killed.[90] Parker, whose mental health was already fragile as a result of his experiences in Vietnam where he had served in the US army film unit, was then flown in by helicopter to take footage of one of the massacres. The sight of the carnage triggered a schizophrenic breakdown that led to Parker having to withdraw from the project for a time so that he could receive treatment.

With Parker absent for a year, Azevedo recruited the Argentinian filmmaker Sergio Solimanov, who came at the recommendation of d'Arthuys. Solimanov directed two films, for which Mulhovo and Langa did the camerawork. The first was *Enxadas* 'Hoes' (1979), the purpose of which was to demonstrate that Mozambique was producing its own hoes in a factory in Machava that had been nationalised. The film shows the factory workers dancing, having lunch and making the hoes and it was taken for projection in farming communities in different provinces. Although Frelimo was trying to make Mozambique more self-sufficient in terms of industrial production, Azevedo pointed out to me that the hoes were in actual fact not of good quality, and eventually the government had to import hoes from China because people refused to buy the Mozambican-made hoes. The second film directed by Solimanov was *Hospital Central de Maputo* (1979). Scenes documented in this film illustrated Frelimo's approach to healthcare, which emphasised preventative medicine and self-sufficiency: a young boy with diabetes is shown learning how to inject himself with insulin.[91] One of the aims of these films was to use them in projections in the northern provinces of the country as demonstrations of the modern developments that were already being established in the south (see Chapter 5).[92]

---

taught Rhodesian Communist Guerrillas of the Zimbabwean African National Union (ZANU) how to make movies. The idea was that after the majority Black Africans had won their fight against the minority White Rhodesians, my students would set up a film and TV Institute in the new country, Zimbabwe. Our course was all day for two years, so definitely, there are tales to tell!'

[90] Attacks by Rhodesian army forces in 1978 an 1979 include: 11 December 1978: bombing of military barracks in Beira killing 26 persons and wounding 73; aerial bombing using napalm in Tete Province between 29 November and 8 December 1978; 19 February: aircraft bombing and strafing of a storage complex in Chimoio area; 1 March 1979: bombing of a ZANLA base in Mutarare; 12 March 1979: bombings at Chokwe and Barragem in Gaza; 16 March: air strike at Dondo; 17 March: air strikes on guerrilla bases in Chimoio. Keesing's Record of World Events (formerly Keesing's Contemporary Archives) (1979). *Rhodesian Raids on Targets in Mozambique, Zambia, Botswana and Angola*, 25, April: 29577. Available at http://web.stanford.edu/group/tomzgroup/pmwiki/uploads/3004-1979-04-KS-a-DIR.pdf.

[91] Interview with João Azevedo, Lisbon, 3 December 2016.

[92] Email correspondence with João Azevedo, 28 December 2017.

1. Poster for *Behind the Lines* (1971), directed by Margaret Dickinson. Courtesy of Margaret Dickinson.

2. Lennart Malmer with Ingela and Lisa Romare filming in Cabo Delgado, 1971. Printed in *Mozambican Revolution*, 49, 1971. Courtesy Lennart Malmer.

3. Samora Machel addresses Frelimo guerrillas in *Nachingwea* (1975), directed by Dragutin Popović. Courtesy INAC.

4. Stills from '25' (1975), directed by José Celso and Celso Luccas. Courtesy INAC.

5. Stills from *Maputo: Meridiano novo* (1976), directed by Santiago Álvarez. Courtesy ICAIC.

6. Josué Chabele using a Steenbeck film editing suite, 1976. Courtesy Margaret Dickinson.

7. Gabriel Mondlane and Ismael Vuvo, INC, 1976. Courtesy Margaret Dickinson.

8. Mário Felix, Margaret Dickinson, Miguel Chambule, Eusebio Mfumo, Josué Chabele, Enoque Mate, José Cabral and Ismael Vuvo, INC, 1976. Courtesy Margaret Dickinson.

9. Sara Mabombo conforming 35mm film in the INC laboratory, 1981. Courtesy Ophera Hallis.

10. Manuel Malo at work in the INC laboratory, 1981. Courtesy Ophera Hallis.

11. Seated at front: two Soviet technicians, unknown, INC Director Americo Soares, Gabriel Mondlane, Ophera Hallis, Henrique Caldeira and others unknown; middle: unknown, Luísa Lourenço, João Ribeiro, Lidia Muianga, unknown, José Cardoso; above: Alberto Chemane and others. Courtesy Ophera Hallis.

12. Ron Hallis and Henrique Caldeira mount a screen on the cantina wall at the collective village of Omm, near Xai-Xai. Courtesy Ophera Hallis.

13. Stills from the *Kuxa Kanema* newsreel, including episodes made between 1978 and 1979 and in 1981. Courtesy INAC.

14. *Segunda Mostra do Cinema Cubano* 'Second Programme of Cuban Cinema', Maputo, 25 September 1976, INC. Courtesy INAC.

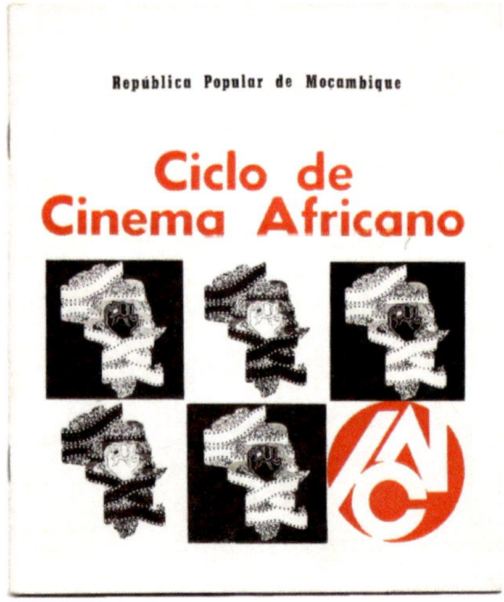

15. *Ciclo de Cinema Africano* 'Season of African Cinema', INC. Courtesy INAC.

16. *Terceira Semana de Cinema Cubano* 'Third Week of Cuban Cinema', Mozambique, July 1980, INC. Courtesy INAC.

17. *Semana de Cinema Argelino* 'Week of Algerian Cinema', Maputo, January 1987, INC. Courtesy INAC.

While these experiments with Super-8 were taking place in 1978, another major figure of the European avant-garde was drawn to Mozambique: Jean-Luc Godard. According to Carlos Jambo, Godard was the first filmmaker to bring the technology of video to the new nation.[93] Godard's concern was not with the cinema *per se* but with the potential of the Mozambican Revolution to re-invent what television could be. His point of contact with the Frelimo government was Minister for Security Jacinto Veloso, who he had first met in Geneva in December 1977.[94] In 1978 Godard and his partner Anne-Marie Miéville were asked by the Mozambican government to carry out research into the possibilities for a liberated form of television broadcasting. By the late 1970s, Godard had left mainstream commercial film production and the collective work he had done with the Dziga Vertov group, and he and Anne-Marie Miéville set up the company Sonimage in Switzerland. Godard was fascinated by the possibilities that video offered in terms of allowing Sonimage to operate autonomously and allowing them to control the entire production process. In the mid-1970s, Sonimage began working on video for television broadcast, although the television series they produced – *Six fois deux: sur et sous la communication* (1976) and *France/tour/détour/deux/enfants* (1978) – deconstructed the conventions of television broadcasting.[95] The Mozambican Revolution enabled Godard to conceive a radically democratised form of television production using video that was unimaginable in Europe, precisely because in Mozambique television did not yet exist.

Little remains of the work Sonimage did in Mozambique except for an article by Godard that was published in *Cahiers du Cinéma* in 1979. In the article, Godard argued that Sonimage was engaged in a struggle to maintain its independence in the face of the colonisation of visual and sonic registers by capitalist interests and ideologies. The Western world comprised societies in which there were already 'too many images' so that the field of the audio-visual was already occupied and saturated by consumerism.[96] His perception of Mozambique was that it was a site where there was still some freedom of manoeuvre to create alternative kinds of collective experiences through the cinema screen. Godard saw a parallel with what Sonimage aimed to do on a smaller scale from its base on the Swiss border, away from the commercialism of the Paris film world. The new nation

[93] Carlos Jambo interviewed by Nicole Brenez (2004). 'Sept rendez-vous avec Jean-Luc Godard'. Youtube video, available https://www.youtube.com/watch?v=Jx-1IVfhIPA.

[94] Godard recounted this encounter in an interview with Nicola Brenez in 2004. Jacinto Veloso confirmed that it was he who invited Godard to Mozambique in a telephone conversation with me in Maputo in 2010. Jean-Luc Godard interviewed in Brenez (2004).

[95] Daniel Fairfax (2010). 'Birth (of the Image) of a Nation: Jean-Luc Godard in Mozambique'. *Film and Media Studies*, 3: 60.

[96] Jean-Luc Godard (1979a). 'Le dernier rêve d'un producteur'. *Cahiers du Cinéma*: 73–77.

was involved in a struggle to create social relations and conditions of production liberated from exploitation, to define what 'Independence' meant on its own terms and to take action against the threat of neocolonialism.

The activity of research, and the activity of filmmaking as research, had profound political underpinnings in Godard's radicalisation during the events of Paris 1968. This saw the beginning of his engagement with Maoism, which insisted on the importance of theoretical knowledge being produced through situated practices, and with currents of feminism, combining critique of patriarchy with self-criticism. In an interview for *Tempo* in 1978, Godard cited Mao to argue for the need for research in Mozambique to be carried out simultaneously and coordinated between different fields of print media, radio and cinema, emphasising the criticality and self-reflection necessary to produce new forms and non-exploitative relations.[97] His own project was designed to 'take advantage of the audio-visual situation of this country so as to study television before it exists, before it inundates (even if only in twenty years) the entire social body and terrain of Mozambique'.[98] The task was thus to think about what might prevent television taking on its conventional role as a commercial medium offering a private, socially isolating experience with a flow of banal reactionary images and sounds. The project explored the technological, aesthetic and social possibilities of video, but with an awareness of the production of knowledge and spaces of critical thought at intersections between different social collectivities and types of textual surface, be it the moving images of film and video, photography, text or assemblages of these.

Intriguingly, Godard's title for the *Cahiers du Cinéma* article, 'North against South or Birth (of the image) of a Nation', cites the title of D. W. Griffiths' film *Birth of a Nation* (1915). Griffith's film is credited with consolidating narrative fiction feature films as the dominant model in Hollywood, but it is also infamous

[97] 'I think that in the area of Information there needs to be more people dedicated to research, just as in industry. In industry it is perfectly admissible that part of a factory or a large company should have a research department where people can carry out research in whatever direction they like. In the industry of cinema, in Information, in the media, research departments don't exist where new forms, forms that were never used before, can be experimented with. Different ways of interviewing people, of working . . . I think that all this should be studied. As President Mao says, "One shouldn't speak without first doing research." Before going to the peasants it is necessary to do a study of the peasants. Even if sometimes the person who is doing the research is herself of peasant origin. This has to be studied, because knowledge has to be given to other people that Mozambique exists. For this, the different parts of Mozambique have to be shown to other parts of Mozambique. Maybe the first time it is shown it will be done badly, or maybe not . . . but the most important thing, above all, is to show.' See Jean-Luc Godard (1978). 'Aprender e ensinar a Imagem no Moçambique independente'. *Tempo*, 408: 32–33

[98] Jean-Luc Godard (1979b). 'Nord contre Sud ou naissance (de l'image) d'une nation'. *Cahiers du Cinéma*, 300: 73–129.

for its deeply offensive representation of African Americans and its racist idealisation of the Ku Klux Klan, which precipitated a number of race riots.[99] The film stands as a symbol of the marginalisation and stereotyping of non-white people in American commercial cinema, through its representations, the technologies it employed and its industrial relations. *Birth of a Nation* culminates in a series of rescue sequences in which the screen is filled with an image of rioting black bodies that are flushed from the screen by the Ku Klux Klan, who enter from the top of the screen like a white wave. In this film the ideology of a nation – the United States – is created around a singular identity and through repeated acts of racialised violence. Godard inserts the words 'of the image' in brackets in the middle of Griffith's title, suggesting that the moving image has the potential to interrupt the consolidation of the nation-state around a singular notion of identity.

An initial section of the *Cahiers du Cinéma* article describes the series of five films Godard envisaged to complete the project. The first would involve an actor and actress interviewing a filmmaking team with figures that represent different sides of the cinema industry. The other films were planned to be like 'note books' on the journey of each of these through Mozambique, the home movie of a businessman; a film shot on video of interviews with people giving their responses to seeing their own image for the first time; one made up of stills, and another dedicated to analysis of the photographic image. On p. 4, the text 'Essai d'actualités mozambicaines' hovers between a photograph of a Mozambican man with a video camera in the top half and a scene of runners meeting on the track in the bottom half. The importance of a people being able to stand behind the camera as well as in front of it are the two sides of a project to use video to document everyday life.

The article describes meetings at the INC, at Radio Mozambique and in Niassa, where the project was carried out, and gives an indication of the methods through which 'the image' and 'the desire of images' was studied by training different groups to use filmmaking equipment. Filmmakers, journalists, peasants, children, state functionaries, factory workers and women in collective villages were questioned about their responses to the new images and sounds being transmitted by the revolution, focusing on what images of themselves they wanted to produce. The article goes on to combine images with shorter aphoristic texts that make provocative statements about empowerment, the global cinema industry, its technological systems and about the relationship of these to the politics of producing images – the 'right to look', the 'right to speak' – in the context of the new kinds of voices emerging with independence.[100]

[99] Linda Williams (2002). *Playing the Race Card: Melodramas of Black and White from Uncle Tom to O.J. Simpson*. Princeton: Princeton University Press.

[100] Williams (2002): 110–111.

Alongside a picture of Miguel Alencar holding a video camera while a black Mozambican man looks at the images that it has just captured, the text points out that there are 'always 2 to make 1 image'. Film production is inherently collective, but its relations of power are not equal. As Raquel Schefer points, in this image the white man holds the technology of moving-image production, while the black man learns how to use it. [101] In this pedagogical scenario the redistribution of the means of production – a task crucial to decolonisation – is underway but is yet incomplete. Other lines reveal Godard's engagement with the kinds of questions raised at the INC over what equipment was appropriate for the situation of decolonisation, given the ways in which film technology had historically been shaped by the racism of the societies that produced them. The manufacture of audio-visual equipment by corporations such as Kodak or Sony meant that, as Fairfax argues: 'imperialist dominance over Mozambique's sound and image production was already implanted – true independence is still a long way off, even, or especially, on a cultural level.'[102] Technologies are embedded within an uneven geopolitics, and therefore choices of equipment have implications that are political. Godard condenses this somewhat reductively into a set of binary choices between different regimes of power: 'Pal or Secam. France or Germany. Senegal or South Africa.'

The phrase the 'image and its secret' accompanies a photograph of a radio journalist looking through the viewfinder at an image (perhaps of herself, as Godard has just been in conversation with her about the music she is choosing to broadcast).[103] The system of instant feedback in video inserts itself into the process of decolonisation, offering a means to close the circle between the one who films, the one who is filmed and the one who views the film. The gesture of crossing out suggests that the revolutionary process of decolonisation involves demystifying the production of images so that people can grasp its forms and create new audio-visual languages, holding in suspension its complexity without erasing its 'secret'. And on the pages that follow:

> All the children are actors.
> All the women know how to make *mise en scène* (record that which works, and compare it with that which doesn't).[104]

[101] Raquel Schefer (2016). 'Comment faire une télévision qui puisse servir le peuple sans desservir le pouvoir en place: Sonimage dans le Mozambique révolutionnaire et un film mozambicain de Jean-Luc Godard – Part One.' La Furia Umana, available https://tinyurl.com/y5ujfk2u.

[102] Fairfax (2010): 63.

[103] Fairfax (2010): 122–3.

[104] Fairfax (2010): 112–13.

In this vision, filmmaking is an empowering collective practice open, in theory, to anyone. Desire circulates in the intersection of sounds and images, in their conjunction with the emergent forces that constitute the newly independent nation. In Godard's formulation, the 'single force' that is 'the people' is not captured or defined by state mechanisms of reproduction, but has the potential to create the forms and modes of their own appearance through the radical democratisation of the means of production and dissemination of moving images. A series of questions and answers concludes the article with photographs of children who get progressively younger. The Althusserian interpellations, 'On whom does it depend that oppression remains? On us./ On whom does it depend that oppression disappears? On us', locate the human potential for collective action and transformation at the heart of the matter.[105]

Godard's eventual proposal was that communities in Niassa would be trained by his company Sonimage to use video equipment so that people could produce whatever they wanted – this would form the basis of television production in Mozambique. As José Luís Cabaço points out, the video training project could have provided material so that 'we could have created little by little a Mozambican cinema capable of really interacting with people.'[106] The Ministry of Information rejected the plan as too impractical. The proposal to use a foreign company to train people to make their own films on video was thought to be expensive and the new technology of video unproven. Godard's sense was that his own private company, by operating outside the Paris film industry, was analogous to the new nation-state of Mozambique. This comparison sits uneasily with his privilege and distance from the lived realities of most Mozambicans.

Godard's article for *Cahiers du Cinéma* communicates a certain hope for the possibility of creating an image of change and for challenging existing systems of producing the moving image. Some years later, Godard made a video-film for the French television company Arte called *Changer d'Image* 'To Alter the Image' (1982). The work in part comments on the political situation in France following the presidential election of François Mitterrand in 1981, whose election campaign slogan 'Change Life' soon rang hollow in the face of economic stagnation and the French government's turn to embrace neoliberal globalisation. Godard appropriates the slogan to reflect on the futility of his own attempts to enact change through the image in Mozambique. Over opaque scenes of a man being tortured, the voiceover talks about a European filmmaker who is invited to a Third World country as an 'expert' on how to change the image. The voiceover describes the filmmaker as an 'idiot', perhaps expressing Godard's disillusionment with the idea that an image of change could be produced within a wider system that was becoming authoritarian. An image

[105] Fairfax (2010): 127–128.
[106] Cited in Schefer (2016).

of change can only emerge from within circuits of image production, or as the voiceover puts it in *Changer d'Image*: 'the image did not exist, only chains of images.' The mode of production Sonimage envisaged involved a decentring that was at odds with Frelimo's centralised chain of command.

Yet Godard's apparent despair at the failure to use video to radically democratise moving-image production was not entirely vindicated in what followed. In these years of 'first contact' with the moving image in the Mozambican Revolution, certain seeds of emancipatory and self-reflexive filmmaking practices, of attention to unscripted moments of everyday life and of democratising moving-image production had been sown that would re-emerge at various times and in different guises in the years that followed. These early years of the INC can be understood as a moment in which there were a number of attempts at radical experimentation that had transnational significance, before this space of relative freedom was foreclosed. While these experiments with bringing cinema to 'the people', documenting everyday life and passing on the means of production were being carried out and would continue, the core productions of the INC were increasingly orientated towards performing a different task. From 1976, Mozambique was increasingly embroiled in a war with Rhodesia, in which the Rhodesian army repeatedly made bloody incursions into Mozambican territory in the name of stamping out ZANU guerrillas. Rhodesia's Central Intelligence Organisation (CIO) was also beginning to organise a combat unit made up of Mozambican dissidents with the aim of destabilising the new nation. The INC was entering a 'battle of information' that required it to produce films that would counter the media dominance of Rhodesia and South Africa. Yet the 'enemies of the people' were not only beyond Mozambique's borders. As discussed in the next chapter, when Frelimo made the shift from an anti-colonial front to a vanguard Marxist–Leninist party in 1977, its directives on cinema became more explicitly militant in terms of the need to adhere to the party line without ambivalence. The battle of information had begun.

4 Who Exactly is the Party? Didacticism, the Battle of Information and the Vanguard Party, 1977–1979

By 1977, the INC was functioning as an institute in command of acquisition and distribution, the profits from which were channelled into the production of films made by a team that included young people who would have been cut off from the possibility of becoming filmmakers under colonialism. The equipment purchased by Ron and Ophera Hallis had made it possible to shoot films on the cheaper format of 16mm that could then be transferred to 35mm for projection in the cinemas. Taking cinema to 'the people' and collectivising production involved not only building up the INC's institutional capacity but also dismantling the hierarchies that had structured the colonial film production. Chapter 3 examined how a number of filmmakers explored the emancipatory potential of capturing scenes of everyday life on film. However, such projects played a minor part in comparison with the bulk of the INC's productions, which sought to harness cinema to the work of political education and the dissemination of information.

This chapter addresses the didactic purpose of many of the INC's film productions, the role that cinema was understood to play in the 'battle of information', and the ways in which films made during these years address their audiences as learners. The battle of information referred in part to the effort to keep Mozambicans informed about the radical changes taking place across the country, explaining the reasons for the challenges they faced and the ways Frelimo intended to address problems of supplies and logistical difficulties in the face of natural disasters and the ruination of infrastructure caused by the colonial war and acts of sabotage by departing Portuguese. In 1977, Frelimo announced that it was transforming into a vanguard Marxist–Leninist party, aligning itself more closely with the Soviet Union and the Eastern Bloc. The dissemination of information to Mozambicans thus also involved instruction on how to participate in the revolution that was unfolding in the correct way. This chapter analyses how short documentaries and the first version of the *Kuxa Kanema* newsreel that was produced in 1978 and 1979 answered to this demand, exploring the extent to which forms of cinema pedagogy may be understood as anticipatory rather than necessarily authoritarian. The battle of information also involved the crucial work that film could perform in challenging the narratives about the region that were circulated by the white minority regimes in Rhodesia and South Africa. As the Rhodesian army accelerated its attacks in Mozambique, the INC responded with a number of documentaries that presented visual evidence of the atrocities and explained the Rhodesian aggression in terms of the history of imperialism in Southern Africa. Murillo Salles's film *Estas São as Armas* 'These are the Weapons' (1978), made in response to the massacre at Nyazônia in 1976 when the Rhodesian army attacked a refugee camp in Mozambique, not only provides a mode of didacticism based on emotive sensorial devices associated with propaganda, but also outlines a pedagogical reading of images, instructing the viewer on how to make a decolonial interpretation of the colonial archive that runs against the grain of their intended purpose. Finally, the chapter considers the hardening of Frelimo's political line and the consequences this had for filmmaking, focusing on Ruy Guerra's *Mueda, Memória e Massacre* 'Mueda, Memory and Massacre' (1979). This film documents a re-enactment of the massacre of civilians that took place in Mueda, Cabo Delgado, in 1960, an event that is credited with precipitating the formation of Frelimo and the armed struggle for independence. *Mueda, Memória e Massacre* encompasses theatrical performance, audience participation, eye-witness testimony, carnivalesque elements, such as the costumes and exaggerated gestures used to depict the former colonial masters, and ethnographic detail. As this chapter will argue, through these means the film is self-reflexively concerned with the constitution of a new set of histories filtered through revolutionary nationalism, the transference of memory across generations through pedagogy and the capture in film of a grassroots form of cultural expression as a moment in which collective memory is harnessed by the state.

One of the short films made by trainees under Margaret Dickinson's supervision, *As Eleicões* 'The Elections' (1977), demonstrates how political education in Mozambique in the years immediately following independence involved taking account of the specific needs of audiences who had no prior experience of cinema and were participating in forms of popular democracy for the first time. *As Eleicões* is about the first elections ever held in Mozambique to select candidates for the *assembleias populares* 'popular assemblies', which were forums for local political participation. Crucially, according to Dickinson, the film shows real differences of opinion being voiced through lengthy scenes of debate between competing candidates, calling in question the assumption that Western democracies provide the only valid model of political participation.[1] Dickinson points out that the film crew faced severe shortages of equipment and skills, where success was measured by 'if the cameraman could hold the

[1] Interview with Margaret Dickinson, London, 13 October 2005.

camera still enough to get the shot'.[2] In this situation, aesthetic questions were not given much attention because of the sheer complexity of carrying out basic filmmaking. Nevertheless, an article in *Tempo* that was published on the film's release argues that *As Eleicões* sought to empower Mozambican audiences by meeting their needs.[3] The article analyses how each scene is constructed out of a number of long, wide-angle shots that allow viewers to take in the entire situation, and only then moves in to pick out and follow certain details, avoiding rapid montage or extra-diegetic sound.[4] The film was projected in *bairros*, factories and other locations where the elections were yet to happen so as to mobilise participation, providing instruction on how to participate in the new forms of political decision-making.

In 1977, changes were afoot within Frelimo that would further shape both the structures of government and the role of cinema in furthering the Mozambican Revolution. In addition, the external threat of aggression from the neighbouring white minority-ruled countries of Rhodesia and South Africa loomed large, as dissenters from Frelimo began to organise themselves over the border. Following the assassination of Eduardo Mondlane, a faction within Frelimo that identified with Marxist–Leninism had come to dominate the leadership and had succeeded in ousting those who deviated from the 'correct line' (see Chapter 1). While at independence, Frelimo was greeted with euphoria as the rightful government-in-waiting, its shift to a centralised form of socialism, the seizure and collectivisation of private property and the draconian punishments meted out to dissenters led to resistance from parts of the population and even from within Frelimo. By 1977, defectors led by André Matsangaice were promoting the idea of an opposition force based in Rhodesia. The radio broadcast Voz da África Livre 'Voice of Free Africa' that was set up with the help of the Rhodesian Security Services created the impression that this was a well organised force and that a substantial military campaign against the Mozambican government was imminent.[5] While at that point in time this was far from the truth, the Rhodesian government was beginning to reconsider its reluctance to support a large-scale opposition force headed by an indigenous leader. At the time of Mozambican independence, a commando unit called Resistência Moçambicana, or Remo, made up of members of the Portuguese armed forces, had been set up by Ken Flowers, the head of the Rhodesian Secret Services, to gather intelligence and carry out attacks across the border. However, an attack in January 1977 was considered to have been a fiasco and, while Remo continued to carry out

[2] Interview with Margaret Dickinson, London, 13 October 2005.
[3] 'As Eleições em Cinema'. *Tempo*, 371, 1977: 28–30.
[4] 'As Eleições em Cinema'. *Tempo*, 371, 1977: 28–30.
[5] João M. Cabrita (2000). *Mozambique: The Tortuous Road to Democracy*. Basingstoke: Palgrave Macmillan: 148.

attacks over the following year, Frelimo defectors, who had been launching their own small raids on re-education camps, began to appear to be a more viable alternative. Voz da África Livre attracted more Mozambican defectors, including Afonso Dhlakama, the son of a Ndau traditional leader from Sofala, who had been serving with Frelimo's armed forces in Beira. Within six months of arriving in Rhodesia in July 1977, Dhlakama had become the leader of the Mozambican National Resistance (MNR), which would later become Renamo.[6]

At the Third Congress in February 1977, Frelimo declared that it was transforming itself from an anti-colonial Front formed out of a broad alliance into a Marxist–Leninist vanguard party, bringing it closer ideologically to the Soviet Union and the Eastern Bloc. During the armed struggle, Frelimo used Marxist terminology to describe the racial humiliation and exploitation of colonialism and promote a nationalist agenda of rapid modernisation.[7] It now announced its commitment to 'scientific socialism'. As a vanguard party, Frelimo became more selective in its membership. At independence *grupos dinamizadores* had taken responsibility for running businesses, *latifundios* and industry abandoned by the Portuguese and, according to some commentators, functioned as 'direct democratic organs'. Increasingly, however, as power became centralised, they came to operate as a conduit for the implementation of policy dictated from above by the party.[8] This process of centralisation aimed to tackle the economic crisis caused by the massive shrinkage of the white settler community, the collapse of businesses and damage to infrastructures. It was also a response to the threat posed by Rhodesia and South Africa and to a more shadowy figure that was increasingly looming large in Frelimo's discourse and policy – that of the *inimigo interna* 'the internal enemy', a category of traitors to the revolution that came from within Mozambique.

Frelimo's Guidelines for a People's Democracy, which was launched at the Third Congress, comprised seven theses, which reiterated the Party's aim to defeat 'internal reactionaries' who continued to threaten the building of a socialist society.[9] As well as demanding the transformation of the economy, the third thesis proclaims that at this stage of the revolution:

> the ideological struggle is accentuated, so as to build the New Man, the socialist Man, the Man free from all superstitious and obscurantist subservience, the Man

[6] Cabrita (2000).

[7] David Robinson (2003). 'Socialism in Mozambique? The "Mozambican Revolution" in critical perspective'. *LIMINA*, 9: 131–151.

[8] Hans Abrahamsson and Andres Nilsson (1995). *Mozambique: The Troubled Transition: From Socialist Construction to Free Market Capitalism*. London: Zed Books: 16.

[9] Frelimo (1977). 'Frelimo's Guidelines for a People's Democracy'. *African Communist* (published by the South African Communist Party), 69, Second Quarter, 1977.

> who dominates science and culture and assumes the fraternal and collective relations and duties of society.[10]

The Seventh Thesis concludes that the role of the vanguard party is to lead the 'worker–peasant alliance'. Defining a new, centralised structure of power, Frelimo declared that the party must:

> guide, mobilise and organise the broad masses in the task of building People's Democracy, carry out the construction of our state apparatus which materialises the power of the worker–peasant alliance and serves as an instrument for the construction of the ideological, political, economic, cultural and social base of the socialist society.[11]

The following year in June 1978, Frelimo officials met in Beira for the Second National Conference of Ideological Work to hammer out a strategy for mobilisation and political education. Central to the role that cinema would play was the plan for a national newsreel called *Kuxa Kanema*. As well as providing an educational news service for the entire country, *Kuxa Kanema* was intended to weave a cohesive image of national identity that would cut across ethnic and linguistic differences. The name means 'Birth of Cinema', from *kuxa*, the word for 'birth' in Ronga and Changanga, and the word *kanema*, which signifies cinema in Chichewa and Makua. These indigenous languages were combined to symbolise the unity of the nation. The newsreel was initially produced in 1978 in occasional thirty-minute episodes and focused on one or two themes per edition. In this format, *Kuxa Kanema* covered current events through reports that investigated subjects in depth.[12] In the absence of television, *Kuxa Kanema* was distributed across the country by mobile cinema units that served rural communities as well as in cinemas in towns and cities. As the vast majority of the population had no means of accessing urban movie theatres, for many it was their first experience of cinema.

The political ambitions for *Kuxa Kanema* are laid out in the *Documentos* of the Second Ideological Conference.[13] The newsreel would:

1. provide incentives for increasing 'production and productivity', by showing the 'national dimension of work' and how each worker and each factory could have a beneficial effect for the country as a whole;

[10] Frelimo (1977).
[11] Frelimo (1977).
[12] Frelimo (1978). *II Conferência Nacional do Trabalho Ideologico: Documentes*, Beira, 5 to 10 June: 91.
[13] Frelimo (1978): 91.

2. cover the difficulties encountered during the revolutionary process, such as food queues, so as to explain their causes and suggest solutions by 'linking them to the need to increase production';
3. show each phase of social-economic development of the country, from state production sectors to sanitation and education centres;
4. mobilise the 'labouring masses' to give them a sense of the importance of 'collective life', in particular in communal villages, collective *machambas* and cooperatives;
5. develop in the workers an 'elevated spirit of the cultural heritage of our People';
6. explain the establishment of the Solidarity Bank and what it could do in the face of natural disasters and other emergencies;
7. explain national events and the political development of the country by focusing on the government's campaigns for such things as vaccination and literacy;
8. encourage a spirit of militant solidarity with the International Proletariat and the struggles of other peoples, particularly in Southern Africa.[14]

The Resolução Sobre Cinema called on the INC to 'take cinema to rural zones', but 'not any old cinema', warning that unlike urban spectators, those of the rural areas 'haven't yet been deformed by bad cinema, and the INC should not be the instrument of this deformation'.[15] The aim of the *Kuxa Kanema* newsreel, therefore, from its very inception, was to maximise the political impact of cinema in the creation of a new revolutionary nation.

Ten *Kuxa Kanema* were made between 1978 and 1979, directed by Fernando Silva and João Costa. The artistry and depth of these episodes contrasted not only with the colonial newsreels that preceded them, but also with the weekly version of *Kuxa Kanema* that was made in the 1980s (see Chapter 5). The colonial newsreels produced in Mozambique during the 1960s were made by small outfits, sometimes with only one or two camera operators that competed with each other for commissions from the Centro de Informação e Turismo. They documented state visits by officials and foreign dignitaries and comprised little more than a few shots overlaid with martial music. The initial *Kuxa Kanema* newsreels, by contrast, are tightly scripted episodes that demonstrate considerable care and skill. Luís Carlos Patraquim, who had been involved in the initial conception of the INC (see Chapter 2), provided much of

[14] Frelimo (1978): 89–91.

[15] 'não estão ainda deformados pelo mau cinema, e não pode ser o Instituto Nacional de Cinema o instrumento dessa deformação'. Frelimo (1978): 92.

the voiceover and wrote the scripts. These were structured around events that allowed for the newsreel to give ideological instruction and show the collective effort of the nation to transform Mozambican society. While the credits reveal that recent trainees including Ismael Vuvo, Miguel Chambule and Josué Chabele were involved with operating cameras, editing and sound, the participation of experienced *cooperantes* such as editor Ophera Hallis ensured high quality.

Editions of this first version of *Kuxa Kanema* cover topics including the nationalisations, the formation of cooperatives, cultural and sporting events, plans for maximising production, political mobilisation campaigns, natural disasters and the Treaties of Friendship that Mozambique signed with countries of the Eastern Bloc after committing itself to Marxist–Leninism. As such, they provide a lens onto the way in which Frelimo understood its task of building a socialist society in Mozambique. They also demonstrate how *Kuxa Kanema* made a social intervention by offering a kind of instruction on how to understand the connection between processes and systems that viewers might encounter in their own lives, the work of the party and the contribution that the Mozambican Revolution was making to a global struggle against imperialism. The aim of this in-depth approach was to educate *Kuxa Kanema* audiences on aspects of everyday life that were rapidly changing and informing them of events taking place on a national scale. Through the moving image, *Kuxa Kanema* gave audiences a connection to the world beyond their immediate community, encouraging them to identify with the agenda of the revolutionary nation-state and its politics of internationalism. In so doing, it also consolidated and institutionalised a Marxist–Leninist rhetoric, which reflected Frelimo's shift to becoming a vanguard party.

Episode 2, for example, focuses on the First National Conference of Planning and sets out to demonstrate the urgent need for effective planning in different sectors. After a brief section on a state visit by Vice-President of North Korea Pak Song-Choi, the newsreel turns to scenes of fruit trees, fields and factories. These are presented as examples of the 'material base for the construction of a new society', in which Mozambican workers 'struggle day and night to overcome the difficulties and disruption left by the colonialists'. In this context, the voiceover asserts: 'Planning will be our tool of construction and progress.' Interviews with workers and factory managers follow, which highlight the challenges of logistics and the acts of 'economic sabotage' by departing Portuguese, such as the mass slaughter of cattle that were left to rot in the fields. Workers at a canning factory perform the Makwayela, and the manager José Sitoe discusses various challenges facing production such as shortages of materials. The episode then turns to the transport sector, where shortages of spare parts for buses were leading to an inadequate service. The commuters are stoical, one of them commenting: 'We are still a young country. When we have buses that run on time, we'll be fine.'

An inter-title then introduces the National Conference of Planning. Interspersed with shots of cranes and other signs of industry, the sequence that follows presents speeches made at the conference by Marcelino dos Santos and Samora Machel. Dos Santos situates the challenges facing the country as the inheritance of colonialism, imperialism and racism, against which Frelimo acts as the vanguard of the Mozambican people. His discourse reinforces the lesson on the importance of planning that was previously demonstrated through the examples of agriculture and transportation. Machel's speech also helps audiences to understand the connection between specific examples and socialist ideology, arguing that planning is 'rooted in socialist practice'. In Mozambique it will involve the nationalisation of industry, the formation of agricultural cooperatives, and a re-organisation of social relations through the collectivisation of everyday life: 'Building communal villages', he declares, 'is THE dominant motto to improve our life on its way toward socialism. The struggle continues. Socialism will win!'

The newsreel then cuts to an interview with Júlio Candido Tembe, Secretary of the administrative commission at the state-run farm called '3rd of February', who reports on the difficulty of complying with production targets due to a lack of planning. The final sequence features images of goods being loaded onto ships and trains at a harbour, while the voiceover explains the importance of planning to the good running of infrastructures that connect the different sectors of the economy: 'Corn and sunflower from the communal village should reach the factories so that the communal village can receive cornmeal and cooking oil in return. For this exchange process, a transport infrastructure should be planned.' Planning, the voiceover argues, is a guard against economic sabotage, and 'will mean liberation of the economy from external dependence'. In addition, 'it will further strengthen our support for the struggle of the people of Zimbabwe.' Over images of industry, the episode closes with the sound of the chitende, signalling a Mozambican industrialisation.

Episode 3 educates audiences on the centrality of culture to the revolution, reporting on the first Festival Nacional de Dança Popular. In so doing, it presents a lesson on how Frelimo's victory against colonialism is the culmination of an entire history of cultural resistance manifested in dance and song. The voiceover highlights the fact that the Festival was also part of a larger project to re-invent forms of cultural expression to serve the Mozambican Revolution. Certain dances and songs are presented as authentic expressions of the Mozambican people. At the same time, the newsreel demonstrates how the very format of the Festival was transforming those same cultural forms, stripping them away from their traditional function within spiritual rituals and the role they played in reinforcing gender hierarchies. In the Mozambican Revolution, dance troupes were no longer permitted to select their members according to affiliations of tribe and lineage. Instead, they were required to be open to everyone who wanted to participate, so that their dances could become articulations of national culture. This process of re-invention had begun during the armed struggle, when guerrillas from different parts of the country taught each other the dances and songs of their regions. Armed struggle films such as *Behind the Lines* presented this as an organic process of sharing between the guerrillas, whereas in fact Frelimo controlled and instrumentalised these cultural exchanges. The liberation front scripted new lyrics filled with the histories, watchwords and slogans of Frelimo, integrating certain dances and songs into their school system and mobilisation campaigns as a means of ideological instruction and to encourage nationalist identification (see Chapters 1 and 2). The Festival can thus be understood as a means of consolidating this process on a national scale, promoting unity through mass participation. The Statement from the Ministry of Education and Culture published in the Festival programme declares:

> The First National Festival of Popular Dance is a milestone in the History of our People and will have an important impact on national life. The whole People will participate in it, from the Circle to the Nation, and it will be a testament to the choice of the Mozambican People to make a Revolution, to construct Socialism, to make culture a weapon to annihilate capitalism, imperialism, neo-colonialism and feudalism.[16]

Beginning in January 1978 with performances across the different regions of Mozambique, it culminated in a spectacle on the Day of Independence at Machava Stadium in Maputo, which was attended by President Samora Machel and featured some 600 musicians and dancers, 60 representing each of the ten provinces.[17] The organisation of the Festival thus replicated, as Paolo Israel points out, the 'pyramid' of the nation-state's administrative structure.[18] The dances and songs performed were not only being represented, but also had to be transformed. The phrase 'from the Circle to the Nation' refers not only to the move from the village to the capital, but also to changes in the choreography of the dances to fit the layout of the Festival performances. Dance troupes had to adapt the movements they had previously performed ritualistically within the village circle to a linear format arrayed before the leaders' podium in which the dances were presented as the new signifiers of the Mozambican nation.

The *Kuxa Kanema* episode begins in Inhambane Province, orientating the viewer with an image of a road-sign to Quissico, 'Land of the Ngoto and the Timbila', as the voiceover informs. The camera follows young women, some

[16] República Popular de Moçambique (1978). *Programma: 1° Festival Nactional de Dança Popular*. Maputo: Instituto Nacional do Livro e do Disco: 8.

[17] http://www.micultur.gov.mz/index.php/ix-festival-nacional-da-cultura/historial

[18] Paolo Israel (2014). *In Step with the Times: Mapiko Masquerades of Mozambique*. Athens: Ohio University Press. 162.

carrying babies, as they walk to where they can watch the performers rehearse. The voiceover describes the different instruments used by the Chopi, the people of this region – the huge wooden xylophones known as timbila, the *ngoma* drums and the bamboo flute ximbeca. At the same time, a sequence of images that show villagers in a circle around the timbila players, with children sitting on the branches of a tree above. The musical piece they play, the *Msaho*, is more than mere entertainment but rather is an expression of collective life: 'Poetry, music and dance contribute to a harmony, in which social life can be expressed, cultural values can be criticised or confirmed.'

The film then cuts to the village of Modunda, in the district of Mueda in Cabo Delgado, where villagers are gathered to watch the energetic masked dance of the Mapiko. An old man sitting in a chair explains the significance of the Mapiko – a dance central to puberty initiation ceremonies. These practices had previously been shrouded in secrecy and were a means through which the Makonde negotiated hierarchies of gender and generational difference.[19] Close-up images of the dancer show an example of the sacred masks that traditionally were worn by men and kept hidden from women, followed by an image of the women facing away, performing a gesture of fear. Finally the camera captures the Mapiko dancer advancing, and as men sway and drum, the dance begins. While colonial anthropology sought to understand indigenous rituals in order that the colonisers might better control local populations, in the post-colony the act of unmasking seeks to destroy traditional belief systems that were seen as upholding obscuratism and social inequality, emptying the gestures of their original power and filling them with new meanings.

The next location featured on the newsreel is Matimo, where the 'dance of resistance of the Marracuene' is performed. The camera pans along a line of men dressed as warriors. Holding spears, animal skin shields and wearing headdresses of feathers, they dance and chant. A member of the film crew asks: 'Comrade, what does it mean, this dance, where does it come from?' To which the dancer responds:

> The dance is called Mutini. Mutini were warriors of the King who scouted the enemy when he was drawing in. Others were sitting on trees to observe the enemy. When the enemy came, they sent messages to the King and he gave the order to inhibit the invasion. When the battle was won, the warriors assembled with the Mutini. They praised each other, they danced and sang.

This explanation is then contextualised with historical drawings that show the attack on the colonial fort of Lourenço Marques that took place on 14 October 1894. Cutting to a brief sequence of warriors charging in attack from the film

[19] For an in-depth analysis of the evolution of the Mapiko, see Israel (2014).

Chaimite (see Chapter 2), the voiceover describes a history of resistance by the people of Marracuene that stretches back to 'the times of the Monomatapa', the Kingdom of Mutapa, which was founded in 1430 and stretched from the Zambezi and Limpopo rivers to the Indian Ocean. Prompted by the film crew, the dancer continues: 'This dance reminds us of the help given by Ngungunhane when Matibejana Zixaxa had to flee to Magude, after the attack on Lourenço Marques.' Another dancer describes how: 'When the soldiers returned from the war, they were danced in remembrance of the battles. Like our ancestors, we were excited about our soldiers going to war.' The dances are thus presented not as timeless relics, but as shifting cultural responses to specific events in the history of Mozambican resistance to foreign occupation. Not only has the language of this song of resistance changed over time but its meaning has evolved to reflect present-day political victories: 'At times of resistance it was sung in Zulu. Today they sing in Changana. The words say: Thanks to you, Samora, for your deeds.'

The voiceover expands upon this, arguing that the Festival accelerates such transformations in cultural expression, stripping away the myths and magical thinking of traditional belief systems so that dance forms can be re-invented for the new Mozambique: 'The Festival, with its peak in Maputo in June is a victory of the people's culture from tradition to revolution. Because in dancing, too, ideologies are fighting.' Images show women and men inter-mingling as they dance the Banguza from Zavala, a dance that previously was performed only by men, to the sound of timbila and drums. Moving to Inhambane, the film shows a performance of the frenetic *Nguinha*, presented by a village elder as an example of cultural resistance to hard labour: 'This is a song from the colonial time of our parents who sang while they were building streets and bridges.'

These energetic dance forms, which are imbued with histories of Mozambican resistance, are contrasted to the forms of culture that were commodified under colonial rule. The neon light of Bar Luso signals a shift in the film, and a woman's voiceover announces the scene of Mozambican culture prostituted in a colonial cabaret: 'Rua Major Araújo. Street of prostitution. Street of colonialism. This Marrabenta performed in a cabaret is a culture of the oppressed, of the assimilated – faked folklore.' In Frelimo's account of cultural authenticity, the Marrabenta, which developed in Lourenço Marques in the 1930s and 1940s through the fusion of Mozambican rhythms with Portuguese folk music, was associated with the decadence of capitalist colonial urban life. The colonial cabaret, she goes on to explain, was 'an institution of colonial fascism. A place where the erotic feelings, which are there in every dancing body, are set free only to turn always into estrangement and passivity.' In contrast to the rural dances, which involve the participation of the entire community, here predominantly white audiences seated at tables to watch black performers on a stage, while young black women in mini-skirts drinking sodas linger in darkened rooms. The newsreel then switches to a painting of Catholic worshippers, which symbolises the hypocrisy of the fascist regime's claim that colonialism was a civilising mission: 'The sword in one hand, the cross in the other, to spread the faith and the empire. Such spectacles can only be understood as perversion, when our cultural heritage is presented as cabaret.' In stark contrast, the film ends by switching back to the village, where, in an image of rural wholesomeness, children stand amid the trees eating berries. Dalcírio Bento Alexandre, the *responsável* for culture and education in Inhambane, explains how the Festival fulfils the party's directives of the Third Congress of Frelimo, in that it involves 'our entire people from Rovuma to Maputo'. The Festival, he claims, furthers research into Mozambican dance cultures and serves the causes of 'national unity and the erection of people's power on the way to socialism.' The final sequence shows children with their legs decorated with bells as they dance the *Ngalanga*. Party ideology reverberates through dance and song, these 'authentic' dances and histories forming the new symphony of the nation.

Episode 4 of *Kuxa Kanema* reports on the floods that devastated Tete, Manica, Zambeiza, Sofala in 1978, and gives an account of Frelimo's restructuring as a vanguard Marxist–Leninist party, seen in the newsreel through activities of mobilisation and recruitment in various localities. While the initial aerial images of vast flood plains show the extent of the inundation, the biggest to affect the country in the twentieth century, the newsreel argues that the losses have 'brought about the active solidarity of all Mozambican workers and the international community'. Indeed, the rescue efforts of the Mozambican army provides a powerful example of its service to the people. A *responsável* from Zambezia Province describes how lines of communication failed to reach remote communities, who experienced severe flooding when the Cahora Bassa dam was opened. Vast operations are needed to transport stranded livestock, while children whose schools were destroyed are waiting to be rehoused.

The newsreel moves swiftly on to the topic of party organisation, in which depictions of the transformations taking place at the micro level of everyday life are interspersed with the discourse of *dinamizadors* and interviews with workers. A shoemaker discusses how he and his peers have benefitted from organising themselves into a cooperative. A *dinamizador* from Inhambane is interviewed as he travels by bus to take part in a party recruitment campaign. Arriving at a new collective village in Panda district, an official gives a speech outlining the process for joining Frelimo and the need for applicants to have 'a sound and moral lifestyle in order to be a party member.' Villagers line up to become members, giving their fingerprints as identification to the officials. Children and men sing as they plough the fields with oxen, while women hoe the fields in a line – an example of an 'organised peasant population'. 'Out of people who did not know each other before, emerge houses, a school and an administrative building.' As women sweep the ground, men are depicted constructing the new administrative building located at the centre of the village. Images from *Venceremos* (see Chapter 1) create a lineage that begins with Frelimo's organisation of the liberated zones and culminates in the collectivisation of the countryside led by the vanguard party. A plethora of slogans and metaphors reinforce the idea of Frelimo as a force that harnesses natural resources: 'The armed struggle was like a great river of mobilised and organised people.' 'Today there more seeds to sow. Today there are new enemies, because of Rhodesia and the enemies that are within us.' 'The Party is the seed and the gun.' The newsreel then switches to footage of Machel announcing Frelimo's transformation into a Marxist–Leninist party, presented as contiguous with the preceding images of the armed struggle. A report follows from a collective village called 'Julius Nyerere', where eighty applicants for party membership are being considered. Party officials comb through their files and analyse their behaviour; they are asked to present themselves before a jury of the people.

The episode concludes with lines drawn from one of Bertolt Brecht's *Lehrstück* 'Learning Plays':

> Who exactly is the Party?
> The Party is us.
> You and me, us, all of us.
> It is how you live, what clothes you wear, you have it in your mind.
> Where it lives, there is your home.
> When you are attacked, the Party fights back.[20]

Punctuating this episode on the organisation of Frelimo as a vanguard Marxist–Leninist party, the quotation from Brecht re-animates an earlier revolutionary moment when socialism was on the march in Germany in the 1920s. Brecht's ideas about socialist learning are worth lingering on because they offer an alternative interpretation to the idea that Frelimo's pedagogy merely consisted

[20] 'Wer aber ist die Partei' forms part of a second version of Brecht's *Maßnahme* or *Lehrstück* (a theatre play translated as *The Measures Taken* or *The Decision* in the English translation based on the first version). It was published in Paris in 1934 in the collection of poems *Lieder Gedichte Chöre*, and under the title 'Wir Sind Sie' in *Hundert Gedichte* in Berlin in 1951. I am grateful to Adriana Liedtke, Benedict Seymour, Filipa César and Mark Washcke for their help with identifying this passage.

of a 'script' of 'readymade ideas' (see Chapter 1).[21] Roswitha Mueller argues that there is a fundamental distinction between the *Lehrstück* and Brecht's earlier and later plays because he understood the Weimar Republic in the 1920s to be a society in transition to socialism.[22] Bypassing the bourgeois contradiction inherent in the separation of the producers of theatre, the means of production and the audience, the *Lehrstück* involved specific groups, such as a school class or a worker's choir, who were given an active role: 'Thus, structurally as well as thematically, the *Lehrstück* has left bourgeois society behind. The *Lehre* themselves, learned in practical exercises, are concerned with the acquisition of a number of attitudes – not specific political decisions – that are necessary for a strategy in the political struggle towards a socialist society.'[23] The learning works through imitation that allows the chorus to test out the theoretical tenets of Marxist–Leninism, which, in Brecht's understanding, are general statements about political action and strategy. The disciplined learning of particular attitudes, gestures and new behaviours is thus, according to Mueller, anticipatory rather than authoritarian.[24] This theatrical pedagogy involves an actualisation of new behaviour through imitation and practice rather than a passive acceptance of political dogma as eternal truths. The Maoist emphasis on self-criticism within Frelimo's pedagogy can be seen to resonate with the rigid structure of the learning plays, in that the slogans can be replaced when necessary.[25] While the Leninist model of the vanguard party leading the masses is authoritarian, in that the insistence on discipline risks turning pedagogy into an instrument of indoctrination, this Brechtian understanding emphasises the active role of the audience/actors in the process of social change. Through the inter-title in this episode of *Kuxa Kanema*, this anticipatory concept of militant learning is brought into relation with the work of political education taking place in Mozambique.

[21] Borges Coehlo. 'Liberation Script', in Assubuji, Rui, Paolo Israel and Drew Thompson (2013). *Notes on The Liberation Script in Mozambican History*, special issue of *Kronos: Southern African Histories*, 39, November: XXXX; Maria Benedita Basto (2012). 'Writing a Nation or Writing a Culture? Frelimo and Nationalism during the Mozambican Liberation War', in Eric Morier-Genoud (2012). *Sure Road? Nationalisms in Angola, Guinea-Bissau and Mozambique*, African Social Studies Series, Vol. 28. Leiden and Boston: Brill: 103–126.

[22] Roswitha Mueller (2006). 'Learning for a New Society: The Lehrstück', in Peter Thomson and Glendyr Sacks (2006). *The Cambridge Companion to Brecht*. Cambridge: Cambridge University Press: 101–117.

[23] Mueller (2006): 108.

[24] Mueller (2006): 110–114.

[25] Mueller (2006): 112.

Further episodes of *Kuxa Kanema* provide instruction on nationalisations and internationalist foreign policy. Episode 7 reports on the government takeover of Sena Sugar, a vast company with its headquarters in London that controlled plantations and processing facilities across central Mozambique, which employed some 14,000 workers (see Chapter 2). Since 1920, the voiceover describes menacingly, 'an enormous crocodile grew – one part in Sofala, one part in Zambésia'. Workers at Sena Sugar gather to hear a letter requesting that the London Stock Exchange put the company into liquidation. The voiceover explains that since independence sugar cane has been left to rot in the fields, one of various acts of sabotage by Sena Sugar factory managers that constitute 'an economic crime'. A headline from *Notícias* reads: 'Sena Sugar taken under control of the state', and images follow of Frelimo officials explaining to workers that an administrative commission is being set up to oversee the company takeover. Luxurious houses inhabited by foreign technicians during colonialism are contrasted to the reed huts of the Mozambican workers: 'This is racism.' Unlike the foreign technicians who rapidly left at independence: 'The comrades of the commission taking control of the Sena Sugar estates are OUR PEOPLE.' An old man talks about the differences in wages before and after independence; now that Frelimo are in power pay has increased from less that 100 escudos to 4,500 escudos. The newsreel ends with the slogan: 'Victory of Production!'

The final three episodes, which were made between 1978 and 1979, profile visits by foreign leaders for the signing of Treaties of Friendship with socialist countries of the Eastern Bloc and African states such as Angola, who shared the common enemies of the white minority regimes in Rhodesia and South Africa. In the context of the Cold War, the Soviet Union and its satellites had supported socialist liberation movements in Africa so as to shift the balance of power in the region. The Treaties of Friendship were for Frelimo a means by which to build alliances that would support economic development and regional security. The pageantry of these visits and the ceremonial rituals they involved mean that these last episodes of the first version of *Kuxa Kanema* are less discursive and more focused on Frelimo's aesthetics of power.[26] Episode 9, which reports on the visit of the president of the Popular Republic of Bulgaria and the Day of Nationalisations, concludes with scenes of Samora Machel addressing a mass rally at Machava Stadium. The president discusses the closing down of private health clinics and the transformation of healthcare into a public service that prioritises preventative medicine and programmes

[26] Episode 8 features the visit to Mozambique by Angola's President Agostinho Neto and a report on the state of the papabichas, the buses that many urban commuters depended on to get to work. Along similar lines, episode 10 reports on the visit to Mozambique by DDR President Eric Honecker

of vaccination for babies. Looking out over the crowds, Machel faces a massive banner showing a stencilled picture of his own face. Rather than the people seeing images of themselves participating in the process of liberation, in this scene of the rally the masses are caught in a cathexis between the charismatic leader and his iconic image.

The 1978 to 1979 *Kuxa Kanema* newsreels report on some of the everyday struggles facing Mozambicans, situating these difficulties in the context of building a new society and instructing the public on how they may resolve them through collective will and mass participation in the revolution. Aside from occasional references to solidarity with the Zimbabwean liberation struggle, they make little mention of the attacks by Rhodesia that were already sapping the euphoria that followed independence. Ron Hallis reported in an article, published in *Cinema Canada* after his return, that when he arrived in Mozambique in 1978 to start work at the INC there were three short films in production: *Offensiva Culturae* 'Cultural Offensive' (1978), a sixty-second 'spot' about a worker's cultural festival; *Cheias* 'Floods' (1978), a ten-minute documentary about the floods in the Limpopo River Valley that occurred in 1977; and *Chimoio* (1978), a ten-minute documentary about an attack in 1977 by the Rhodesian army on a collective farm housing Zimbabwean refugees near the town of Chimoio.[27] Hallis recalls the horror of seeing the images that began to come through the INC laboratory: 'Sitting among the lab workers, Malo, Malumba, Castigo, Vasco and Magaia, I watched the horrifying images of countless bodies of murdered women and children strewn over the rain-soaked ground and piled in huge open graves.'[28] Violent incursions by the Rhodesian army into Mozambican territory began immediately after independence, one of the worst atrocities being the attack carried out by the Selous Scouts in 1976 on the Nyazônia refugee camp, in which 1,028 young unarmed Zimbabweans were killed.[29] The Selous Scouts were a military unit that led a counter-insurgency campaign through terrorist warfare including bombing private houses, abductions, laying mines, sabotage of infrastructure, blackmail, extortion and the use of car bombs in an attempt to assassinate Joshua Nkomo. Rhodesia had sought to control the international perception of the Nyazônia attack in advance, placing articles in newspapers that claimed that the refugee camp was a military base run by the Zimbabwe African Liberation Army (ZANLA), from which guerrillas were planning attacks on white settlers. Fernando Silva's film *O Massacre de Nyazónia* (1977) was the INC's initial refutation of Rhodesian reporting of the massacre, which Western media outlets tended to rely upon.

27 Ron Hallis (1980): 19–20.

28 Ron Hallis (1980): 20.

29 Paul Moorcraft (2011). *Mugabe's War Machine: Saving or Savaging Zimbabwe*. Barnsley: Pen & Sword Military: 53.

Silva's documentary features shocking footage of corpses strewn across the ground, presented without voiceover or musical accompaniment, forcing the viewer to confront the full horror of the images without commentary. This use of the moving image as an instrument of combat would accelerate in the years that followed as new 'enemies' of the Mozambican Revolution, both external and internal, were identified.

In 1978, a year after *O Massacre de Nyazónia* was made, the INC released a feature-length documentary in response to Rhodesian attacks, which was directed by Brazilian *cooperante* Murilo Salles. Titled *Estas são as Armas* 'These are the Weapons' (1978), the documentary denounced Rhodesia's ongoing aggression, placing it in the context of their military operations with the Portuguese army in Mozambique during the armed struggle and the historic alliance between the colonial powers of Britain and Portugal. The novelist Luís Bernardo Honwana, whose short story from the collection *We Killed Mangy Dog* had already been adapted to the cinema screen by Barbosa before independence (see Chapter 2), wrote the film script. Honwana drew for his title on a speech made by Samora Machel in the liberated zones, in which he brandished weapons that Frelimo had captured from the Portuguese army during the first attack that launched the armed struggle in 1964. Machel uses the weapons to galvanise his audience of peasants and guerrillas, instructing them on how this initial act of seizing the enemy's weapons and turning them on their foe led to subsequent victories. This gesture of appropriation and instruction is replicated throughout *Estas são as Armas*, which is best understood as a compilation film, a genre historically associated with propaganda in which archival materials are reworked and ascribed with new meanings to make a forceful argument through juxtaposition, repetition and voiceover. Although the first compilation film is usually credited as Fritz Hippler's anti-Semitic Nazi propaganda *Der Ewige Jude* 'The Wandering Jew' (1940), the method was widely harnessed to the cause of anti-imperialism by filmmakers working for socialist film institutions, including notably the Cuban Santiago Álvarez and Algerian Farouk Beloufa. In this trajectory, montage is a didactic principle that finds its genealogy in the disjunctive synthesis of Vertov and Eisenstein and may be understood as an aesthetic of internationalism.

Instead of editing together new footage, Salles therefore worked with images and sounds from both the colonial and the anti-colonial archives. Included within *Estas são as Armas* are excerpts from armed struggle documentaries that were made with Frelimo, such as *Behind the Lines* and *A Luta Continua*, together with drawings, photographs, colonial newsreels and films produced by *Radiotelevisão Portuguesa* and the Cinematographic Services of the Army. As Robert Stock argues, a particular feature of *Estas são as Armas* is the way in which the archive images have a function that extends beyond mere illustration.[30] Rather, images are presented to the viewer as 'objects of scrutiny', the voiceover providing the viewer with instruction on how to make a decolonial reading of them.[31] Walter Benjamin argued that the caption of a photograph could wrench the image from 'the ravages of modishness' and grant it 'revolutionary use-value'. Here, the voiceover works with the repetition and juxtaposition of colonial propaganda and images of colonial aggression to subvert the claims of imperialism and make an indictment of its violence.[32] In *Estas são as Armas* images are weapons in an ongoing struggle against imperialism, as the film is directed at challenging the dominance in the international media of narratives about region constructed by the white minority regimes in South Africa and Rhodesia.

If the voiceover is crucial to the re-interpretation of images that takes place in *Estas são as Armas*, then so too is silence. Right from the outset, the film experiments with what happens when images are stripped of verbal commentary and the emotional conditioning of the soundtrack. The film begins in silence, with an inter-title that reads 'Tete during the armed struggle', followed by sequences from *Viva Frelimo!* showing women and children weeping after an attack on their village (see Chapter 1). Still in silence, another inter-title 'Nyazônia Agosto 1976' introduces footage from Fernando Silva's *O Massacre de Nyazónia* of dozens of corpses and a shot in which the camera scans over shoes scattered across the ground. With no distraction from the soundtrack, the film forces the viewer to confront these images as visual evidence, in its full horror. Finally, the inter-title 'Why do they attack us?' provides the segue to a rare interview with Eduardo Mondlane: 'Why do they attack us?' he asks. 'They

[30] Robert Stock (2016). 'Cinema and Conflict in Postcolonial Mozambique: Archival Images as Illustration and Evidence in *Estas São as Armas* (1978)', in Adriana Martins, Alexandra Lopes and Mónica Dias (eds) (2016). *Mediations of Disruption in Post-Conflict Cinema*. London: Palgrave Macmillan: 79–81.

[31] Stock (2016).

[32] 'What we must demand from the photographer is the ability to put such a caption beneath his picture as will rescue it from the ravages of modishness and confer upon it a revolutionary use-value.' Walter Benjamin (1934). 'The Author as Producer', in Walter Benjamin (2002). *Selected Writings Volume 4 1938–1940* (trans. Edmund Jephcott *et al.*). Cambridge, MA, and London: Harvard University Press. In 'The Work of Art in the Age of its Technological Reproducibility', speaking of the hidden political significance of Atget's photographs, Benjamin wrote: 'They demand a specific kind of reception. Free-floating contemplation is no longer appropriate to them . . . For the first time, captions become obligatory. And it is clear that they have a character altogether different from the titles of paintings. The directives given by captions to those looking at images in illustrated magazines soon become even more precise and commanding in films, where the way each single image is understood appears prescribed by the sequence of all the preceding images.' Benjamin (2002): 258.

attack us because they are the enemies of freedom. They don't want Mozambique to be independent.'

Saxophone music accompanies images of Mozambican resistance to colonial violence, chiefly the battle in 1895 between the Gaza empire and the Portuguese army led by General Mouzinho de Albuquerque. The figure of Mouzinho de Albuquerque appears in the colonial film *Chaimite*, which celebrates the defeat of Ngungunhane through a fictional depiction of the battle, and in Celso and Luccas's '25', which includes sequences from *Chaimite* and footage of the General's statue being toppled at independence (see Chapter 2). *Estas são as Armas* presents photographs of Mouzinho de Albuquerque with his family and servants, a photographic portrait and his statue in the central Praça of Lourenço Marques. These images represent a colonialist account of the Portuguese presence in Mozambique as a noble civilising enterprise. However, a male voiceover intervenes to demolish this mythology: five hundred years of Portuguese colonialism has been, he insists, 'principally a war of occupation. The true face of colonialism is aggression. The colonial armies are armies of aggression. Aggression to ensure domination to enable exploitation.' Lines of soldiers marching are juxtaposed to workers without shoes planting rows of seeds.

At this point in the film, the male voiceover gives way to a female voiceover. While earlier films made with the Serviço de Cinema such as Celso and Luccas's '25' had featured inter-plays between male and female voiceovers, their content and interpretation of the visual material presented to the viewer was not markedly different (see Chapter 2). The male voice in *Estas são as Armas* has, as Stock points out, familiar qualities associated with an authoritative voiceover in documentary – it is rich in tone and has a Standard Portuguese accent. The female voiceover, by contrast, has a more pronounced Mozambican accent and makes repeated use of a collective inclusive address: 'we', 'our', 'us'. This discourse includes the viewer within an imagined community of Mozambicans who have suffered colonial violence, and, as Stock argues, represents a 'feminising' of the revolutionary nationalist project.[33] It is the voice of the 'New Woman' in the Mozambican Revolution, embodied in the figure of Josina Machel, who sought not only to destroy colonialism, but was also associated with education and the effort to dismantle traditional rituals and practices that maintained women in subordinate roles.[34] The role of the female voice here is significantly different in relation to the images. While the male voice pronounces historical truths, the female voice instructs the viewer on how to interpret the colonial images that the film presents, and in so doing radically changes their meaning from the original intended purpose.

[33] Stock (2016).

[34] See discussion of Josina Machel in Israel (2016): 189–190.

Images of Mozambican peasants cultivating cotton provide an opportunity to explain how the colonial regime enforced this form of agriculture, leading to widespread hunger: 'Our sweat served to enrich the proprietors.' The voiceover then takes an overtly pedagogical approach: 'The colonial powers plotted to make their methods of exploitation more efficient. Let us look at the images of one of these encounters.' The film then switches to an episode of the newsreel *Actualidades de Moçambique*, which was produced by the company of Melo Pereira. Titled 'Visita do Governador Geral da Federação', it documents the visit of the Governor-General of the Federation of Rhodesia and Nyasaland, the semi-independent Federation of southern African territories made up of the self-governing Southern Rhodesia and the British protectorates of Northern Rhodesia and Nyasaland. A jaunty male voiceover gives a commentary on the meeting, reporting on a factory visit and a banquet, at which the British Governor-General and the Portuguese Governor Manuel Sarmento Rodrigues give congratulatory speeches over glasses of champagne, confirming the friendship between Britain and Portugal. *Estas são as Armas* then repeats the images of the banquet, but stripped of the newsreel soundtrack. Instead the female voiceover gives an alternative interpretation: 'These images of the meeting that we have just seen don't show exploitation or oppression, but that is what they were dealing with. It was this that occupied the Portuguese and British colonialists. Colonialism is an instrument of imperialism.'

The following sequence provides further opportunities for deconstructing the propaganda of the previous regime, through yet more footage of visits by other governors of colonial Mozambique. Amid a soundtrack that features a lugubrious Portuguese song, the film shows footage of another governor, Baltasar Leite Rebelo de Sousa, who, with his wife by his side, is borne through the streets of Ilha de Moçambique in a carriage pushed by a Mozambican man. Ilha de Moçambique, an island of the coast of Cabo Delgado strongly influenced by its historical connection to the Arab world and Swahili culture, was an area of the country that was relatively prosperous under Portuguese rule; within Frelimo's discourse it was often pointed to as an example of colonial corruption.[35] A crowd gathered to greet the governor carries a sign saying 'The population thanks you'. Portuguese officials meet and greet African soldiers recruited into the colonial army. In this instance the claim to historical truth of these images is undercut not by the voiceover, but through juxtaposition. Without commentary, the film switches to footage of police dogs attacking a black man. A startling close-up

[35] Séverine Cachat's research reveals that even long after independence nostalgia for colonial times persisted among certain sections of the population of the island. Séverine Cachat (2009). 'Un héritage ambigu: L'île de Mozambique, la construction du patrimoine et ses enjeux'. PhD Thesis. Université de la Réunion. Available: https://tel.archives-ouvertes.fr/tel-00955661v1/document.

of a *palmatória* rears into view, a sudden crash zoom making it seem as if the implement is hitting the viewer. The *palmatória*, a perforated paddle that was used on the plantations to inflict maximum scarring and pain upon forced labourers, was synonymous with colonial labour abuses. More images follow of police officers and soldiers marching with dogs, and the scene of the dog attack is repeated again. Large aggressive dogs were specially bred and widely used by white minority regimes across Southern Africa to protect white privilege and quell black revolt.[36] Indeed, Honwana's short story *We Killed Mangy Dog* was just one of a number of literary works produced in Angola, Mozambique and South Africa in which dogs function as symbols of both the perpetrators and the victims of colonial oppression.[37] These scenes of dog attacks and displays of ferocity are more than potent symbols of white aggression: through the editing the images assault the viewer. While colonial propaganda presents images of conviviality, the truth of colonialism is brutality and terror, evoked through the triggering of a sensorial collective memory of violence.

These images of the *palmatória* and the dogs are alarming to encounter, but to understand their cumulative affect in this sequence a wider context of moving-image production in the region needs to be considered. Unlike the Portuguese colonial regime, the Rhodesian government commissioned films specifically for African audiences, though their racist convictions about the vulnerability of African peoples to the persuasive effects of film meant that their efforts often backfired. J. M. Burns argues that by the late 1970s the Rhodesian regime had recognised that its efforts to use films addressed to African audiences failed to convince them that white minority rule was in their best interests.[38] Abandoning attempts at persuasion, the Rhodesian Information Service (RIS) turned to the production of films that presented graphic images of violence that were intended to intimidate. The film *Vigil* that was produced some time after 1972, for example, presents Rhodesia's white communities as being threatened by communist violence. It includes a re-enactment of a Rhodesian army raid on a

[36] Aggressive dogs had been imported into Southern Africa by European settlers and the British military over the centuries of colonialist expansion. The role of large fierce dogs in protecting white property and privilege in South Africa and Rhodesia accelerated after the Second World War as rapid urbanisation coincided with the rise of militant black resistance. According to Lance van Sittert and Sandra Swart, the number of dogs used by police forces increased in direct relation to the escalation of black rebellion in the years following 1960, and in 1964 a military dog unit was established by the South African army to assist in 'sniffing out' guerrillas. This South African practice was replicated in neighbouring settler states including Mozambique. Lance van Sittert and Sandra Swart (2003). 'Canis Familiaris: A Dog History of South Africa'. *South African Historical Journal*, 48: 1: 150–3, 163–5.

[37] I am grateful to Afonso Ramos for his insights into this wider context.

[38] J. M. Burns (2002). *Flickering Shadows: Cinema and Identity in Colonial Zimbabwe*. Athens: Ohio University Press: 205.

guerrilla base 'behind the iron curtain' in Mozambique.[39] The film emphasises the superior military technology of the Rhodesian army, whose helicopters, airplanes, tanks and explosives enable them to defeat the insurgents. The camera lingers on the dead bodies of guerrillas, one of them clutching a book by Chairman Mao Tse-Tung, an 'unsuspecting African' who had been 'lured by promises of free education'.[40] Frederiske describes another untitled film that was destroyed by the Rhodesian government in 1980 just before Zimbabwe's independence, which featured a horrifying scene of a hyena on a leash ripping apart the mutilated bodies of three guerrillas.[41] The camera lingers on this obscene image, before closing with a black screen and the sound of hyenas laughing. Burns describes the resistance to this wave of films as 'unprecedented': 'Mobile cinema operators who worked during the middle and late 1970s live in constant fear of attack and reprisals for showing them . . . In the border regions of the colony, which had the heaviest incidents of guerrilla infiltration, freedom fighters often attended the shows.'[42] Rather than intimidate, the RIS productions only inflamed the anger of viewers who recognised the staged nature of the films and refused the Rhodesian government's version of events.[43]

The effect of the images of colonial violence in *Estas são as Armas* is incendiary. Immediately following this visceral sequence, the female voiceover channels its affect. Instead of being terrorised into submission, she insists that: 'Our people always resisted. Our history is a history of many revolts.' A montage of images of contemporary and historical resistance to colonialism gives way to footage of Samora Machel's 'These are the Weapons' speech, followed by footage of Mondlane and Machel together in the liberated zones and finally the sequence from the beginning of *A Luta Continua* that announces the beginning of the armed struggle (see Chapter 1). 'With the founding of Frelimo,' the female voice comments, 'colonialism felt very threatened. They prepared their forces for combat and reinforced their alliances.' Footage of armoured vehicles driving past crowds of white settlers and soldiers mounted on horses are followed by a single photograph showing Ian Smith and Salazar shaking hands. 'Who is this talking with Salazar?' the female voice asks rhetorically. 'It is Ian Smith. They have many interests in common.' Indeed, in the year that Frelimo launched the armed struggle, Smith visited Lisbon, where Salazar, furious at Britain's relinquishing of its African colonies, offered him support if he were to

[39] Burns (2002): 203.

[40] Burns (2002): 203–204.

[41] J. Frederiske (1991). *None but Ourselves: Masses vs Media in the Making of Zimbabwe*. Harare: OTAZI/Anvil: 95, cited in Kedmon Nyasha Hungwe (2005). 'Narrative and Ideology: 50 Years of Film-making in Zimbabwe'. *Media, Culture & Society*, 27, 1: 83–99.

[42] Burns (2002): 204.

[43] Burns (2002): 205.

unilaterally form a white minority state. The following year, on 11 November 1965, Smith issued a Unilateral Declaration of Independence for Rhodesia in defiance of the British government.

Estas são as Armas concludes with a series of sequences showing footage from the armed struggle. In contrast to imperialist violence, Frelimo's struggle is presented as having a higher cause. The female voiceover explains: 'Frelimo did not limit itself to recruiting combatants, it transformed life, it liberated initiative.' Over images from *Behind the Lines*, she states: 'The armed struggle was the highest form of anti-colonial resistance. The armed struggle was the affirmation of our culture and of our nationality.' Sinister electronic sounds accompany scenes of Portuguese officials, soldiers marching and bombing campaigns, while the liberated zones are presented with soft guitar music over scenes of agricultural cultivation, construction of houses and forest schools. While the visual presentation in *Estas são as Armas* depicts relations between the colonisers and the colonised in terms of racial conflict, the voiceover clarifies that decolonisation requires more than reversing racial privilege: 'All the sacrifices are not just to replace a white exploiter with a black exploiter. Our struggle isn't just against colonialism, it is against all forms of exploitation and domination.'

Images of Mondlane and Machel in *Estas são as Armas* serve to vindicate the truth of their words. By contrast, when Caetano is shown claiming that there is no such thing as colonial war in Mozambique and that the 'overseas provinces are peaceful', images of Portuguese soldiers in combat and being carried wounded from the battlefield demonstrate that this is untrue. Machel is depicted as a dignified figure on the international stage, shown giving his address to the United Nations, at which he lays out Frelimo's principles of internationalism and their determination to stand up to foreign aggression. Finally, the film returns again to Machel's speech in the liberated zones, in which he holds up the weapons that began the armed struggle in Cabo Delgado: 'The canons and bazookas that you have come from these weapons. The products that you have today, cashews and peanuts, come from these weapons.' The film concludes with the choral hymn 'Viva Frelimo!' and the words 'A Luta Continua'.

Estas são as Armas marks a hardening of anti-imperialist rhetoric in response to Rhodesian aggression at a time when Frelimo was also becoming increasingly suspicious of departures from the party line. These tensions emerged more starkly in the making of another major INC production: Guerra's *Mueda, Memória e Massacre*. In the first two years after his return to Mozambique in 1977, Guerra directed a number of documentaries and contributed to the strategic discussions taking place within the INC about what technologies of the moving image were appropriate for a newly independent nation that had embarked upon the path of socialist revolution. In 1978, at the suggestion of Camilo de Sousa, Guerra and a team of INC filmmakers set off to Cabo Delgado

Province to document a community re-enactment that had taken place annually since 1976 of a massacre by Portuguese soldiers of hundreds of protestors in the town of Mueda.[44] The Mueda massacre took place on 16 June 1960, when the colonial official in charge of the district ordered soldiers to open fire on protestors who had gathered in front of the administrative building. While it was reported in the colonial press at the time that only fourteen protestors had died, the figure cited by Frelimo was in the region of six hundred. Like the mass killing of strikers at the docks of Pidijuiti in Guinea-Bissau on 3 August 1959 and the Baixa de Cassanje revolt in Angola on 4 February 1961, this atrocity came to be understood as the trigger for anti-colonial insurrection.[45] Few of the atrocities committed by the colonial regime were documented, a fact that led filmmakers working with Frelimo during the armed struggle to re-use repeatedly a small number of trophy photographs that were actually taken by Portuguese soldiers in Angola (see Chapter 1). Frelimo was keen for the INC to make an 'epic' film that would commemorate this event as the pivotal moment that precipitated the armed struggle for independence.[46]

The non-professional actors, some of whom were survivors of the massacre, followed a script written by Calisto dos Lagos. However, as João Borges Coelho points out, the carnivalesque performance is permeated with the ritual practices of the Cabo Delgado region, particularly the permeable border between actor and audience.[47] As well as depicting the re-enactment, the film incorporates testimonies from eye-witnesses. In addition, the film is framed at the beginning and end by scenes of everyday life in the Mozambican Revolution, manifested in the construction of houses, adult education and agricultural labour. In an article in *Tempo*, Guerra describes how the power of the enactment compelled the film crew to make an 'imperfect cinema' out of an 'imperfect theatre', referring to Espinosa's essay 'For an Imperfect Cinema' (see Chapter 3).[48] Guerra shared Espinosa's view that filmmakers should insert themselves into the realities of societies in transition to socialism, using whatever technological means were

[44] Camilo de Sousa was then still overseeing the political use of film in the province of Cabo Delgado. He had known Guerra before independence, and while he was visiting the province de Sousa suggested that Guerra should return with a film crew to document the re-enactment. Conversation with Camilo de Sousa, Lisbon, 2017.

[45] An account of the massacre by Alberto Joaquim Chipande was published in *Mozambique Revolution* in 1970. Chipande led the first attack by Frelimo on the colonial post at Chai that began the armed struggle. Alberto Joaquim Chipande (1970). 'The Massacre at Mueda'. *Mozambique Revolution* 43: 12–14.

[46] José Luís Cabaço cited in Vavy Pacheco Borges (2017). *Ruy Guerra: Paixão Escancerada*. São Paulo: Boitempo Editorial.

[47] João Paulo Borges Coelho (2011). 'Mueda – memoria e massacre'. *Views of the World: Films from the Archive of INAC, Maputo: Mozambique*: 20–21.

[48] 'Memória e Massacre de Mueda'. *Tempo*, 418, 1978: 35.

at hand. Despite being a major production, *Mueda* was shot on the cheaper format of 16mm black-and-white film as Guerra preferred its aesthetic effect to colour. 'Imperfect' also refers to the idea that the film is incomplete without the active response of the audience, and here revolutionary aesthetics meets with the cultural practice of Mapiko, the song and dance of the Makonde people traditionally associated with initiation rituals which had been radically transformed and politicised during the armed struggle. According to Paulo Israel, Mapiko is 'marked by a double inclination to naturalistic perfection and grotesque exaggeration'.[49] In Mapiko the performers are both the masked dancers who move acrobatically, but also their 'audience', the members of their community encircled around them, who respond with gestures of fear or provocation. The mask allows the dancer to embody other identities, both representing and absorbing alterity through mimesis. The re-enactment of the massacre documented in the film displays many traits associated with Mapiko. Actors playing the roles of colonial officials wear exaggerated white pointed noses and adopt a comical gait. Performers move in and out of the circle of people that surrounds the administrative building where the re-enactment takes place. These features insist upon the fictionality of the performance and draw attention to moments of comedy and ambivalence.

An article published in *Tempo* in 1978 cites Guerra as claiming that the film crew followed the imperative of 'imperfect cinema' by inserting themselves into the unfolding enactment, with the filmmaking causing very little alteration to the organic process of the play. Indeed, the filmmaker asserts that the film crew felt that there was 'a total understanding between us and the participants' and that 'the presence of the cameras did not produce disturbances or alterations in . . . the comportment of the actors'.[50] While the actors may have been undeterred by the presence of the film crew, the same cannot be said of the audience, whose direct looks to the camera and responses to the unfolding drama are captured on film, breaking the cinematic illusion of non-interference by the filmmakers that is often maintained in observational documentary. Such sequences provide a clue that the process of documenting the performance is in itself having a transformative effect on this enactment of collective memory.

Portuguese colonial anthropologists Jorge and Margo Dias, who had conducted the only ethnographic study in the region prior to the making of the film, stressed the social function of Mapiko in sustaining gender hierarchy, representing Makonde culture as static and as if it existed outside of history.[51]

[49] Israel (2014): 11.

[50] 'Memória e Massacre de Mueda'.

[51] See Harry West (2006). 'Invertendo a Bossa do Camelo. Jorge Dias, a sua Mulher, o seu Intérprete e eu', in Manuela Ribeiro Sanches (2006). *Portugal Não é um País Pequeno: Contar o 'Império' na Pós-colonialidade*. Lisbon: Livros Cotovia: 141–192.

The rapid evolution of the Mapiko during the armed struggle demonstrated the error of this assumption and reflected the central role that the Makonde played in initiating and participating in the armed struggle. But relations between Makonde guerrillas and other Frelimo combatants were not without conflict. The schism within the liberation movement that erupted in violence in 1968 was in part due to the actions of a group led by Lázaro Nkavandame. His advocacy for a revival of 'Makonde consciousness' set it on a collision course with Frelimo's anti-tribalist stance (see Chapter 1). To what extent would this pre-history of contestation and rebellion unsettle Frelimo's desire to construct a narrative of resistance to colonialism that would promote national unity?

The film begins with a black screen and the sounds of a lesson in which the pupils repeat by rote a narrative of Mozambican history dictated by their teacher, a new curriculum centred on the history and geography of the nation rather than Portugal that recites the genealogy of peoples already living in the region when Portuguese explorers arrived in 1498.[52] *Mueda, Memória e Massacre* thus opens with the question of how we learn about the past – what is the narrative that is passed down? Traces of violence are in evidence in the fabric of everyday life: the first image shows a window, a spider suspended next to a bullet hole in the pane of glass, and as the camera begins to pan around it reveals a wooden building in a state of decay. The camera falls upon a bugle, which the trumpeter Filipe Gunoguacala picks up. His sounding of the bugle announces the beginning of the play. An inter-title explains that *Mueda, Memória e Massacre* is shot at the original location and with survivors as actors and audience, and the film cuts to a shot taken with a camera positioned within the audience. A man leads the cries 'Viva Frelimo!' in Shimakonde and then begins a set of instructions to the crowd on how they should conduct themselves during the filming:

> We will tell the history of the massacre that took place here in Mueda in 1960. They will record it. Everybody, wherever they are standing, has to take up a posture, like a well-organized person. For now we are independent. It's not the moment to yawn or to let yourself go. When you start scratching yourselves here and there, outsiders might laugh about it and that would be bad. They have seen our movies that we watched at night. Today it would be good if everybody maintained a good posture. Keep quiet, and behave like a well-organized person, so that people can say: 'Yes

52 'When the Portuguese came to Mozambique . . . in the year 1498 . . . they encountered . . . an Arabian chief . . . by the name . . . of Moussa Mbiki . . . on the Ilha de Moçambique. Man of the languages . . . that we speak . . . belong . . . to the Bantu . . . The first inhabitants . . . of Southern Africa . . . including us Mozambicans . . . were the Khoisan . . . people of small stature . . . nomads. After the Khoisan . . . came the Hottentots . . . a people with an advanced social structure . . . The Khoisan fled . . . into the Kalahari . . . Where they are still living today.

> sir, this person knows how to behave.' For now we are independent. So, when we start our play, they will start shooting in the middle. And when they start shooting we have to go back all together. Don't go back all the way to your houses, it's only a matter of a few steps. And then you return to your position, until we are allowed to leave . . . There shouldn't be sudden exits. That wouldn't be good. These films will go far away, even to Europe. Viva Frelimo! Viva! Now we will make room . . . so they can film . . . as the sun is already blazing. Viva Frelimo! Viva!

The camera, which has been lingering within the circle of the audience, then pans backwards and turns to a group of men seated on the ground by a tree. It fixes on Romão Canapoquele, who rises to his feet, suitcase in hand, assuming the role of Faustino Vanomba, a nationalist recently returned from Tanganika. The camera follows his face in close-up as he walks forward, in role, and approaches the colonial administrators building. Faustino asks to speak to the white men, and the *cipaio* Tac Tac Mandusse, played by Baltasar Nchilema, tells him to wait.

The drama unfolds to its crescendo of violence through a sequence of encounters in which nationalist activists request to enter the administrative building so as to demand independence. The camera thus follows the actors playing the nationalists into an interior space that the audience cannot enter, and which functions more like a film set. This movement signals the shift taking place with the cinematographic recording of the performance, which will transform it from popular re-enactment into a film that will travel beyond the circle of that particular community – a local memory becoming national narrative. They are ushered into the building by *cipaio*, one of whom acts as the translator. The nationalists make their demands in Shimakonde, and the colonial officials strut about, making racists slurs and pontificating on the superiority of Europeans and the history of colonialism. Much of the comedy is derived from the exaggerated gestures of the actors who play the oafish colonialists, with their pointed fake white noses and high-stepping gait. The *cipaio* Tac Tac Madusse is another source of comedy, his buffoonish subservience to the colonialists and the beatings he receives for his foolish errors providing a cathartic release. The mimicking of the Europeans and their lackeys, conducted with such verve and so clearly not illusionistic, provokes laughter, a bodily excess that punctuates the interactions between the Europeans and the Africans that culminates in the massacre. But there are also extraordinary moments of slippage in the mimesis, as when one of the colonial officers asks the translator: 'Aren't you black?' This seems to propel the actor playing the translator into a *mise en abyme* of imitation. He hesitates, as if for a moment uncertain.

Raquel Schafer argues that such elements constitute a 'sensory' re-enactment of the experience of colonialism.[53] This sensory collective work of memory competes with other elements in the film that provide different registers of narrative, including eye-witness testimonies from survivors and, in the version of the film held at INAC, uniformed soldiers who provide a meta-narrative that forefronts the massacre as a foundational event in the history of Frelimo. In recent years, careful research by Raquel Schefer and Caterina Simão has located different versions of *Mueda, Memória e Massacre* and begun the work of re-constructing its complicated production history. Schefer reports that when the Minister for Information Jorge Rebelo saw the film in 1979 he objected to the presence of the eye-witness testimony of Raimundo Pachinuapa, veteran of the liberation struggle, member of the Frelimo and, at the time, Governor of Cabo Delgado Province.[54] Pachinuapa appears in military uniform, which was interpreted by Rebelo as conferring on his testimony the status of official history and giving a 'disproportionate' role to the Makonde in the struggle for independence.[55] He attempted to convince Guerra to re-shoot these scenes with an actor. When Guerra refused, the film was partially re-shot and re-edited without his supervision by Licínio Azevedo, a Brazilian filmmaker and journalist who arrived in Mozambique in 1977, having spent time reporting on the Carnation Revolution and independence in Guinea-Bissau.[56] Eventually a version of the film was released in 1980 without these replacement scenes as they were deemed to be of insufficient quality for international distribution. This final version won the People's Friendship Union and Film Culture awards at the Tashkent Film Festival in 1980, and was projected at other international events in different parts of the world.

Schefer argues that *Mueda, Memória e Massacre* is a 'dissensual object' and that the history of censorship that her research has uncovered demonstrates that the multiple layers of history in evidence in the film could not be contained by Frelimo's official version of history. According to this argument, the discourse of the military appropriates the anti-colonial resistance of the people of Mueda to legitimise the new regime. *Mueda, Memória e Massacre* is indeed structured through a series of enclosures – the circle of the audience and the building of the colonial administrator – that might also represent the containment of the narrative of the massacre within an officially ratified historical discourse. Yet

[53] Raquel Schefer (2017). 'Between the Visible and the Invisible: Mueda, Memória e Massacre by Ruy Guerra and the Cultural Forms of the Makonde Plateau', in Maria do Carmo Piçarra and Teresa Castro (eds) (2017). *(Re)imagining African Independence: Film, Visual Arts and the Fall of the Portuguese Empire*. London: Peter Lang: 48.

[54] Raquel Schefer (2018), 'Ruy Guerra's *Mueda, Memoria e Massacre*: The Lost Images', *The Journal of African Cinemas*, 10, 3: 205–223.

[55] Schefer (2018).

[56] Schefer (2018).

the film also shows these structures of containment continually being breached, both by the actors who move between the building and the outside, and between the circle of the audience and the inner area of the re-enactment. Also crossing these boundaries is the camera, in its sweeping circular movements as well as the moments when its gaze penetrates through windows and crevasses, or after the end of the performance when it follows the crowd dispersing into the village.

In contrast to the representations of colonial anthropology, in *Mueda, Memória e Massacre* the Makonde are agents of history and their forms of cultural expression dynamically reflect their central role within the struggle for independence. The ethnographic scenes at the end of the film, which depict women taking literacy classes, construction and agricultural work, show the Mozambican society in a process of radical transformation, in transition to socialism. Part of that transformation is the appropriation of the play within Frelimo's nationalist discourse through the making of the film. Seen through the moving image, the yearly re-enactment is no longer open to subtle shifts in memory. Instead this interpretation of history is shown in the process of becoming fixed, precisely through its documentation and the historical narration that frames it. Ironically, despite the complex play with representational codes and aesthetic form in *Mueda, Memória e Massacre*, the film came to serve as a substitute for the lack of visual evidence of the massacre, ironically becoming a testament to the effectiveness of film as a tool to control the collective memory of a contested history.

Mueda, Memória e Massacre thus marked a moment in which the possibilities for what might constitute an aesthetic of liberation and what kind of narratives cinema could tell began to narrow. At the same time, the project of democratising film production as part of a process of decolonisation migrated away from the INC to be taken up in the 1980s by other institutions. The demand for adherence to the 'correct line' of the vanguard party resulted in a number of casualties at the INC. The efforts to deconstruct the inequalities produced by colonialism within filmmaking examined in Chapter 3 coincided with a hardening of anti-imperialist rhetoric and an intensification of efforts to re-educate and eradicate counter-revolutionary elements. Some of those who came to the INC from the ciné-clubs began to experience hostility directed towards those who had occupied a position of privilege within the colonial order, even if they had been active anti-colonialists. Patraquim, who left Mozambique in the 1960s as a political refugee only to return in 1975, suggests that the effort to recruit and train black Mozambicans might be understood as a kind of 're-Mozambicanification', but that it was, according to his interpretation:

> a euphemism that hid the suspicion or conflict between staff members, mostly Mozambicans from an urban environment and imbued with a cinephilia tradition

> . . . they were regarded as 'petit bourgeois' and cosmopolitan in transition – in transition between the 'old Lourenço Marques' and the Maputo of independence.[57]

The fate of José Baptista's film *Madrugada Suburbana* 'Suburban Dawn' produced between 1977 and 1978 is exemplary for Patraquim of the way in which the potential for certain filmmakers to develop was cut short by the imperative to make films that provided a clear political line. Baptista had trained as a sound technician at the INC and *Madrugada Suburbana* was his first film in the role of director. This short film, which according to Patraquim revealed Baptista's talent for realist documentary, followed the trajectories of inhabitants of the *subúrbios* as they attempted to make their way to work in the city centre.[58] In revealing the everyday struggles that these protagonists faced as a result of a failing transportation infrastructure, the documentary was at odds with official rhetoric, which insisted that conditions were improving. As a result, Rebelo censored the film and Baptista left Mozambique to pursue his career in Europe.[59] In 1979, Fernando Silva left for Brazil and Americo Soares departed for Portugal after having been 'humiliated' politically.[60] Soares's assistant Samuel Matola was promoted to be the new director of the INC.

Guerra's film thus marks both the foreclosure of the INC's early years of experimentation and the onset of a new decade that would begin with a drive for increased efficiency and professionalism as cinema in Mozambique continued its battle of information. The INC's contribution to this struggle for revolutionary pedagogy and its dissemination encompassed didacticism of different kinds – from newsreel delivery of information and the staging of official politics, instructional films, documentary interventions that sought to reveal how present-day violence was rooted in colonialism and white supremacy to the genre-defying *Mueda*, which reflects on the transmission of knowledge across generations and its harnessing to the narrating of the history of the nation-state. These various experiments with didacticism reveal competing urgencies that required different film aesthetics and strategies – ranging from the desire to present the transition to socialism to acts of détournement in which the intentions of the colonial archive are put into reverse through the cultivation of a decolonial film viewer. What emerges in these years is a continual tension and slippage between gestures that anticipate a new socialist society and those that reinforce totalitarian forms of power, the revolutionary scene becoming a crystalline image that refracts other times and places *en abyme*. The circular shots in *Mueda* recall those in Celso and Luccas's film '25', another film made

[57] Luís Carlos Patraquim, 'The New Series of Kuxa Kanema: The Institutionalized Revolutionary Discourse.' INAC. *Views from the World: Films from the Archive of INAC*: 13.

[58] Interview with Luís Carlos Patraquim, Lisbon, 18 December 2016.

[59] Interview with Luís Carlos Patraquim, Lisbon, 18 December 2016.

[60] Interview with Luís Carlos Patraquim, Lisbon, 18 December 2016.

by filmmakers associated with the New Latin American cinema who came to contribute to the Mozambican Revolution (see Chapter 2). Within this tradition of filmmaking, the circular shot is understood as an emancipatory tendency that expresses a revolutionary desire. It is a device that situates the filmmakers within the scene of revolution on the same continuum of radical upheaval. Schefer suggests that the circular shots in *Mueda* are in fact incomplete, arguing that this indicates that, unlike the horizontal organisation of the militant film collectives, the hierarchy of the director as author of the artistic vision is re-asserted.[61] However, and as this chapter has also explored, the breaking of the circle can also result in the formation of a line that faces the revolutionary leader, who is the embodiment of a new power.

[61] Schefer (2017).

5 A New Symphony: Cinema and Television in the 'Decade of Development', 1980–1984

On 21 December 1979, the Lancaster House Agreement settled the terms of Zimbabwe's independence and announced the end of the armed struggle, which Frelimo had supported by offering sanctuary to the liberation movement ZANU (see Chapter 6). The elections in February 1980 resulted in a landslide victory for Robert Mugabe and it was anticipated that, without the support of the Rhodesian security forces, the MNR (known as Renamo after 1984) would wither away. It soon became apparent that this was not the case. Indeed the MNR quickly found a more powerful sponsor in the form of P. W. Botha's government in South Africa and attracted recruits who were disaffected by Frelimo. But at the advent of this new decade, it seemed that Mozambique would be able to build on the achievements of the first few years of independence, when forms of local democratic participation had been established, access to education and healthcare increased and the work of national reconstruction had begun. In November 1980, the first annual meeting of the Southern African Development Coordination Conference (SADCC) placed Mozambique at the heart of a plan to break regional dependency on South Africa through regional economic cooperation (see Chapter 6).[1]

Within Mozambique, 1980 saw the launch of Frelimo's ten-year Prospective and Indicative Plan (PPI) that set out targets for increasing national production and industrialisation (though in fact it only remained in place until 1983). Intended to implement a great leap forward to modernisation, it proposed expanding industry to produce more basic consumer goods, transforming the countryside through the formation of collective villages and continued state control of abandoned farms that were mechanised and required centralised management. In 1980, Mozambique cemented its independence from the former regime with the introduction of a new currency – the metical – that replaced colonial money with banknotes and coins with portraits of Samora

[1] Joseph Hanlon (1991). *Mozambique: who calls the shots?* Bloomington: Indiana University Press and London: James Currey: 17–18.

Machel and Eduardo Mondlane. For the time being it seemed that Mozambique's sovereignty was secure.

In 1979, with peace in the region finally in sight, Samora Machel had declared that the 1980s would be 'the decade of victory over underdevelopment'. However, five years after independence the new nation was still in economic crisis and production had not returned to pre-1975 levels. Now that the war with Rhodesia had ended, Machel turned his attention to problems that were internal to the country. At a rally in Beira on 11 January 1980, he launched a new 'social offensive, for justice, for respect for revolutionary legality, and the combat to dislodge slave mentalities indebted to foreign ideas'. Beira, which was perceived by Frelimo to be a stronghold of colonialism, was to be the 'point of departure for the offensive against banditry, corruption and counter-revolution'.[2] INC filmmakers were on-hand to capture this latest venture. Camilo de Sousa, who had been executive producer of *Mueda: Memória e Massacre*, directed *Ofensiva* (1980), which tracks Machel as his campaign took him to industrial sites, factories, schools, hospitals and state-run shops. In a scene filmed at the docks Machel accosts the 'enemy', but in a different form, rooting out 'economic saboteurs' who have infiltrated the supply system to paralyse the economy. Mountains of products lie rotting in warehouses as the people queue for hours to buy basic goods, only to find the shelves are empty. Machel berates and heckles officials, leaning forward and wagging his finger at them, or standing shoulders back, feet wide apart in the midst of a crowd of dock-workers, joking, scolding and propounding.

Malyn Newitt notes that Machel's rhetoric after independence continued in the vein that he had begun to use during the armed struggle, adopting a discourse characterised by 'moralistic homilies' that attributed economic failings to a lack of discipline and weak revolutionary moral fibre.[3] While some of Frelimo's greatest successes relied on high levels of voluntarism, Machel adopted an increasingly puritanical approach to the kinds of behaviour that the 'New Man' and 'New Woman' of the revolution should embody. Thus in *Ofensiva*, exhorting the workers to take pride in their work, he urges them to continue to increase production, discipline and cleanliness. In so doing, he sketches out a diagram of power. Within this frame, the work of each individual is dedicated not to furthering personal ambitions but, above all, to the collective task of national reconstruction administered by the revolutionary state. The threat to the Mozambican Revolution, according to Machel, comes from those who deviate from this path. In *Ofensiva*, his message is clear: 'The enemy's agents have infiltrated the state apparatus. Who are they? They are . . . those who were

[2] Transcript of speech by Samora Machel, *Tempo*, 485, 25–26.

[3] Malyn Newitt (2017). *A Short History of Mozambique*. London: Hurst: 157.

being prepared by colonialism to take over, who have remained here as long-range booby-traps.'[4]

This chapter examines film production in the early 1980s, at the beginning of the so-called 'decade of development', which saw not only a great expansion in the number of documentaries and newsreels made by the INC, but also a radical overhaul of the institution itself to increase professionalism and efficiency. While the INC's response to the violence that quickly engulfed the country and interventions through filmmaking in regional geopolitics will be addressed in Chapter 6, this chapter focuses on efforts to harness filmmaking to the projects of development, collectivisation and national unity. It considers various attempts to develop filmmaking practices that were appropriate to the lived realities of most Mozambicans, for whom cinema was still a new phenomenon, and that would assist in the campaign against 'underdevelopment' in terms of literacy, health, agriculture and industrial production. Explorations of what technologies of the moving image would be appropriate to the Mozambican context that had begun in the late 1970s continued, both through the launch of Televisão Experimental and in more marginal filmmaking projects that used video to support rural development. This took place in the context of growing anxiety about Renamo's attacks and infiltration by the 'internal enemy'. The chapter examines films that address how Frelimo dealt with 'counter-revolutionary' behaviour, both through re-education and rituals of public confession.

The first two years of the new decade, from 1980 to 1981, were the most productive years for the INC in terms of documentary filmmaking, and the chapter makes a close analysis of a number of key film productions in terms of how they embody conflicting ideas of national identity and how they support the cause of socialist transformation. These films demonstrate how the INC offered certain individuals opportunities to hone their skills as directors with documentaries that project singular accounts of the Mozambican Revolution. Ruy Guerra's *Um Povo Nunca Morre* 'A People Never Dies' (1980) documented the return to Mozambique from Tanzania of the bodies of fallen combatants of the armed struggle, contributing to the narration of national history through a cult of military heroes. José Baptista's *Madrugada Suburbana* 'Suburban Dawn' (1980) focuses on the daily plight of urban inhabitants who struggle to get to work on a failing transportation system, a realist approach that was perceived as a criticism by Frelimo. José Cardoso's *Canta Meu Irmão, Ajuda-me a Cantar* 'Sing My Brother, Help me to Sing' (1981) takes the Festival of Traditional Song and Dance as the premise for an intimate cultural portrait of the nation, while

[4] Speech given in Maputo on 18 March 1980 that launched the internal offensive. Translated from Samora Machel (1980). 'Deslojemos o Inimigo Interno do Nosso Aparelho de Estado'. *Palavras de Ordem*, 19. Maputo: Edição do Partido Frelimo, in Barry Munslow (ed.) (1985). *Samora Machel, An African Revolutionary*. London: Zed Books: 86–103.

Moira Forjaz's *Um Dia Numa Aldeia Communal* 'A Day in a Communal Village' (1981) is a rare example of an INC film that focuses on gender, examining the harsh lives of women living in a collective village. In the early 1980s, the INC continued to receive delegations of filmmakers from other socialist countries including Cuba and North Korea, and the films they made in Mozambique demonstrate contrasting versions of what a socialist cinema could be.

In 1980, José Luís Cabaço replaced Jorge Rebelo as Minister for Information. Although the INC had succeeded in setting up a part-nationalised integrated system of production, acquisition and distribution, Cabaço identified a number of problems with the INC's operations that he claimed were preventing the institution from being truly 'independent' and serving the cause of development in Mozambique. He initiated changes at the INC that were outlined in a speech he delivered to staff in 1981. Focusing on the image as a medium of communication rather than artistic expression, Cabaço suggested that all forms of image production should be centralised under the control of the Ministry of Information, including cinema, television and what in Portuguese is referred to as '*audiovisuais*' – a term that includes photography, slide-shows and posters that might perform a supportive role in using the moving image for didactic purposes. A new weekly version of the *Kuxa Kanema* newsreel was proposed, which was to be the INC's core production and at the heart of plans to develop television broadcasting for the nation.

While certain factions within Frelimo sought to rein in the INC's autonomy, the project organised by TBARN and CEC at Eduardo Mondlane University persisted, in part due to its more marginal status. While in the late 1970s the team had focused their efforts to use filmmaking in rural development on the region around Maputo, in 1980 they began working in the northern region of Niassa in the far more impoverished and isolated district of Mavago. Drawing on testimonies of key participants, the chapter examines how they moved on from Super-8 to experiment with video so as to facilitate 'exchanges of experiences' between different communities as a means to inspire and empower villagers in the task of setting up cooperatives.

Though Machel's cinematic allure remained untarnished, these years in fact saw a waning of his command of government, as the difficulties that Frelimo experienced in terms of both domestic and foreign policy led to increasing paranoia about security and sabotage. In the early 1980s filmmakers at the INC documented Frelimo's approach to dealing with dissent through re-education and rehabilitation at a time when the Mozambican government came under pressure over human rights abuses. Ike Bertel's *Treatment for Traitors* (1983) edited together some of the public confessions made at the Meeting of the Compromised in 1982 by people accused of collaborating with the colonial authorities, as a precondition for re-entering society. While the party line emphasised rehabilitation and social transformation, certain figures within the political elite manoeuvred to gain more control and quell dissent. The restructuring of the INC and other initiatives, such as the setting up of a private production company called Kanemo, can be understood as part of a project of bringing moving-image production under the tighter control of the Ministry of Information and the Security Services and the beginning of a shift away from a socialist command economy towards the free market.

While changes were afoot at the turn of the decade, within the INC the first two years of the 1980s saw the release of an unprecedented number of documentaries, the strongest of which present compelling visions of what a Mozambican cinema could be, grounded in an attempt by filmmakers to address the lived realities of Mozambicans. In 1980, José Baptista's documentary *Madrugada Suburbana* was finally projected, after having been shot between 1977 and 1978.[5] According to Luís Carlos Patraquim, this was a remarkable short film that, in its depiction of the attempts of urban inhabitants from the suburbs of Maputo to navigate their way to work in the city centre, showed an affinity with Italian neorealism. Baptista was one of the INC's younger filmmakers who had trained within the institution and had participated in Rouch's workshops at Eduardo Mondlane University in 1978. However, his artistic affiliations were clearly with the cinephilic tradition of the intellectuals of the ciné-clubs that had been a site of resistance under colonialism. The depiction of lived realities in *Madrugada Suburbana* set it at odds with Frelimo's claim that conditions for Mozambicans were improving through the implementation of socialist policies. The film was censored for showing the transportation system as failing, and Baptista soon left Mozambique to pursue a career in filmmaking in France.[6] By contrast, Ruy Guerra's *Um Povo Nunca Morre* documented a ceremony on 3 February, the Dia dos heróis 'day of heroes', which marked the return from Tanzania to Mozambique of the remains of Frelimo guerrillas who had died abroad during the armed struggle. The film thus contributed to the myth of the birth of the nation through the sacrifices of revolutionaries during the armed struggle.

José Cardoso's *Canta Meu Irmão, Ajuda-me a Cantar*, which was released the following year, gives another account of Mozambican cultural identity that takes as its point of departure the Festival da Canção e da Música Tradicional de Moçambique 'Festival of Song and Traditional Music', which took place in Maputo over the course of eight days, from 28 December 1980 to 6 January 1981. The Festival was part of the Campanha Nacional de Preservação e Valorização da Cultura 'Campaign for the Preservation and Valorisation of Culture' that had been launched two years previously by the Ministry of Culture, led by Graça Machel. Cardoso was planning the production of a film about the festival, when

[5] Luís Carlos Patraquim (2011). 'The New Series of Kuxa Kanema: The Institutionalized Revolutionary Discourse'. *Views of the World: Films from the Archive of INAC*: 13.

[6] Interview with Luís Carlos Patraquim, Lisbon, 2017.

he discovered that the Ministry of Culture had arranged for a Portuguese film crew, led by director José Fonseca e Costa, to make a documentary. Fonseca e Costa was born in Angola and raised in Portugal, but due to his anti-fascist sympathies he left to study filmmaking in the United Kingdom, before moving to Italy for a time to work with Michelangelo Antonioni. During the Carnation Revolution, he threw himself into the collectivisation of film production, contributing to the making of *As Armas e o Povo* (1975), then turned to the subject of decolonisation in Angola with the documentary *Independência de Angola, o Governo de Transição* (1977). These films confirmed his politics as resolutely anti-colonial and revolutionary.

Fonseca e Costa's film about the festival, *Música, Moçambique!* (1981), was made as a co-production between the INC and the Portuguese production company Filmform, with funding from the Calouste Gulbenkian Foundation and the Instituto Português de Cinema.[7] *Música, Moçambique!* focused on the spectacle of the performances in the pavilion of the Clube de Desportos do Maxaquene and various other sites in Maputo. It includes an interview with the Minister for Culture Graça Machel, footage of the South African singer and exiled ANC activist Miriam Makeba, who was a guest of the Festival and an international star, and scenes shot at the house-studio of the artist Malangatana Valente. Fonseca e Costa had not met Malangatana prior to the shooting, but he was struck by Malangatana's dedicated attendance at the Festival and wanted to convey the cultural connection between his paintings and the musical expression of Mozambique's indigenous cultures.[8] The film also includes commentaries by the Brazilian ethnomusicologist Martinho Lutero and the Zambian anthropologist Professor Mponda, who assert the international Pan-African significance of the Mozambican musical culture on display. As Maria do Carmo Piçarra points out, *Música, Moçambique!* bears comparison with William Klein's documentary *First Pan-African Cultural Festival of Algiers* (1969), which performed an important diplomatic role in promoting Algeria as the centre of new cultural politics grounded in both internationalism and Pan-African solidarity with anti-colonial liberation movements.[9]

[7] L. P. (1981). '"Música, Moçambique" – novo filme sobre 1. Festival de Música e Canção Tradicionais'. *Tempo*, 554, 24 May: 7.

[8] Maria do Carmo Piçarra (2018). '*Música, Moçambique!* (Fonseca e Costa, 1981)'. E-book: *A colecção (anti-)colonial da Cinemateca Portuguesa. Campo, contracampo, fora-de-campo.*

[9] Piçarra (2018). For an in-depth analysis of William Klein's film and its cultural politics, see Olivier Hadouchi (2011). '"African culture will be revolutionary or will not be": William Klein's Film of the First Pan-African Festival of Algiers (1969)', in Kodwo Eshun and Ros Gray (2011). *The Militant Image: A Ciné-geography*, special issue of *Third Text*, 108, 1, 25, January: 117–128.

Faced with the dilemma of another film in production that had been commissioned by the Ministry of Culture, Cardoso decided take an entirely different approach. While *Música, Moçambique!* represents the cultural richness of Mozambican music that is brought to the capital, Cardoso opted instead to go to the provinces where the musicians came from and make a film that would study their instruments, stories and cultures *in situ*.[10] The fact that the film was shot in colour on 16mm is an indication that the documentary was an important production for the INC, as colour film stock had to be sent to Harare for processing. Cardoso's film *Canta Meu Irmão, Ajuda-me a Cantar* is ethnographic, intimate and poetic rather than spectacular. It includes explanations of how traditional Mozambican instruments were made, how the musicians train and how music was woven together with dances and songs for particular purposes in specific locales and communities.[11]

The film begins with a dedication: 'To the artists, to the musicians of our country, who sing the sounds of the earth, who do their work and teach us to sing.' An image of a meadow of yellow flowers and the sound of birds cuts to a man sawing a branch off a tree, singing in time with his movements. From the block of wood he begins to carve and hollow out a drum. Finishing the instrument, he begins to beat a rhythm. The film proceeds to take the viewer behind the scenes of the spectacle, not to the bustle and superficial conviviality of the changing rooms and hotel rooms where the performers are filmed as in *Música, Moçambique!*, but to the villages that nurture these forms of cultural expression. If *Música, Moçambique!* showcases Mozambican culture to the world and depicts Maputo as a cosmopolitan site of Pan-African culture, *Canta meu Irmão, Ajuda-me a Cant*a faces inwards, weaving a nationalist sensibility through the sharing of songs and the stories behind them.

It is worth pausing to consider the use of the address 'brother' as it is indicative of an attempt to constitute a particular feeling of national unity that is distinct from other appellations that were widely used in Mozambique at the time, such as 'comrade'. Jodi Dean writes that the term 'comrade' denotes an 'emancipatory egalitarian communist horizon'.[12] 'Comradeship', she adds, 'binds action and in this binding works to direct action toward a certain future.' It is thus not an identity so much as a shared politics and suggests a common course of action directed to the actualising of a utopian future. To be addressed as a comrade cuts

[10] Conversation with Laura Cardoso, Maputo, 6 August 2016.

[11] As the INC did not have the capacity to process in colour, the film was sent to Zimbabwe for processing. For a time, the laboratory in Zimbabwe was closed in the chaos that accompanied independence, and the original film negatives were lost. Conversation with Laura Cardoso, Maputo, 6 August 2016.

[12] Jodi Dean (2017). 'Four Theses on the Comrade'. *e-flux*, 86, November. Available http://www.e-flux.com/journal/86/160585/four-theses-on-the-comrade/.

across familial or neighbourly ties and so, from a Marxist–Leninist perspective, it overrides kinship in the same way that in the transition to socialism the vanguard party subsumes and exceeds many of the roles previously held by traditional or colonial authorities. While being a comrade is not dependent on proximity (indeed, arguably it may require a certain distance from the murky emotions of friendship), to call someone 'brother' implies intimacy and warmth. In an interview with me in 2017, Luís Carlos Patraquim suggested that the term '*irmão*' also expresses deference, making it a respectful supplication by the urban filmmaker to the rural indigenous musicians.[13] With the term 'brother', fissures in the new nation between an assimilated urban culture and rural indigenous traditions are condensed to the level of the personal, the conversational and the familiar, even while the film perpetuates patriarchal gender exclusions, as when the voiceover refers to the film crew as '*os homens de cinema*' 'the men of cinema', which overlooks the women who were part of the film crew and the female staff who played a crucial role at the INC. The title of the film thus makes a request from the filmmakers of the INC to musicians from across the country to perform their songs, and in doing so teach the nation to sing a song that henceforth will be shared.

A brief sequence of images from the Festival, showing crowds entering one of the venues and clips from the performances, accompanies an invitation to the musicians:

> A country is born. Five years later your music is as old as the people playing it, dancing it, singing it, loaded with function and meaning. Your music, five years later, is the topic of a festival. Bringing along your instruments and your art. Behind the gestures we, the men of cinema, sense your true rhythm, determined by sowing and harvest, by the sun and the rain, following the calendars of the stars and the birds.

The film cuts to a scene at the INC, where Cardoso and other members of the crew are gathered around a table, looking at images and a large map. 'We, the men of cinema, are going to visit you. With our equipment, our curiosity, our desire to learn.' Cardoso marks a red line between Maputo and Inhambane: 'We decided on a route and we set off.'

This self-reflexivity about the filmmaking process and the foreignness of moving-image technology to most Mozambicans continues in the scene that follows. Here the film crew are shown seated on the ground with a timbila band preparing for the shoot. Henrique Caldeira, clapboard in hand, speaks through a translator to the head musician to explain the purpose of the film and how it will allow people from across the country to learn about the traditional music of the new nation. As the musicians begin the play, the camera pans out

[13] Interview with Luís Carlos Patraquim, Lisbon, 18 December 2017.

to include the film crew, camera and sound boom, before cutting to close-ups of the timbila players and then panning around behind the timbilas to capture the singer-dancers who perform the Msao in front of the band. The rotational gesture of the circular panning shot, already associated with revolutionary self-reflexivity in films such as '25' and *Mueda, Memoria e Massacre* (see Chapters 2 and 4), inscribes the film crew within the mise en scène. Images of the musicians are then intercut with scenes of everyday life – tranquil village streets, women taking water from a well, children playing in the sea with wooden sailboats in the background.

Chapter 4 discussed how in *Estas são as Armas* the female voiceover personified the 'New Woman' of the Mozambican Revolution – one who is liberating herself and others through a decolonial pedagogy that involves deconstructing the myths perpetuated by colonialism. In Cardoso's documentary, the female and male voiceovers perform different roles. The male voiceover provides explanation of the making of the documentary and information about the local musical traditions that the film captures. He seems to embody the position of the film director, addressing the musicians and the audience with the familiar pronoun *tu*. By contrast, the female voiceover is more poetic and includes herself within the indigenous community, whom she addresses using the pronoun *nos* 'we'. While the female voiceover in *Estas são as Armas* evokes a shared experience of colonial abuse, the female voice in *Canta meu Irmão, Ajuda-me a Cantar* romantically evokes strands of local tales that are part of a collective culture that has nurtured Mozambique's traditional music. The film reveals a desire to use filmmaking to constitute an inward-looking nationalism as opposed to the cosmopolitan internationalism represented by the film of Fonseca e Costa. The nationalism of *Canta meu Irmão, Ajuda me a Cantar* is one that is grounded in the cultures of the indigenous peoples of Mozambique but seeks to include those white settlers and assimilated urbanites who had committed themselves to national reconstruction.

In contrast to the idealised images of harmonious rural existence in Cardoso's film, Moira Forjaz's documentary *Um Dia Numa Aldeia Communal* presents an account of village life that focuses on the labour and struggles of women. In the late 1970s, Forjaz had worked as a photographer on the major ethnographic research project that studied Mozambican migrant labour to South African mines, led by scholar and ANC activist Ruth First.[14] Like Baptista, Forjaz had been among those who attended Rouch's Super-8 workshops in 1978, before starting to work at the INC.[15] By 1981, Forjaz had already made a short film on 16mm called *Mineiro Moçambicano* 'Mozambican Miner'. Using a voiceover in

[14] Ruth First (1981). *Black Gold: Mozambican Miner, Proletarian and Peasant*. Brighton: Harvester Press.

[15] Interview with Moira Forjaz, Lisbon, 2005.

Portuguese and interviews in local languages, *Um Dia Numa Aldeia Communal* describes daily life in Vigilância, a communal village that was then only three years old and is populated by nearly a hundred women and their children and only four men. The voiceover describes how, because so many of the men had to work in the mines in South Africa or had been conscripted into the army, the labour required to build the village and cultivate the *machambas* falls to the women, who also had to raise the children and fetch water – a gruelling task in such an arid area. As such *Um Dia Numa Aldeia Communal* addresses the wider social impact of Mozambican men's migration, depicting the lives of the women they are forced, by economic necessity, to leave behind. Despite the harsh conditions of life in the village, the film endows its protagonists with dignity. Even functional shots that track the workings of basic technologies used for conserving water, such as a gutter that runs along a hut into a well, are gracefully composed and paced. *Um Dia* includes an animated sequence to explain the government's policy of collectivisation and depicts the construction of this particular village. At the end of the day, villagers gather around a fire to sing songs about their collective strength, their joy at being free from forced labour and their hopes for the future. Yet the 'vigilance' of the villagers and armed forces protecting them was not enough. In an interview with me in 2005, Forjaz recounted that a few years after the film was released Renamo attacked the village and almost every person who appears in the film was killed.[16]

That same year, delegations from Cuba and North Korea overlapped at the INC, offering training and, in the process, to make films. Both films celebrated Frelimo's charismatic leader but were different in tone and approach. 'Everyone wanted to work with the Cubans', Pedro Pimenta, then Director of Production, recalled to me in an interview in 2005, as ICAIC then was the hub of a kind of revolutionary filmmaking that was seductive and lyrical as well as effective as propaganda.[17] The North Korean co-production was called *Moçambique em progresso sob a direcção do Presidente Samora Moisés Machel* 'Mozambique Advances under the Leadership of President Samora Moisés Machel' (1981), the title of which gives an indication of the film's dogmatic tone. By contrast, the Cuban team made a film called *Nova Sinfonia* (*The New Symphony*, 1981), which took as its starting point Machel's habit of breaking into song at the beginning of Party meetings.[18] Santiago Álvarez, who led the Cuban delegation, had developed a dynamic and innovative mode of documentary aesthetics that was a new departure in political filmmaking during the 1960s and 1970s. Often combining different kinds of archival material syncopated to dynamic music, a method that he had already put to work in Mozambique in 1976 for *Maputo: Meridiano novo*

[16] Interview with Moira Forjaz, Lisbon, 2005.
[17] Interview with Pedro Pimenta, Johannesburg, 30 June 2005.
[18] Interview with Pedro Pimenta, Johannesburg, 30 June 2005.

(see Chapter 3), Álvarez's film worked on the revolutionary promise of montage for disjunctive synthesis. Its juxtapositions of un-reconciled images and sounds breaks the illusion of continuity associated with bourgeois films and involves the viewer in the construction of a 'new symphony' in the connecting of its disparate parts. The fact that these two delegations coincided in Mozambique in 1981 is an indication of the extent to which the INC was perceived internationally as an important site for militant filmmaking. By the early 1980s its film production had increased substantially, a cohort of technicians had received training and were working on film productions, and the remaining privately owned cinemas from the colonial era had been nationalised, so completing an integrated system that ensured that the INC could maintain financial autonomy from the state. Nevertheless, changes were afoot that would involve a substantial restructuring of the institution so that moving-image production would come under more direct control of government.

When José Luis Cabaço was appointed Minister of Information, he replaced Jorge Rebelo, who had held the post since independence but had been promoted to run the Department of Ideological Work. As a young man in Lourenço Marques, Cabaço had befriended Americo Soares and Ruy Guerra. In 1971 he departed for Italy, where he studied sociology at the University of Trento, then a hotbed of student activism, and was involved with Frelimo's clandestine network.[19] At independence he had been appointed Minister for Transport and Communications. Under Rebelo, the INC had enjoyed a degree of autonomy even though they were ultimately answerable to the Ministry of Information. As Minister for Information, Rebelo's concern had been with mass propaganda rather than artistic expression and he favoured radio rather than cinema as the most effective means of communicating with the largest possible number of Mozambicans.[20] Radio was cheap, could reach across vast distances to remote regions and could be broadcast locally in different languages. Rebelo thus had little enthusiasm for the state flooding its resources into expensive filmmaking projects, let alone television broadcasting, which he believed could only benefit the tiny urban minority who could afford a television set – a luxury good out of the reach of most Mozambicans.[21] By contrast, Cabaço believed it was essential to centralise moving-image production and to take pre-emptive action to prevent television corroding the collective experience of cinema and alienating

[19] The University of Trento was pedagogically innovative and attracted socially engaged students from across Italy. The Red Brigade, Western Europe's most notorious armed communist organisation, began at the University of Trento in the late 1960s and was led by Renato Curcio and his wife Margherita 'Mara' Cagol, both of whom studied sociology.

[20] Interview with Jorge Rebelo, Maputo, 20 September 2005.

[21] Interview with Jorge Rebelo, Maputo, 20 September 2005.

Mozambicans from their own cultures. In September 1980, Cabaço began a study of moving-image production, and this resulted in the development of a 'global strategy for the image' in Mozambique.[22]

Some months later in 1981, Cabaço made a speech to INC employees that laid out his findings and plans for restructuring and centralising image production so that the organisation would oversee research and development of film, television and other audio-visual forms of communication such as posters and photography to meet the specific needs of Mozambicans. Within this vision, the purpose of the image in the Mozambican Revolution was to provide clear instructions and communication that left no room for ambivalence or misunderstanding. Significantly, his speech begins with identifying a series of dilemmas facing the INC resulting from conditions of dependency on foreign technology and experts. There was, Cabaço claimed, a 'grave risk' that comes with working with sophisticated cameras and editing and sound equipment that are 'the result of the cultural and technological development of the countries that manufacture all the equipment we work with'. These technologies are not neutral, but rather filmmakers are 'conditioned' by the equipment they use. Similarly, contact with foreign technicians involved conforming 'to a standardised form of use without considering that [the equipment] must, . . serve our political, social, cultural and revolutionary reality.' At stake was the danger of the INC producing films that would alienate and even endanger Mozambicans.

Cabaço cites examples he encountered at the Ministry of Information that demonstrate how Western codes of visual representation often did not translate well to local audiences in the Mozambican context. For instance, a poster that showed pictures of two latrines – one well constructed and the other badly made – used a cross to show which should be avoided. For many Mozambican viewers, however, the cross symbol was understood as an affirmative sign, with potentially dangerous consequences. Similarly, a traffic sign using the symbol of a blue disc with a white arrow would be easily recognised by urban inhabitants but made little sense to rural people: 'in peasant society this symbol was nothing more than a beautiful thing, "a blue wheel with a white line" with no meaning at all: this symbol does not establish any kind of relation with the life of peasant.' Other examples included the way in which even urban cinema spectators expressed being so dazzled by 'lively' images that they were unable to say what meaning they derived from the film beyond its instantaneous sensorial affect. These case studies, Cabaço argued, demonstrated the danger of an unquestioning use of symbolic systems that originated not in Mozambique

[22] José Luís Cabaço, 'Imagem: Uma arma que aliena ou liberta: Orientaçoes do Ministro da Informação para o estabelecimento de uma estratégia de produção de imagem em Moçambique'. No date. I am grateful to Sol de Carvalho for providing me with a copy of this document.

but in Europe, America, the Soviet Union or East Germany. To fail to know and understand the needs of Mozambicans, Cabaço concludes, means that either the filmmakers are 'alienated' or 'criminals to our people'. Taking the example of how the image might be used to convey public health information about disease assuming a knowledge of Western science and medicine, Cabaço argues that the notion that cinematic language is universal is incorrect:

> The truth is that the image communicates, but it only communicates what we know. For example, peasants who do not know what microbes are and do not have this notion in their cultural heritage will only see in these images their beauty or their ugliness.

If the last fifty years of colonialism had distanced Mozambicans from their culture, then now was the time for filmmakers to come to know their 'objective reality'. The metaphor widely used by internationalist militant filmmakers was of the camera as a 'gun', a weapon to be wielded against imperialism.[23] In the discourse of many militant filmmakers of the time, manipulation of the moving image could be justified if it led to a successful assault on the colonialist regime of signs.[24] However, if proponents of Third Cinema such as Fernando Solanas and Octavio Getino assumed that the camera-weapon was pointed at the imperialists, here Cabaço suggests that images that are difficult to understand could be dangerous to Mozambicans: 'having Mozambique's image in the hand is as big a responsibility as being in control of a cannon. With it we can culturally kill people. We can even kill them physically, triggering processes that lead them to death.'

While the Ministry of Education had responsibility for teaching young people, Cabaço understood the Ministry of Information as having a role in plugging the gap in knowledge and information for generations above school age who would in their lifetimes, according to Frelimo's plan for industrialisation, transition from peasants to workers. Cabaço defined the task of cinema as being

[23] Jonathan Buchsbaum (2011). 'One, Two . . . Third Cinemas', in Kodwo Eshun and Ros Gray (2011). Special issue: 'The Militant Image: A Ciné-geography'. *Third Text* 108, 25, 1, January 2011: 13–28.

[24] In José Filipe Costa's film *Red Line*, a documentary about the making of the film *Torre Bela*, the director Thomas Harlan makes a robust defense of the way in which he 'manipulated' the unfolding event of the land occupation through the presence of the camera and the way in which he encouraged the villagers to enter the Duke's palace, which led to one of the most memorable and controversial scenes of the film. Similarly, in an interview with Olivier Hadouchi, Fernando Solanas defended using staged sequences in *Hour of the Furnaces* that were presented as if they were recordings of actual events, arguing that the images portrayed a wider truth about neocolonial conditions. Gabriela Trujillo and Olivier Hadouchi (2012). 'Conversation avec Fernando Solanas'. *La Furia Umana*, 19. Available at http://www.lafuriaumana.it/index.php/47-archive/lfu-19/165-gabriela-trujillo-et-olivier-haduchi-conversation-avec-fernando-solanas.

'an instrument of development', assisting the population in moving beyond 'obscurantism'. While Frelimo's campaign against tribalism was articulated in terms of the unmasking of superstition, here Cabaço identified ways in which cinema could be mystifying for an audience that was new to the technology and its conventions. Taking the example of karate films, a genre popular with Mozambican cinema-goers, he argued that many viewers did not yet have the ability to recognise the 'magical' abilities of the moving image: 'the fact that a karate movie actor jumps from three meters high. . . . The actor who "died" in this week's movie and is seen very much alive in another film – he has a "cure" for death.' The role of the INC was to explain these phenomenon through a 'literary campaign' directed at teaching people how to 'read' the image. This would put cinema to work in the process of development and liberation rather than maintaining it as an instrument of manipulation and domination.

For Cabaço, the first edition of the *Kuxa Kanema* newsreel provided examples of the kinds of errors that were made in the INC's first few years. The mistakes that were made fell into three interlinked categories. The first involved inefficient use of resources, for example, the cost of salaries resulted in too small a number of films that were useful in a Mozambican context. The second concerned over-reliance on foreign *cooperantes*, who, Cabaço claimed, had influenced the INC to produce film were sometimes not suitable and stayed only for a year or two, their departures leaving the institution without an adequate number of trained staff to be self-sufficient. The third error lay in the uncritical adoption of film forms that originated in contexts that were very different to the Mozambican Revolution. For instance, Cabaço argued, the first version of the *Kuxa Kanema* newsreel appropriated a model that developed in Europe in the 1950s for the purpose of conveying information, but this format had largely disappeared with the advent of television. Similarly, the documentaries of Santiago Álvarez, another important influence at the INC, served a certain purpose in the context of the Cuban Revolution despite the fact that the Caribbean island already had television broadcasting, but his mode of filmmaking might have little relevance beyond a small urban elite in Mozambique who were familiar with his signature form of rapid montage agitprop documentary.

To answer to the needs of most Mozambicans who were new to the moving image, Cabaço claimed, it would be necessary to make films about their realities that were 'extremely simple'. Of course, the idea that it was necessary to make educational films for African audiences in a simplified way was not new. British colonial film policy in Ghana and Tanzania was based on a set of racist and paternalistic assumptions about colonised peoples being, in the words of Manthia Diawara, 'too primitive to follow the sophisticated narrative techniques of mainstream cinema', an ideology that stood in the way of British filmmakers recognising that the educational films they made were so 'boring and clumsy' that audiences rejected them.[25] Similarly in Rhodesia many films commissioned by the white minority government specifically for African audiences failed because they were too simplistic or manipulative (see Chapter 4). The Portuguese colonial regime made no such attempt to use films directed specifically at indigenous audiences for pedagogical purposes, and local film production in Mozambique prior to independence was focused on propaganda newsreels and pornography (see Chapter 2). In light of this, it is significant that Cabaço draws on the language of the armed struggle to explain the INC's role and situation and to justify his proposals. The INC would fulfil its role in the 'vanguard' of the revolution by building up the image literacy of the population. While 'popularism' is content to condemn *o Povo* to underdevelopment and ignorance, the vanguard drives the revolutionary process forward through education and research. Cabaço insisted that the INC should be self-sufficient, meaning that its own employees would have the capacity to produce a weekly newsreel with the equipment they already had at their disposal without external support. This would enable the INC to establish a 'liberated zone' for a national production of the image. Cabaço is quick to point out that the purpose of this is not nationalistic chauvinism, but rather the 'Mozambicanization' of consciousness:

> In this liberated zone we will shape the Mozambicanization of the consciousness of filmmakers. And it is only with a Mozambican head that the machine will also be Mozambicanised. This means that it is only with the consciousness of our revolution that the machine becomes a revolutionary instrument. Because if the head is empty it is the machine that dominates.

Cabaço's plan for restructuring the INC involved a new version of *Kuxa Kanema*, a weekly edition standardised at 11 minutes in length, which would henceforth be the centrepiece of the INC's production. Further documentary films would be made to answer to needs as they arose, such as to respond to attacks from South Africa, but the priority would be to maintain weekly delivery of the newsreel whatever the circumstances. Still adopting the language of armed struggle and Marxist–Leninist propriety, Cabaço argued that this was necessary 'to consolidate the liberated zone and not embark on cinematographic adventurism'. Television would be developed in partnership with the INC. This constituted another departure from the European model, where television had historically been connected with radio broadcast rather than cinema, resulting in a bifurcation into two different kinds of image production. Cabaço was determined that Mozambique would not make the 'mistake' of two regimes of image-making developing in parallel, but rather that television would draw on

[25] Manthia Diawara (1992). *African Cinema: Politics and Culture*. Bloomington: Indiana University Press: 4.

the expertise developed at the INC. The speech also outlined the important role of audio-visuals, which would be developed by the Instituto de Comunicação Social (ICS) to support communication to the rural populations. He envisaged that posters and slides with spoken explanation could be used to explain the content of films projected by mobile cinema units to rural communities to support their understanding of the moving images. In addition, many of the tasks of image communication could be performed through audio-visuals at much less of a cost than film. All these different kinds of image production would come under the responsibility of a new director-general of production, whose role it would be to direct the 'overall image strategy' for the entire nation.

Citing Mao Tse-Tung's mantra 'No investigation, no right to speak', Cabaço proposed the setting up of a study centre to coordinate, energise and centralise research.[26] This would not involve 'three or four intellectuals closed off in an office to make small grants of self-sufficiency'; rather, it would aim to be 'the place where all the practice of production is synthesised and later becomes operational, from the point of view of knowledge.' The Centre of Studies would not be a cluster of academics but a centre of activists. One of the INC's key activities – the running of the mobile cinemas – was identified as an area in need of further research. Cabaço had withdrawn the mobile cinemas donated by the Soviet Union in 1978 from circulation so as to rethink its role, and in his speech he posed the question: 'What is the difference between the colonial *cinema ambulante* and the *cinema móvel*?' According to Marcus Powers, a group of advertisers conceived *cinema ambulante* as a means of promoting consumer goods to the indigenous population.[27] From the late 1960s, the Centro de Informação e Turismo granted them permission to organise projections to rural communities in the regions of Manica, Sofala, Gaza and Lourenço Marques.[28] While granting that the colonial *cinema ambulante* had very different economic and ideological objectives, Cabaço argued that the *cinema móvel* had not done more than function as a mobile station that went to certain sites to project films. The scope for improvement here was immense: 'Mobile cinema is the permanent contact point of our communication policy with the image of the people.' *Cinema móvel* needed to be conceived with broader set of objectives to increase image literary, assessing what the existing level of literacy was and to 'write' films at a level that people could understand and so as to improve their 'reading' ability. Cabaço argued: 'The mobile cinema must be the centre for capturing and agitating with the moving image, using the image of the people to

[26] Mao Tse-Tung (2014). 'Preface and Postscript to Rural Surveys' (March and April 1941), *Selected Works*, Vol. III. Oxford: Pergamon: 13.

[27] Marcus Powers (2004). 'Post-colonial Cinema and the Re-configuration of Moçambicanidade'. *Lusotopie*: 268.

[28] Powers (2004): 268.

prepare the people for the films they will see next.' Within the INC, the training of filmmakers would continue and be standardised, with all employees doing stints in both cinema and television.

Cabaço's rhetoric makes a strident distinction between what the revolutionary situation required of the INC and modes of filmmaking that were 'alienated' from Mozambican realities and indulgent of 'cinematic adventurism' by individual directors. Such 'bourgeois' forms of cinema exacerbated dependency on foreign film aesthetics, technologies and expertise. However, the speech made two important concessions. Cabaço acknowledged that the INC would continue to benefit from the contributions of *cooperantes* 'with good technical and political-cultural qualities' to advise the director-general. He also stated that those who aspired to direct films were invited to put forward their proposals. These would be considered, Cabaço promised, and when the opportunity arose they would be produced. The possibility of the INC nurturing auteur directors was thus left open, though the question of who would be able take on this most prestigious of roles within tradition filmmaking hierarchy was presented as being a matter of individual 'capacity' and 'aspiration' rather than something that was shaped by privileges of class, race, gender and access to higher education.

Cabaço lobbied the Italian government to give material and financial support to make broadcasting possible and initiated a radical overhaul of the INC with implications across the entire field of audio-visual production.[29] Under the new scheme, production at the INC was to focus, for the time being, on two areas: the *Kuxa Kanema* newsreel and documentaries. While José Cardoso had been appointed Production Director in 1978, he had no passion for management and hankered to direct films as he had begun to do in the context of the colonial film clubs in Beira in the 1960s (see Chapter 2).[30] In 1980 Pedro Pimenta took on the role of director of production, while Samuel Matola remained as the director of the INC. The new role of director-general of production is described in the speech as having the function of centralising control of the strategy for the image for the entire nation. In the years that followed this function was performed by the Minister of Information himself, who thus exercised overarching control over the entire spectrum of image production. A third arm of this front came into being with the establishment in 1983 of the company Kanemo, set up by Ruy Guerra and others as a commercial enterprise that would function as the state's interface with the capitalist world outside.

A key objective of Cabaço's plans was to maintain the INC as the central productive force in making films of and for the people of Mozambique.[31] On

[29] Interviews with Sol de Carvalho, Maputo, 12 September 2005, and Luís Simão, Maputo, 17 September 2005. See Appendix.

[30] Interview with José Cardoso. Maputo, 2005.

[31] Interview with Sol de Carvalho. Maputo, 2005.

1 May 1981, *Kuxa Kanema* was relaunched as a shorter weekly newsreel. Ten copies of each edition were printed by the INC laboratory and distributed to each region of the country. Sol de Carvalho, a journalist from *Tempo*, was selected by Cabaço to reconceptualise *Kuxa Kanema* and was expected to direct all episodes. Carvalho resigned before the newsreel was launched, and it was decided that all INC filmmakers should be involved in directing *Kuxa Kanema*.[32] All production staff had to follow an intensive training course, based on the handbook *Stages of Production*, which was written by Carvalho and based on materials developed by the Brazilian *cooperantes* Alberto Graça and Vera Zaverucha. The newsreel provided an important opportunity for INC filmmakers to hone their skills in documentary, which was recognised as the basis of INC film production, even though the economic crisis resulted in the format of *Kuxa Kanema* stagnating.[33]

An article by Alves Gomes that was published in *Tempo* in June 1981 reviewed the new version of *Kuxa Kanema* following fives weeks of regular weekly projections, finding it an 'agreeable surprise'.[34] Acknowledging that the newsreel did not present great achievements technically, and noting numerous faults, gaps and that sections of the reels were badly filmed, Gomes comments that the INC had clearly committed itself to making a newsreel within the 'capacities that we have' rather than try to create a 'new "Hollywood" in Maputo'.[35] 'This organ of information proves', Gomes concludes, 'that finally we have people who can use film cameras to keep us informed.'[36] The weekly newsreel reported on current affairs, though the shorter format meant that it did not provide the same level of commentary as the first version made in 1978 and 1979. Among the themes that were regularly highlighted, including developments in healthcare, education and production, international solidarity continued to be a frequent topic, with new allies such as Nicaragua coming to the fore, with reports on visits from cultural delegations. The victory of the Sandinistas in Nicaragua followed on from the defeat of Portuguese colonialism in Angola, Mozambique and Guinea-Bissau and coincided with ZANU's ascent to power in Zimbabwe, constituting a significant socialist surge in the Third World. Mozambique and Nicaragua in particular seemed to open up the possibility of new societies emerging, based on non-alignment, anti-racism and socialism.[37]

[32] Carvalho later returned to work on the newsreel for a year. Interview with Sol de Carvalho.

[33] Interview with Sol de Carvalho, Maputo 2005 and Skype conversation, 2016.

[34] Alves Gomes (1981). 'Kuxa Kanema: Uma Surpresa Agradável'. *Tempo*, 557, 14 June: 60–1.

[35] Gomes (1981): 61.

[36] Gomes (1981): 61.

[37] Hanlon (1991): 3.

While the INC was at the heart of Frelimo's attempts to centralise moving-image production, the project initiated by TBARN and CEC in the late 1970s was able to develop independently for a time, in part because of its more marginal status within the Eduardo Mondlane University. In 1980, TBARN and CEC shifted the location of the project from the region around Maputo to the northern province of Niassa, responding to the decision by the Fourth Session of Frelimo's Central Committee in 1978 that the TBARN project should be enlarged to cover other rural areas. The primary aim of the project, of encouraging peasant communities to form cooperatives, was in tune with shifts in emphasis in Frelimo's approach to agricultural transformation. Barry Munslow argues that by the late 1970s Frelimo realised that the focus on large state-run mechanised farms had led to smaller agricultural cooperatives being neglected, to the detriment of raising national production to pre-independence levels.[38] The 'Land Law' instituted in 1979 not only codified state ownership of the land that had been declared in the 1975 Constitution, but also sought to 'encourage the integration [of farmers] into cooperatives'.[39]

The team selected the district of Mavago in Niassa, where they developed a project from April to October 1980. The area had been a key liberated zone during the armed struggle and the villages of Mzawise, Nkalapa and Chilolo had all been under Samora Machel's control during the armed struggle. Indeed, some of the participants feature in Margaret Dickinson's film *Behind the Lines*, which was shot in Niassa in 1970 (see Chapter 1). João Paulo Borges Coelho, Arlindo Mulhovo, João Azevedo and Russell Parker were among those who ran the project, with support from the University of Paris X Nanterre and UNICEF.[40] While the TBARN team had initially used the Super-8 equipment provided by Rouch, they moved on to a Kodak video machine that was donated by the French government. Inhabitants of Mavago – a remote district – generally relied on small radio transistors to pick up news from the outside world.[41] The films that CEC and TBARN had made in Maputo and the surrounding district in the previous two years were projected so as to allow the people of the Mavago

[38] Munslow:

[39] Eléusio Filipe and Simon Norfolk (2017). Understanding Changing Land Issues for the Rural Poor in Mozambique. London: International Institute for Environment and Development: 23. Available http://pubs.iied.org/pdfs/17594IIED.pdf.

[40] Russell Parker was part of an older generation of radicals. He had studied at Berkeley and had been a cameraman in Vietnam before coming to Europe. See the interview with João Paulo Borges Coelho, 16 August 2005, in Maputo, Mozambique. See the Appendix in Ros Gray (2007). 'Ambitions of Cinema: Revolution, Event, Screen'. PhD Dissertation, London: Goldsmiths, University of London.

[41] Centro de Estudos de Comunição and Centro de Tecnícas Básicas para o Aproveitamento dos Recursos Naturais (1980). *Catálogo dos Filmes de Mavago*. Maputo: Universidade Eduardo Mondlane: 2.

district to learn about the social transformations that had been taking place in the south and about life in the different regions of the country (for instance, while cows were central to farming in the south, they were unknown to many people in Niassa as oxen did not exist there).

As discussed in Chapter 3, while the French filmmakers associated with Rouch were interested in capturing everyday life to make ethnographic narratives, this group moved beyond the notion of filmmaking having merely a 'documentary' purpose. While they saw themselves as continuing in the spirit of Rouch's proposal, the TBARN project had a more interventionist approach grounded in a liberationist pedagogy that understood learning as a two-way process. In an interview with me, João Azevedo explained that the films they made in the north were very different because of the extreme poverty of the communities they were working with, who urgently needed to mobilise themselves to improve living conditions.[42] The films completed in Niassa totalled around twelve hours and covered subjects ranging from female empowerment to the formation of cooperatives and techniques of production.[43] They included a film that showed blacksmiths forging metal products and another depicting the making of bread, for which they experimented with different mixtures of sorghum and cassava to tackle shortages of wheat.[44] There was also a film about brickmaking, as TBARN assisted villagers in setting up a brick-making cooperative and negotiated with the local authorities to ensure that they would buy the bricks from the farmers. Though the spirit of voluntarism that had animated the liberated zones during the armed struggle still existed at that time, the project arranged for the workers to be paid. In an article that was published in *Tempo* in 1980 Borges Coelho argued that the cooperatives improved the income of its members.[45] This level of participation from the crew in the task of development marks this project as distinctive, the usual protocols of observational documentary dictating that the filmmakers should stay behind the camera rather than making interventions to change the communities they were filming.

The films that were made in Mavago were also deliberately 'non-triumphalist'. Rather than basing their filmmaking on a model of cinema that was 'abstract and universal', the text in the *Catálogo dos Filmes de Mavago* stresses that: 'On the contrary, these films were produced in a particular moment, in particular conditions, using a particular technology.' As a result:

> Sometimes the camera happened to be present when something was happening. At other times it was absent. In any case, the filming was not staged and did not

[42] Interview with João Azevedo, Lisbon, 3 December 2016.

[43] Interview with João Azevedo, Lisbon, 3 December 2016.

[44] Interview with João Azevedo, Lisbon, 3 December 2016.

[45] João Paulo Borges Coelho (1980). 'Crónica do Niassa: Mavago – os problemas da transformação'. *Tempo*, 508, 6 July.

> attempt, through the artifice of montage, to make 'cinema' following any model. Sometimes the narrative is not always very clear. Other times, words are more important than images. In this case, the volume of communication depends on the protagonists of the films, what they say about what happens. This also explains the long duration of some of the shots.[46]

While professional camera operators took the footage, the villagers had a strong say in how the films were edited, and where and when they were screened.[47] Production and display thus involved in-depth negotiation with local communities over technical and 'artistic' aspects such as camera angle, length of shot and editing, which had different significance for people who read the moving images according to other criteria. Often they demanded that the time of the image be as close as possible to 'real time' and that rapid montage and the cropping of human figures be avoided. These could be confusing or even, when parts of a person's body had been cut out of the frame, offensive. Such negotiations involved collaboration to overcome the vast cultural differences and economic inequality between the filmmakers and the villagers, who came from radically different worlds. João Azevedo recounted to me an incident that occurred at the end of a day of filming in Chiolo, when the villagers asked the filmmakers to record them making a final victory cry. When the moment came, they called out 'Abaixo o Desenvolvimento!' – 'Down with Development!' rather than the slogan 'Down with Underdevelopment'. 'Development' was, of course, the aim of the film, and their mistake demonstrated how the villagers were being forced by the new regime to use Portuguese, a language that was foreign to them. The incongruence of pursuing a radical agenda of empowerment from the grassroots within the frame imposed by the vanguard party is perhaps symbolised by an incident recalled to me by Borges Coelho that occurred during the project. Government Minister Oscar Monteiro came to visit one of the villages where the project was operating. Arriving by helicopter, he exited the aircraft, only to find that the gusts of wind from the landing had blown the roof off from the hospital he was coming to visit!

As in the earlier iterations of the project, a key aim was local empowerment. Their films were intended to inspire social transformation rather than offer precise technical instructions, and through this project the mobile cinema screen became a means of empowering people to find ways of working together cooperatively using new techniques of production and of sharing their experiences with communities that were geographically remote. The

[46] Centro de Estudos de Comunição and Centro de Tecnícas Básicas para o Aproveitamento dos Recursos Naturais (1980): 3.

[47] Centro de Estudos de Comunição and Centro de Tecnícas Básicas para o Aproveitamento dos Recursos Naturais (1980): 3.

filmmakers sought to build different kinds of relations and alternative processes of production with the communities participating in the projects, drawing on their other skills as artists, architects and designers, as well as what they observed through their engagement with the village communities, rather than using film as an instrument for unilateral dissemination. Indeed, they saw themselves as learning from the villagers about local indigenous techniques and knowledge of materials and conditions, as evidenced by the grain storage silos that they designed based on vernacular structures, models of which still stand in the grounds of Eduardo Mondlane University.[48] They contrasted their liberationist pedagogy and interdisciplinary approach with *Kuxa Kanema*, which they believed reinforced authoritarian power structures. Borges Coelho explained to me that by achieving their aims of transforming the communities they were working with and empowering them to benefit directly from increasing production, they upset local hierarchies that underpinned party support. Whether it was because of this, or due to the fact that 16mm film projections were becoming more widespread in remote areas, which meant that the TBARN was less likely to be allocated funds, the project was brought to a close in 1982. According to Borges Coelho, within days of their departure, the villages they had worked in were attacked, and the district became a base for Renamo.[49] The films were stored at the Centre for Cooperative Development in Changara, Tete Province, but in the mid-1980s a grenade attack destroyed the laboratory, the projector and most of the copies of the films.

Television in Mozambique began when the Italian government provided the technological and financial resources to set up Televisão Experimental (TVE). On 3 February 1981, the first emissions of a speech by Samora Machel were broadcast to Maputo. At the outset, the party presented its policy on television as motivated by the desire to make what was conventionally a private commodity accessible to the people, arguing that they were preventing television from becoming a means by which foreign commercialism could colonise audio-visual

[48] See Ângela Ferreira's photographs in Ângela Ferreira (2013). *Political Cameras*. Edinburgh: Stills Scotland's Centre for Photography.

[49] Borges Coelho explains that 'the problem was precisely that we were developing the cooperative and doing really well . . . the young people . . . were making some money in the village, but it was the elders who were the representatives for Frelimo. They had previously made clay pots to sell, and suddenly the young were doing these bricks and making money out of it, and the old guard were accusing us of bringing in capitalism because we were introducing money. . . . We always kept a very clean relationship with the government, but one day the governor called us and said, "Wonderful job you have been doing, but you cannot expect me to go against my men, the old people, so you have to leave . . . you did a wonderful job, but you have to go." That is how we left. And the day after we left Renamo took the village . . . and it became a provincial base for Renamo. Interview with João Paulo Borges Coelho, 16 August 2005, in Maputo, Mozambique

registers and kill off collective experiences of the screen. Television sets were installed in the *bairros*, where audiences of hundreds gathered to watch. Licínio Azevedo, Moira Forjaz and Miguel Arreas made a documentary called *Televisão nos bairros* (1981), filmed in a hall where several hundred people gathered to watch television for the first time. The filmmakers interviewed children, party *dynamizadores*, nursing mothers and other members of the audience. Although a Frelimo representative gives the party version of what the project was intended to achieve, responses from the crowd tell another story. Many of the viewers could hardly even see the screen or, if they could, did not identify with the foreign images they saw, suggesting the action was little more than a gesture. The programme was broadcast once, but was immediately taken out of circulation because of the criticism it gave voice to.[50]

In the 1980s, TVE also broadcast material that was produced by teams who trained up local people in the spirit of Godard's proposal, though the content was much more controlled than the French filmmaker had envisioned. The ICS first began training *correspondentes populares* to run community radio stations and write articles for *O Campo*, a newspaper created by the ICS for rural communities. Felisberto Tinga described to me how they sought visual languages that would be effective for people not familiar with a Western regime of signs, working out practical solutions in the field, which formed the basis for theorising their activities afterwards.[51] Tinga gave the example of how a film that was made to educate people about the causes of malaria failed because audiences were not able to interpret the scale of the images. On seeing the hugely magnified diagrams of mosquitoes, people assumed that there was no need to worry, because they did not have mosquitoes that big in their village! The emphasis of the ICS was on transmitting practical information through which communities could increase production, access education and combat disease. The newspaper *Campo* was published in simple Portuguese and made substantial use of visual forms of communication such as photo-stories, diagrams and cartoons, which semi-literate people could understand more easily. These illustrated agricultural techniques, health education and news of development projects, often told through stories that made pedagogical use of situations and characters that rural people could relate to. Some narratives focused on family dilemmas, including children being kidnapped by Renamo, while others taught readers skills such as how to process sunflower oil, a cast of regular characters appearing in different editions. However, a cartoon in *O Campo* illustrates the strategy whereby, under the auspices of information, government organs of

[50] I am grateful to Moira Forjaz for finding and giving me access to a copy of the documentary, which has since been deposited at ANIM, the archive of the Cinemateca Portuguesa.

[51] Interview with Felisberto Tinga, Maputo, 4 August 2005. See Gray (2007).

mass communication were made integral to the material and social fabric of collective life. A village celebrates a marriage at the information centre set up by the ICS. The loudspeakers that usually make announcements and broadcast community radio play special music for the wedding. However, at other times the speakers had a regulating function, blaring out instructions to villagers about what time to get up and how to work the fields.[52]

From 1983 the ICS worked with the INC, training *correspondentes populares* to make reports on video, which were then broadcast on Canal Zero. Among those who made short programmes with *correspondentes populares* were Licínio Azevedo and Brigitte Bagnol, a French anthropologist who trained as a filmmaker with a radical political group in Italy. Azevedo's experience of working as a journalist in Brazil under the military dictatorship meant that he had great skills in weaving stories based on testimonies that could convey truths without risking the safety of the individuals he interviewed. By this time Renamo's attacks were becoming more widespread. According to Bagnol, the short video films they made with villagers during these years were 'stories of hope', transmitting messages of resistance to Apartheid aggression.[53] *Escola em Armas* is about schoolchildren taking up guns to defend their school against a Renamo attack, while *A Coluna* follows one of the armed convoys people had to travel in because of the danger of ambush outside the cities. Other films were more experimental or had a cultural focus. *Melancólico* 'Melancholia' (1986) is inspired by a poem and celebrates women's bravery to make a critique of polygamy. *O Poço* (1986) was an experiment in making a silent film in an attempt to explore solutions to the problem of making instructional films in a country where people speak different languages. It teaches how to maintain the cleanliness of a village well, but without recourse to the spoken word.

The transformations at the INC initiated by Cabaço culminated in 1982 with an event that celebrated Frelimo's successes through the achievements of the INC. From 26 to 30 June, a *Retrospectiva do Cinema Moçambicana* marked the twentieth anniversary of the formation of Frelimo in Maputo.[54] It included films about Frelimo's armed struggle such as *Venceremos*, *Ten Days with the Guerrillas in Mozambique*, *Nachingwea*, '*25*', *A Luta Continua* and *Do Rovuma ao Maputo*. In addition, cinema-goers were able to see films made prior to independence and more recent works by the INC, including *Xilembene*, *Angoche*, *E temos a floresta*, *Visor Moçambicano*, *Catembe*, *Madrugada suburban*, *Operação Leopardo* and *Limpopo*, *III Congresso*, *Mueda*, *Mueda*, *Memória e Massacre*,

[52] Interview with João Paulo Borges Coelho; Gray (2007).

[53] Television was only broadcast to the Maputo area at first. Interview with Brigitte Bagnol, Maputo, 7 July 2005; Gray (2007).

[54] 'Comemorações da Independência: Cinema moçambicana retrospectiva'. *Notícias*. 24 July 1982.

Obrigado Zimbabwe, Pamberi ne Zimbabwe, Massacre de Chimoio, Moçambique avança sobre a liderança do Presidente Samora Machel and various editions of *Kuxa Kanema*.

At the same time as the INC was celebrating its achievements, Cabaço and Guerra were discussing new filmmaking initiatives that would operate under tight government control to communicate Frelimo's ideological position.[55] Labi Mondonça, one of the Brazilians involved, describes how Guerra recruited a number of Brazilian filmmakers who were 'ideologically "recommended"' to work in a private company that would be run commercially to make films on commission just like 'any other Western production company'.[56] Kanemo provided Guerra with a base from which to continue making films in Mozambique despite the conflicts over resources that had arisen at the INC as a result of his projects. In 1982, Machel approved the plan. The company would interface with the open market of transnational capitalism, thus, according to Mendonça, adapting the modes of the struggle on the 'cultural front' to a world that was becoming increasingly characterised by globalisation.

The following year, in 1983, Kanemo was set up with funds from the Bank of Mozambique and Socimo, the government's commercial company that had been established after independence.[57] Socimo was intricately linked with security forces and became one of the main shareholders of Kanemo, along with Guerra himself and the Brazilian company Tropic, a partner of Socimo. The company's close ties to the secret service were controversial, some seeing Kanemo as a front for the Mozambican intelligence services.[58] Mendonça was appointed General Director and Carlos Alberto, who was General Director of Socimo, was put in charge of finances. Jacinto Veloso, the Minister for State Security and a close friend of Guerra, acted as a 'security shield' for Kanemo to carry out its work and protect the company against internal and external attacks. Between 1983 and 1988, Kanemo produced documentaries and educational fiction films commissioned by the government, the Red Cross and UNICEF. Chico Canciro and Labi Mendonça's *Pequenos Herois* (1984), a film shot in black and white on 16mm, depicted rural children who had to take their herds of cattle to the city by themselves, relying on their own resources. Canciro's *Lixo Urbano – Um Problema de Todos* (1985), shot in black and white on 16mm, addressed the

[55] Labi Mendonça, 'Text sobre a Kanemo Produção e Comunicação', an undated report sent by email on 19 September 2005: 2.

[56] Labi Mendonça: 6

[57] At the same time a sister film production company, Austra, was set up in Brazil. Labi Mendonça.

[58] Mendonça's response is that: 'In any case, in a country at war, everything goes through Security! It's obvious that there were personel from Intelligence infiltrated into everything and on all sides! Including Kanemo. But this was normal for the times.' Labi Mendonça: 11.

problem of urban waste and exhorted audiences to keep the streets clean. Mário Borgneth's *Karingana* (1985), shot in black and white on 16mm, explored the contribution to Mozambican literature of José Craveirinha. Alongside these activities, Kanemo created an archive of black and white photographs and participated in developing the use of video.

In 1982, Kanemo launched an ambitious project to document the public confessions of *os comprimetidos* 'the compromised', which was the name given to Mozambicans who were accused of collaboration with the colonial regime. The idea of 're-education' was a central tenet of Frelimo's commitment to revolutionary social transformation through the creation of a 'New Man', but Frelimo was by then coming under criticism from the international community because of alleged human rights abuses at its re-education camps. In 1981, during the Political and Organizational Offensive, Machel made a tour of the re-education camps in Chaimite and Ruárua and was alarmed by conditions in the Ruárua camp. Historian João Cabrita, who presents this period from the perspective of Renamo, argues that Machel's campaign, which blamed rogue elements within the security forces, in fact deflected attention away from key figures who were responsible for the camps during a period when leading dissenters and members of their families were being executed.[59] Kanemo's closeness to the security services did not make it immune from the climate of suspicion into which the Mozambican Revolution was descending as the war of destabilisation grew. Although Kanemo was a private enterprise, it was permitted to use the INC's resources, and this single project involving three cameras operated simultaneously used up the institute's entire film stock for the year. This led Pimenta to resign in protest, as he had already opposed decisions taken without consultation with the INC regarding the commissioning of *Musica, Moçambique!*[60] Later, the idea was developed of using some of the footage for a television series directed by Guerra and titled *Os Comprimentidos: Actas de um Processo de Decolonização* 'The Compromised: Acts in a Process of Decolonisation'. According to Chico Carneiro, the project continued until 1984, but the topic came to be considered too politically sensitive and only the first two episodes were broadcast.

[59] In June 1982, less than a year after the launch of the Political and Organization Offensive, Celina Simango (the wife of Uria Simango) was executed. While some security personnel were either dismissed or detained as a result of the investigation, other officials remained in place or were promoted. For example, Salésio Nalyambipano, who set up the Ruarua re-education, remained as vice-minister of security and was awarded a medal. João M. Cabrita (2000). *Mozambique: The Tortuous Road to Democracy*. Basingstoke: Palgrave Macmillan: 101–3.

[60] Email correspondence with Pedro Pimenta, 1 March 2019.

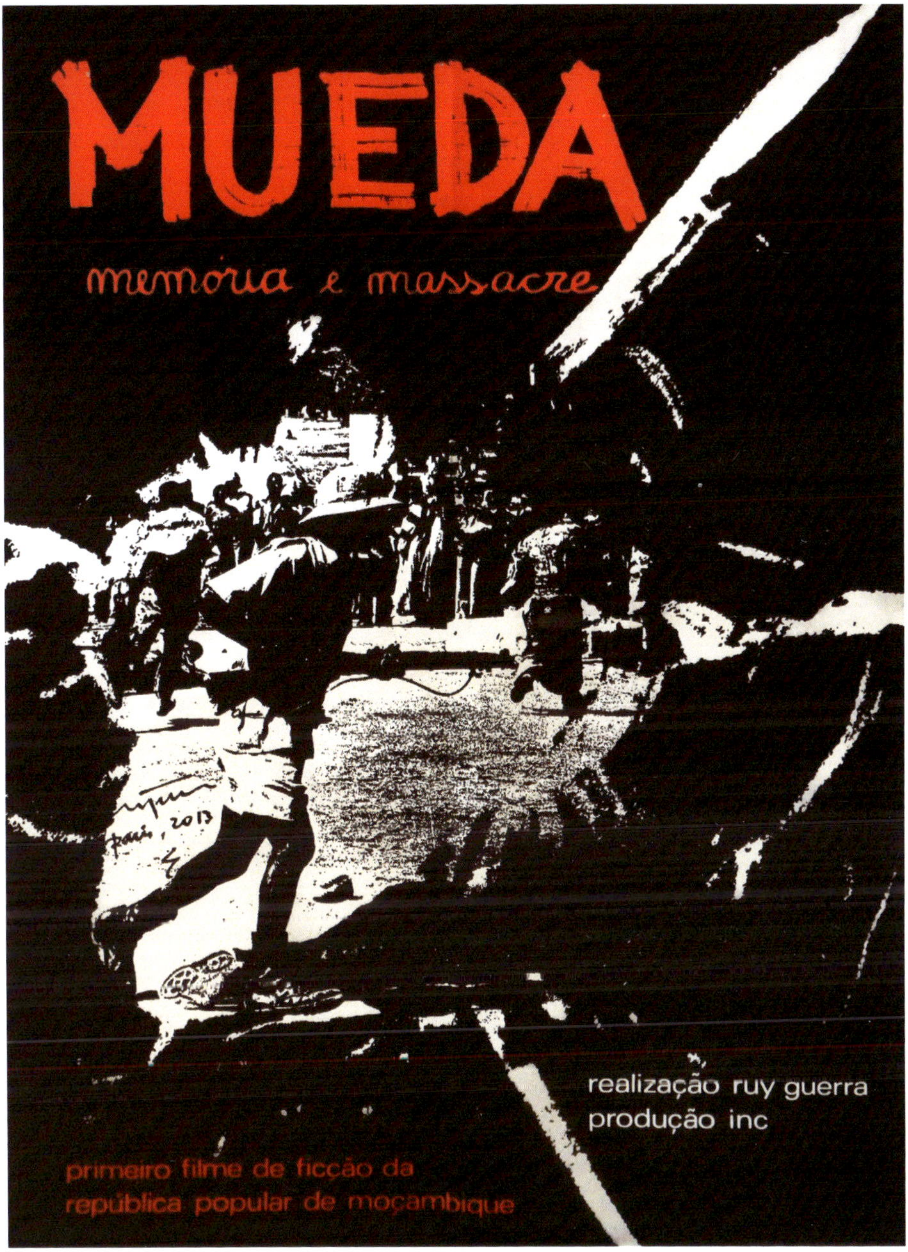

18. Poster for *Mueda, Memória e Massacre* (1979), directed by Ruy Guerra. Courtesy INAC.

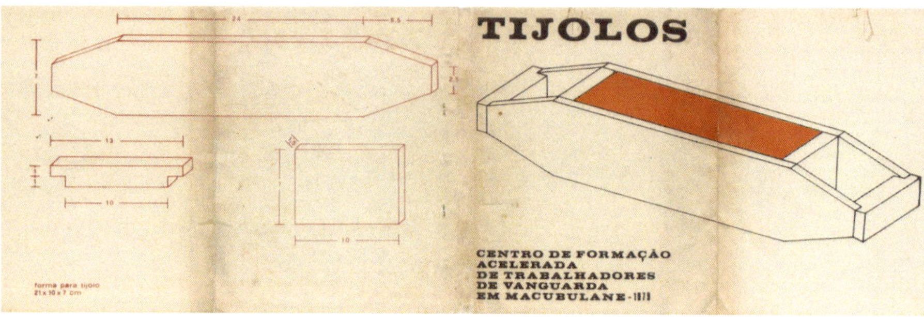

19. Cover of the book *Tijolos* (1979), Centro de Formação Acelerada de Trabalhadores de Vanguarda em Macubulane. Courtesy João Azevedo.

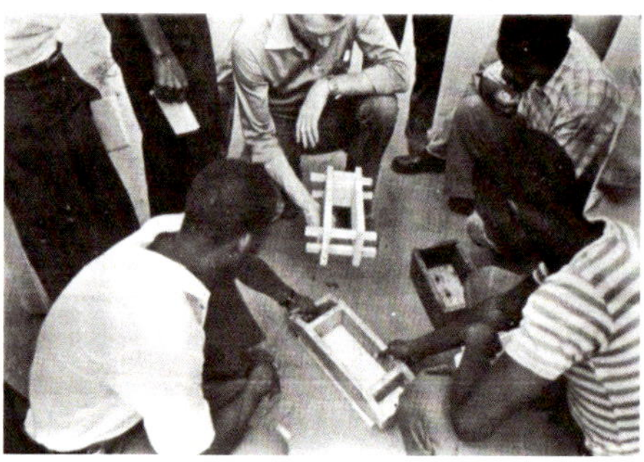

20–21. TBARN experiments with brick moulds. Photographs from *Tijolos* (1979). Courtesy João Azevedo.

22. Samora Machel interrogates a Mozambican who served in the Portuguese army in *Treatment for Traitors* (1983), made by Ike Bertels from archive material from the INC. Courtesy Ike Bertels and INAC.

23. An image of two young children overlaps buildings in Harare and a statue of Cecil Rhodes, *Pamberi ne Zimbabwe* (1980), directed by João Costa and Carlos Henriques. Courtesy INAC.

24. Vitor Henriques, João Costa, Camilo de Sousa, Licínio Azevedo, three MPLA soldiers, Francisco Henriques and their driver at Cahama, Angola, September 1981, for the shooting of *Cinco Tirors de Mause* (1981), directed by Licínio Azevedo and Camilo de Sousa. Courtesy Licínio Azevedo.

25. Still from *O Tempo dos Leopardos* (1985), directed by Zdravko Velimrović, with Ana Magaia in the role of Ana and Santos Mulungo in the role of Pedro. Courtesy INAC.

26. José Cardoso, Camilo de Sousa and Lucrécia Paco, among others, on the set of *O Vento Sopre do Norte* (1987), directed by José Cardoso. Courtesy João Cardoso.

27. Meeting of some of the crew of *O Vento Sopre do Norte*. Left to right: Isabel Noronha, João Machado da Graça, Camilo de Sousa, José Cardoso, unknown and João Costa. Courtesy João Cardoso.

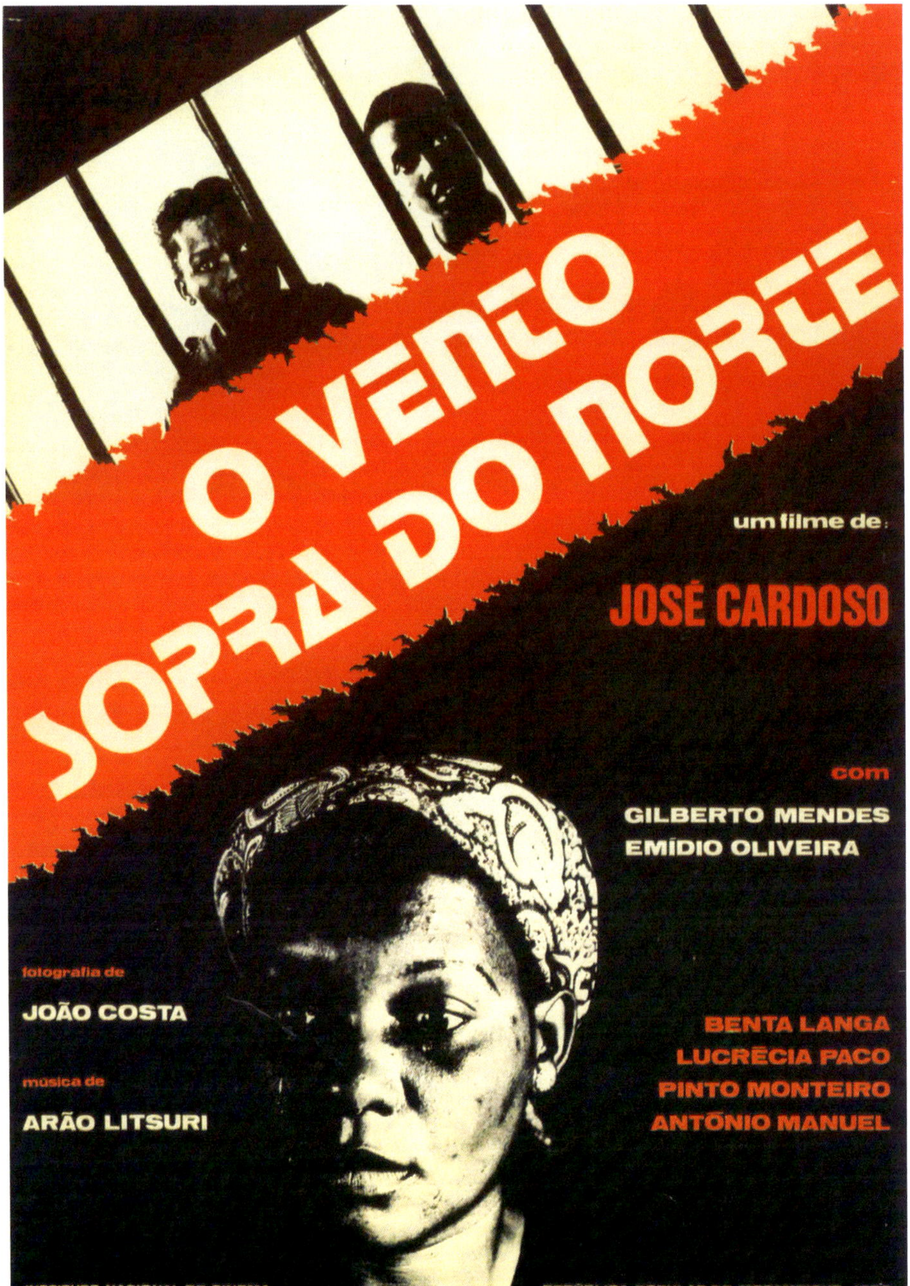

28. Poster for *O Vento Sopre do Norte* (1987). Courtesy family of João Cardoso and INAC.

In the meantime, the Dutch filmmaker Ike Bertels purchased footage of the public confessions from the INC, and she and Wim Louwrier edited the material into *Mozambique: Treatment for Traitors* (1983).[61] This film presents documentation from a week of confessions by individuals who had collaborated with the colonial regime, either by working for PIDE, participating in political organisations that were permitted by the fascist state, such as the Associação dos Negros Moçambicanos (AMP) or Acção Nacional Popular, or by serving in the Portuguese army. Held at the Escola Secundária Josina Machel in Maputo, the accused are seated together, grouped according to which colonial organisation they were affiliated with. Samora Machel and his government ministers sit on the stage, below a huge banner that reads: 'When we liberated Mozambique those who collaborated with colonialism also won a country'. From here, Machel interrogates individuals as they make their confessions. The film begins with images of the photographs and biographies of the *comprometidos* that were hung up for the purposes of public identification in their places of work, a policy that was implemented after 1978, when it was found that members of Acção Nacional Popular had infiltrated Frelimo.[62] The voiceover points out that this process of rehabilitation initiated within the Mozambican Revolution offers the accused the possibility of re-entering the new society and participating in national reconstruction, when they might in other situations have faced the firing squad for their crimes. The film is book-ended by speeches by Machel, which set out the stakes of the proceedings. Based on the conviction that the people can be transformed and 'reborn', the process is an attempt by the new nation to come to terms with history, using the act of personal confession as a means to restore the accused to their families and to the nation, so that the country can move forward together in constructing their shared future.

Treatment for Traitors then presents four individuals who are interrogated by Machel. The collaborators stand to the side of the room below the stage, from where they can be surveilled by the government ministers and President Machel. For his part, Machel, dressed in military uniform, is frequently shot from below, elevating and monumentalising his stature as head of state. The first confession is by Jaime Mateus, who describes how he spied on fellow African students involved in anti-colonial activities on behalf of PIDE in return for the Portuguese government funding his studies. Machel asks him to describe in detail his steps down 'the path to treason', until finally he is confronted with two of the men he betrayed. 'Forgive me', he pleads, before Machel abruptly calls

[61] Conversation with Chico Carneiro, Maputo, September 2005.

[62] Robert Stock (2017). 'The Many Returns to Wiriyamu': Audiovisual Testimony and the Negotiation of Colonial Violence', in Maria do Carmo Piçarra and Teresa Castro (eds) (2017). *(Re)imagining African Independence: Film, Visual Arts and the Fall of the Portuguese Empire*. Oxford: Peter Lang: 94.

the confession to an end. Machel denounces the psychological warfare that the colonial regime pursued, through which collaborators 'lost their personalities'. Next, Enoch Libombo, a member of the AMP fervently confesses to his collaboration with the colonial regime and the many public speeches he made defending their record. Machel, now wearing somewhat intimidating sunglasses, probes him further, at times laughing at his subservience to the Portuguese and pointing out that now the tables have turned. He explains that Frelimo 'teaches us to value human life' and that the aim of the rehabilitation process is 'complete identification with our people, with our Nation'. He then evokes other lengthy revolutionary struggles, including the Soviet Union from 1917 to 1934, China's struggle against the Japanese and Chaing Kai-Shek and Vietnam's victory against US imperialism, episodes in history that have totalitarian as well as anti-imperialist connotations. While individuals can betray their country, Machel argues, '*o Povo* can never commit treason. *O Povo* never dies.' At the end of Libombo's confession Machel approaches him and shakes him by the hand.

Finally, two Mozambicans who had served in the Portuguese army describe their roles in the massacre at Wiriyamu in December 1972. Machel's demeanour oscillates between threatening, sombre and even, at times, jocular – at one point asking the group of commandos how long it would take them to kill the paratroopers with their bare hands. Victor Igreja argues that Machel's interest in the commando's narratives is somewhat superficial, and so of limited value in terms of determining the truth of how many villagers were killed in the massacre.[63] Following Igreja, Robert Stock proposes that, despite the claims that *Treatment for Traitors* makes, Frelimo was developing a new kind of revolutionary rehabilitation programme that 'does away with the age-old distinction between collaboration and resistance', the show trials had another intention, which was to identify trained military personnel who could be sent to fight Renamo. According to this argument, the 'forced testimony' was a means to achieve the 'political-military project' of re-integrating former enemy soldiers who would be sufficiently hardened to fight in a situation of civil war. Indeed, the end of the film seems to confirm that by making their confessions the accused are re-entering a collective project of defending the nation. The confessions have allowed people to be 'reborn', enabling them to accept 'the values of the new society and bury the past'. Machel concludes: 'Let us all unite and stand together and stand in defence of our country. The struggle continues. The Revolution will be victorious.' Finally, the president invites the accused to throw down the signs that identify them as colonial collaborators, and with palpable relief they join together in applause and song.

[63] Victor Igreja (2010). 'Frelimo's Political Ruling through Violence and Memory in Post-colonial Mozambique'. *Southern African Studies*, 36, 4: 797.

The following year, in 1984, the INC held a Festival of Mozambican Films, expanding on the Retrospective held in 1982. However, by the mid-1980s the hopes that this would be the 'decade of development' had evaporated. Combined with the impact of the 1982–1983 drought followed by floods in 1984, the scale of destruction being wrought by Renamo meant that the country was in crisis, facing widespread famine and many people displaced from their homes (see Chapter 7). Until 1984 Frelimo had sought to realise the aspirations of independence through the pursuit of non-aligned foreign policy and the building of a socialist society that served the needs of the *o Povo* rather than an elite few. The central flank of its foreign policy was to support the struggle of the ANC against the Apartheid regime, just as it played a crucial role in supporting ZANU in the 1970s. In addition, according to Joseph Hanlon, in its first nine years the Frelimo government took steps to safeguard national sovereignty. It barred most foreign NGOs and 'negotiated clear relationships' with those that were permitted to operate.[64] Mozambique did not seek to join the IMF, the World Bank or the Lomé convention, which is the agreement that structures relations between the European Community and many African, Caribbean and Pacific countries. In 1984, however, two decisions signalled that the Frelimo government had come to the conclusion that these principles were no longer tenable. On 16 March, the governments of Mozambique and South Africa signed the Nkomati Accord. This proclaimed that Frelimo would cease to offer sanctuary to the ANC, and South Africa would stop supporting Renamo. On 24 September, Mozambique joined the IMF and began negotiating the terms of structural adjustment.

[64] Hanlon (1991): 1.

6 Let Them Come! Filmmaking on the Frontline against Apartheid, 1980–1989

This chapter examines Mozambique's role in regional filmmaking collaborations of the 1980s, which sought to make an intervention against South Africa's campaign of destabilisation that targeted the independent nations around its border. It considers how Southern African films such as *Pamberi ne Zimbabwe* 'Forward Zimbabwe' (1981), *Fronteiras de Sangue* 'Borders of Blood' (1986) and *Corridors of Freedom* (1987) attempted to shift global narratives about the region that privileged the perspectives of white minorities and the former colonial powers. Mozambique and other countries of the region saw themselves as part of a collective 'frontline' against Apartheid. The Frontline States alliance was first formally recognised by the Organisation of African Unity in April 1975, following visits by Samora Machel to Zambia and Tanzania during the period of transition to Mozambique's independence (see Chapter 2).[1] These countries, which had supported Frelimo and People's Movement for the Liberation of Angola's (MPLA) armed struggle for independence, recognised the ongoing threat to their national sovereignty posed by the white minority regimes of Rhodesia and South Africa, and that their fates were entangled with the organisations that were resisting them – the ANC in South Africa, SWAPO in Namibia and ZANU and ZAPU in Rhodesia.

Despite independence in Angola, Mozambique and Zimbabwe, South Africa continued to dominate the region economically and had the power to disrupt energy and food supplies across Southern Africa. In response to this situation, the Southern African Development Coordination Conference (SADCC) made up of the state members of Angola, Botswana, Lesotho, Malawi, Mozambique, Swaziland, Tanzania, Zambia and the newly independent Zimbabwe was held to develop economic cooperation (see Chapter 5). The Conferência Africana de

[1] In early May 1975, Machel made an eight-day farewell tour of Tanzania, visiting nine Tanzanian regions to thank the Tanzanian people for their support of Frelimo during the armed struggle. His four-day visit to Zambia took place between 12 and 15 May 1975, at the invitation of President Kenneth Kaunda. C. B. Thompson (1985). *Challenge to Imperialism: The Frontline States in the Liberation of Zimbabwe*. Harare: Zimbabwe Publishing House: 16.

Cooperação Cinematográfica that took place in Maputo in 1977 had seen the launch of the Associação Africana de Cooperação Cinematográfica (AACC), which was the first attempt to re-organise the cinema industry at a regional level (see Chapter 3). But in fact little ensued in terms of cinematographic collaboration until 1980, when Zimbabwe gained independence. To understand the significance of this moment for Mozambique and the entire region, it is necessary to make a detour back through the entangled history of resistance to colonial and white minority rule in the Southern African region.

By the late 1970s, the defence of white minority rule in Rhodesia threatened to draw the entire region into an international war involving numerous powers, including the United States, the Soviet Union and China, which were on opposing sides of the Cold War and the Sino–Soviet split. In 1963, Ndabaningi Sithole, Herbert Chitepo, Robert Mugabe and Edgar Tekere had founded the Zimbabwean African National Union (ZANU). For much of the next ten years Sithole, Mugabe, Tekere and other leading figures were imprisoned, while Chitepo led the armed struggle from Zambia. In 1975, Chitepo was assassinated and Mugabe, who was then in Mozambique, seized the leadership of ZANU, while many of the cadres of Ndebele ethnicity followed Joshua Nkomo to form a rival independence movement called the Zimbabwe African People's Union (ZAPU). ZAPU was designated an 'authentic' national liberation movement by the Organisation of African Unity and after independence in Angola the MPLA supported the Zimbabwe People's Revolutionary Army (ZIPRA), the army of ZAPU.[2] ZAPU, on the one hand, had bases in Zambia and Angola and received military instruction and equipment from Cuba and the Soviet Union, which favoured conventional warfare. Frelimo, on the other, supported and offered sanctuary to ZANLA, the armed wing of ZANU, which was dominated by the Shona majority. ZANU benefitted from the Sino–Soviet split as its search for patrons coincided with China's desire to cultivate client organisations in Africa, and from Nyerere's frustration with Nkomo.[3] Some of ZANLA's leading officers received military training in China, and Chinese instructors taught ZANLA guerrillas at the Itumbi Training Base in Tanzania.[4] Although Machel's government was at first suspicious of Mugabe and kept him under house arrest, they were eventually won over by his commitment to armed struggle and socialist transformation. Mozambicans living near the border with Zimbabwe shared linguistic and historical roots with Mugabe's Shona-speaking guerrillas,

[2] Sabelo J. Ndlovu-Gatsheni (2010). 'Angola–Zimbabwe Relations: A Study in the Search for Regional Alliances'. *The Round Table*, 99, 411: 637.
[3] Ndlovu-Gatsheni (2010): 637–638.
[4] Ndlovu-Gatsheni (2010): 638.

so solidarity with the ZANLA fighters was felt at the grassroots as well as within Frelimo's political elite.[5]

In 1976, under pressure from other African leaders, the two forces united to form a Patriotic Front, with the Zimbabwe People's Army (ZIPA) as its armed wing. Despite this, Alfred 'Nikita' Mangena and Rex Nhongo (*nom de guerre* of Solomon Mujuru), the respective heads of ZIPRA and ZANLA, maintained that they would field separate forces and rarely launched joint offensives.[6] Indeed, ZANLA guerrillas sometimes fought against ZIPRA forces within Rhodesia.[7] Meanwhile, other Zimbabwean nationalists formed parties, including Sithole's ZANU-Ndonga and Bishop Abel Muzorewa's United African National Council (UANC), which denounced armed struggle and sought power sharing agreements that granted the white minority disproportionate power. During the final years of Zimbabwe's armed struggle, the Rhodesian army and Selous Scouts accelerated their devastating attacks across the Mozambican border. Their attacks on ZANU camps and Mozambican infrastructure resulted in mass killings (see Chapter 5). As the dissolution of white minority rule in Rhodesia came to be seen as inevitable, the Frontline States were keen to reconcile the ethnic divide within the Patriotic Front and became concerned that a hostile government in Harare involving a coalition between Muzorewa's UANC and Smith's Rhodesian Front could strengthen South Africa.[8] Britain's Conservative government led by Margaret Thatcher favoured recognising elections in April 1979 that would have put UANC and the Rhodesian Front in government. However, the 1979 elections were condemned by the United Nations, and, under pressure from US President Carter, the British government ultimately rejected the result. In September 1979, negotiations between the British government, the Patriotic Front and the transitional Zimbabwe–Rhodesian government led by Smith and Muzorewa began at Lancaster House in London. Mugabe initially resisted a settlement as he wanted to be able to claim an outright military victory. However, Mozambique could no longer bear the cost of hosting ZANU.[9] As Mugabe's host, Frelimo was in a position to put pressure on ZANU. The talks

[5] Clinarete Victoria Luis Munguambe (2017). 'Nationalism and Exile in an Age of Solidarity: Frelimo–ZANU relations in Mozambique (1975–1980)'. *Journal of Southern African Studies*, 43, 1: 161–178.

[6] Paul Moorcraft (2011). *Mugabe's War Machine: Saving or Savaging of Zimbabwe?* Barnsley: Pen & Sword: 52.

[7] Munguambe (2017): 168.

[8] By mid-1979, senior officers in the Rhodesian army including General Peter Walls stated publicly that Rhodesia could not win the war. In the run up to the elections in 1980, elements within the Rhodesian army proposed plots to assassinate senior ZANU figures including Mugabe, Nhongo, Tongogara and Nkomo. David Martin and Phyllis Johnson (1981). *The Struggle for Zimbabwe*. London: Faber: 311.

[9] Munguambe (2017): 161 and 177.

led to a negotiated settlement in 1979 to hold multi-party elections that would be overseen by the British government in 1980.

As these first democratic elections loomed, therefore, the stakes involved in achieving national reconciliation in Zimbabwe could not be higher, not only for the internal parties but also for the neighbouring Frontline States that had supported them. It was in this context that the MPLA and Frelimo governments agreed to a project that became perhaps the most important and influential film made at this crucial juncture: *Pamberi ne Zimbabwe* 'Forward Zimbabwe' (1981), the first South–South co-production in Southern Africa. *Pamberi ne Zimbabwe* documented the transition to independence in Zimbabwe in 1980 and was made by Angolan and Mozambican filmmakers as a gift from the two governments to the new nation. The Angolan Carlos Henriques, who worked for Televisão Popular de Angola (TPA), and João Costa of the INC undertook the direction of *Pamberi ne Zimbabwe*. Both had experience of camera work in situations of conflict. The rest of the crew was made up of Mozambican and Angolan filmmakers, as well as some international *cooperantes* working at the INC, such as the Canadian editor Ophera Hallis and Simon Hartog, who play an instrumental role in securing funds from Libya. The film was shot in 16mm, which meant that the negatives had to be processed in Harare as the INC laboratory only had the facilities to develop black and white.

Pamberi ne Zimbabwe is of historical significance because it tells the story of the transition from the perspective of ordinary Zimbabweans as well as their political leaders. It thus situates Zimbabwe's independence in terms of regional geopolitics and Pan-African affiliations, rather than from the point of view of the white minority and without the condescension of the British officials overseeing the transition, which dominated Western media reporting.[10] It reflected the importance of representing this historic event from an African perspective. International awareness of the need to decolonise a media system that was entering a new stage of globalisation had been mounting.[11] In 1978, UNESCO published a study entitled *The New World Information Order*, which diagnosed a persistent colonial bias in global information systems, produced by a 'profound imbalance between developed and developing countries'

[10] This bias is still prevalent in the historical analysis of Zimbabwe's transition to independence. See Sue Onslow (2013). 'The Man on the Spot: Christopher Soames and Decolonisation of Zimbabwe/Rhodesia'. *Britain and the World*, 6.1: 68–100.

[11] As Frederic Jameson argues in *The Geopolitical Aesthetic*, in the late 1970s alarm about the way in which global networks were dominated by shady alliances between Western governments and corporations manifested culturally in the paranoid Hollywood thrillers of the late 1970s. Significantly, though, the upheavals of Third World revolutions barely register in Jameson's account of the 'world system'. Frederic Jameson (1992). *The Geopolitical Aesthetic: Cinema and Space in the World System*. Bloomington: Indiana University Press.

and affecting 'news agencies, radio and television, films, reviews, books and illustrated mass circulation magazines, data banks and advertising firms.'[12] *The New World Information Order* called for transformation of a transnational communication system that is 'an amalgam of disorders', including 'flagrant quantitative imbalance between North and South' in terms of news generated; inequality of information resources such as access to radio frequencies and copyright law; lack of information on developing countries; and, on the part of Western powers, a 'will to dominate' global information flows. The study argued that:

> The present-day information system enshrines a form of political, economic and cultural colonialism which is reflected in the often tendentious interpretation of news concerning the developing countries. This consists in highlighting events whose significance in certain cases is limited or even non-existent; in collecting isolated facts and presenting them as a 'whole'; in setting out facts in such a way that the conclusion to be drawn from them is necessarily favourable to the interests of the transnational system; in amplifying small-scale events so as to arouse unjustified fears; in keeping silent on situations unfavourable to the interests of the countries of origin of these media. In this way, world events are covered only insofar as it suits the interests of certain societies.[13]

This situation of colonial bias not only led to cultural alienation within the Global South, but also, as Sue Onslow argues, had the potential to shape international affairs in ways that would disadvantage the Frontline States, as it led to governments in the West taking political decisions on the basis of information that was skewed.[14]

Pamberi ne Zimbabwe opens with images of the stone ruins of the medieval city of Great Zimbabwe. A voiceover scripted by Luís Carlos Patraquim sketches out a historical context for the struggle for independence in Zimbabwe, starting with the Kingdom of Mutapa, which stretched from the Zambezi through to the Limpopo and the Indian Ocean and was founded by the descendants of the people who constructed Great Zimbabwe.[15] The voiceover then explains the colonisation of Zimbabwe by the British South Africa Company and the founding in 1895 of Rhodesia, named after the company's instigator Cecil Rhodes. Using

[12] Mustafa Masmoudi (1978). *The New World Information Order*. Washington, DC: UNESCO: 1.

[13] Masmoudi (1978): 4.

[14] Sue Onslow with Simon Bright (2013). '"The Battle of Cuito Cuanavale": Media space and the end of the Cold War in Southern Africa', in Artemy Kalinovsky and Sergey Radchenko (2013). *The End of the Cold War and the Third World*. London: Routledge: 277–296.

[15] Kingdom of Mutapa (Monopotapa in Portuguese, Mutapa in Shona or more commonly Munhumutapa).

colonial photographs, the film describes the building of the railways to facilitate the extraction of natural resources. It recounts how Zimbabweans responded to British imperialism with the first *chimurenga* 'revolutionary revolt' against the British South Africa Company during the 1890s. This introductory section then outlines Rhodesia's unilateral declaration of independence and the formation of ZANU and the subsequent split into the faction led by Robert Mugabe from Mozambique and ZAPU led by Joshua Nkomo from Zambia. Finally it describes the ZANU–ZAPU alliance, the Lancaster House negotiations and the birth of the new nation of Zimbabwe.

What then follows is an extraordinary document of meetings between ZANU and ZAPU forces and the Rhodesian army at the assembly points (the designated places where returning guerrillas were instructed to gather), Zimbabweans participating in the country's first democratic elections, the independence ceremony and street celebrations. The story of the transition is told through footage, often shot from shoulder height in the midst of crowds in the street, at polling stations and at places of work and rural labour. The aesthetic approach is clearly Third Worldist, chiming with the imperative articulated by ICAIC's Julio García Espinosa that truly revolutionary filmmaking practice does not aim for technological perfection. Rather, the revolutionary 'imperfect cinema' of the Third World involves filmmakers inserting themselves into the revolutionary situation with whatever means are available to them (see Chapter 3).[16] Interspersed through *Pamberi ne Zimbabwe* are excerpts from an interview with Robert Mugabe, who sets out how the armed struggle was responsible for the collapse of the white minority regime and how ZANU is poised to take over government. He stresses that the incoming administration intends to move gradually towards socialist transformation rather than immediately dismantle the capitalist economic system. Mugabe emphasises that this is a 'moment of anxiety' as the defeated power is still in place. At a later moment in the film, he speaks about the centrality of political education within the armed struggle, a militant pedagogy that sets out to advance 'political confidence at all levels, the people and the party merged as one'. The result of the armed struggle is a political settlement: 'the trajectory of our guns is political – towards political objectives, control of political and economic power by our people.'

While the inclusion of these excerpts privileges Mugabe's account, the film is careful to acknowledge the cross-party effort to work for a peaceful transition, emphasising the role of Joshua Nkomo and General Peter Walls, the commander of the Rhodesia Security Forces, in persuading their troops to be reconciled with their former enemies. Moreover, most of the interviews in the film are not with political or military leaders but people who range from whites, who are visibly

[16] Julio García Espinosa translated by Julianne Bruton (1979). 'For an Imperfect Cinema'. *Jump Cut*, 20: 24–26.

tense and anxious about the future, to jubilant black youths who express their joy and hopes for an emancipated Zimbabwe. Importantly, the film aligns itself with the people who are being liberated by independence. This affiliation is evident in the scene of the meeting on 26 March 1980 between officers from the Rhodesian army and ZANLA guerrillas at Foxtrot, also known as Dzapasi Camp in Buhera, which was the largest of sixteen assembly points.[17] While the Lancaster House Agreement set out the terms for the civilian transition to democratic elections, the task of reconciling three rival military forces of ZANLA, ZIPRA and the Rhodesian army was left to the incoming government. As Knox Chitiyo and Martin Rupiya point out: 'In military terms, the three armies remained in place, each with its own intelligence and command-and-control structures still intact. This constituted real potential for civil war if the political environment was not handled correctly.'[18] Dzapasi was one of sixteen assembly points stipulated in the Lancaster House Agreement, where guerrillas would gather with their arms in the run up to the election. British Foreign Secretary Lord Carrington, who chaired the Lancaster House Conference, admitted that the assembly points were a 'tricky' proposal that could determine the success or failure of the agreement.[19] The scene opens with ZANLA Commander Rex Nhongo leading his guerrillas in a rendition of 'Nyika yeZimbabwe' 'Our country Zimbabwe'. Arriving at Dzapasi by helicopter as the soundtrack fills with sound of guerrillas singing, the Rhodesian army officials stand around with their arms crossed as Nhongo addresses the crowd in Shona. Magnanimous and expansive, Nhongo explains to his forces the difference between members of the Commonwealth Monitoring Force, who wear armbands on their sleeves and are present to maintain the ceasefire, and the 'local soldiers' – the Rhodesian Security Forces and British South African Police (BSAP). The question of how to begin to construct relations with these former enemies is addressed with bawdy humour through the metaphor of courtship. 'How', he asks rhetorically, 'are we going to

[17] Rhodesian troops withdrew to bases that were mainly in the centre of the country, with some moving to assembly points close to the border. The guerrilla troops were thus sandwiched between Rhodesian army rendezvous points, meaning that if attacked their escape routes to Mozambique or Zambia would be blocked. Between 28 December and 4 January, more than 25,000 ZANLA and ZIPRA guerrillas registered at the assembly points. Patience Murava (2016). 'Assembly Points: The Forgotten History'. *The Patriot*, 28 January. Available https://www.thepatriot.co.zw/old_posts/assembly-points-the-forgotten-history/.

[18] Knox Chitiyo and Martin Rupiya (2005). 'Tracking Zimbabwe's Political History: The Zimbabwe Defence Force From 1980 to 2005', in Martin Rupiya (2005). *Evolutions and Revolutions: A Contemporary History of Militaries in Southern Africa*. Pretoria: Institute for Security Studies: 354–356.

[19] Alexander Kanengoni (2016). 'Dzapasi Assembly Point . . . the forgotten story'. *The Patriot*. 28 January. Available at https://www.thepatriot.co.zw/old_posts/dzapasi-assembly-point-the-forgotten-story/.

figure out the *sahwira* ["close bond"]?' Emphasising that the conflict has resulted in a draw in which neither side was defeated, he teases his troops:

> Maybe they are the wife and you are the husband, or maybe you are the wife and they are the husband. . . . How can we get to the point where we can sleep in the same bed together?

The musician Dick Chingaira Makoni, otherwise known as 'Comrade Chinx', steps out from among the guerrillas and leads a choir of *chimbwido* (young civilian women who assisted the ZANLA guerrillas) in the song 'Maruza Imi vapambepfumi' 'You have been defeated, you imperialist exploiters'.[20] The full lyrics of this choral song give an account of ninety years of settler domination, chronicling the devastation of colonial subjugation. It describes the emergence of the nationalist movement and the guerrilla war, detailing the harsh conditions in the training camps in Tanzania and Mozambique, the massacres committed by the Rhodesian Security Forces and the final victory of the armed struggle at Lancaster House.[21] In this sequence, and in contrast to Nhongo's conciliatory tone, Chinx freestyles a series of jibes against the Rhodesian troops, who have been 'defeated' and who have 'lazy wives from the land of misery', jabbing with his hand at the sky to indicate those who have flown here in their 'flashy' helicopters. The Rhodesian army official addresses the guerrillas stiffly: 'The war is now finished. We as soldiers can stop this war, and that is why we have come today, so that we can start to build a trust between the ZANLA forces and the Rhodesia Security Forces.' One of Nhongo's men asks whether they will be housed together with the Rhodesians at the assembly point camp, and he replies by returning to the courtship analogy: 'If you meet a girl you like, you don't just grab her breast or bum, you take your time, and then you get to do everything else.' Another guerrilla steps out to lead the song 'Chikwama chababa' 'Father's Wallet', which again expresses the antagonism that Nhongo's discourse seeks to smooth over.[22] And to the beat of this war cry, the guerrillas dance, the chorus running through the provinces of Zimbabwe, underlining that some of their number wanted to continue to fight on for a military victory.

The central section of the film depicts the election process, including interviews with officials who describe the voting procedure and, with Bob Marley's song 'Zimbabwe' (1978) on the soundtrack, scenes of lengthy queues

[20] During the armed struggle Cde Chinx led the Takawira Choir, which later became the Zimbabwe African National Liberation Army (ZANLA) Choir.

[21] Geoffrey Nyarota gives a moving account of Comrade Chinx and description of a performance of 'Maruza imi vapambepfumi' in Geoffrey Nyarota (2006). *Against the Grain: Memoirs of a Zimbabwean Newsman*. Cape Town: Zebra: 83–84.

[22] The song is also known as 'Hondo kuManyika' ('war in Manica'). I thank Arnold Chamunogwa for his help with translations of Shona dialogue in *Pamberi ne Zimbabwe*.

at polling stations. A black election official speaks of voters feeling intimidated by armed soldiers and policemen from the Commonwealth Monitoring Force. Other scenes include the merging of Selous Scouts and ZIPRA guerrillas at army camps, with interviews with white officers and black guerrillas, one of whom speaks optimistically about the possibility of the former enemies now calling one another 'comrade' and 'brother'. Documented just days before the election, the subsequent scene shows Joshua Nkomo addressing ZIPRA troops, asking them to join together with their former enemies. In contrast to Rex Nhongo's informal rapport with his troops, Nkomo speaks in English, suggesting a more hierarchical relation with ZIPRA soldiers, who were much more of a professionalised army than ZANLA. This is followed by a speech by General Peter Walls, the commander of the Rhodesian Security Forces. In the weeks approaching the election Walls had in fact been considering an attack to crush ZANU and assassinate key figures including Mugabe, but ultimately he renounced the plan and threw his weight behind reconciliation. Walls says to the ZIPRA soldiers: 'We fought each other. That is history. Let this be a good start to our future together. It's a wonderful country. Let us together make it the best one in the world. I don't mind what it's called, because it's such a damned good place. And so I say to you Pamberi ne Zimbabwe.' The film cuts to a close up of the faces of two ZIPRA fighters, whose surly expressions suggest that they are unimpressed. In the next scene a British official reads out the elections results. As he concludes, the images switch to celebrations in the streets, interviews with ecstatic ZANLA supporters and muted responses from whites, who stand nervously in doorways.

The soundtrack is crucial to the political meaning and power of the film, which repeatedly makes use of overlapping in the editing to carry music and sometimes Mugabe's voiceover into the subsequent set of images, thus functioning as a connective device between different moments of the transition. Zimbabwean Chimurenga songs set the scene for the Rhodesian army officials' tense encounters with the guerrillas, emphasising that the white minority regime is in the position of humiliating defeat even though their stiff deportment suggests residual feelings of superiority. As well as Chimurenga music, the songs of Bob Marley weave through the soundtrack. Marley's 1978 song 'Zimbabwe', had, as Tsitsi Ella Jaji argues, become an anthem of global solidarity with ZANU and ZAPU.[23] Like many of his other songs about black suffering and resistance, 'Zimbabwe' conjures a Pan-African imaginary that crosses the Black Atlantic, extending the aesthetics of the film to encompass a transnational Third Worldism. As a 'black vernacular intellectual', in Grant Farred's phrase, Marley's music functioned as a mode of intervention into the

[23] Tsitsi Ella Jaji (2014). *Africa in Stereo: Modernism, Music and Pan-African Solidarity*. Oxford: Oxford University Press: 1–7.

dominant public sphere.[24] Its prominence on the soundtrack echoes the way in which *Pamberi ne Zimbabwe* sought to have a powerful impact on international understanding of what independence in Zimbabwe meant for its people and for the world.

In a memorable sequence that follows the depiction of the election results, the entire track of Marley's 'Redemption Songs' plays over images that juxtapose the luxurious existence of the white settlers with the poverty of black Zimbabweans. This simple device of juxtaposition displays the reality of segregation and racial violence – travelling shots of lavish suburbs are contrasted with the destitution of slums, black women cook on wood fires in the street while the kitchens of the white bourgeoisie are well stocked with alcohol, soldiers patrol the city streets in armoured vehicles, white men play golf followed by their black caddies, children carry and chop firewood while white girls play hockey. Finally, as the song moves into its final chords, an image of two black infants is superimposed over Harare's skyscrapers and colonial buildings, and as the images glide over one another, one of the children momentarily seems to hold the statue of Cecil Rhodes in his hands. The sequence recalls moments in a number of films made at Mozambique's transition to independence that were endlessly projected in cinemas and by the mobile cinema units, not least Robert van Lierop's *O Povo Organizado*, which makes an acute diagnosis of the challenges Frelimo faced in reconciling the contradictions and segregation produced by colonialism, particularly in the urban areas (see Chapter 2). In *Pamberi ne Zimbabwe*, however, there is no overbearing analytical voiceover but rather a kaleidoscopic portrait of a nation fused out of seemingly irreconcilable parts. Marley's music on the soundtrack endows the sequence with an emotional depth that has an almost spiritual dimension, echoing the revolutionary mysticism of Celso and Luccas's '25' (see Chapter 3).

The final section of the film portrays the independence ceremony, starting with Prince Charles descending from his British Royal Air Force plane to be greeted by Zimbabwean officials. A white choir sings as the British flag is lowered and there is a sudden cut to a dramatic performance of a Shona *Muchongoya* dance as the colonial flag is returned to Prince Charles by Nobert Chimombe, otherwise known by his *nom de guerre* as Agnew Kambeu, who then raises the Zimbabwean flag. Other foreign heads of state are shown entering the stadium, including Kenneth Kaunda of Zambia and Indira Ghandi of India, followed by shots of a performance of *Isitshikitsha*, a ceremonial dance of the Ndebele people. *Pamberi ne Zimbabwe* follows with a short sequence from Marley's performance at the independence ceremony, which the reggae superstar

[24] Grant Farred (2003). *What's My Name: Black Vernacular Intellectuals*. Minneapolis: University of Minnesota Press.

funded himself.[25] With Chief Justice Hector McDonald and Lord Soames on the podium, the first President of Zimbabwe Canaan Banana calls on Mugabe to be invested as the nation's first prime minister. The film finishes with a choir bursting into a Chimurenga song, which continues into the final credits as the sun sets over Great Zimbabwe. In the years that followed, *Pamberi ne Zimbabwe* came to function as a resource of collective memory, its sequences endlessly appropriated into new films and television broadcast. But the documentary was also important for future regional film production cooperation in that it forged professional relations between particular individuals, showcasing their professional skills and a style of documentary featuring hand-held camera work and local and international genres of popular music as a powerful generator of meaning. *Pamberi ne Zimbabwe* forged a Southern African aesthetic that brought documentary images into relation with a multilingual, musical soundtrack that that crossed genres and expanded beyond national boundaries as an expression of emancipation.

While the independence of Zimbabwe seemed to offer some relief to the Frontline States, the Apartheid regime was still entrenched in South Africa and continued to menace the region. In November 1980, leaders of the majority-ruled neighbouring nations, now nine in number, met for the first Southern African Development Coordination Conference (SADCC) to organise cooperation between states forging independent paths of development. Their declaration emphasised that 'future development must aim at the reduction of economic dependence not only on the Republic of South Africa, but also on any single external State or group of States'. They stressed a commitment to non-alignment and to dismantling 'the artificial links' with South Africa that had been built through Portuguese colonialism and Rhodesia's white minority rule.[26] Frelimo's pursuit of a non-aligned foreign policy and socialist economic development depended on maintaining its sovereignty and regional cooperation. With the election of Margaret Thatcher in 1979 and Ronald Reagan in 1981, two powerful governments became further entrenched in the view that Mozambique and Angola posed a communist threat. Their administrations sought to block sanctions against South Africa and, in the United States, Chester Crocker advocated the policy of 'constructive engagement' with the Apartheid

[25] In fact the moment was a tense one, as the first song 'War' was interrupted when security forces fired tear gas at ZANLA guerrillas who had congregated outside, frustrated at being denied entry. Marley gave another free concert the following night for all those who had not been able to get into the stadium. For an account of the concert and analysis of Marley's songs, see Farred (2003): 216–220.

[26] Joseph Hanlon (1991). *Mozambique: who calls the shots?* Bloomington: Indiana University Press and London: James Currey: 17.

regime. This was interpreted by Pretoria as a license to continue and extend its attacks on neighbouring Marxist–Leninist states.

The regional cooperation on filmmaking that developed in the 1980s became chiefly directed towards exposing South African aggression across the region. South Africa was conducting large-scale military operations across Southern Africa, which the Apartheid government wanted to keep secret from its own population and out of the attention of the international community. While in the late 1970s the principal external threat to Mozambique had been attacks by the Rhodesian army, Angola had been subjected to numerous invasions by South African troops, who were supporting the União Nacional para a Independência Total de Angola 'National Union for the Total Independence of Angola' (UNITA). In September 1980, a few months after the filming of *Pamberi ne Zimbabwe*, Camilo de Sousa, João Costa and Licínio Azevedo went to Angola during one of the South African invasions.[27] According to Camilo de Sousa, they spent several weeks in trenches in southern Angola filming under fire to make *Cinco Tiros de Mauser* (1981) with Carlos Henriques's brothers Vitor and Francisco, accompanying MPLA soldiers.[28] The film was an act of internationalist solidarity, as de Sousa explained to me in 2005:

> We wanted to show that it was the same fight we were involved with together against Apartheid. This is something important that you should know. Our struggle wasn't about nationalism. It may sound strange these days, but their struggle was our struggle too.[29]

Just as Pretoria justified its attacks on Angola in part because the MPLA was supporting the Namibian liberation movement SWAPO, so too Mozambique became a target because it gave sanctuary to political exiles of the ANC. By 1980, the ANC had built up a network of safe houses in Mozambique and some of its leading figures, such as Joe Slovo, Ruth First, Jacob Zuma, Alpheus Manghezi, Albie Sachs and a large number of cadres were living in Maputo and the surrounding areas.[30] Just ten days after the inauguration of President Reagan, in the early hours of 30 January 1981, truckloads of South African commandos crossed over the border into Mozambique. The South African Defence Force (SADF) attacked three ANC safe houses in the Maputo suburb of Matola, killing fourteen members of Umkhonto we Sizwe, the military wing of the ANC. They also killed a Portuguese electrician, whom they mistook for

[27] Interview with Pedro Pimenta (1983). *Jump Cut*, 28, April 1983: 30-31. https://www.ejumpcut.org/archive/onlinessays/JC28folder/MozambPimente.html.

[28] Conversation with Camilo de Sousa, Maputo, August 2005.

[29] Conversation with Camilo de Sousa, Maputo, August 2005.

[30] Nadja Manghezi (2009). *The Maputo Connection: ANC Life in the World of Frelimo*. Johannesburg: Jacana Media.

Joe Slovo.[31] Henrique Caldeira's *30 de Janeiro* (1981) documented the carnage. Survivor Matthews Thombela managed to kill one of the commandos, who turned out to be a British mercenary named Mike Hedgerson. *30 de Janeiro* includes an image of his helmet, which was painted with swastikas and the words 'sieg heil'.[32] Hanlon argues that the attack was probably 'testing the water'. [33] The US government did not object to the raid and shortly afterwards held talks between the Pentagon and high-ranking South African intelligence officials as part of Reagan's policy of 'constructive engagement' with the Apartheid government.

The official response from Mozambique was defiance. Journalists and politicians in Maputo argued that, with their experience of conducting a successful 'people's war', the Mozambican people would meet the threat posed by South Africa head on.[34] José Cardoso's documentary *Que Venham!* (1981) captured a powerful speech by Samora Machel at a rally in the Praça de Independencia in Maputo on 14 February 1981. Beginning with gruesome images of the scene at Matola, including the bodies of the ANC cadres tangled in debris, the film then makes the connection between European imperialism and the racist regime in South Africa through a newspaper image of a Mirage fighter jet and the caption 'La France, fournisseur quasi exclusif de l'armée de Pretoria'. *Que Venham* combines close-up shots of Machel giving his speech with sweeping panoramas of the crowds gathered to listen to him, with banners with slogans and iconic portraits of the president, creating a powerful image of unity and authority. Standing on the podium with Oliver Tambo, Machel renewed Mozambique's commitment to support the ANC and offer sanctuary to its political exiles. Machel's speech included some self-criticism that Frelimo had lowered its guard after the end of the war in Rhodesia and as a result had underestimated the threat posed by South Africa. Eight prisoners accused of collaborating with South Africa and 'opening the door' to the attack were presented to the crowd one by one on a plinth, the president promising that, as soon as the investigation was complete, all 'criminal enemy agents' would be

[31] A fifteenth ANC member, Vuyani Mavuso, was kidnapped and later executed when he refused to cooperate with the Apartheid security agency. See http://www.thepresidency.gov.za/national-orders/recipient/matola-raid-martyrs-1981.

[32] Manghezi quotes the testimony of Matthews 'Mabena' Thobela. Manghezi (2009): 102–103.

[33] Hanlon (1986). *Beggar Your Neighbours: Apartheid Power in Southern Africa*. London: James Currey: 27.

[34] For example, Carlos Cardoso argued that the Apartheid system could not comprehend the nature of 'people's war': 'The combatants of liberty are not uniformed soldiers that can be distinguished from the masses. They *are* the masses and in Mozambique and South Africa there are 35 million soldiers. Who is afraid after all?' Quoted in Paul Fauvet and Marcelo Mosse (2004). *Carlos Cardoso e a Revolução Moçambicana*. Maputo: Ndjia: 121.

put before the Revolutionary Military Tribunal. Challenging the South Africa government to declare outright war on Mozambique, Machel declared '*Que Venham!*' 'Let them come!' 'Let all the racists come! Let them come! We will liquidate the war once and for all. That way there will be true peace in the region. Not this artificial peace we're living in. Let the South Africans come, but they should know that the war will end in Pretoria!'[35] As Paul Fauvet and Marcelo Mosse point out, the 'enemies' were identified, and come they did, but not in the way they were expected.

The attack in Matola marked an acceleration of Botha's 'total strategy for survival', which had been an official state policy since 1978 and included plans to destabilise the entire region so as to expand and consolidate South Africa's dominance.[36] Internally, Pretoria was attempting to restrict black people to ten designated 'tribal homelands' or *bantustans*. Regionally, they sought to replicate this structure by bringing the majority-ruled neighbouring states within South Africa's orbit of control. More immediately, the international aims of the 'total strategy' were to ensure that regional states refused to allow liberation movements to operate in their territories, that they break economic and military ties with socialist countries and that they deepen their economic dependence on South Africa and refrain from calling for sanctions against the Apartheid regime.[37] The independence of Zimbabwe and the formation of SADCC were major blows to Pretoria's campaign to reshape regional politics according to its will, and it responded with further military assaults on neighbouring states.

South African attacks continued to damage infrastructure in Mozambique in the months that followed in 1981, with a further incursion over the border by SADF troops on 17 March, followed by the bombing of bridges in the Beira corridor on 29 October and in its port on 13 November.[38] However, these more spectacular attacks by SADF were only part of Botha's 'total strategy'. The theory of destabilisation was developed by Deon Geldenhuys, a professor of political science at Rand Afrikaans University in Johannesburg who was close to National Party strategists and ideologues. It involved a combination of military assault and economic pressures applied by the South African government in different combinations across the region in order to defend the Apartheid system.[39] In January 1981, the same month as the Matola raid, Geldenhuys published a study entitled 'Some Strategic Implications of Regional Economic Relations for the

35 Cited in Fauvet and Mosse (2004): 122.
36 Robert Davis (1985). *South African Strategy towards Mozambique in the Post-Nkomati Period: A Critical Analysis of Effects and Implications*. Uppsala: Nordiska Afrikainstitutet: 10.
37 Davis (1985): 11.
38 Hanlon (1986): 19–27.
39 Hanlon (1986): 29

Republic of South Africa', which was commissioned by the Institute for Strategic Studies of the University of Pretoria, one of the recipients of secret government money.[40] In the study, Geldenhuys explored how South Africa could use economic coercion to force shifts in the policies of neighbouring governments.[41] A further paper, 'Destabilisation Controversy in Southern Africa', was published in September 1982, in which Geldenhuys set out to establish South Africa's right to destabilise the region for its own purposes.[42] His proposals included manipulation of food supplies, limiting or prohibiting access to South Africa's trade routes, regulating energy and supporting 'disaffected groups in the target state' by providing arms, training rebels, recruiting mercenaries and 'sending out military personnel as advisors, or as combatants blended into the local forces, or as a force in its own right'.[43] He argued for the need to provide rebels with their own radio station and stressed that 'psychological means are crucially important in a destabilisation campaign'.[44] Geldenhuys's studies provided insight into South Africa's policy of destabilisation even while Pretoria was officially denying that such efforts were afoot.

While Frelimo expected the Mozambican National Resistance (MNR) to collapse following independence in Zimbabwe, the greatest devastation was to come when support was taken up by the South African Military Intelligence. Indeed, South Africa stepped up this 'technique of coercion' in response to Zimbabwean independence and SADCC's stand against its 'total strategy'.[45] While South Africa viewed some countries in the region, such as Swaziland and Malawi, as being relatively compliant, Pretoria saw regime change as the only way in which Mozambique would fold. South Africa thus set about to weaken Mozambique's economy and damage or destroy SADCC's projects through its sponsorship of Renamo.

Camilo de Sousa's documentary *Operação Leopardo* (1981) told of the return home of a contingent of Mozambican volunteers who had been fighting the racist regime in Rhodesia and how the Mozambican army then had to launch an operation against a MNR base in Manica set up with support from South African and remaining Rhodesian forces. The title refers to FAM's campaign against Renamo that covered an area between the Save river to the south and the Beira corridor to the north. Since 1978, Dhlakama had consolidated support

[40] Hanlon (1986): 30.

[41] Deon Geldenhuys (1981). 'Some Strategic Implications of Regional Economic Relations for the Republic of South Africa'. Pretoria: Institute for Strategic Studies of the University of Pretoria.

[42] Deon Geldenhuys (1982). 'Destablisation Controversy in Southern Africa'. S A Forum Position Paper. Johannesburg.

[43] Geldenhuys (1982).

[44] Geldenhuys (1982).

[45] Davis (1985): 12.

for MNR in Gorongosa, but he was coming under pressure from South Africa to move its centre of operations southwards closer to Maputo. Operation Leopard culminated in the bombing of an MNR base at Sitatonga in which FAM was supported by the Zimbabwean army and Cuban and Soviet military advisors.[46] While the film sought to present the FAM soldiers in a heroic light, João Cabrita argues that the Sitatonga attack failed to deal a fatal blow to Renamo's activities. Instead MNR continued to operate in Sofala and Manica.[47] Over the course of 1982 and 1983, MNR caused devastating damage, which was made worse by a series of natural disasters as the country was ravaged by drought followed by flooding. Major incidents included the destruction of an oil tank farm in Beira in 1982 and an air raid on Maputo on 23 May 1983, in which suburbs of the city were bombarded with fragmentation rockets. Frelimo officials estimated that 140 villages, 840 schools, 900 rural shops and other 200 public health installations had been destroyed, the cost of the destruction being put at US$3,8 billion.[48]

On 13 July 1983, eight of the nine heads of state of the SADCC nations met in Maputo. They issued a joint statement, pointing out that: 'South Africa can invade and occupy sovereign states, blow up vital installations, and massacre populations at no apparent cost to its relations to its main allies.'[49] They suggested that 'friends of South Africa' in the West who continued to 'provide the racist regime with the capital, technology, management skills, and weapons necessary to carry out such a policy also seek to improve their relations with SADCC', and that they could do so by using 'their influence to check the aggression being waged against SADCC member states'.[50] While negotiations between Mozambique and South Africa began in secret in 1983, at the same time Machel turned to the international community and embarked on an intense diplomatic campaign. In October 1983, Machel visited Western Europe and won sympathy from the British, French and Portuguese governments by appealing for their diplomatic assistance and indicating that Frelimo was willing to open up Mozambique to foreign investment. As discussed in Chapter 5, by 1983 elements within Frelimo's elite had begun to argue that the country needed a

46 João M. Cabrita (2000). *Mozambique: The Torturous Road to Democracy*. Basingstoke: Palgrave Macmillan: 174–175. Cabrita argues that the Soviet military training to FAM since independence had been focused on conventional warfare ill-suited to counter-insurgency campaigns. Some of Cabrita's claims, such as that of FAM being supported by Cuban troops, is disputed by other authors, who argue that Cuban assistance was limited to military advisors, *cooperantes* working in civilian fields, and grants for Mozambicans to study in Cuba. See Gillian Gunn (1987). 'Cuba and Mozambique'. *CSIS Africa Notes* 80, 28 December.

47 Cabrita (2000): 174–175.

48 Davis (1985): 15.

49 Hanlon (1986): 35.

50 Hanlon (1986): 35.

new economic policy that would be more open to the free market, in order to address the national debt. Machel's trip led to European powers putting more pressure on the United States and South Africa to resolve the conflict and was seen as a success, though Thatcher also insisted that Mozambique should try to improve relations with South Africa. When Pik Botha followed in Machel's footsteps shortly afterwards, he was told that South Africa was risking European investments, and within the Apartheid regime questions were asked about the economic cost of the destruction caused by destabilisation.

On 16 March 1984, the governments of Mozambique and South Africa signed the Nkomati Accord of 'Non-Aggression and Good Neighbourliness'. The pact stipulated that Mozambique would end ANC operations within its territory and South Africa would cease its military assaults and sponsorship of MNR. Frelimo argued that without South African support, MNR's attacks would wither away and the economy would recover and open up to foreign investment. Yet while Frelimo tried to insist that the Nkomati Accord represented a victory for its 'socialist policy of peace', Botha's government regarded it as a 'miracle' that vindicated their 'total strategy'.[51] Most SADCC members reacted to the Accord with dismay, seeing it as a capitulation to Apartheid and a betrayal of the ANC. Frelimo honoured the agreement by expelling large numbers of ANC members and permitting only a limited number of diplomatic representatives to continue in Maputo. By contrast, although SADF personnel ceased entering Mozambique to assist MNR fighters directly and *Voz Africa Libre* went off air, South Africa continued to support them by supplying arms, maintaining camps in South Africa and providing indirect support through a network of front companies.[52] In the months that followed the Nkomati Accord, MNR in fact accelerated its attacks and changed its name to the Portuguese Resistência Nacional Moçambicana (Renamo) to signal that it was a Mozambican organisation with a firm foothold within the nation.

Mozambique applied to join the International Monetary Fund in 1984, seeking to build on the reputation the country gained diplomatically following the Nkomati Accord by actively seeking support from Britain and the United States. As discussed in Chapter 5, elements within Frelimo's political elite had already begun to shift away from Marxist–Leninism and, in the field of film production, Kanemo was created with support from Minister of Security Jacinto Veloso to interface with the free market. From 1984, Kanemo's energies and resources were increasingly taken up with a documentary directed by Mário Borgneth titled *Fronteiras de Sangue* 'Borders of Blood' (1986). A press release explained that the documentary set out to 'fill the information gap that exists in the West' on a regional conflict often analysed internationally from

[51] Davis (1985): 17.
[52] Davis (1985): 21–22.

the perspective of the Cold War without due consideration of 'those in the front lines of the political process taking place in Southern Africa'.[53] *Fronteiras de Sangue* exposes South Africa's strategy of destabilising the independent countries at its borders chiefly through interviews with heads of state, including Eduardo dos Santos of Angola, Robert Mugabe of Zimbabwe, Kenneth Kaunda of Zambia, Quett Massire of Botswana, former president of Tanzania Julius Nyerere and his successor Ali Hassan Mwinyi. Oliver Tambo of the ANC and Sam Nujoma, the leader of SWAPO, are also interviewed as the leaders of liberation movements fighting for majority rule in South Africa and Namibia. Finally, on the Mozambican side, Prime Minister Mário da Graça Machungo and Joachim Chissano, who became president during the film's production, describe the massacres of peasants in collective villages and how the violence was destroying the nation's capacity to enjoy the fruits of its workers' labour. Archival footage, including interviews with Machel, provide insights into Mozambique's armed struggle and emphasise that, unlike the Apartheid system, their post-independence revolution aims to create a multiracial society. SADCC leaders describe the impact that South Africa's policy of destabilisation is having on their efforts to build independent economies and call on the international community to assist in resolving the crisis, with Nyerere stressing that only the abolition of Apartheid can provide a solution.

With spiralling costs, production of *Fronteiras de Sangue* was nearly halted when Samora Machel was killed on 19 October 1986, as a plane carrying the president and his entourage back from a diplomatic meeting in Zambia crashed mysteriously on South African territory. [54] Soviet experts who worked with the Mozambican authorities in their investigation of the crash argued that it was caused by the Soviet pilots flying the plane being lured off course by a fake beacon set up by the South African Secret Service.[55] Rather than halting the project, however, Borgneth's team re-orientated the film so that it opens with footage of the aeroplane wreckage. Archival images are used to narrate how Rhodesia worked to set up a network of 'eyes and ears' in Tete even before independence, at a time when Ian Smith was presenting the white minority regime as a bulwark against the spread of communism in Southern Africa. According to Chico Caneiro, who was Director of Photography, the most important coup during the film's production came when the Kanemo team

[53] Kanemo (1986). *Borders of Blood: A Film about the Struggle for Peace in Southern Africa*. Maputo: Kanemo: 3.

[54] The original budget for the film was US$250,000, but this rose to over 600,000 with the huge number of archive images that had to be purchased from Portugal, the UK, Zimbabwe and other countries. Labi Mendonça, 'Text sobre a Kanemo Produção e Comunicação', an undated report sent by email on 19 September 2005.

[55] South Africa orders new probe into Samora Machel crash'. BBC News, 12 December 2012. https://www.bbc.co.uk/news/world-africa-20694109.

interviewed Ken Flowers, the former director-general of Rhodesia's Central Intelligence Organisation.[56] Flowers gives a detailed account of how he set up MNR with former PIDE officers and Mozambican army deserters as an intelligence gathering operation designed to foil ZANU. Flowers nonchalantly claims he had no interest in creating a viable opposition force in Mozambique, but that following independence in Zimbabwe, the South African government became MNR's main sponsors. This interview alone gives the lie to the claim that the organisation had its origins as a genuine Mozambican opposition force born out of local resistance to Frelimo, a point that was crucial for Frelimo to drive home at a time when the Reagan administration was trying to claim that Renamo were home-grown anti-Communist freedom fighters. Later in the documentary, visual evidence is provided to show how South Africa was contravening the Nkomati Accord by supplying arms and sophisticated communications equipment to Renamo's base in Gorongosa.

The final sequence of the documentary reconstitutes the political scene leading up to the plane crash with a dramatic series of events: Machel denouncing South African violence, mobilisation for the defence of Maputo against imminent South African attacks and meetings with heads of state in the region that Machel travelled to in his last frantic diplomatic mission to bring peace to Mozambique. Then follow scenes of the mass outpouring of grief on the streets of Maputo and images of Machel's state funeral, where mourners included political leaders from across the world (see Chapter 7). The film culminates with Chissano's inauguration as president of the People's Republic of Mozambique. When *Fronteiras de Sangue* was finally released it played an important role in galvanising support among a growing international body that was outraged by the situation in Mozambique.

While Kanemo was occupied with *Fronteiras de Sangue*, other collaborations through film production attempted to shine a light on the economic and infrastructural impact of destabilisation on the region, building on the professional alliances formed in the making of *Pamberi ne Zimbabwe*. In 1983, INC *cooperante* Simon Hartog made a documentary for Channel 4 titled *Cinema as Foreign Exchange*. Broadcast in the UK in 1984 as part of Channel 4's African Cinema season, the documentary examined the film industry and cinema in Zimbabwe, Madagascar and Mozambique. It revealed that the INC was something of an anomaly within the region, as it had succeeded in building a national film industry centred on documentary filmmaking that supported production through distribution and exhibition receipts. *Cinema as Foreign Exchange* presented the INC as an open-minded institution orientated by socialism but not adverse to importing Western films. Despite severe budgetary

[56] Conversation with Chico Caneiro, Maputo, August 2005.

constraints, as Pedro Pimenta asserts in his interview, the INC had cultivated a 'Mozambican cinematography' based on short documentaries. Indeed when Julius Nyerere stood down as president of Tanzania in 1985, the INC was in a position to send a crew including Camilo de Sousa and Luís Simão to document his final state tour, though the fact that the footage was never edited into a film was an ominous sign that the INC's financial autonomy was at risk.[57] By contrast, Zimbabwe was still flooded with American and British films that alienated cinema-goers from their own culture and deprived local filmmakers of financial support.[58] Zimbabwean filmmakers wanted to address this situation by creating a new film culture, and they began to organise meetings, film screenings and reaching out to potential allies in government and approaching the French cultural attaché so that they could connect with West African filmmakers. In 1984, Simon Bright, Steven Chifunyse and Steve Chigorimbo set up a Southern African Regional Film Workshop, inviting Pedro Pimenta from the INC, as well as Ethiopian US-based director Haile Gerima and the Senegalese director Djibril Diop Mambety. Their plan was to learn from other parts of the continent to lay the basis for a Zimbabwean film industry that would build on regional connections.[59]

While at a governmental level regional film production found scant support, in 1986 the making of the documentary *Corridors of Freedom* (1987), which was directed by Zimbabwean Simon Bright, enabled filmmakers from across the Frontline States to collaborate. Bright became involved in the project after meeting Ingrid Sinclair, who was then working for the Trade Films Workshop in the UK. They sought out funding from development organisations in Norway, Holland and Sweden, as well as from Channel 4. In an interview with me in 2017, Bright explained how he travelled to Mozambique in 1983 to find the filmmakers who had worked on *Pamberi ne Zimbabwe* to recruit them to work on the film alongside professionals from Angola and Tanzania.[60] This was the first crew made up of individuals from four SADCC countries to make a film about the organisation's resistance to Apartheid through regional collaboration. Bright and Sinclair were impressed by João Costa and Carlos Henrique's camera work in *Pamberi ne Zimbabwe* and they came to appreciate the professionalism of staff who had trained with the INC, such as sound engineer Gabriel Mondlane.[61] They worked with a Tanzanian producer and commissioned Comrade Chinx to compose the soundtrack. As it turned out, the constitution of this film crew

[57] Interview with Luís Simão, Maputo, 17 September 2005.
[58] In Madagascar, a boycott by the MPEA was stifling the entire cinema industry.
[59] Interview with Simon Bright, 12 January 2017, London.
[60] Interview with Simon Bright, 12 January 2017, London.
[61] Email correspondence with Simon Bright, 10 August 2019.

drawn from across the Frontline States was a huge advantage in the making *Corridors of Freedom*.

The documentary explores the operations and geopolitical importance of SADCC, describing the recent history of anti-imperialist alliance between Southern African nations through footage of leaders such as Nyerere, Kaunda, Mugabe and Machel. It includes interviews with key officials in SADCC and national leaders, as well as instructors and workers on the ground, highlighting the different ways in which the nations involved in the organisation were participating and developing projects in energy, transport infrastructure, manufacturing and agriculture. Transport infrastructures built by colonial powers in the region were key to the extraction and export of raw materials in the region, and this made them a target during the armed struggle. But now the independent Southern African nations urgently needed infrastructure and organisations that would facilitate trade between themselves to avoid having to conduct their economic relations via South Africa. In Mozambique particularly, South African attacks regularly targeted railways, which gave access to the Indian Ocean, providing routes that were cheaper than moving goods through South Africa. Disruption due to the wars of destabilisation was severe, and security and bureaucracy at borders repeatedly threatened to obstruct filmmaking. The crew could draw on its members' skills in negotiating in multiple languages and communicating effectively with officials of differing ranks and ethnicities, as they moved across war zones.[62]

While *Corridors of Freedom* highlights ambitious large-scale infrastructural, energy and industrial projects, it also emphasises the urgent needs of ordinary people living in extreme poverty in the Southern African region, stressing the importance of grassroots participation and community education in SADCC's projects. Thus a sequence on the benefits to the region of developing infrastructure for exporting Angolan oil across the region is followed by a section that points out that most of the Southern African population is still dependent on firewood as its chief form of energy. The documentary then focuses on an older woman explaining to some children how to gather firewood responsibly, as part of a community project to promote sustainable forestry. *Corridors of Freedom* concludes that, when ordinary people can identify a specific item, service or experience in their daily life with SADCC, then SADCC will be judged as having been successful.

The optimism of *Corridors of Freedom*, which was released in 1987, contrasts strongly with *Limpopo Line* (1989), a documentary made in Mozambique by Sinclair and Bright just two years later. This time they worked with Valente Diamante as sound engineer and again with João Costa on camera, while Camilo

[62] Interview with Simon Bright, 12 January 2017, London.

de Sousa was employed as an editor. *Limpopo Line* focuses on the railway line that runs across southern Mozambique, which was at constant risk of attacks by Renamo and was essential for Zimbabwe's export trade. It is worth recalling that British colonial documentaries in particular reveal an obsession with industrial infrastructure, with films such as *West Africa Calling* (1927), which was made in Ghana by British Instructional Films (BIF), asserting white superiority through the celebration of infrastructure that facilitated the extraction of natural resources from African territories. Brian Larkin describes this as an example of a technological 'colonial sublime', which overlooked the terrible suffering and exploitation that these vast projects involved in terms of African labour.[63] *Limpopo Line* repurposes colonial archive footage of the building of the colonial railways as part of an effort to reclaim, repair and redirect infrastructure as an essential part of the struggle against Apartheid and its supporters in the West. *Limpopo Line* draws attention to the human as well as the economic cost of the civil war in Mozambique. Following the route of the Limpopo line, often with footage shot from an armoured train, the documentary captures the testimonies of railway workers facing perilous conditions. It highlights the plight of refugees displaced by the conflict, connecting these local stories both to a longer history of the colonial construction of the railway and to the present-day, wider geopolitical struggle against the Apartheid regime.

By the late 1980s, regional cooperation in film production that was achieved reflected solidarities forged during the struggle for independence and in the support Mozambique gave to other liberation struggles, as well as the necessity for SADCC nations to present a united front against Apartheid. In this context, news reporting and documentary-making were weapons on the cultural front against imperialism and white minority rule, in a battle in which the flows of information needed to be seized and reshaped so that voices from the region could be heard across the world. *Pamberi ne Zimbabwe* not only provided aesthetic inspiration for making documentaries that would intervene in international media to give African perspectives as part of the struggle against white minority dominance in Southern Africa. It was also important in that it led to a series of collaborations that showcased the professional skills of filmmakers in Angola, Mozambique and Zimbabwe. As the state institutions and socialist aspirations of those nations crumbled, these South–South collaborations persisted through the 1990s and were sustained by the connections forged between individual filmmakers in these crucial years rather than as a result of the support of their governments. Even as the INC faced the mounting crisis in Mozambique, the ideas for regional cooperation that were first discussed at the Conferência Africana de Cooperação Cinematografica in Maputo in 1977 were taken up

[63] Brian Larkin (2008). *Signal and Noise: Media, Infrastructure, and Urban Culture in Nigeria*. Duke University Press: 16–47.

and elaborated collaboratively in Zimbabwe, leaning to the First Frontline Film Festival in Harare in 1990 and other projects. What would emerge across the region in the coming decade were new hybrid modes of filmmaking, some of which built on techniques of documentary to make fiction films, while others used techniques of fiction to make documentaries. These allowed previously unacknowledged voices to be heard. They would include the perspectives of women, articulating their struggles within patriarchal societies. Thus when João Costa was employed as a cameraman on Ingrid Sinclair's feature film *Flame* (1996), a fictionalised account of ZANU's armed struggle that for the first time acknowledged the sexual assault experienced by many female guerrillas, Costa recreated the very scene of the gathering at Dzapasi assembly point that he had himself first captured on film in 1980.

7 The Time of the Leopards: The End of Socialist Fictions and the Beginnings of the Docu-Drama, 1985–1991

In 1985, the INC's first fiction feature, *O Tempo dos Leopardos* 'The Time of the Leopards' (1985), was premiered in Maputo at a magnificent ceremony to celebrate ten years of independence. The film is a fictional account of the anti-colonial war that contributes to a mythic narrative about the founding of the nation through armed struggle and an idea of authentic Mozambican identity based on Frelimo's values of disciplined militancy and self-sacrifice for the good of *o Povo*. Zdravko Velimirović, the Yugoslav director of the film, was in attendance for the occasion. The film's stars – Santos Mulungo and Ana Magaia, who played the heroic couple Pedro and Ana – were invited to the reception after the projection, as was the other leading actor Simião Mazuze, who played the love rival and flawed Frelimo guerrilla Januario. In the years that followed, Velimirović recounted an incident at the reception that stayed with him: Samora Machel presented Mulungo with a gift of a pair of trainers and Magaia some fabric. When it came to Simião, however, the president berated him, asking how it was that he was not ashamed after everything he had done in the film and threatening to have him arrested as a traitor to Frelimo.[1] Machel's strong sense of political theatre seems to have come to the fore in this blurring of art and life. It is telling that the most reviled character in the film was not one of the Portuguese colonisers, who are shown committing mass killings of civilians and torturing captured Frelimo guerrillas. Rather, the most dangerous character is embodied by the figure of the traitor – 'the enemy within'.

It is worth recalling that the first film made with Frelimo, Dragutin Popović's *Venceremos*, was also both a production made with Yugoslavia and a response to fears of betrayal, motivated in part to assuage the concerns of Frelimo's foreign supporters following the assassination of Eduardo Mondlane in 1969 and the upheavals of discontent that had torn through the movement in the previous year (see Chapter 1). *Venceremos* and the other armed struggle films made in the early 1970s presented Frelimo as the only legitimate and authentic Mozambican liberation movement dedicated not just to ending colonial rule, but also to

[1] Interview with Dušan Ninkov, Belgrade, May 2018, with translation from Serbo-Croat by Mark Brogan.

destroying the colonialist mentalities that threatened the emancipation of the Mozambican people. Ironically, in 1985, ten years after independence, Frelimo's revolution had perhaps never been more endangered, despite the signing of the Nkomati Accord with South Africa in the previous year, which Frelimo had hoped would lead to Renamo's efforts to destabilise the country withering away. By mid-1982, Renamo had moved south beyond Manica and Sofala into Inhambane and Gaza, and north into southern Tete. Research carried out as early as 1983 to 1984 by French anthropologist Christian Geffray, while criticised by Frelimo supporters, suggested that Renamo was tapping into discontent caused by unhappiness with the government's policy of 'villagisation'.[2] After the signing of the Nkomati Accord, South Africa continued to break the terms of the agreement, providing arms and logistical assistance to Renamo. As a result the conflict accelerated, Renamo spreading through Inhambane towards the coast, where they were pushed back by Frelimo forces.[3] Meanwhile, Dhlakama began to develop a political platform, announcing an anti-communist line that would reinstate respect for traditional beliefs and power structures. The organisation began using the Portuguese name and acronym of Renamo (Resistência Nacional Moçambicana) rather than the English abbreviation of MNR (Mozambican National Resistance), to signal that it had moved inside Mozambique and was Mozambican. Renamo continued to build a more centralised military organisation and to attract domestic support, and Frelimo responded with increased coercion towards the civilian population, which paradoxically aided Renamo, just as colonial oppression had played into Frelimo's hands during the armed struggle.[4] While support for Frelimo remained strong in certain regions, particularly where Renamo's activities were limited to tactics of sabotage and attacks on civilians, in its strongholds it was beginning to build organisational structures and added political persuasion to its repertoire of violence.[5]

While previously Frelimo had blamed the country's economic difficulties on various factors including worker's lack of discipline, paucity of skilled managers and logistical problems, after 1983 the government laid the blame for the hardships in Mozambique firmly with Renamo, as well as the drought that

[2] See Patrick Chabal (2002). *A History of Postcolonial Lusophone Africa*. London: Hurst: 217.

[3] Margaret Hall (1990). 'The Mozambican National Resistance Movement (Renamo): A Study in the Destruction of an Africa Country.' *Africa: Journal of the International African Institute*, 60, 1: 39–68.

[4] M. Anne Pitcher (2002): *Transforming Mozambique: The Politics of Privatization, 1975–2000*. Cambridge: Cambridge University Press: 118.

[5] Pitcher (2002): 119; see also Justin Pearce (2010). 'From Rebellion to Opposition: Unita in Angola and Renamo in Mozambique', in Wafula Okumu and Augustine Ikelegbe (2010). *Militias, Rebels and Islamist Militants: Human Insecurity and State Crises in Africa*. Pretoria: Institute for Security Studies: 365–388.

lasted from 1982 to 1983 and the floods of late 1984.[6] In 1983, *Operação Produção* 'Operation Production' was launched as a national campaign that involved rounding up any unemployed or itinerant people living in the cities, who were described as 'undesirables and parasites', and relocating them to remote rural areas, where they were expected to contribute to agricultural production, though often they lacked basic knowledge of farming.[7] Although in principle Operation Production was supposed to be voluntary, in fact government officials often used coercive tactics. The project to 'unify the habits, customs and traditions' of 'our People' to 'give them a revolutionary dimension', as articulated by Frelimo in 1975, had come to justify the rooting out of any counter-revolutionary behaviours that were considered treacherous, including promoting ethnicity and racism, anti-social behaviour and economic exploitation.[8] In 1985 Frelimo relaunched its political and organisational offensive that it had first launched in 1980–1981 (see Chapter 5), but this time it was more blatantly militaristic, with the government vowing to liquidate the 'armed bandits', whom, the Council of Ministers argued, were 'criminals paid by the old colonial and capitalist bosses' whose objective was to 'recolonize Mozambique'.[9] According to Lars Buur, while it is not known how many people classed as 'internal enemies' were 'sent away' to re-education camps, estimates range from 30,000 to 50,000.[10]

Velimirović's anecdote from the reception for *O Tempo dos Leopardos* reveals the extent to which this war epic was as much a reflection of its times as it was a fictional depiction of history. Indeed, the animal symbolism in the title of Adam Yussuff's analysis of post-colonial Mozambique from 1975 to 1990 is telling: Mozambique had 'Escape[d] the teeth of the crocodile and fall[en] into the mouth of the leopard'. [11] From this perspective, the leopards of the film's title can be understood in relation to the multiple threats facing the nation in the context of the mid-1980s as well as the violence of the colonial war that is represented in the film. Unlike that other large feline predator, the lion, which tends to symbolise power and strength, or the greed of the colonial crocodile, the leopard is associated with ferociousness and is known to lie in wait for its victims, remaining silent and unseen until launching its voracious attack.

[6] Pitcher (2002): 103.

[7] H. Matusse (1983). 'Operação Produção: Evacuados vão recever familiares'. *Tempo*, 678, 9 October: 22–24.

[8] Lars Buur (2010). 'Xiconhoca: Mozambique's Post-Independence Traitor', in Sharika Thiranagama and Tobias Kelly (2010). *Traitors: Suspicion, Intimacy, and the Ethics of State-Building*. Philadelphia: University of Pennsylvania Press: 31–32.

[9] 'Relançar a Ofensiva Política e Organizacional para resolução das nossas dificuldades actuais'. Reprinted in *Tempo*, 756, 7 April 1985: 21–24; Pitcher (2002): 120.

[10] Buur (2010): 25.

[11] Adam Yussuf (2005). *Escapar aos dentes do crocodilo e Cair na boca do leopard: trajectoria de Moçambique pós-colonial (1975–1990)*. Maputo: Prómedia.

This context grounds the emergence of the INC's first fiction films, a mode that had previously been viewed as less essential than documentary, newsreel and propaganda for furthering the Mozambican Revolution. It would seem that during the mid-1980s Frelimo was involved in maintaining certain fictions of socialism – the foundational myth of the birth of the nation through armed struggle, ideals of selfless disciplined militancy, and the need for constant vigilance against 'enemies of the people' – simultaneously attempting to strengthen links with sympathetic socialist countries while courting Western financial institutions, opening up to the free market and seeking to attract foreign investment. Two major fiction films set in recent history were made by the INC during this time of unprecedented crisis: Velimirović's *O Tempo dos Leopardos*, a big budget war epic made on 35mm in the tradition of the partisan film, and José Cardoso's *O Vento Sopre do Norte* 'The Wind Blows from the North' (1987), which exemplifies auteur filmmaking on 16mm as a nationalist demonstration of independence. Both engage with a number of different fictions of socialism and founding myths of the birth of the nation through resistance to colonial rule. Each, in its own way, involved negotiating what was possible to articulate in conditions of political paranoia, widespread violence and economic collapse. The death of Samora Machel in 1986 came to symbolise the beginning of the end of Frelimo's socialist project, and the mythic stature of Mozambique's first president was reinforced by the film *Samora Vive* 'Samora Lives' (1986), which documented his funeral. With the making on video of Licínio Azevedo and Brigitte Bagnol's *A Colheita do Diablo* 'The Devil's Harvest' (1988), however, another model of filmmaking emerged just at the moment when the fall of socialism loomed and the state was initiating a process of withdrawal from its previous role as commissioner of cultural production. This new mode of fictional realism on video made use of non-professional actors to portray the resilience and everyday struggles of the people who play the protagonists. As such, the film can be understood as a precursor to the genre of the docu-drama that emerged in the 1990s. These people were, of course, vital to Frelimo's revolutionary project, but as the docu-dramas that would follow demonstrate, the meaning of their lives also exceeded it.

In 1983, the INC was given responsibility for producing content for Televisão Experimental de Moçambique and was granted permission to begin making fiction films.[12] Already in his speech to INC employees in 1981, Minister of Information José Luís Cabaço had affirmed that anyone who aspired to direct films should put their ideas forward for consideration, indicating an

[12] The Channel 4 documentary *Cinema as Foreign Exchange*, which was made in 1983 by Simon Hartog and John Ellis and broadcast in the UK in 1984, documents a dinner to celebrate the INC's eighth year and reports on Frelimo's decision to expand the INC's remit.

openness to films that expressed an artistic vision as well as the collective model of documentary production that was exemplified at the INC by the *Kuxa Kanema* newsreel. Fiction, however, was a new departure. Luís Carlos Patraquim, interviewed in 1983 for Simon Hartog and John Ellis's Channel 4 documentary *Cinema as Foreign Exchange*, drew a distinction between those making films at independence in 1975, who were 'preoccupied with creating an image that was propagandistic and politically correct', and those eight years later, who, while maintaining their cinema's militancy, wanted to consider 'the other side: the needs of the viewers'.[13] Referring to the 1982 seminar on audio-visual media convened by Cabaço, Patraquim raised the possibility of 'a two-way communication, in which people can recognise themselves in the communication and speak for themselves and not just listen to propaganda, even if it's a propaganda message that we agree with'. Paradoxically, however, this desire to pluralise the narratives that Mozambican films could tell coincided with a period of increased authoritarianism and coercion, as Frelimo responded to the maelstrom caused by the combined effects of economic crisis, natural disasters and the war with Renamo.

In 1985 the INC began working with Yugoslav Avala Films to make Mozambique's first major fiction film production to commemorate ten years of independence. Avala Films selected the well-known Yugoslav film director Zdravko Velimirović as director, while the INC proposed Camilo de Sousa to take on the role of assistant director. The resulting fiction feature, *O Tempo dos Leopardos* (1985), can be understood as the last gesture of solidarity manifested through film production between Mozambique and the European, non-aligned socialist state. The 'socialist friendship' between Mozambique and Yugoslavia had begun during the armed struggle when Dragutin Popović made the films *Venceremos*, *Nachingwea* and *Do Romuva ao Maputo* with Frelimo (see Chapters 1 and 2). These collaborations came to an end following independence, as the costs of these productions led the newsreel company Filmske Novosti to exceed the budget it received from the Yugoslavian government. Following Frelimo's 1977 decision to become a Marxist–Leninist vanguard party, ties with the Soviet Union and the Eastern Bloc were strengthened (see Chapter 4). By the mid-1980s, East German advisers had come to dominate the Mozambican security services, and higher education and commercial agreements had been signed with other countries in the Eastern Bloc such as Bulgaria. Frelimo was dependant on military advisors and supplies of arms and aid from the Soviet Union, while Cuba provided *cooperantes* in the fields of education and healthcare, as well as sending filmmakers from ICAIC to carry out training at the INC (see Chapters 3 and 5). By comparison, the relationship with Yugoslavia

[13] Simon Hartog and John Ellis (1984). *Cinema as Foreign Exchange*. Channel 4.

seemed more tenuous. What, then, motivated this final collaboration between Mozambique and Yugoslavia?

Yugoslavia was one of the founding nations of the non-aligned movement, which, though defined by ideals of anti-imperialism, self-determination and international cooperation, included countries with a range of political systems and ideological orientations, from multi-party democracies to one-party communist states. Through the 1960s Marshal Tito used Yugoslavia's prestige within the movement to bolster its policy of 'self-managed socialism', resisting dependency on both the West and the Soviet Union.[14] Instead, Yugoslavia invested in a number of large infrastructure projects in non-aligned African countries. However, by the late 1970s, these had proved unprofitable. Soviet and Cuban interventions in Angola and Ethiopia were carving out 'spheres of influence' and their governments sought to assert that there was a 'natural' alliance between Third World liberation movements and Marxist–Leninism[15] Following Tito's death in 1980, Yugoslavia's geopolitical significance as the predominant Balkan state within the non-aligned movement was further undermined as Eastern Bloc nations strengthened their economic and diplomatic ties with socialist African nations.[16] Mozambique signed commercial agreements with Bulgaria and East Germany in 1981 and, as documented in the *Kuxa Kanema* newsreel, received visits from their respective Presidents Zhivkov and Honecker (see Chapter 5). Despite Yugoslavia's influence waning, the desire within parts of the government to maintain the country's commitment to non-alignment remained.

Testimony from the Yugoslav film crew who worked on *O Tempo dos Leopardos* suggests that, while the importance of the non-aligned movement was diminishing, the project still had diplomatic significance to both countries. The Yugoslav film crew was made up of filmmakers from all eight republics within the federation, representing national unity at a time when tensions between the different regions were mounting.[17] In terms of motivations for the

[14] Zachary Irwin (2016). 'The Untold Stories of Yugoslavia and Nonalignment', in Gorana Ognjenović, Jasna Jozelić (2016). *Revolutionary totalitarianism, pragmatic socialism, transition. Volume One, Tito's Yugoslavia, stories untold.* New York: Palgrave Macmillan: 140.

[15] Irwin (2016): 152–154.

[16] Irwin (2016): 156–157.

[17] Yugoslavia's film industry was set up after the Second World War, not as a single national film institute, but eight studios that serviced different parts of the federation of republics, as part of an effort to preserve the balance between 'unity and diversity' that the nation was built on. These federal units made films in minority languages as well as Serbo-Croat. Jurica Pavičić, 'Titoist Cathedrals: The Rise and Fall of the Partisan Film', in Gorana Ognjenović *et al.* (2016). *Titoism, Self-Determination, Nationalism, Cultural Memory: Volume Two, Tito's Yugoslavia – Stories Untold.* New York: Macmillan Palgrave: 37–38.

collaboration on the Mozambican side, cinematographer Dušan Ninkov, who worked closely with camera operator João Costa, recalls that:

> In Mozambique we heard the story of how Yugoslavia had been selected as the partner for this project so that the politics of non-alignment would be confirmed on the world stage. Of course this was only a mask because Mozambique at that time depended mostly on the Eastern Bloc, especially the USSR and East Germany.[18]

Association with Yugoslavia, it would seem, was politically expedient for Mozambique at a time when Machel was conducting his high-stakes diplomatic campaign to woo sympathy and support from Western nations for Frelimo's fight against Renamo, which the Reagan and Thatcher administrations were continuing to present as a legitimate anti-communist force (see Chapter 6).

Beyond international diplomacy, Yugoslavia had a well-regarded film industry with a strong tradition of making films about the partisan struggle that had founded the Balkan nation. Velimirović was an experienced film director whose credits included a biographical film about Marshal Tito entitled *Tito-Vrhovni Komandant* 'Tito – Commander-in-Chief' (1972) and partisan films such as *Vrhovi Zelengore* 'The Peaks of Zelengora' (1976) and *Dvoboj za Južnu prugu* 'Duel for the Southern Railway' (1978). In contrast to other revolutionary aesthetics that influenced the INC, such as the Cuban notion of 'imperfect cinema' (see Chapters 3 and 4), Yugoslav cinema production strove to emulate the Hollywood studio system in terms of professional directing and acting practices, technological effects, dramaturgy and the way in which they adapted the aesthetics of foreign genres such as the Western to their own cinematic myths about the birth of the nation. As such, Jurica Pavičić argues, in Yugoslavia cinema functioned as 'a social metaphor for modernisation'; it was part of a wider process of revolutionary modernisation involving the acquisition of technology and technological skills to put this formerly colonised socialist country on a par with the West.[19] The partisan film was perhaps the most quintessential and frequently produced genre in Yugoslavia. These dramas revolving around armed partisan resistance to the Nazi occupation provided a founding myth for the nation and were a channel for overt expressions of Titoist ideology, as well as sometimes more critical explorations of contemporary political questions through the veil of history. Over the forty-year period in which partisan films were produced they included a wide range of narrative forms – from historical epic to urban spy thriller, and from the psychological chamber piece to action movies. However, all shared the same historical setting and recognisable iconography. In the wake of the Second World War, the memory of the partisan experience had contributed to the political solidarity

[18] Interview with Dušan Ninkov, Belgrade, May 2018, with translation by Mark Brogan.
[19] Pavičić (2016): 38.

felt in Yugoslavia towards African armed struggles for independence. By the mid-1980s, however, the partisan film had entered its final 'baroque' phase and was becoming anachronistic.[20] Jurica Pavičić argues that as tensions within the federation mounted and the economic crisis began to cause shortages for the first time since the Second World War, Yugoslav cinema audiences ceased to believe the myths of the nation that were required to sustain further production of the genre. The making of *O Tempo dos Leopardos*, in which the liberation struggle in Mozambique is retold through the filter of a Manichean plot, also revealed some of the limits of this identification with African liberation filtered through the ideals of non-alignment.

Other statements by Yugoslav and Mozambican filmmakers who worked on *O Tempo dos Leopardos* confirm that this 'socialist friendship' involved uneven power relations that at times became quite fraught, with tensions exacerbated by the difficulty of filmmaking in conditions of war, economic crisis and political sensitivity. The Yugoslav government provided the bulk of the finances, film stock and the colour-processing facilities, and their scriptwriters, directors and technicians oversaw proceedings. Each member of the Yugoslav film crew had a Mozambican counterpart whom they had responsibility to train where necessary. Lacking a large pool of professional actors, many of the leading stars, extras and technicians were members of the Grupo Amador de Teatro (GAT), established in Maputo in 1983, or associated with performing arts venue Casa Velha.[21] In addition to filmmaking equipment and supplies, the Yugoslav crew brought with them two large containers of food, because by 1985 famine had taken hold in Mozambique and there were severe shortages of food, water and electricity even in urban areas.[22] Although the story the film tells is set in the north of Mozambique, Frelimo was not able to guarantee security outside the major cities, and this presented a problem in terms of where to shoot the scenes of armed struggle combat. An initial suggestion of filming these scenes in a city park was rejected as unworkable. The Yugoslav crew were waiting for the weekly flight to take them back to Yugoslavia without making the film, when it was proposed that the film crew could be flown by helicopter over to Inhaca, a small forested island in the Indian Ocean off the coast of Maputo that had been a tourist attraction before independence.[23] Renamo lacked naval capacity and Frelimo maintained a firmer grip on coastal areas, so Inhaca was considered a

[20] Pavičić (2016): 62.

[21] Guido Convents (2011). *Os Moçambicanos Perante o Cinema e o Audiovisual. Uma História Politica-cultural do Moçambique Colonial até à República de Moçambique (1896–2010)*. Maputo: CP: 493.

[22] Interview with Dušan Ninkov.

[23] Interview with Dušan Ninkov.

safe place in which to film. All the interior scenes were shot later at Avala Film in Belgrade.

Although the film has retained its popular appeal in Mozambique, some of the Mozambican filmmakers who were involved in the project have since stated that *O Tempo dos Leopardos* was not the kind of film they wanted to make.[24] According to Camilo de Sousa, the project began 'with great difficulties, since they started from different perspectives'.[25] Luís Carlos Patraquim and Licínio Azevedo wrote the first draft of the script, drawing on *Relatos do Povo Armado* 'Stories of the People Armed' (1982) a collection of stories by Azevedo based on testimonies of the armed struggle gathered from people from the Makonde Plateau who participated in the fight.[26] Azevedo had in fact written the book with a view to adapting it to the cinema screen and envisioned a kind of cinema that would involve storytelling that would be truthful to the lived experience of guerrillas who had contributed to Mozambique's struggle for independence. But according to Azevedo and Patraquim, the script they submitted to the scriptwriters at Avala Films was returned to them with changes that made it almost unrecognisable.[27] Azevedo claims that the Yugoslav scriptwriters proposed dramatic helicopter battle scenes that bore little relation to how the struggle had been fought by villagers and guerrillas on the ground. Furthermore, they suggested that the film should open with a scene that Azevedo and Patraquim considered absurd: a scantily clad female guerrilla running through the forest, watched by two Portuguese soldiers, one of whom falls in love with her at first sight.[28]

Ninkov reports that, when the Yugoslav crew arrived in Mozambique, they had the distinct feeling that they were unwelcome and that 'the Mozambicans would have been happier if we had been Russians or East Germans'.[29] Executive Producer Mihajlo Rašić tried to impose some time-keeping discipline on the film crew, but found himself under arrest on the charge of 'neo-colonial conduct'; imprisoned for four days, he was eventually released after an intervention by

[24] Azevedo and Patraquim distance themselves from the film and describe how their original script was transformed in Margarida Cardoso's documentary *Kuxa Kanema*. Interviews with Licínio Azevedo and Camilo de Sousa.

[25] Camilo de Sousa (2013), 'The Time of the Leopards', in *O Mundo em Imagens: Filmes do Arquivo do Instituto Nacional de Audiovisual e Cinema, 1 O Tempo dos Leopardos*. Arcadia Film Produktion.

[26] Republished as Licínio Azevedo (1995). *Coração Forte: Relatos do Povo Armado*. Lisbon: Ediçoes Dinossauro: 7.

[27] Interview with Licínio Azevedo, Maputo, 2005. Interview with Luís Carlos Patraquim, Lisbon, 18 December 2016.

[28] Azevedo and Patraquim gave these examples of the conflicts over the script in interviews with me, but they are also described in the interviews they gave to Margarida Cardoso that are included in her documentary *Kuxa Kanema* (2004).

[29] Interview with Dušan Ninkov.

the Yugoslav ambassador.[30] Further accounts suggest that the experience of 'socialist friendship', though sometimes tinged with paternalism, also led to mutual respect and trust between the Mozambican and Yugoslav filmmakers. Gabriel Mondlane was one of two sound engineers who worked with Hanna Preuss in Inhaca and later at the post-production stage at the CFS Košutnjak audio-editing studios in Belgrade. At first, as Mondlane recounted to me in an interview in 2004, he found he had to prove his competence before being allowed to operate the equipment unsupervised.[31] Hanna Preuss recalls: 'I was told my job was to train Mr Mondlane, but I actually quickly realised he possessed considerable knowledge of the profession already. Gabriel displayed great sensitivity and interest in the sound matter, and it was a pleasure working with him.'[32]

O Tempo dos Leopardos is a fictional account of the anti-colonial war told from the perspective of the colonised.[33] While drawing on recognisable tropes of the partisan film, such as combat sequences and chamber piece interrogation scenes, what distinguishes the film thematically is the emphasis on key aspects of Frelimo's modernist revolutionary ideology, particularly militant discipline, revolutionary self-sacrifice for the collective good and a refusal of essentialism based on ethnicity. The narrative revolves around the confrontation and eventual bonding between Pedro (played by Santos Mulungo), a Frelimo commander, Armando (played by the journalist Marcelino Alves), a white psychiatrist employed by the Portuguese army to provide a psychological profile of the charismatic revolutionary. Pedro and his lover, a guerrilla named Ana (played by Ana Magaia), are first shown defending a village from an attack by Portuguese soldiers. The couple are exemplary militants who are prepared to sacrifice their lives to the struggle. Their integrity is in contrast to another Frelimo guerrilla, Januario (played by Simião Mazuze). Januario is also in love with Ana, but he sees the struggle as a battle of revenge against white people and he manifests some of the key flaws that were repeatedly criticised in Frelimo's official discourse, such as impetuous adventurism. The film reveals Januario's personal motivations to be misguided and dangerous to others as his recklessness leads him to be ambushed by the Portuguese. Under interrogation he betrays Pedro and Ana, which results in their capture. The psychiatrist Armando, of Portuguese origin but born in Mozambique, now has his opportunity to come face to face with the legendary Pedro. Eventually, through intense dialogue, Pedro wins him over to the nationalist cause, and Armando comes to realise that his identifications are

30 Interview with Dušan Ninkov.

31 Conversation with Gabriel Mondlane, Maputo, September 2004.

32 Email correspondence with Hanna Preuss, 20 June 2018.

33 In this it resembles Flora Gomes *Mortu Nega* and Sarah Maldoror's *Sambizanga*. See Chapter 2.

as a Mozambican rather than with the colonial regime. Frelimo guerrillas storm the barracks, showing that commitment to the struggle lives on in others, but they are too late to save Ana and Pedro, who have been tortured and killed. The film concludes with a gruesome shot that displays Pedro's dead body silhouetted against a window as if crucified, revealing the Christian resonances embedded within the Manichean concept of heroic sacrifice to revolutionary nationalism. The consolidation of nationalist myth through quasi-Christian sacrifice was commonplace in Yugoslav partisan films and in war fiction produced across the Southern African region, but the other biblical theme of treachery had particular significance in Mozambique in the mid-1980s. Echoing speeches given by Machel at the time that warned of the need for vigilance to root out the internal 'traitors', the narrative demonstrates that the flawed revolutionary – the enemy within – is an even greater danger to the revolution than the foreign enemies that Frelimo can defeat head on.

In the years that followed, the film proved to be a huge success with Mozambican audiences. Having demonstrated with *O Tempo dos Leopardos* that they were capable of taking on a full-length feature, the INC determined that their next fiction film should be made entirely as a Mozambican production so as, in the words of Camilo de Sousa, to demonstrate their 'independence ... in the realm of cinema'.[34] It was decided that the INC's most senior filmmaker, José Cardoso, should direct a fiction feature, and he began working on the script. Although Cardoso's fiction feature was nearly abandoned following the death of Machel, the resulting film, *O Vento Sopre do Norte*, demonstrates how Cardoso's background and formation within a local amateur auteur tradition of filmmaking (see Chapter 2) was distinct both from the militant newsreel and documentary-making practice associated with *Kuxa Kanema* and from the heroic narrative of nation-building through revolutionary struggle of *Os Tempos dos Leopardos*. His documentary *Canta Meu Irmão, Ajuda-me a Cantar* had already suggested an intimate approach to Mozambican nationalism distinct from the internationalist focus of other documentaries (see Chapter 5). Cardoso also made a number of short fiction films in the early 1980s: *O Papagaio* 'The Parrot' (1982), *Frutos da nossa colheita* 'Fruits of Our Harvest' (1984) and *10 Passos Para o Futuro* '10 Steps to the Future' (1985).[35] His earlier amateur fiction films made under colonial rule aspired to a complex and personal symbolic language through which he was able to address subjects such as sexuality and

[34] Camilo de Sousa (2013), 'The Time of the Leopards', in *O Mundo em Imagens: Filmes do Arquivo do Instituto Nacional de Audiovisual e Cinema, 1 O Tempo dos Leopardos*. Arcadia Film Produktion.

[35] Silva Vieira (2018). 'José Cardoso: O Homem e o Cineasta', in Jorge Seabra (2018). *Cinemas em Português. Moçambique. Auto e Heteropercecões*. Coimbra: Impresa da Universidade de Coimbra: 78.

militarism that were subject to censorship by the New State. By contrast, for the short fictions he made at the INC in the early 1980s, Cardoso developed a slower rhythm and a simpler visual narration, which he thought could be more easily understood by audiences with little exposure to Western traditions of the moving image. In this regard, he followed the thinking articulated in Cabaço's speech to INC employees in 1981, which stipulated that it was necessary to make films that are 'extremely simple' for Mozambican spectators (see Chapter 5). He was disappointed when *Frutos da Nossa Colheita* was shown at the Festival of Aveiro and received negative responses, including the painful accusation that he had 'lost his creativity'.[36] It would seem that simplifying films ran the risk of underestimating his audience.

When *O Vento Sopre do Norte* was made in the mid-1980s, it offered a glimpse of yet another version of what a Mozambican 'national cinema' could be, one that would give form and voice to the collective desires and memory of *o Povo* through the filter of a personal vision grounded in the director's experience growing up in colonial Beira. Cardoso has since claimed that in writing a script denouncing colonial society over ten years after its demise he was in part motivated by the fact that this would be acceptable to the authorities and that he compromised the film's aesthetic complexity in order to produce a more simplified, patriotic narrative.[37] The director had already addressed themes of poverty, sexuality and the violence of settler society in his early experimental amateur films *Raizes*, *O Anuncio* and *O Pesadelo*, albeit in a somewhat coded fashion (see Chapter 2). However, it was only after ten years of independence that Cardoso was able to make a fiction feature that could express more explicitly how colonial society was sustained through violence and oppression, his purpose being to communicate the experience of that time to a new generation who had not lived through it.[38]

The script was based on a story by the Mozambican journalist José Carlos Areosa Pena, which was entitled *O Costa Barrigudo* and was one of his *Quatro Crónicas* published between 1967 and 1981.[39] The novel is set in the small town of Xai-Xai, four years after the beginning of the armed struggle, by which time there was, according to Cardoso, 'a certain alarm among the settlers, the beginning of the abandoning of the country. And in parallel . . . the awareness [*tomada de consciência*] among the Mozambicans about the situation in the

36 Teresa Sá Nogueira (1986). 'Cinema Moçambicano'. *Tempo*, 17 August: 44.
37 See interview with José Cardoso in Margarida Cardoso's documentary *Kuxa Kanema* (2003).
38 Nogueira (1986): 44.
39 Hélio Nguane (2014). 'Cineasta José Cardoso: um homen sonador'. *Notícias Online*, 14 October. Available http://www.jornalnoticias.co.mz/index.php/caderno-cultural/24879-cineasta-jose-cardoso-um-homem-treparardor.html?device=desktop.

country, the necessity of the struggle for independence.'[40] Some of the actors in *O Vento Sopre do Norte* had trained with the theatre group Casa Velha and gained experience of acting for film through their participation in the making of *Os Tempos dos Leopardos*.[41] As with his earlier amateur films made during the colonial period, Cardoso also worked with non-professional actors, although, according to Convents, he struggled to find enough white people to fill the politically unappealing roles of colonial settlers and police officers, many people promising to take part, but failing to appear for the filming.[42] *O Vento Sopre do Norte* focuses on João (played by Gilberto Mendes) and Zita (played by Lucrécia Paco), a young couple who, with their circle of family and friends, attempt to resist the colonial authorities. Significantly, the film portrays the sexual assault of black women as both a manifestation of fascist ideology and a tool of colonial violence.

Set in 1968, when the armed struggle was in its fourth year, the film presents the liberation struggle as a repressed tremor running through colonial society. The winds of change that 'blow from the north' are audible in the first scene as the crackled sounds of A Voz de Moçambique, Frelimo's radio station, which João and his friend Renato (played by Emídio Oliveira) listen to in secret. Shortly afterwards a railway clerk is arrested on suspicion of carrying out clandestine work for Frelimo, and rumours of his arrest circulate back to the *bairros*. The film shows the climate of violence and fear affecting both the colonisers and the colonised. It seeps into every aspect of daily life, infecting the games European children play as they stalk each other with toy guns through the picket fences that surround the affluent villas of the settlers. This latent violence erupts in the attempted rape of Zita by the drunken Portuguese police officer Gomes. Back at the family home, Zita's father consoles her. He connects her assault to the wider conditions facing Mozambican women and how sexual violence is enacted through the colonial system, but his own experience of persecution leads him to urge João to be cautious and not to seek vengeance. In the meantime, João and Renato become more hardened in their resolve to find a way to resist.

In its portrayal of a colonial society on the cusp of revolution, *O Vento Sopre do Norte* builds a cumulative picture of collective memory with a narrative that connects different social groups and individuals. This tactic is evident at the level of the shot, as less use is made of shot-reverse-shot, which characteristically functions in Hollywood movies to master the screen, filling its cinematic space with shots that dramatise psychological confrontation, the camera inhabiting the viewpoints of opposed individual subjectivities. By contrast, in *O Vento Sopre do Norte* the camera often weaves through spaces, taking in snatches of

[40] Nogueira (1986): 44.
[41] Convents (2011): 495–496.
[42] Convents (2011): 496.

conversations and lingering with marginalised social figures – the houseboy who silently prunes the hedge while Portuguese children play with toy guns and their mothers gossip over the garden fence, or the little boy in a café scene who moves from table to table, his begging largely ignored. Sequences move between the different spaces that divide the colonial city: the shacks of wood and corrugated iron in the *bairros*; the PIDE headquarters at Villa Algarve; villas owned by Portuguese settlers and tended by black servants; and a café scene in the city centre, where Europeans fret and bluster about the armed insurrection but continue to treat the colonised with contempt. While the epic narrative of *Os Tempos dos Leopardos* is structured around a linear plot, *O Vento Sopre do Norte* segues between different temporalities. For instance, the discussion of the railway clerk's arrest by the friends as they sit outside their home prompts a flashback to Zita's father's own experience of imprisonment at Villa Algarve. Individual memories from different generations are folded into the narrative, so that they come to signify collective memories as well, to make an indictment of colonial society and signify the desire that lay hidden within it for radical change.

A key sequence in the film comes after the family have comforted Zita. She, João and Renato go to a party, where couples dance to a Marrabenta band. As Zita and João dance together, Zita weeps as she tells her lover that she knows he is planning to join the armed struggle. They retreat outside, and while Zita initially resists, João persuades her to make love with the words: 'We are free, the land is ours.' The following scene depicts the friends' visit to the beach the next day. Racial segregation on the beach is evident, with white families lounging by the sea, while Zita, her younger brother, João and Renato sit together among the palm trees. They comment on Renato exchanging glances with a white girl, but this moment of inter-racial desire remains unfulfilled. Scanning the beach, Zita exclaims: 'Will it end one day – racism, poverty, the rich and the poor?' To which Renato replies: 'Lots of African people are liberating themselves. Colonialism is in its final days. Believe it, Zita!' João argues that while the Portuguese see the freedom fighters as terrorists, he is certain that one day Mozambique will be independent. Looking up, Zita comments that the cries of the sea birds are sad, but their movements are happy. The birds, at least, are free.

Meanwhile, Officer Gomes plots with the governor to root out Frelimo sympathisers. Flanked by a number of policemen, he ambushes João and Renato as they walk along the beach at night with sacks slung over their shoulders. Accusing them of smuggling arms, he thrusts his hand into one of the sacks, only to find himself bitten by a large crab. The young men run off laughing. Shortly after, Zita comes to João's mother with a letter from her son explaining that he has gone to join Frelimo. They read the letter together, only to be interrupted by a PIDE raid. Officers search the house, throwing the family belongings on the floor and tearing up a mattress. The senior officer, a sinister figure played by INC employee Guilhermo Afonso, sexually assaults Zita and finds João's letter hidden in her blouse.[43] While the film cuts to João and Renato in guerrilla uniform engaging in combat, the concluding scene shows Zita and João's mother imprisoned, watching the birds flying free outside from behind bars. While the narrative of *O Vento Sopre do Norte* centres on the sexual violence suffered by black women under colonialism, the sexual politics of the film remain patriarchal. Only the male characters are allowed the agency of participating in anti-colonial armed resistance while the women remain passive victims, a detail that runs counter to historical accuracy as women participated in combat as well as many other aspects of the armed struggle.

The use of black and white 16mm film in *O Vento Sopre do Norte* effectively conjures time past, adopting the modes of filmmaking that still predominated in the late 1960s. In fact, though, this choice of format was the only way the INC could make the film as a Mozambican production, colour-processing being beyond the capacity of the INC laboratory.[44] While East Germany provided the 16mm film stock, the INC laboratory developed the negatives. Even then, the wider economic crisis and conditions of severe shortages threatened the production of *O Vento Sopre do Norte*. In an interview with me in 2005, Luís Simão, who was the INC's Director of Production during the making of the film, recalled that, while adequate results were achieved in processing most of the film, a power cut in the INC's laboratory spoilt some of the footage for the crucial sequence on the beach.[45] This crowd scene had been filmed on the beach at Costa do Sol, an area on the outskirts of Maputo, and had been so complicated to set up that it was impossible to reshoot. Convents reports that water shortages also threatened to halt development of the negatives.[46] In some ways *O Vento Sopre do Norte* marks the climax of the INC's efforts to create an independent cinema, making films with characteristics specific to Mozambique without foreign technical support. Its budget was less than half that of *Os Tempos dos Leopardos* and the INC drew on the professional skills of their own staff, who made use of equipment that they had mastered during the first ten years of independence. When the film was released in July 1987 it excited huge interest

[43] Guilhermo Alfonso was a veteran of the colonial ciné-club of Lourenço Marques and in fact had worked as a policeman in Portugal before moving to Mozambique. I am grateful to him for giving me access to his large personal collection of press cuttings about the INC when I met him at his house in Maputo in 2005.

[44] Even after the decision was taken to shoot in black and white, the choice not to send the film abroad for processing was controversial. Luís Simão, then director of production, insisted they should depend entirely on the professional ability and resources at the INC, rather than send the film to be developed in East Germany, which was the other option that had been discussed. Interview with Luís Simão, Maputo, 2005.

[45] Interview with Luís Simão, Maputo, 2005.

[46] Convents (2001): 496.

from the public.[47] According to Convents, in the first days following the release of *O Vento do Norte*, more than 8,000 people attended projections at Cine-África, a large cinema in Maputo, and the film was shown at international film festivals in the Soviet Union, Portugal, Brazil and elsewhere. However, by then the political and economic situation had worsened to such an extent that *O Vento Sopre do Norte* was the last gasp of a dream that could not be sustained.

The aeroplane crash that killed Machel and most of his entourage on 18 October 1986 threw the entire nation into disarray. His death precipitated a mass outpouring of grief that was captured in the film directed by Ismael Vuvo and scripted by Fátima Albuquerque entitled *Samora Vive!* 'Samora Lives!' (1986). The tribute begins as a compilation film, with an assemblage of footage of Machel gleaned from documentaries made during the armed struggle and the transition, including *Viva Frelimo!* and *Do Rovuma ao Maputo*. Over footage of Machel marching through the forest with Marcelino dos Santos and other commanders, saluting and fraternising with the guerrillas, the voiceover pays homage to the deceased president as a revolutionary hero: 'Samora Machel was a fighter for the just cause of the people, whose glowing star will never be extinguished.' The film tells the story of how Machel rose through the ranks due to his 'exceptional courage', stressing his 'connection to the people' and 'faith in the masses', as well as his 'dedication' and 'surpassing competence'. Moving to footage of Machel's triumphal journey to Maputo at independence, the voiceover stresses his importance as an orator, describing how he 'mobilised people by the power of his gestures and words'. Images from INC newsreels and documentaries including *Que Venham!* and *Ofensiva, Samora Vive!* highlight key moments such as Machel's election as president when Frelimo became a vanguard party in 1977, his campaigns against corruption, his speeches to small groups in the streets and factories, and to massive crowds at stadiums, where he is shown galvanising support for other Southern African freedom struggles. Other 'historic images' show Machel greeting foreign heads of state, addressing the press at the White House with Ronald Reagan, and giving a speech at the United Nations on the subject of Apartheid. The film then shows the last images taken of Samora Machel at the Fifth Session of the Central Committee of Frelimo, and his attendance at the Non-aligned Summit in Harare, where he denounced that 'terrorism' continued despite the signing of the Nkomati Accord. The voiceover begins to speak of his final meeting with neighbouring heads of state to discuss regional cooperation, when suddenly the film cuts to a black screen – 'Mozambique is in morning.'

Samora Vive moves from images of the plane wreckage to scenes of mass grief on the streets of Maputo that were captured by camera operators Jacinto

[47] Convents (2011): 497.

Bai-Bai, Henrique Jorge and Ahmad Ali on the occasion of Machel's funeral. Interspersed with testimonies about Machel from people who knew him and from mourners in the street, the film follows the funeral entourage, taking in the long queues of people who waited to pay their respects. World leaders including Julius Nyerere, Yasser Arafat and Thomas Sankara attend the funeral, the shock and shared grief palpable in their facial expressions and intense embraces with Frelimo officials. Finally, the film shows the transportation of Machel's body to its final resting place at the Praça dos Herois, site of the eternal flame, where it is laid to rest alongside Eduardo Mondlane, the 'architect of the nation'. *Samora Vive!* concludes with Marcelino dos Santos's rousing eulogy that ends: 'We will never say goodbye. A nation cannot destroy its own history. Samora Lives! A Luta Continua!'

Throughout the mid-1980s, the Instituto de Comunicação Social continued to make short documentaries on video that were broadcast on the weekly television programme 'Canal Zero'. Over a five-year period, Licínio Avezedo lead a team of filmmakers, who included Edérito Armindo, Horácio Come, Jorge Ferrão, João Luís Fonzo and Tomé Ntchenya, although other filmmakers based at the INC also contributed on an occasional basis.[48] By the late 1980s, the focus of their productions had shifted from short documentaries about struggles of everyday life in the countryside, such as difficulties of food distribution in Ana Sitói and Bunamade Assane's *Como Abastecer a População* 'How to Feed the Population' (1985), to testimonies of how people were surviving the violence and displacements of the war. In 1987, Come and Azevedo made *O Cidadão de Orelhas Cortadas* 'The Citizen with Cut Ears' (1987), which documented the testimonies of victims of a Renamo attack in Zambezia, and *Espera do Regresso* 'Hope of Return' (1987), which included interviews with medics and the Irish Oxfam consultant John Cosgrave, who discusses the problem of contaminated water and the risk this poses to child health in a refugee camp; finally, *Os Deslocados* 'The Displaced' (1987) reported from a refugee camp in Zambezia.

In 1988 Azevedo and Bagnol made the first Mozambican fiction feature on video, *A Colheita do Diabo* 'The Devil's Harvest' (1988). It tells of a village menaced by drought and defended by five veterans of the armed struggle from the new threat of 'armed bandits', as Renamo was still described. The film opens with the villagers watching an armed struggle film, indicating the importance of cinema to their collective life. A feature characteristic of Azevedo's later fiction films is the peppering of the story with small details that give a texture of the lived experience of the times, such as an old woman peering inside the mobile cinema van to try to understand how the moving images appear. *A Colheita do Diabo* is interspersed with recurrent motifs such as static shots of village

[48] Convents (2011): 477.

women working the fields in a straight line to a collective rhythm. A soldier carves a Makonde sculpture while telling a young boy about the fight against colonialism and the current violence, articulating how the villagers' survival is a collective project that involves culture, ecology and politics. *A Colheita do Diabo* ends with the armed bandits defeated and the arrival of the rains. Along the way, however, the young boy steps on a landmine and is killed, and the radio announces the death of Samora Machel.

Although Machel's death marked a turning point, the erosion of socialism in Mozambique was already underway. Throughout the mid-1980s, the capacity for state intervention was in decline. While some commentators have presented the shift from command economy to the free market as a form of recolonisation that was imposed by external powers such as the IMF and the World Bank, Anne Pitcher argues that from 1983 the socialist economy was also eroded by the Mozambican government permission of, and participation in, commercial activities, 'assiduously courting the West and Western financial institutions.'[49] In 1984, the government created an institution within the Ministry of Planning with the mandate to attract foreign investment and revived the trade fair FACIM to promote Mozambique's productions to the outside world and to exhibit foreign commodities.[50] Soviet support evaporated with Gorbachev's accession to power, and in 1986 the USSR announced that it was no longer interested in political involvement in Southern African countries. When Frelimo had become a vanguard party in 1977, rules were drawn up stipulating that members should live 'exclusively from the fruits of their work'.[51] With Machel's death, the Mozambican state was suddenly stripped of the model for this kind of exemplary conduct. At a meeting of the Central Committee of Frelimo in 1986, the Party changed its rules so that members could amass property for profit. [52] Private enterprise re-surfaced and with it the prestige accrued to personal wealth. This negation of the principles of the 'New Man' and its collective vision opened up the floodgates to increased corruption. Meanwhile, key institutions through which Frelimo's one-party state had operated began to be dismantled, such as the Revolutionary Military Tribunal, which was abolished in 1988. In 1989, the fifth Frelimo conference formally renounced the Party's Marxist–Leninist position, revoking its status as a vanguard party and announcing constitutional reform that would pave the way for multi-party democratic elections.

[49] Pitcher (2002): 101–105.

[50] Pitcher (2002): 108.

[51] Frelimo, 'Programa e Estatutos', Chapter 2, Article 7: 42.

[52] The decision was taken at the Central Committee meeting in 1986. José Luís Cabaço (2001). 'The New Man (Brief Itinerary of a Project)', in Anteonia Sopa (2001). *Samora: Man of the People*. Maputo: Maguezo Editores: 109.

The economic crisis caused by the war and the fading away of the government's collective project, compounded by the withdrawal of support from Soviet Bloc countries, meant that during the 1980s the INC's profits were increasingly appropriated for other uses by the state.[53] By 1986 the mobile cinema units had effectively ceased their programme of projections in rural areas, due to the difficulty of travelling safely to remote parts of the country.[54] Articles in the press expressed outrage as cinemas in the cities began falling into disrepair.[55] By 1990 the financial situation became so bad that two films were cancelled in mid-production.[56] In 1986 Teodata Hunguane replaced Cabaço as the Minister for Information, and direction of the INC was taken over by the former Kanemo director Matias Xavier, who had previously worked for State Security. Kanemo was the government's first foray into film production on a free market rather than command economy model, and its management worked closely with the Mozambican Security Services (see Chapter 5 and 6). When I met him in Maputo in 2010, Xavier described to me that his chief task as the new director of the INC was to push through privatisation of the film industry. [57] By the early 1990s the shift away from the command economy had accelerated into a systemic process of transformation that involved lowering people's expectations of what government should be held responsible for.[58] One of the requirements of structural adjustment across all sectors was that those holding more senior management roles should have completed higher education. As a result, a number of INC employees who had risen up through the post-independence training programmes were effectively demoted and replaced in the senior roles by younger staff from more privileged backgrounds, partially restoring the pattern of privilege that had been in place in the colonial era.[59] In place of film production being centralised within the INC and funded by cinema ticket sales, private companies would have to seek funding for their own productions on the open market.

The first collaboration between independent Mozambican filmmakers and foreign investors, a fiction film entitled *Child from the South* (1991), was, however, fraught with disasters. Zimbabwean Chris Austin wrote the script, which was based on the life of musician Chude Mondlane, the daughter of Eduardo and

[53] Interview with Polly Gaster, Maputo, 11 June 2005. See the Appendix in Gray (2007).

[54] Convents (2011): 425.

[55] 'Devido à crise financeira, problemas afectam salas de cinema', in *Notícias*, Friday 6 April 1990: 8.

[56] Suspension of the production of *Severino* and *A Solidão* because of a lack of funds is reported in Bento Balói (1990). 'INC suspende preparação de dois films moçambicanos'. *Domingo*, 7 July 1990: 3.

[57] Conversation with Matias Xavier, Maputo, 2010.

[58] Pitcher (2006): 128.

[59] Conversation with Isabel Noronha, Maputo, 2010.

Janet Mondlane, whom Austin persuaded to return to Mozambique so that she could take the starring role.[60] Channel 4 offered funding, and local businessman Aurelio de Bon invested heavily in the production. The shooting began in October 1990 using the INC equipment, but soon fell behind schedule. Chude Mondlane walked out of the production, Austin was sacked and replaced by Sérgio Rezende, a Brazilian director then working for Kanemo. The version of the film that was finally released was classified as a 'television movie'. Aurelio de Bon was declared bankrupt, which made it more difficult to drum up local investment in filmmaking in the years that followed. Midway through this first foray into independent film production another disaster struck. On the night of 12 February 1991, seemingly as a result of an electrical fault, the INC was engulfed by fire.

[60] Chude Mondlane had lived in New York following the assassination of her father. I am grateful to Karen Boswall for the information she provided to me about the production history of *Child of the South*.

Conclusion

I began this book by recounting my first visit in 2004 to the building that housed the INC and the way in which Gabriel Mondlane evoked a collective experience of cinema that persisted in ruins. Later I discovered that some months earlier the Portuguese filmmaker Margarida Cardoso was similarly shown around the INC building by Mondlane when she was in Mozambique for the shooting of her fiction film *A Costa dos Murmúrios* 'Murmuring Coast' (2004), one of the first feature films in some twenty years to address the trauma of the colonial wars that Portugal fought in Africa.[1] Moved by the state of the film archive and the dedication of the remaining INC staff and filmmakers still active in Mozambique, Cardoso made the documentary *Kuxa Kanema: The Birth of Cinema* (2004), which told the story of the INC through archival footage and interviews with some of the key protagonists. The documentary played an important role in drawing international attention to the recent history of Mozambican cinema and to a unique body of cinematic work that was in danger of decay. Critically, too, *Kuxa Kanema: The Birth of Cinema* conveys a strong sense that the filmmakers who built the INC recognised that they had been involved in a project that was historically significant, but which was at risk of being lost to the world. When Isabel Noronha is interviewed in the documentary, she describes the building of the INC as being 'a thing that exists without existing'. Over images of the film reels on the shelves at the INC, Noronha says: 'everything that was made was not destroyed but also does not exist.'[2] Suspended in a state of limbo, the reels of film and the ruins of the INC become a synecdoche for the political condition of the entire nation, the promise of its revolution still present but foreclosed. The documentary concludes with images of Maputo streets at night, the flickering lights in the windows of apartment blocks signalling the dispersal of the collective experience of cinema, a nation fragmented and privatised by an individualist consumerism symbolised by the television screen.

[1] Estela Vieira points out that Cardoso has been production assistant João Botelho's film *Um Adeus Português* (1985), which was the first fiction feature film to represent Portugal's colonial wars in Africa. Estela Vieira (2013). 'Politics and the Aesthetics of Absence in Margarida Cardoso's Cinematic Work'. *Hispanic Research Journal*, 14, 1: 67–85.

[2] Vieira also draws attention to this juxtaposition of image and voice. Estela Vieira (2013): 71.

This book has presented a history of 'cinemas' of the Mozambican Revolution spanning the years 1968 to 1991, and thus culminates with the conflagration that, like the aeroplane crash that killed Machel, has become an overdetermined moment. This refers in part to the confluence of events and forces that produced both these tragedies, and which the preceding chapters have sought to unravel. But I wish the term 'overdetermined' also to suggest that if these two events are understood as decisive moments of ending, there is a risk that the afterlives of the Mozambican Revolution and its manifestations through cinema are displaced. Drawing on Kristin Ross, I use the term 'afterlives' to signal that the effects of the cinemas of the Mozambican Revolution are shifting and endure.[3] Ross points out that events such as the Mozambican Revolution cannot be 'considered separately from the social memory and forgetting that surrounds them'.[4] As this conclusion will explore, the films of the Mozambican Revolution still carry the potential to denaturalise dominant narratives about the conditions of the present, but equally they are being harnessed to maintain the status quo. The films thus cannot be disentangled from the ways in which the memory of the Mozambican Revolution is managed, at times through neglect, but also through strategic re-animation.

The fire on the night of 12 February 1991 did indeed destroy part of the INC's building, much of its filmmaking equipment and some of the film archive. In the climate of accelerated liberalisation of the economy that followed, the role of the INC as the centre of moving-image production, distribution and exhibition in Mozambique withered away.[5] The INC was renamed the Instituto Nacional Audiovisual e Cinema (INAC), and its responsibilities changed to those of archiving audio-visual material, regulating and promoting film distribution, and promoting research. Meanwhile, filmmakers have voiced the opinion that the government has failed to provide a supportive climate for local film production, with laws obliging filmmakers to pay taxes on their production and complaints of state censorship.[6] Filmmakers found themselves in a situation were in order to continue to make films they had to establish their own private production companies. In 1991, Licíncio Azevedo, João Sol de Carvalho, Pedro Pimenta and José Luís Cabaço founded the production company Ebano, with a view to making their own films and providing facilities for other filmmakers.[7] In the late 1980s and early 1990s, a number of INC filmmakers, including Orlando Mesquita and João Ribeiro, had gone to study

[3] Ross (2002).
[4] Ross (2002): 1.
[5] Ute Fendler (2014). 'Cinema in Mozambique: New Tendencies in a Complex Mediascape'. *Critical Interventions*, 8, 2: 247.
[6] Fendler (2014): 248.
[7] Fendler (2014): 250.

at the Escuela Internacional de Cinema y Televisión de San Antonio de Los Baños (EICTV) in Cuba, and on their return they also joined Ebano, as did the British musician and filmmaker Karen Boswall.[8] In 1993, Sol de Carvalho left Ebano to create another film production company called Promarte, with Chico Carneiro.[9] Not all INC employees were so fortunate: while some were able to find employment at Televisão de Moçambique, others were forced to leave the film industry, some falling into low-paid, casual labour. Isabel Noronha's documentary *Sonhos Guardados* 'Guarded Dreams' (2005) features an interview with one such former-INC employee who had to resort to working as a night-guard.

On 4 October 1992, Frelimo and Renamo signed the Rome General Peace Accord, ending the sixteen-year conflict. This paved the way for multi-party elections overseen by the United Nations, which Frelimo won decisively. With low incidents of violence, Mozambique's transition to democracy was judged by the international community to have been a success. The discourse of the global financial elite began to change, with the country championed as an exemplary recipient of international aid and investment despite the fact that rapid GDP growth had less of an impact in terms of poverty reduction. In the 1990s Ebano and Promarte produced numerous award-winning documentaries and the docu-drama emerged as an important genre, in which non-professional actors perform stories very close to their own lives. One of Ebano's earliest documentaries, Licínio Azevedo's *Adeus RDA* 'Farewell DDR' (1992), drew attention to the sudden deportation of a large number of Mozambican workers and a rise in xenophobia and neo-Nazi activity after the reunification of Germany. As well as focusing on the affective legacy of the socialist friendships between Eastern Bloc and African socialist countries, the documentary went against the grain of the dominant Western narrative about the fall of communism being a triumph of freedom against totalitarianism.[10] Initially the BBC and Channel 4 invested in film productions such as *Marracuene: Two Banks of a Mozambican River* (1990) and *A Àvore dos Antepassados* 'The Inheritance Tree' (1994), both of which were directed by Azevedo and depict the stories of refugees in the aftermath of the war. Other documentaries of the 1990s addressed the crucial work of removing the thousands of mines left strewn across the countryside and portrayed how communities responded to drought and sought to protect local

[8] Convents (2011): 533 and 548.

[9] For further information about other film production companies that were set up in the 2000s, see Fendler (2014).

[10] For further discussion of *Adeus RDA*, see Ros Gray (2011). 'Haven't You Heard of Internationalism?'.

ecologies.[11] The protagonists of these films are involved in efforts to empower their communities, through the sustainable management of the land, water and other natural resources and the struggle to achieve economic autonomy and access to services such as healthcare, electricity and education. The docu-drama proved to be an effective way for filmmakers to engage with the diversity of Mozambican peoples, cultures and histories so as to make socially engaged films that create and renew national identity, and a focus on the resilience of women fighting against patriarchal behaviours and traditions is a recurrent theme. Azevedo's docu-drama *Desobediência* 'Disobedience' (2002) focuses on the true story of a woman named Rosa from Chimoio, who is accused by her in-laws of causing the suicide of her husband by having a 'spirit-husband' and forced to submit to two trials: one by a traditional healer, and the other by court of law. The protagonists play themselves, with the dead husband performed by his twin brother. *Desobediência* is notable for its use of self-reflexive devices, such as the inclusion of the film crew in the shot and interviews with the cast at the end of the film, who give their opinion on whether they think the filmmaking process resulted in a fair representation.

As interest in Mozambique as a post-conflict news story waned and Channel 4 turned to more populist programming, Mozambican filmmakers were forced to vie for commissions from NGOs and other, mainly European, funding bodies. NGOs tended to release funding for topics such as public health, particularly HIV prevention and treatment, community empowerment and environmental issues, and these themes came to dominate Mozambican films, reflecting the agendas of those organisations. Some of these collaborations were successful in terms of allowing filmmakers to explore sensitive social issues with dignity. For example, Gabriel Mondlane's docu-drama *A História de um Mineiro* (2001), co-directed with Nic Hofmeyer, is a moving account of Joaquim's return to his first wife and son after four years away working in the mines in South Africa, where he has lived with another wife and contracted HIV. The film highlights how people are forced to navigate the difficulties of economic migration and the expectations of traditional family life in the context of the HIV/AIDS crisis. However, Ute Fendler points out that filmmaking to commission from NGOs that dominated production between 1991 and 2010 sometimes negatively affected overall aesthetics. She cites the example of Noronha's documentary *Maciene* (2010), whose intensely poetic depiction of daily life in a village is

[11] *A Guerra da Àgua*, 1995; *Rosa Castigo*, 2002; *O Acampamento de Desminagem*, 2004. Licínio Azevedo and Orlando Mesquita also co-scripted and co-directed *Histórias communitarias* ('Community Stories', 2002), six short documentaries or docu-dramas set in rural areas of Mozambique in the provinces of Nampula and Cabo Delgado. For discussion of the series, see Fernando Arenas (2010). *Lusophone Africa: Beyond Independence*. Minneapolis: University of Minnesota Press: 113.

broken by interviews with representatives and project leaders from the NGO that funded the documentary.[12] The global economic crash of 2007 and the austerity policies that followed led to cuts that put European NGO sponsorship of filmmaking in jeopardy, meaning that other forms of collaboration with different parts of the world, such as Brazil and South Africa, became increasingly important. At the same time as the Mozambican government was trying to revitalise the country's reputation as a tourist destination for wildlife safaris and beach holidays, Azevedo's documentary *Hóspedes da Noite* 'Night Lodgers' (2007) focused on the 3,500 squatters living in squalid conditions in the ruined Grande Hotel in Beira. An elderly blind man who was once a hotel steward reminisces nostalgically about the hotel's former colonial glory, but the paradox is that he literally cannot see the resourcefulness of the thousands of people all around him who are busy organising their lives, as both the building and the state infrastructures that should support them fall apart through neglect. Only a few years later, in 2010, a sharp rise in food prices, the result of a drought that affected wheat production Russia, brought the tensions caused by gaping social inequality to a head. Riots engulfed the capital, leading to the city centre being cut off from the rest of the country for a number of days.

During the 2000s Mozambique's relatively unknown landscapes and the pool of skilled professionals began to draw major international film productions, such as Sydney Pollack's *The Interpreter* (2005), which starred Nicole Kidman, and Edward Zwick's *Blood Diamond* (2006), which starred Leonardo DiCaprio. Both these blockbuster thrillers feature narratives that revolve around stereotypes of Africa as a hopelessly war-torn continent afflicted by the HIV/AIDs epidemic and apparently endless violence, in which 'white saviour' heroes, played by major Hollywood stars, redeem themselves. *Blood Diamond* is actually set in Sierra Leone, while *The Interpreter* features an unnamed African country that seems to be an amalgam of Zimbabwe, Angola, Mozambique and parts of West Africa. Other international productions have, however, been dedicated to the cinematic representation of Mozambican stories. For instance, Teresa Prata's *Terra Sonambula* 'Sleepwalking Land' (2007) features a plot revolving around a displaced child's friendship with an old man that is set during the civil war and is an adaptation of the celebrated novel of the same name by Mozambican writer Mia Couto. A small number of Mozambican filmmakers have managed, against the odds, to secure funding for feature-length fiction films that have had some international distribution. Ribeiro's *O Último Voo do Flamingo* 'The Last Flight of the Flamingo' (2010) adapted another novel by Mia Couto, while Sol de Carvalho's *No Jardim do Outro Homem* 'Another Man's Garden' (2006), which was financed by a consortium of international funders plus the Conselho

[12] This example is cited by Fendler (2014): 251.

Nacional pelo Combate à Sida 'National Council for the Fight against HIV/AIDS', tells the story of a school girl who wants to study medicine but has to deal with the objections of her boyfriend and family and a corrupt teacher who is a sexual predator. Licínio Azevedo's two feature-length fiction films set after independence suggest a new departure for Mozambican cinema, in that they depict some of the more painful episodes of the Mozambican Revolution. *Virgim Margarida* 'Virgin Margarida' (2013) is based on the testimony of women from the Baixa area of Maputo who in 1975 were indiscriminately arrested as sex workers and sent to remote re-education camps, with powerful performances from the leading actors. While uncovering the brutality often involved in the revolutionary government's attempts to 're-educate' its citizens and 'free' them from the vices of colonialism, the film was also widely seen as a critique of present-day patriarchy in Mozambique. *Comboio de Sal e Açucar* 'The Train of Salt and Sugar' (2017), which was entered for an Oscar, is set in 1989 and follows a trainload of passengers, including soldiers, refugees and traders, on a perilous journey to Malawi through rebel-held territory. Over the course of the journey, a recent graduate from nursing school named Rosa encounters the violence of the final years of the civil war at first hand. The film depicts the horrors of the conflict unfolding across spectacular Mozambican landscapes, but also, through the depiction of Rosa's resourcefulness and her romance with Taiar, one of the soldiers assigned to guard the train, offers a glimpse of hope for a future beyond the war.

Another way in which former INC employees have sought to nurture Mozambican cinema culture is through building distribution capacity and creating public platforms for film screenings and discussion. Many of the cinemas that were run by the INC have since closed down or are used for other purposes, and those that remain are private businesses that tend to show mainstream Hollywood and European blockbusters rather than local productions. The spaces available for non-commercial film screenings in Maputo are few, though cultural organisations and academic institutions play an important role in hosting such events. In 2006, Pedro Pimenta launched the first edition of *Dockanema*, an international documentary film festival that for a number of years drew filmmakers from across the world, and provided an international audience for local film productions, as well as numerous workshops and opportunities for screenings of work by a new generation of artists and filmmakers, such as Camila de Sousa, whose installation and short film *Mafalala Blues* (2010) was shown at the Centro Cultural Franco-Moçambicano. While Pimenta no longer organises the Dockanema festival, in 2011 Diana Manhiça of the film production company Zoom launched a short film festival called Kugoma, which includes fiction films in its programmes. With support from Eduardo Mondlane University, Manhiça led a project to open a Museu de Cinema at the Forteleza in Maputo, which has hosted seminar programmes with invited filmmakers, film scholars and historians. Opportunities for training in filmmaking within Mozambique remain limited, and despite the establishment of a number of workshops and university programmes, students who have the option often choose to study abroad.[13]

In recent years some of the films held at the INC have been re-animated from their condition of latency. In 2009 the Portuguese Cinemateca sent a team of archivists to assess the conditions of the INC film archive. They succeeded in making an inventory of film reels that could be salvaged and found that most of the films made by the INC had survived the fire, it being mainly the collection of international films that had been destroyed.[14] After nearly two decades of neglect, the Frelimo government began to take a renewed interest in the country's recent audio-visual heritage. The year 2010 saw the inauguration of INAC's programme to restore the INC building and its film storage facilities, and salvage historical film reels at risk of decay. The timing of this project that was funded by the government suggests a politically motivated strategic interest in the moving image in the run up to the fortieth anniversary of the founding of Frelimo. The DVDs that have so far been issued by INAC are predominantly films of the armed struggle, which reinforce the nationalist status of Frelimo's political elite. To make this point even more explicit, the cover of *I vårt land börjar kulorna blomma* features a present-day image of President Armando Guebuza, who appears briefly in the film as a young cadre. However, it would seem that the reviewing of the films about the armed struggle decades after the event is politically ambivalent. Following a screening of Margaret Dickinson's *Behind the Lines*, which took place at an international symposium held at Eduardo Mondlane University in 2010, Isabel Noronha asked pointedly: 'Whatever happened to this vision of Mozambican identity?' As Ute Fendler points out:

> The government is now willing to preserve material that evokes political ideas with which the majority of the population would agree. Relatively harmless, they offer up nationalist ideas and mythologize the past. At the same time, the younger generation is now forced to confront their great disillusionment with the outcomes of the neoliberal policies of the last two decades. In their search for new models and ideas, many of them have turned towards ideals of the era of independence. Imbedded in the historical material many see the basis for the critique of the neoliberal politics of the standing government, which is so at odds with the socialist ideals proclaimed during the 1970s and early 1980s.[15]

[13] Fendler (2014): 257–258.

[14] José Manuel Costa (2008). 'Mission in Maputo: Saving the Film Collection at INAC'. *Journal of Film Preservation*, no.76, 1 April: 25–28.

[15] Fendler (2014): 248.

It is also perhaps significant that it is predominantly the documentaries about the armed struggle made by foreign filmmakers that have been prioritised in the process of digitisation coordinated by INAC, rather than the films produced by the INC after independence. While the armed struggle films include footage that presents a number of elder statesmen in a heroic light, some of the INC productions include visual evidence that implicates members of the present government in policies that they might prefer to forget. It would seem that the choice of films to digitise and circulate is politically expedient. Frelimo continues to maintain its hold on the reins of government in the face of mounting questions about its legitimacy. Renamo declared the peace accord to be annulled in 2013, following an army attack on its base in Gorongosa. In 2016, it was revealed that Frelimo had been covering up the existence of secret loans to companies owned by the government's intelligence agency, which meant that the country was some US$2 billion in debt, with large sums unaccounted for.[16]

In varying material configurations, the films of the armed struggle and those made after independence by the INC continue to have potency despite the very different political conditions. As well as INAC's DVD editions, a number of international projects have been involved with restoration and digitisation and have sought to nurture academic and artistic research, as well as wider public debate around questions of decolonisation and the politics of the images. In 2013, INAC collaborated with Ute Fendler of the University of Bayreuth, FLCS and the Instituto Cultural Moçambicano-Alemão (ICMA) on the project *Views from the World – Images from the Archive of INAC* to digitise a number of *Kuxa Kanema* editions and some of the documentary and fiction works produced at the INC, and this resulted in a collection of DVDs that has made these films far more accessible. The Living Archive project curated by Tobias Hering, which is run from the Arsenal in Berlin and receives funding from the Goethe-Institut Johannesburg, has worked on the restoration and digitisation of a number of key works made in Mozambique. Hering has collaborated with Portuguese artist Catarina Simão to restore and digitise Joaquim Lopes Barbosa's *Deixa-me pelo menos subir às palmeiras*, Murilo Salles's *Estas São As Armas* and Ruy Guerra's *Mueda, Memória e Massacre*. The work of technical preservation is accompanied by screenings, publication of DVD editions and discursive events that make a critical contribution to knowledge and its dissemination. Diana Mahiça has also organised a Kugoma DVD edition of José Cardoso's early amateur films made on 8mm, which includes an interview with the filmmaker and archival material relating to the films and the colonial ciné-clubs.

Other projects have sought to re-animate revolutionary films as a more overt provocation. Films including Lennart Malmer and Ingela Romare's *I*

[16] Joseph Cotterill (2017). 'State loans at heart of Mozambique debt scandal'. *Financial Times*. 25 June. Available at https://www.ft.com/content/805d2b58-59a2-11e7-b553-e2df1b0c3220.

vårt land börjar kulorna blomma and Robert van Lierop's *A Luta Continua* are among the documentaries and news reports from the Swedish television archives that feature in Goran Hugo Olsson's *Concerning Violence* (2012). This film edits together documentary footage that shows the cruelty, violence and racism of European imperialism in Africa, as well as scenes of armed struggle in Angola and Mozambique. Taking aesthetic cues from the tradition of the militant essay-film, the images are divided into chapters and accompanied by an assertive reading of excerpts from Frantz Fanon's *Wretched of the Earth* by the American singer-songwriter Lauryn Hill, and with a preface by post-colonial philosopher Gayatri Chakravorty Spivak. The filmmaker intended to make a powerful indictment of a generalised global condition of immiseration and oppression caused by neoliberalism, counting on the footage and Fanon's words read by Hill to resonate strongly in the present day. Unlike the films made with Frelimo during the armed struggle, which were circulated through activist networks with carefully produced educational materials that guided viewers on how they could contribute to the campaigns of particular political organisations, this film's distribution was to film festivals, academic institutions and art house cinemas. *Concerning Violence* is strong on affect but weak on a more precise analysis of the pressing question of how decolonisation might be understood today. Olsson has acknowledged that the films sampled in *Concerning Violence* are at times problematic, and that they include distressing and objectifying representations of the victims of colonial violence. Yet the armed struggle documentaries he includes in his film were at least produced and circulated with a clear sense of how they would make a political contribution to emancipation. In the context of Frelimo's ongoing attempt to control the narrative of the nation-state in Mozambique, it is clear that these assemblages of sound and image retain a power beyond the decay or mutation of the political project they depict, but to what end?

This book has explored sounds and images animated through cinema of people in Mozambique building a new society, at a unique and unrepeatable moment when a people were becoming aware of themselves as a political constituency for the first time through their own cinematic image. It studies how filmmaking made an intervention for the purposes of nation-building, radical social change and decolonisation. As such, the book argues that the Mozambican Revolution was a crucial site for militant filmmaking internationally, opening up a space for experiments that were aesthetic and social that raised compelling questions about how to decolonise the moving image, how to democratise film production and how to visualise and articulate new subjectivities born out of a commitment of revolutionary nationalism. Attending to the radical moment, as I have argued, involves studying the contradictions, echoes and persistence of forms of oppression even in the instant in which the status quo is ruptured. The book retrieves a politics of internationalism that grounded the cinemas of the

Mozambican Revolution, and in so doing it cuts across categories that organise contemporary film studies such as 'national cinemas' and 'world cinemas', which have become naturalised but in fact emerged in particular conditions of the restoration of capitalism through the neoliberal order. The immediate cinematic legacy of the radical moment of the Mozambican Revolution is to be found in a generation of filmmakers who persist in making aesthetically innovative films that are concerned with social justice and representing the diversity, resilience and cultural richness of the people of Mozambique. This book offers a detailed reading of the cinemas of the Mozambican Revolution so as to not only better understand the history of filmmaking but also recognise what it was that they introduced into the world that was new. To do so is essential to thinking critically about the cinemas of the Mozambican Revolution and their enduring potency.

Bibliography

Anonymous articles

'25'. *Tempo*, 365, 2 October 1977: 50–53.
'Abid Hondo: Fazer com sio um cinema descolonizado "Cinematario de Luta"'. *Tempo*, 316, 1976: 58–59.
'Acta de uma reunião onde se discutiram questões relacionadas com o cinema no período imediatament posterior à independência' [minutes of a meeting given to me by Jorge Rebelo], 12 November 1975.
'Chai: O Massacre que os colonialistas esconderam'. *Tempo*, 364: 35.
'Comemorações da Indepenência: Cinema moçambicana retrospectiva'. *Notícias*. 24 July 1982.
'Conferência Africana de Cooperação Cinematográfica'. *Tempo*, 335, 1977: 63–64.
La Crosse Tribune, Wisconsin, 24 July 1973: 37.
'Dossier'. *Cinéthique*, 25/26, 1980.
'As Eleições em Cinema'. *Tempo*, 371, 1977: 28–30.
'Maputo: Alterada a Toponímia'. *Tempo*, 306, 1976: 4.
'Memória e Massacre de Mueda'. *Tempo*, 418, 1978: 35.
'The Movement for Colonial Freedom & Liberation Archive', 1 May 2014. Available at http://blogs.soas.ac.uk.
'Orphans Tell of New Atrocities'. *The Age*, 23 July 1973: 5.
'Super 8'. *Tempo*, 406, 1978: 13.
[article about Catembe] *Cinéfilo*, 33, 25 May 1974.
[report on Rádio Moçambique conference] *Tempo*. 271, 1975: 60–61.

Correspondence

Letter to Jorge Rebelo, Minister of Information, from Sima Karaoglanović, General Manager, Filmske Novosti, Maputo, 2 July 1976. Archive of Filmske Novosti, Belgrade, Yugoslavia.
Notes from a meeting on 27 January 1976 at Savezni Zavod za Medjunarodnu Naucni, Prosvetno-Kulturnu (Allied Institute for International Scientific, Education-Cultural and Technical Co-operation). Present were: head of the Savezni Zavod, head of Filmske Novosti Sima Karaoglanović, SSIP The Department for International Affairs (responsible for film distribution), and representatives from government departments. Filmske Novosti archive, Belgrade.

Other documents

Abrahamsson, Hans and Andres Nilsson (1995). *Mozambique: The Troubled Transition: From Socialist Construction to Free Market Capitalism*. London: Zed Books.

Adams, John (1978). 'Jean Rouch Talks about his Films to John Marshall and John W. Adams (September 14th and 15th, 1977)'. *American Anthropologist*, 80, 4: 1005–1020. Transcript available at http://www.der.org/resources/jean-rouch/jean-rouch-interview.html.

Althussser, Louis (2005). *For Marx*. London: Verso.

Arenas, Fernando (2010). *Lusophone Africa: Beyond Independence*. Minneapolis: University of Minnesota Press.

Arendt, Hannah (1963). *On Revolution*. Harmondsworth: Penguin.

Assubuji, Rui, Paolo Israel and Drew Thompson (eds) (2013). *Notes on the Liberation Script in Mozambican History*, special issue of *Kronos: Southern African Histories*, 39, November.

Bakari, Imruh and Mbye Cham (1996). *African Experiences of Cinema*. London: BFI.

Balsom, Erika (2017). *After Uniqueness: A History of Film and Video Art in Circulation*. New York: Columbia University Press.

Bamba, Mahomed (2011). 'O Parti-pris Ideológico e Estético de Dois Brasileiros na Formação de um Cinema Pós-colonial em Moçambique (anos 70–80)'. *Curtiba*, 12, 2, July/December: 1–11.

Basto, Maria Benedita (2006). 'Who is Written? The Representation of the Other in Rewriting Experiments during the Portuguese Colonial War and the Mozambican Liberation Struggle'. *Italianistica Ultraiectina*, 1: 68–92.

Benjamin, Walter (2002). *Selected Writings Volume 4 1938–1940*. Cambridge, Mass. and London: Harvard University Press.

Berger, Iris, Tricia Redeker Hepner, Benjamin N. Lawrance, Joanna T. Tague, and Meredith Terretta (2015). *African Asylum at the Crossroads: Activism, Expert Testimony, and Refugee Rights*. Athens: Ohio University Press.

Borges Coelho, João Paulo (1993). 'Protected Villages and Communal Villages'. PhD thesis, University of Bradford.

Borges Coelho, João Paulo (2002). 'African Troops in the Portuguese Colonial Army, 1961–1974: Angola, Guinea-Bissau and Mozambique'. *Portuguese Studies Review*, 10, 1: 129–150.

Borges Coelho, João Paulo (2011). 'Mueda – Memoria e Massacre'. *Views of the World: Films from the Archive of INAC*, Maputo: 20–21.

Borges Coelho, João Paulo (2013). 'Politics and Contemporary History in Mozambique: A Set of Epistemological Notes'. *Notes on The Liberation Script in Mozambican History*, special issue of *Kronos*, 39, November: 13.

Bosgra, Sietse (2005). *Brothers in the West*. Amsterdam and Maputo: Netherlands Institute for Southern Afria and Arquivo Historico de Moçambique.

Bragança Aquino de and Jacques Depelchin (1988). 'From the Idealisation of Frelimo to the Understanding of Mozambique Recent History'. *Review* (Fernand Braudel Center), 11, 1, Winter: 95–117.

Brautigam, Deborah (2009). *The Dragon's Gift: The Real Story of China in Africa*. Oxford: Oxford University Press.
Brecht, Bertolt (1934). *Lider Gedichte Chöre*. Paris: Éditions du Carrefour.
Brenez, Nicole (2005). 'A Propos de Nice and the Extremely Necessary, Permanent Invention of the Ciné-pamphlet'. *Rouge*. Available at http://www.rouge.com.au/7/propos_de_nice.html.
Broomberg, Adam and Olivier Chanaran (2017). 'Performing Change'. *Art Africa* – Masquerade, Performance and Performativity 'A Luta Continua', guest edited by Kendall Geers. March. http://www.broombergchanarin.com/text-performing-change/
Bussotti, Luca and Antonella de Muti (2013). 'Italy and Mozambique: Science, Economy & Society within a History of an Anomalous Cooperation'. *Advances in Historical Studies*, 12, 4: 185–193.
Cabaço, José Luís (1981). 'Imagem: Uma Arma que Aliena ou Liberta: Orientaçoes do Ministro da Informação para o Estabelecimento de uma Estratégia de Produção de Imagem em Moçambique'. Transcript of unpublished speech.
Cabaço, José Luís (2009). *Moçambique: Identidade, Colonialismo e Libertação*. São Paulo: Editora Unesp/ANPOCS.
Cabaço, José Luís (2016). 'Ruy Guerra num Breve Panorama do Cinema Moçambicano no Seculo XX'. *La Furia Umana*, 30. http://www.lafuriaumana.it/index.php/63-archive/lfu-30/662-jose-luis-cabaco-ruy-guerra-num-breve-panorama-do-cinema-mocambicano-no-seculo-xx
Cabral, Amílcar (1969). *Revolution in Guinea: Selected Texts by Amilcar Cabral*. New York: Monthly Review Press.
Cabrita, João M. (2000). *Mozambique: The Torturous Road to Democracy*. Basingstoke: Palgrave Macmillan.
Cachat, Séverine (2009). 'Un Héritage Ambigu: L'île du Mozambique, la Construction du Patrimoine et ses Enjeux'. PhD Thesis. Université de la Réunion. https://tel.archives-ouvertes.fr/tel-00955661v1/document
Centro de Formação Acelerada de Traballhadores de Vanguarda (1979). *Tijolos*. Universidade Eduardo Mondlane: Maputo.
Chanan, Michael (2003). *Cuban Cinema*. Minneapolis: University of Minnesota.
Chipande, Alberto Joaquim (1970). 'The Massacre at Mueda'. *Mozambique Revolution* 43: 12–14
Christie, Ian (2001). 'Charles Cooper: Obituary', *Guardian*, 4 December.
Convents, Guido (2010). *Os Moçambicanos perante o Cinema e o Audiovisual. Uma História Política-Cultural do Moçambique Colonial até à República de Moçambique (1896–2010)*. Maputo: CP.
Cook, Alexander C. (ed.) (2014). *Mao's Little Red Book: A Global History*. Cambridge: Cambridge University Press.
Corrêa, José Celso Martinez, Celso Luccas and Álvaro Nascimento Noilton (1980). *Cinemação*. San Paulo: Cine Olho Revista de Cinema.
Costa, José Filipe (2002). *O Cinema ao Poder: A Revolução do 25 de Abril e as Políticas de Cinema entre 1974–1976: Os Grupos, Instituições, Experiências e Projectos*. Lisbon: Hugin.

Costa, José Manuel (2008). 'Mission in Maputo: Saving the Film Collection at INAC'. *Journal of Film Preservation*, 76, 1 April: 25–28.

Cotterill, Joseph (2017). 'State Loans at Heart of Mozambique Debt Scandal'. *Financial Times*. 25 June. Available at https://www.ft.com/content/805d2b58-59a2-11e7-b553-e2df1b0c3220.

Couto, Mia (1981). 'Ainda o Problema da Linga: Submissão Cultura?' *Tempo*, 536, 18 January: 11.

Cross, Michael (2011). *An Unfulfilled Promise: Transforming Schools in Mozambique*. Addis Ababa: Organisation for Social Science Research in Eastern and Southern Africa.

Cruz, José de Matos (1999).'Cinema Luso-Moçambicano', *Revista Camões*, 6: 40.

Davis, Robert (1985). *South African Strategy towards Mozambique in the Post-Nkomati Period: A Critical Analysis of Effects and Implications*. Uppsala: Nordiska Afrikainstitutet.

De Cuir, Greg (2016). 'Želimir Žilnik's unemployed bodies'. *Jump Cut: A Review of Contemporary Media*, 57. Available at https://www.ejumpcut.org/archive/jc57.2016/-DeCuirZilnic/text.html.

Dean, Jodi (2017). 'Four Theses on the Comrade'. *e-flux*, 86, November. http://www.e-flux.com/journal/86/160585/four-theses-on-the-comrade/

Dhada, Mustafa (2016). *The Portuguese Massacre of Wiriyamu in Colonial Mozambique, 1964–2013*. London: Bloomsbury.

Diawara, Manthia (1992). *African Cinema: Politics and Culture*. Bloomington: Indiana University Press.

Dickinson, Margaret (1972). *When Bullets Begin to Flower*. Nairobi: East African Educational Publishers.

Dickinson, Margaret (1999). *Rogue Reels: Oppositional Film in Britain 1945–90*. London: British Film Institute.

Dyer, Richard (1997). *White: Essays on Race and Culture*. London: Routledge.

Enwezor, Okwui (2003). *Under Siege: Four African Cities*. Hatje Cantz.

Eshun, Kodwo and Ros Gray (2011). *The Militant Image: A Ciné-geography*, special issue of *Third Text*, 1, 108, 25, January.

Espinosa, Julio García, translated by Julianne Burton (1979). 'For an Imperfect Cinema'. *Jump Cut*, 20: 24–26.

Fanon, Frantz (1970). *Towards the African Revolution*. Harmondsworth: Penguin.

Fanon, Frantz (2004). *The Wretched of the Earth*. New York: Grove Press.

Fairfax, Daniel (2010). '*Birth (of the Image) of a Nation*: Jean-Luc Godard in Mozambique'. *Film and Media Studies*, 3: 60.

Farred, Grant (2003). *What's My Name: Black Vernacular Intellectuals*, 2003.

Fauvet, Paul (1984). 'Roots of the Counter-Revolution: The "Mozambique National Resistance'. *Review of African Political Economy*, 29, July 1984: 108–112.

Fauvet, Paul, and Marcelo Mosse (2003). *Carlos Cardoso e a Revolução Moçambicana*. Maputo: Ndjia.

Fendler, Ute (2014). 'Cinema in Mozambique: New Tendencies in a Complex Mediascape'. *Critical Interventions*, 8, 2: 246–260.

Ferreira, Ângela (2013). *Political Cameras*. Edinburgh: Stills Scotland's Centre for Photography.
Filipe, Eléusio and Simon Norfolk (2017). Understanding Changing Land Issues for the Rural Poor in Mozambique. London: International Institute for Environment and Development: 23. Available http://pubs.iied.org/pdfs/17594IIED.pdf.
First, Ruth (1983). *Black Gold: Mozambican Miner, Proletarian and Peasant*. Brighton: Harvester Press.
Frelimo (1971). *Poesia de Combate*. Dar es Salaam: Frelimo.
Frelimo (1972). 'Chinese guests praise Frelimo's successes'. *Mozambique Revolution*, 50: 17–18.
Frelimo (1972). 'Italian Comrades Strengthen Links with Frelimo'. *Mozambique Revolution*, 52: 15–16.
Frelimo (1972). A Priest Describes Portuguese Butchery', *Mozambican Revolution*, 50, January–March: 10.
Frelimo (1973). 'Visitors in Free Mozambique'. *Mozambican Revolution*, 55: 9–10.
Frelimo (1975a). *Documentos da Conferência Nacional do Departamento de Informação e Propaganda da FRELIMO*, Macomia 26 to 30 November. Maputo: Frelimo.
Frelimo (1975b). 'The Nation Celebrates Independence', *Mozambique Revolution*, Independence Issue, 61, 25 June.
Frelimo (1975c). 'The President's Message to the Nation on Independence Day'. *Mozambique Revolution*, 61, 25 June: 21–23.
Frelimo (1977). 'Frelimo's Guidelines for a People's Democracy'. *African Communist*, 69, Second Quarter.
Frelimo (1978). *II Conferência Nacional do Trabalho Ideologico: Documentes*, Beira, 5 to 10 June.
Frelimo (1979). *Estudos e Orientações*, 6, July. Maputo: Frelimo.
Freud, Sigmund (1991). *The Interpretation of Dreams*. London: Penguin.
Funada-Classen, Sayaka (2013). *The Origins of War in Mozambique: A History of Unity and Division*. Cape Town: African Minds.
Gabriel, Teshome (1982). *Third Cinema in the Third World: The Aesthetics of Liberation*. Ann Arbor: UMI Research Press.
Geldenhuys, Deon (1981). 'Some Strategic Implications of Regional Economic Relations for the Republic of South Africa'. Pretoria: Institute for Strategic Studies of the University of Pretoria.
Geldenhuys, Deon (1982). 'Destablisation Controversy in Southern Africa'. S A Forum Position Paper. Johannesburg.
Gikandi, Simon (2016). *The Oxford History of the Novel in English, Volume Eleven: The Novel in Africa and the Caribbean since 1950*. Oxford: Oxford University Press.
Glaude, Eddie S. (2002). *Is it Nation Time? Contemporary Essays on Black Power and Black Nationalism*. Chicago: University of Chicago Press.
Godard, Jean-Luc (1978). 'Aprender e Ensinar a Imagem no Moçambique Independente'. *Tempo*, 408: 32–33.
Godard, Jean-Luc (1979a). 'Le Dernier Rêve d'un Producteur'. *Cahiers du Cinéma*: 73–77.

Godard, Jean-Luc (1979b). 'Nord contre Sud ou Naissance (de l'Image) d'une Nation'. *Cahiers du Cinéma*, 300: 73–129.

Gomes, Alves (1981). '*Kuxa Kanema*: Uma Surpresa Agradável'. *Tempo*, 557, 14 June: 60–61.

Grant, Paul Douglas (2016). *Cinéma Militant: Political Filmmaking and May 1968*. New York and Chichester: Wallflower Press.

Gray, Ros (2007). 'Ambitions of Cinema: Revolution, Event, Screen'. PhD Dissertation, London: Goldsmiths, University of London.

Gray, Ros (2012). 'Haven't You Heard of Internationalism? The Socialist Friendships of Mozambican Cinema', in Lars Kristensen (2012). *Postcommunist Film – Russia, Eastern Europe and World Culture*. London: Routledge.

Gunn, Gillian (1987). 'Cuba and Mozambique'. *CSIS Africa Notes*, 80, 28 December.

Hadouchi, Olivier (2016). *Images of Non-aligned and Tricontinental Struggles*. Belgrade: Museum of Contemporary Art.

Hall, Margaret (1990). 'The Mozambican National Resistance Movement (Renamo): A Study in the Destruction of an Africa Country'. *Africa: Journal of the International African Institute*, 60, 1: 39–68.

Hallis, Ron (1980). 'Movie Magic in Mozambique'. *Cinema Canada*, February: 19.

Hanlon, Joseph (1991). *Mozambique: who calls the shots?* Bloomington: Indiana University Press and London: James Currey.

Hanlon, Joseph (1986). *Beggar Your Neighbours: Apartheid Power in Southern Africa*. London: James Currey.

Hartog, Simon (1973). *Nationalising the Film Industry*. London: ACTT Publications.

Head, Judith (1980). 'Sena Sugar Estates and Migrant Labour'. *Mozambican Studies*, 1: 53–71.

Henriksen, Thomas H. (1978). 'Marxism and Mozambique'. *African Affairs*, 77, 309, October: 452.

Honwana, Luís Bernardo (1969). *We Killed the Mangy Dog*. London: Heinemann.

Howe, Stephen (1993). *Anticolonialism in British Politics: The Left and the End of Empire, 1918–1964*. Oxford: Oxford University Press.

Idahosa, Ehioze (2002). 'Going to the People: Amílcar Cabral's Materialist Theory and Practice of Culture and Identity'. *Lusotopie*, 2.

Instituto Nacional de Cinema (1982). *Retrospectiva do cinema Moçambicana*. Maputo: INC.

Isaacman, Allan and Barbara Isaacman (1983). *Mozambique: From Colonialism to Revolution, 1900–1982*. Boulder: Westview Press.

Israel, Paolo (2010). 'The Formulaic Revolution: Song and "Popular Memory" of the Mozambican Liberation Struggle'. *Cahiers d'Études Africaines*, 50, 197: 181–216.

Israel, Paolo (2014). *In Step with the Times: Mapiko Masquerades of Mozambique*. Athens: Ohio University Press.

Jaji, Tsitsi Ella (2014). *Africa in Stereo: Modernism, Music and Pan-African Solidarity*. Oxford University Press.

Jameson, Frederic (1992). *The Geopolitical Aesthetic: Cinema and Space in the World System*. Bloomington: Indiana University Press.

Jones, Gareth and Florian Zeyfang (eds) (2003). *I Said I love. That is the Promise. The Tvideo Politics of Jean-Luc Godard.* Berlin: b_books.

Joseph, Peniel E. (ed.) (2006). *The Black Power Movement: Rethinking the Civil Rights–Black Power Era.* London: Routledge.

Kalinovsky, Artemy and Radchenko, Sergey (2013). *The End of the Cold War and the Third World.* London: Routledge.

Kanemo (1986). *Borders of Blood: A Film about the Struggle for Peace in Southern Africa.* Maputo: Kanemo.

Kanengoni, Alexander (2016). 'Dzapasi Assembly Point… the forgotten story'. *The Patriot.* 28 January 2016. https://www.thepatriot.co.zw/old_posts/dzapasi-assembly-point-the-forgotten-story/.

Keesing's Record of World Events (formerly Keesing's Contemporary Archives) (1979). *Rhodesian Raids on Targets in Mozambique, Zambia, Botswana and Angola,* 25, April: 29577. Available at http://web.stanford.edu/group/tomzgroup/pmwiki/uploads/3004-1979-04-KS-a-DIR.pdf, accessed 27 July 2019.

Kingdon, Zachary (2002). *A Host of Devils: The History and Context of Making Makonde.* Abingdon: Routledge.

L. P. (1981). '"Música, Moçambique" – Novo Filme sobre 1. Festival de Música e Canção Tradicionais'. *Tempo* 554, 24 May: 7.

Larkin, Brian (2008). *Signal and Noise: Media, Infrastructure, and Urban Culture in Nigeria.* Duke University Press.

Lloyd-Jones, Stewart (2002). 'An End or a Beginning for Portugal? Some Notes on the Legacy of 25 April 1974'. *Lusotopie* 2002/2: 141–147.

Lopes, Frederico , Paulo Cunha and Manuela Penafria (2017). *Cinema em Português – X Jornadas.* . Covilhã, Portugal: Universidade da Beira.

Lowndes Vicente, Filipa (2014). *O Império da Visão: Fotografia no Contexto Colonial português (1860–1960).* Coimbra: Edições 70.

Machel, Samora (1971). 'Sowing the Seeds of Liberation'. *Mozambican Revolution,* 49: 22–24.

Machel, Samora (1980). *Palavras de Ordem,* no.19. Maputo: Edição do Partido Frelimo.

Madeira, Maria João (ed.) (1999). *25 de Abril no Cinema: Antologia de Textos.* Lisbon: Cinemateca Portuguesa–Museu de Cinema.

Malmer, Lennart and Ingela Romare (1971). 'Filming the new society'. *Mozambican Revolution,* 49: 18–19.

Manghezi, Nadja (2009). *The Maputo Connection: ANC Life in the World of Frelimo.* Johannesburg: Jacana Media.

Manning, Carrie L. (2002). *The Politics of Peace in Mozambique, 1992–2000.* Westport: Praege.

Mao Tse-Tung (2014). 'Preface and Postscript to Rural Surveys' (March and April 1941), *Selected Works,* Vol. III. Oxford: Pergamon.

Marcum, John (1969). *The Angolan Revolution, Volume I: The Anatomy of an Explosion (1950–1962).* Cambridge, MA, and London: The MIT Press.

Martens, J., A. Verdaasdonk, J. van Rijen, A.van Kampen and J. Tielemans (1974). 'Diary of Inhaminga'. *Issue: A Journal of Opinion,* 4, 2, Summer: 62–73.

Martin, David and Phyllis Johnson (1981). *The Struggle for Zimbabwe*. London: Faber.
Martins, Adriana, Alexandra Lopes, Mónica Dias (ed.) (2016). *Mediations of Disruption in Post-Conflict Cinema*. London: Palgrave Macmillan.
Masmoudi, Mustafa (1978). *The New World Information Order*. Washington, DC: UNESCO.
Meleiro, Alessandra (2011). *Luso-African Cinema*. Special issue of the *Journal of African Cinemas*, 3, 2.
Mendonça, Labi. 'Text sobre a Kanemo Produção e Comunicação', a report sent by email on 19 September 2005.
Meneses, Maria Paula and Bruno Sena Martins (2013). *As Guerras de Liberatação e os Sonhos Coloniais: Alianças secretas, mapas imaginados*. Almedina.
Michelson, Annette (1966). 'Film and the Radical Aspiration'. *Film Culture*, 42.
Mikhalev P. (1971). 'Angola, Your Son!', *BOKPYT CBETA*, 1 March. Available at http://www.vokrugsveta.ru/vs/article/4525/.
Miller, Toby and Robert Stam (2000). *Film and Theory: An Anthology*. Malden, Mass: Blackwell.
Minter, William, Gail Hovey and Charles Cobb, Jr. (2008). No *Easy Victories: African Liberation and Aemrican Activists Over a Half Century, 1950–2000*. Trenton, NJ and Asmara: African World Press. Available at http://www.noeasyvictories.org/.
Mondlane, Eduardo (1969). *Struggle for Mozambique*. Harmondsworth: Penguin.
Monteiro, Lúcia Ramos (2016). *Africas: Cinema e Revolução*. São Paulo: Caixa Belas Artes.
Monteiro, Oscar (2005). 'Testemunho de um Jovem nas Negociações para a Independência'. *Notícias*, Saturday 25 June: 8 and 33–35.
Morier-Genoud, Eric (2012). *Sure Road? Nationalisms in Angola, Guinea-Bissau and Mozambique*. Leiden and Boston: Brill.
Mozambique Film Project (1975). *A Discussion Guide for the Film* O Povo Organizado *(The People Organized)*.
Munguambe, Clinarete Victoria Luis (2017). 'Nationalism and Exile in an Age of Solidarity: Frelimo–ZANU relations in Mozambique (1975–1980). *Journal of Southern African Studies*, 43, 1: 161–178.
Munslow, Barry (1984). 'State Intervention in Agriculture: The Mozambican Experience'. *Journal of Modern African Studies*, 22: 199–221.
Munslow, Barry (1985). *Samora Machel, An African Revolutionary*. London: Zed Books.
Mwakikagile, Godfrey (2010). *Nyerere and Africa: End of an Era*. Pretoria and Dar es Salaam: New Africa Press.
N. R. (2011) 'Istorija u filmskim depoima'. *Politika*, 5/9. Available at http://www.politika.rs/sr/clanak/190228/Istorija-u-filmskim-depoima.
Ndlovu-Gatsheni, Sabelo J. (2010). 'Angola–Zimbabwe Relations: A Study in the Search for Regional Alliances'. *The Round Table*, 99, 411: 631–653.
Newitt, Malyn (1995). *A History of Mozambique*. Bloomington: Indiana University Press.
Newitt, Malyn (2017). *A Short History of Mozambique*. London: Hurst
Newton, Huey P. (1971). 'Interview with Sechaba'. *Black Panther*, 16 January.

Nyarota, Geoffrey (2006). *Against the Grain: Memoirs of a Zimbabwean Newsman.* Cape Town: Zebra.
Obichere, Boniface I. (1973). 'Eduardo Chivambo Mondlane and the Enigma of Revolutionary Leadership'. *Ufahamu: A Journal of African Studies*, 4, 2: 166–170.
Oudart, Jean-Pierre, and Dominique Terres (1979). 'Une Expérience de Super 8 au Mozambique'. *Cahiers du Cinéma*, 246: 54–59.
Owen, Hilary and Anna Klobucka (2014). *Gender, Empire and Postcolony: Luso-African-Brazilian Intersections.* New York: Palgrave Macmillan.
Pacheco Borges, Vavy (2017). *Ruy Guerra: Paixão Escancarada.* São Paulo: Boitempo.
Parrott, R. Joseph (2015). '*A Luta Continua*: Radical Filmmaking, Pan-African Liberation and Communal Empowerment', *Race and Class*, 57, 1, July–September: 20–38.
Patraquim, Luís Carlos (2011). 'The New Series of Kuxa Kanema: The Institutionalized Revolutionary Discourse'. INAC. *Views from the World: Films from the Archive of INAC*: 13.
Piçarra, Maria do Carmo (2015). *Azuis Ultramarinos: Propaganda Colonial e Censura no Cinema do Estado Novo.* Lisbon: Edições 70.
Piçarra, Maria do Carmo (2018). '*Música, Moçambique!* (Fonseca e Costa, 1981)'. E-book: *A colecção (anti-)colonial da Cinemateca Portuguesa. Campo, contracampo, fora-de-campo.*
Piçarra, Maria do Carmo and Teresa Castro (eds) (2017). *(Re)imagining African Independence: Film, Visual Arts and the Fall of the Portuguese Empire.* London: Peter Lang.
Powers, Marcus (2004). 'Post-Colonial Cinema and the Re-Configuration of Moçambicanidade'. *Lusotopie*: 261–278.
Praça, Afonso, Albertino Antunes, António Amorim, Cesário Borga and Fernando Cascais (1974). *25 de Abril: Documento.* Lisbon: Casaviva.
Prashad, Vijay (2007). *The Darker Nations: A People's History of the Third World.* New York: New Press.
Prashad, Vijay (2002). *Everybody was Kung-Fu Fighting: Afro-Asian Connections and the Myth of Cultural Purity.* Boston: Beacon Press.
Qi, Tan (2009). 'A Personal Memoir of Shooting *The People of Mozambique are Fighting On*', *Popular Cinema*, volume 12, http://doc.qkzz.net/article/f000ae55-993a-4f73-9d46-021273d64b5e.htm.
República Popular de Moçambique (1978). *Programma: 1° Festival Nactional de Dança Popular.* Maputo: Instituto Nacional do Livro e do Disco.
Roberts, George (2017). 'The Assassination of Eduardo Mondlane: Frelimo, Tanzania, and the Politics of Exile in Dar es Salaam'. *Cold War History*, 17, 1: 1–19.
Robinson, David (2003). 'Socialism in Mozambique? The "Mozambican Revolution" in Critical Perspective'. *Limina: A Journal of Historical and Cultural Studies*, 9: 131–151.
Ross, Kristin (2002). *May '68 and its Afterlives.* Chicago and London: University of Chicago Press.
Ross, Kristin (2015). *Communal Luxury: The Political Imaginary of the Paris Commune.* London: Verso.

Rouch, Jean (1969). 'Utilisation des techniques audio-visualles pour la collecte et l'étude des traditions corales en Afrique.' UNESCO colloquim, Porto Novo, Dahomey (now Benin), 14–20 November 1969.
Rouch, Jean (1974). 'The Camera and the Man'. *Studies in Anthropology of Visual Communications*, I.1.
Rouch, Jean (1975). 'Situation and Tendancies of the Cinema in Africa'. *Studies in the Anthropology of Visual Communication*, 2/1.
Rouch, Jean and Ousmane Sembène (1982). 'Jean Rouch–Sembène Ousmane; "Comme des insectes"' *CinémAction*, 17, February: 77–78.
Rucai, Lu (2016). 'Du Jian: witness to the birth of the TAZARA'. China.org.cn, 12 January. Available at http://www.china.org.cn/world/2016-01/12/content_37557692.htm.
Rupiya, Martin (2005). Evolutions and Revolutions: *A Contemporary History of Militaries in Southern Africa*. Pretoria: Institute for Security Studies.
Sabour, M'hammed (1994). *African Perspectives in Development: Voices from the South*. Joensuu: Joensuu University Press.
Salles, Murilo (1988). 'Eu Tinha Que Fazer Um Filme Sobre a Geração 68'. *Filme Cultura: Diretores estreantes – 27 depoimentos sobre a experiência de realizer o primeiro longa-metragem*, 48, November 1988. Available at http://www.murilosalles.com/film/cl_no1.htm.
Sanches, Manuela Ribeiro (2006). *Portugal Não é um País Pequeno: Contar o 'Império' na Pós-colonialidade*. Lisbon: Livros Cotovia.
Savage, Polly (2017). 'Os Bolseiros: Ideology, Internationalism and the Artist in Cold War Era Mozambique'. PhD Thesis, Royal College of Art, London.
Schefer, Raquel (2018). Ruy Guerra's *Mueda, Memória e Massacre* – The Lost Images'. *The Journal of African Cinemas*, 10, 3: 205–223.
Schefer, Raquel (2016). '"Comment Faire une Télévision qui Puisse Servir le Peuple sans Desservir le Pouvoir en Place": Sonimage dans le Mozambique Révolutionnaire et un Film Mozambicain de Jean-Luc Godard – Part One.' La Furia Umana. Available at https://tinyurl.com/y5ujfk2u. Accessed 20 July 2019.
Scott, James C. (1998). *Seeing Like a State: How Certain Schemes to Improve the Human Condition Have Failed*. Boston: Yale University Press.
Sellström, Tor (2002). *Liberation in Southern Africa: Swedish and Regional Voices*. Uppsala: Nordiska Afrikainstitutet.
Sellström, Tor (2002). *Sweden and National Liberation in Southern Africa. Volumes 1 and 2*. Uppsala: Nordiska Afrikainstitutet.
Shields, Rob (1999). *Lefebvre, Love and Struggle: Spatial Dialectics*. Routledge: London and New York.
Shilliam, Robbie (2011). *International Relations and Non-Western Thought: Imperialism, Colonialism and Investigations of Global Modernity*. London: Routledge.
Shohat, Ella and Robert Stam (1994). *Unthinking Eurocentricism: Multiculturalism and the Media*. London and New York: Routledge.
Shubin, Vladimir (2008). *The Hot 'Cold War': The USSR in Southern Africa*. Chicago: University of Chicago Press.

Siegel, Lois (1978). 'Montreal Cowboy'. *Cinema Canada*, 44 February: 17.

Silva, Carlos Nunes(2015). *Urban Planning in Lusophone African Countries*. London: Routledge.

Silva, Isabela Oliveira Pereira da (2010). '"Babaros Tecnizados": Cinema no Teatro Oficina'. MA Dissertation, Faculdade de Filosofia Letras e Ciênias Humanas, Universidade de São Paulo.

Simango, Uria T. (1969). 'Gloomy Situation in Frelimo'. 3 November. Available at: http://macua.blogs.com/moambique_para_todos/2010/01/suponho-nunca-ter-sido-tornado-publico-na-sua-totalidade-o-documento-apresentado-por-uria-simango-em-novembro-de-1969-e.html

Simbine, Graça (1976). 'New Social Relations in Mozambique'. *Ikwezi*, II, IV, December: 50.

Soares, Paulo (1980). 'A Valorização da Musica e Cancão Tradicional em Moçambique'. *Música Tradicional em Moçambique*. Maputo: Ministério da Educação e Cultura.

Sol de Carvalho, João (1980). 'Cinema Kung-Fu: Violência Gratuita ou Ideologia da violênia?' *Tempo* dossier, 2 November: 21–33.

Stroud, Christopher (2002). 'Framing Bourdieu Socio-culturally: Alternative Forms of Linguistic Legitimacy in Postcolonial Mozambique'. *Multilingua: Journal of Cross-Cultural and Interlanguage Communication*, 21, 2–3, January: 247–273.

Sousa Santos, Boaventura de (ed.) (2008). *Beyond Northern Epistemologies: Another Knowledge is Possible*. London: Verso.

Szajkowski, Bogdan (ed.) (1981). *Marxist Governments: A World Survey*. London: Palgrave Macmillan.

Taussig, Michael (1993). *Mimesis and Alterity: A Particular History of the Senses*. New York: Routledge.

Taylor, Ian (2006). *China and Africa: Engagement and Compromise*. London and New York: Routledge.

Thompson, C. B. (1985). *Challenge to Imperialism: The Frontline States in the Liberation of Zimbabwe*. Harare: Zimbabwe Publishing House.

Thompson, Drew (2013). 'Visualising FRELIMO's Liberated Zones in Mozambique, 1962–1974'. *Social Dynamics: A Journal of African Studies*, 39, 1: 24–50.

Trujillo, Gabriela and Olivier Hadouchi (2014). 'Conversation avec Fernando Solanas'. *La Furia Umana*, 19. Available at http://www.lafuriaumana.it/index.php/47-archive/lfu-19/165-gabriela-trujillo-et-olivier-haduchi-conversation-avec-fernando-solanas.

Tsing, Anna (2016). 'Earth Stalked by Man'. *The Cambridge Journal of Anthropology*, 34, 1: 2–16.

US Department of State (1975). 'Frelimo Pardons 240 "Traitors"', Wikileaks Public Library of US Diplomacy (Tanzania Dar es Salaam, March 18) Available at: https://www.wikileaks.org/plusd/cables/1975DARES00806_b.html

Van Lierop, Robert (1971). 'The revolution lives in the hearts of the people'. *Mozambican Revolution*. 49: 16–17.

Veloso, Jacinto (2012). *Memories at Low Altitude: The Autobiography of a Mozambican Security Chief*. Cape Town: Zebra Press.

Vieira, Estela (2013). 'Politics and the Aesthetics of Absence in Margarida Cardoso's Cinematic Work'. *Hispanic Research Journal*, 14, 1: 67–85.
Vieira, Patricia (2013). *Portuguese Film, 1930–1960: The Staging of the New State Regime*. London: Bloomsbury.
Wanono, Nadine (2007). 'Fragmentos da história de Moçambique em Super 8mm'. *Notícias*, 5 September.
Weigert, Stephen (1996). *Traditional Religion and Guerilla Warfare in Modern Africa*. Basingstoke: Palgrave Macmillan.
Williams, Linda (2001). *Playing the Race Card: Melodramas of Black and White from Uncle Tom to O.J. Simpson*. Princeton, New Jersey: Princeton University Press.
Zdravković, Mića and Dragutin Popović (1975). 'Report from the journey to Tanzania and Mozambique' ['Izvestaj sa Puta u Tanzaniju I Mozambik']. 25 April. Belgrade: Filmske Novosti Archive.

Filmed interviews

Carlos Jambo interviewed by Nicole Brenez (2004). 'Sept rendez-vous avec Jean-Luc Godard'. https://www.youtube.com/watch?v=Jx-1IVfhIPA
Jean-Luc Godard interviewed by Nicole Brenez (2004), 'Sept rendez-vous avec Jean-Luc Godard'. https://www.youtube.com/watch?v=Jx-1IVfhIPA

Filmography

10 Passos Para o Futuro (1985). Direction: José Cardoso, INC, Mozambique.
25 (1975). Direction: José Celso and Celso Luccas, colour, SNC, Mozambique.
30 de Janeiro (1981). Direction: Henrique Caldeira, 4 mins, black and white 35mm, INC, Mozambique.

Um Adeus Português (1985). Direction: João Botelho, 85 mins, 35mm, Produções OFF, Portugal.
Adeus RDA (1992). Direction: Licínio Azevedo, video, Ebano, Mozambique.
L'Ange et la Femme (1977). Direction: Gilles Carle, 16mm, Canada.
Ano 1 da Independência (1976). Direction: Fernando Silva, SNC, Mozambique.
Anúncio (1961). Direction: José Cardoso, 18 mins, black and white 8 mm, Beira-64, Mozambique.
As Armas e O Povo (1975). Direction: Colectivo de Trabalhadores da Actividade Cinematográfica, 81 mins, colour, Instituo Portugûes de Cinema, Portugal.

Behind the Lines (1971). Direction: Margaret Dickinson, 50 mins, colour 35mm, Company Films, United Kingdom.
The Birth of a Nation (1915). Direction: D.W. Griffith, 13,058 ft, United States.
Blood Diamond (2006). Direction: Edward Zwick, 143 mins, colour 35mm, USA.
Bom Povo Portugues (1981). Direction: Rui Simões, 135 mins, black and white 35mm, Portugal.
Bronenosets Potyomkin (*Battleship Potemkin*, 1925). Direction: Sergei Eisenstein, 5,709 ft, USSR.

A Canção da Terra (1938). Direction: Jorge Brum de Canto, 115 mins, black and white, Portugal.
Cantar meu Irmão, Ajuda-me a Cantar (1981). Direction: José Cardoso, 70 mins, colour, INC, Mozambique.
Catembe – 7 dias em Lourenço Marques (1964). Direction: Manuel Faria de Almeida, 47 mins, colour 35mm, Mozambique.
Chaimite (1953). Direction: Jorge Brum de Canto, 157 mins, black and white 35 mm, Cinal, Portugal.
Changer d'Image (1982). Direction: Jean-Luc Godard, video, Arte, France.
Cheias (1978). Direction: unknown, 10 mins, INC, Mozambique.
Chimoio (1978). Direction: unknown, 10 mins, INC, Mozambique.
Chronique d'un Été (1961). Direction: Jean Rouch and Edgar Morin. France.
O Cidadão de Orelhas Cortadas (1987). Direction: Horácio Come and Licínio Azevedo, video, ICS, Mozambique.

Cinco Tiros de Mauser (1981). Direction: Licínio Azevedo and Camilo de Sousa, INC, Mozambique.
A Colheita do Diabo (1988). Direction: Licínio Azevedo and Brigitte Bagnol, 52 mins, video, Mozambique.
Colonialism Has Fallen (1979). Direction: Ron Hallis, 25 mins, black and white 16mm.
A Coluna (unknown). Direction: Licínio Azevedo and Brigitte Bagnol, video, ICS, Mozambique.
Comboio de Sal e Açucar (2017). Direction: Licínio Azevedo, colour 35mm, Mozambique.
Como Abastecer a População (1985). Direction: Ana Sitói and Bunamade Assane, video, ICS, Mozambique.
Concerning Violence (2012). Direction: Goran Hugo Olsson, 85 mins, colour 35mm, Sweden.
Corridors of Freedom (1987). Direction: Simon Bright, colour, UK/Zimbabwe/Mozambique/Angola/Tanzania.
A Costa dos Murmúrios (2004). Direction: Margarida Cardoso, 120 mins, colour 35mm, Filmes do Tejo, Portugal.
Cry The Beloved Country (1951). Direction: Zoltan Korda. South Africa.

Deixam-me pelo menos subir as palmeiras (1972). Direction: Joquim Lopes Barbosa, 35mm, black and white 35mm, Mozambique.
Os Deslocados (1987). Direction: Horácio Come and Licínio Azevedo, video, ICS, Mozambique.
Desobediência (2002). Direction: Licínio Azevedo, video, Ebano, Mozambique.
Os Deuses e os Mortos (1970). Direction: Ruy Guerra, 97 mins, Brazil.
Um Dia Numa Aldeia Communal (1981). Direction: Moira Forjaz, 29 mins, 16mm, INC, Mozambique.
Dieci giorni con I guerriglieri nel Mozambico Livro (1972). Direction: Franco Cigarini, 24 mins, 16mm, Reggio Emilia, Italy.
Do Rovuma ao Maputo (1975). Direction: Dragutin Popović, black and white 35mm, Filmske Novosti, Yugoslavia/SNC, Mozambique.
Dvoboj za Južnu prugu (1978). Direction: Zdravko Velimrović, Yugoslavia.

As Eleicões (1977). Direction: Margaret Dickinson, black and white 16mm, INC, Mozambique.
Enxadas (1979). Direction: Sergio Solimanov, Super-8, CEC/TBARN, Mozambique.
Escola em Armas (unknown). Direction: Licínio Azevedo and Brigitte Bagnol, video, ICS, Mozambique.
Espera do Regresso (1987). Direction: Horácio Come and Licínio Azevedo, video, ICS, Mozambique.
Estas São as Armas (1978). Direction: Murillo Salles, black and white 35mm, INC, Mozambique.
Der Ewige Jude (1940). Direction: Fritz Hippler, Germany.

Flame (1996). Direction: Ingrid Sinclair, 85 mins, Zimbabwe.

First Pan-African Cultural Festival of Algiers (1969). Direction: William Klein, 120 mins, colour 35 mm, Algeria.
France/tour/détour/deux/enfants (1978). Direction: Jean-Luc Godard and Anne-Marie Miéville, video, Sonimage, Switzerland.
Fronteiras de Sangue (1986). Direction: Mário Borgneth, colour, Kanemo, Mozambique.
Frutos da nossa colheita (1984). Direction: José Cardoso, INC, Mozambique.
Os Fuzis (1964). Direction: Ruy Guerra, Brazil.

The Great Dictator (1940). Direction: Charlie Chaplin, black and white, USA.
A Group of Terrorists Attacked... (1968). Direction: Michael Sheppard, ITN, UK.

A História de um Mineiro (2001). Direction: Gabriel Mondlane and Nic Hofmeyer, video, South African/Mozambique.
Hóspedes da Noite (2007). Direction: Licínio Azevedo, 57 mins, colour, Ebano, Mozambique.
Hospital Central de Maputo (1979). Direction: Sergio Solimanov, Super-8, CEC/TBARN, Mozambique.

I vårt land börjar kulorna blomma (1971). Direction: Lennart Malmer and Ingela Romane, colour, Sveriges Radio AB, Sweden.
Independência de Angola, o Governo de Transição (1977). Direction: José Fonseca e Costa, Angola and Portugal.
The Interpreter (2005). Direction: Sydney Pollack, 128 mins, colour 35mm, USA.

Jemima and Johnny (1966). Direction: Lionel Nkagane, 31 mins, black and white, Vukani Ventures, UK.

Karingana (1985). Direction: Mário Borgneth, 28 mins, black and white 16mm, Kanemo, Mozambique.
Kuxakanema (1978–1979). Direction: Fernando Silva and João Costa, approx. 20 mins, black and white 16mm.
Kuxakanema (1981–1985). Direction: various, approx. 10 mins, black and white 16mm.
Kuxa Kanema: The Birth of Cinema (2003). Direction: Margarida Cardoso, 52 mins, Portugal.

Ladri di biciclette (1948). Direction: Vittorio de Sica, 89 mins, black and white, Italy.
Last Tango in Paris (1972). Direction: Bernado Bertolucci , 129 mins, colour 35mm, France and Italy.
Lenin in October (1937). Direction: Mikhail Romm and Dimitry Vasilev, black and white, USSR.
Limpopo Line (1989). Simon Bright and Ingrid Sinclair. Zimbabwe/Mozambique.
Listen to Britain (1942). Direction: Humphrey Jennings, black and white, UK.
Lixo Urbano – Um Problema de Todos (1985). Direction: Chico Carneiro, 18 mins, black and white 16mm, Kanemo, Mozambique.

A Luta Continua (1972). Direction: Robert Van Lierop, 36 mins, 16mm, African Information Unit, USA/Mozambique.

Maciene (2010). Direction: Isabel Noronha, video, Ebano, Mozambique.
Madrugada Suburbana (1980). Direction: José Baptista, INC, Mozambique.
Mafalala Blues (2010). Direction: Camila de Sousa, Mozambique.
Makwayela (1977). Direction: Jean Rouch, colour 16mm, INC, Mozambique.
Makwayela Mozambique (1978). Direction: Ron Hallis. 20 minutes, black and white 16mm.
Maputo: Meridiano novo (1976). Direction: Santiago Álvarez.
The March of Freedom (1968). Direction: Yuri Egorov, USSR/PAIGC, Guinea Bissau.
O Massacre de Nyazónia (1977). Direction: Fernando Silva, INC, Mozambique.
Melancólico (1986). Licínio Azevedo and Brigitte Bagnol, video, ICS, Mozambique.
Meridiano novo (1976). Direction: Santiago Álvarez.
Moçambique, Documento vivo (1975). Direction: Viriato Barret. Mozambique.
Moçambique em progresso sob a direcção do Presidente Samora Moisés Machel (1981). Direction: unknown. North Korea/Mozambique.
Moi, un Noir (1959). Direction: Jean Rouch. France.
Mueda, Mémoria e Massacre (1979). Direction: Ruy Guerra, 80 mins, black and white, 16mm, INC, Mozambique.
Música, Moçambique! (1981). Direction: José Fonseca e Costa, 91 mins, colour 16mm, Filmform, Portugal/INC, Mozambique.

Nachingwea: a intelligência e a mão (1975). Direction: Dragutin Popović, black and white, Filmske Novosti, Yugoslavia/CNS, Mozambique.
No Jardim do Outro Homem (2006). Direction: Sol de Carvalho, colour 35mm, Fado Films, Portugal/Films du Mai, France/Promarte,Mozambique.
Nova Sinfonia (1981). Santiago Álvarez, 16mm, ICIAC, Cuba/INC, Mozambique.

Ofensiva (1980). Direction: Camilo de Sousa 33 mins, black and white 35mm, INC, Mozambique.
Operação Búfalo (1978). Direction: Ruy Guerra, black and white, INC, Mozambique.
Operação Leopardo (1981). Direction: Camilo de Sousa, 20 mins, 35mm, INC, Mozambique.

Pamberi ne Zimbabwe (1981). Direction: João Costa and Carlos Henriques, 50 mins, colour 35mm, TPA, Angola/INC, Mozambique.
O Papagaio (1982). Direction: José Cardoso, INC, Mozambique.
O Parto (1974). Direction: José Celso and Celso Luccas, black and white, Oficina Samba, Brazil/Portugal.
The People of Mozambique are Fighting On (1971). Tan Qi. China/Frelimo, Mozambique.
Pequenos Herois (1984). Direction: Chico Carneiro and Labi Mendonça, 16 mins, black and white 16mm, Kanemo, Mozambique.

O Pesadelo (1969). Direction: José Cardoso, 6 mins, black and white 8mm, Mozambique.
O Poço (1986). Direction: Licínio Azevedo and Brigitte Bagnol, video, ICS, Mozambique.
Um Povo Nunca Morre (1980). Direction: Ruy Guerra, INC, Mozambique.
O Povo Organizado (1976). Direction: Robert van Lierop, 67 mins, colour 16mm, African Information Unit, USA.

Que Venham! (1981). Direction: José Cardoso, 25 mins, black and white 35mm, INC, Mozambique.

Raízes (1968). Direction: José Cardoso, 8 mins, black and white 8mm, Mozambique.
A Revolução La Famba (1979). Direction: Ron Hallis, 25 minutes, colour 16mm.

Samora Vive (1986). Direction: Fatima Albuquerque and Ismael Vuvo, black and white 35mm, INC, Mozambique.
Six fois deux: sur et sous la communication (1976). Direction: Jean-Luc Godard and Anne-Marie Miéville, video, Sonimage, Switzerland.
Sonhos Guardados (2005). Direction: Isabel Noronha, video, Ebano, Mozambique.
Streets of Early Sorrow (1963). Direction: Manuel Faria de Almeida, 8 mins, black and white, UK.

Televisão nos bairros (1981). Direction: Moira Forjaz and Lícinio Azevedo, TVE, Mozambique.
O Tempo dos Leopardos (1985). Direction: Zdravko Velimirović, 91 mins, colour 35mm, Avala Films, Yugoslavia/INC, Mozambique.
Tijolos (1978). Direction: Arlindo Mulhovo, 60 mins, Super-8. CEC/TBARN, Mozambique.
Tito-Vrhovni Komandant (1972). Direction: Zdravko Velimrović, Yugoslavia.
Torre Bela (1977). Direction: Thomas Harlan, 119 and 240 mins, colour 16mm, Era Nova, Portugal.
Tracção Animal (1978). Direction: Bento Sitoe, Super-8, CEC/TBARN, Mozambique.
Treatment for Traitors (1983). Direction: Ike Bertels, 51 mins, The Netherlands/INC, Mozambique

O Último Voo do Flamingo (2010). Direction: João Ribeiro, 90 mins, colour 35mm, Mozambique.

Venceremos (1968). Direction: Dragutin Popović, 30 mins, black and white, Filmske Novosti, Yugoslavia/Frelimo, Mozambique.
Virgim Margarida (2013). Direction: Licínio Azevedo, colour 35mm, Mozambique.
Viva Frelimo! (1971). Direction: Yuri Egorov and Leonid Maksimov, 17 mins, colour 35mm, USSR/Frelimo, Mozambique.
O Vendedor (1974). Direction: Fernando Silva and Courinha Ramos, 90 mins, 35mm, Sonar Films, Mozambique.

O Vento Sopre do Norte (1985). Direction: José Cardoso, 100 mins, black and white 16mm, INC, Mozambique.

Vrhovi Zelengore (1976). Direction: Zdravko Velimrović, Yugoslavia.

West Africa Calling (1927). Direction: 859ft, black and white 35mm, BIF, UK.

Year III: Communal Village (1981). Direction: Madeleine Taylor.

Zé do Burro (1971). Direction: Eurico Ferreira, 96 mins, black and white, FILMLAB, Mozambique.

Index

Page numbers are in roman, plate numbers are in *italic*.

AFRICAN ARTICULATIONS

ISSN 2054-5673

Previously published

Achebe & Friends at Umuahia: The Making of a Literary Elite
Terri Ochiagha, 2015. Winner of the ASAUK Fage & Oliver Prize 2016

A Death Retold in Truth and Rumour: Kenya, Britain and the Julie Ward Murder Grace A. Musila, 2015

Scoring Race: Jazz, Fiction, and Francophone Africa Pim Higginson, 2017

Writing Spatiality in West Africa: Colonial Legacies in the Anglophone/Francophone Novel Madhu Krishnan, 2018

Written under the Skin: Blood and Intergenerational Memory in South Africa Carli Coetzee, 2019

Experiments with Truth: Narrative Non-fiction and the Coming of Democracy in South Africa Hedley Twidle, 2019

At the Crossroads: Nigerian Travel Writing and Literary Culture in Yoruba and English Rebecca Jones, 2019

Forthcoming

African Literature in the Digital Age: Class and Sexual Politics in New Writing from Nigeria and Kenya Shola Adenekan, 2020